theSOCIALIST TRADITION

the SOCIALIST TRADITION

From **Crisis** *to* **Decline**

CARL BOGGS

Routledge
New York London

Revolutionary thought/
Radical movements
Series Editor: Roger S. Gottlieb

Published in 1995 by
Routledge
29 West 35 Street
New York, NY 10001

Published in Great Britain in 1995 by
Routledge
11 New Fetter Lane
London EC4P 4EE

Library of Congress Cataloging-in-Publication Data
Boggs, Carl.
  The socialist tradition: from crisis to decline / by Carl Boggs.
  p.   cm.   —   (Revolutionary thought/radical movements)
  Includes index.
  ISBN 0-415-90669-5.   —   ISBN 0-415-90670-9 (pbk.)
  1. Socialism. 2. Post-communism. I. Title. II. Series.
HX44.5.B63   1994   94-12024
320.d5'31—dc20   CIP

For my brother, Dennis

Contents

Preface

THE FAMILIAR LITANY OF REPORTS ON THE DEATH OF SOCIALISM IN THE WAKE OF
the Soviet-bloc collapse during 1989 and 1991 may have been greatly exag-
gerated. If we take the entire global situation into account, the term "decline"
may be a more appropriate substitute for the long-standing and hackneyed
theme of "crisis" and its apocalyptic connotations of a fatal ending. To speak
of the corrosive decline of such a deeply-embedded intellectual and political
tradition, as I do in this book, is not to suggest that a century-long epoch
has finally reached its nadir. While much of the tradition lies in ruins, there
is a good deal more to the story: crushed in some regions and clearly forced
on the defensive around the world, the historic struggle for radical social
transformation survives as both discourse and practice—in the form of dispersed social movements, non-governmental organizations (NGOs), leftist
parties, anti-colonial struggles, and urban insurrections.

Of course the extent to which anti-system forces are shaped by any socialist outlook remains more unclear than ever, but critical elements of the tradition—the values of social equality, community, popular sovereignty,
human rights, and so forth—do come into play with great regularity. Yet the
socialist legacy today appears to have less ideological credibility and coherence than at any time since the birth of European social democracy in the
1890s. One might readily conclude that this rich and variegated history has
been exhausted with the eclipse not only of the Soviet and Chinese models
but, from all indications, of the European socialist experience *tout court*.

Still, surprisingly durable residues of these and other Marxist theories, movements, and parties live on, typically in the fragmented milieu of a postmodern world that resists totalistic schemas like those associated with communism and socialism. This book explores the complex patterns of socialist politics in the twentieth century that gave rise to a fragmented, decentered phenomenon far removed from what Marx, early socialist thinkers, and even more recent partisans of anti-capitalist politics could have imagined.

Yet to speak of socialist "decline" in this fashion is to refer to the passing of a world of ideas, strategies, and even goals that has less and less relevance to the contemporary scene. While many leftists try to explain away socialist failures and disasters as a function of passing historical conditions and fads, I argue that anti-system movements on a global scale are now leaving behind the socialist paradigm with its universalist, class-based, productivist vision of change. That paradigm cannot assimilate the explosive dynamics of conflict shaping the modern landscape: bureaucracy and claims to democratic empowerment; the global ecological crisis; erosion of the family and struggles around gender relations; the process of deindustrialization stemming from fierce global economic competition; technology and the communications revolution; the growth of violence, crime, and personal alienation. To have any chance of success, future strategies of change must adapt to a rapidly changing political matrix where disparate sites of conflict and change negate the socialist penchant for identifying single or "leading" agencies of transformation. New strategies will, therefore, no longer be socialist in any conventional meaning of the term. But they will probably be more anti-bureaucratic, pluralistic, ecological, and feminist than anything experienced within the vast history of Marxian socialism. This point can be stretched even further: The very decline of socialism, whether Leninist or reformist or some other path, can be traced in large part to its fatal encounters with these powerful sources of social conflict.

Even in such a post-Marxist era, however, many traditional (and some not-so-traditional) leftists view the socialist project as salvageable insofar as a viable alternative to capitalist plundering on a world scale *must* be found. But the political reality of disparate countries suggests yet another trend. Since the 1970s, and in many cases sooner, nominally "socialist" movements, parties, and governments have moved to dismantle, in one way or another, virtually every ideal historically linked to Marxian socialism. Whether in China or Italy, Vietnam or France, the trend has been more or less the same: flight toward privatization of resources and "free markets"; acceptance of social inequality, poverty, and bureaucracy; willingness to collaborate with the multinationals; retreat on social and cultural issues. If socialism always meant collective mobilization of human and economic resources for purposes of social equality, it would appear that socialism has lost sight of its historical mission. The hopes and promises of a more optimistic, earlier period seem to have vanished as triumphant capitalism reasserts itself with a vengeance. No strategy—insurrectionist, electoral, or radical—has been able to penetrate the vast web of capitalist material and cultural hegemony, at least for any substantial period of time. This profound waning of collective belief in a moral and political alternative to the international status quo stands as one of the depressing hallmarks of the very late twentieth century. The new ideological shift has been celebrated in some quarters as the "end of history"—the moment when liberal capitalism has finally managed to conquer every challenge of the period.

Even with the collapse of communism and the ascendancy of a capitalist new world order, however, this prediction seems ridiculously premature; anti-system movements, however fragile and defensive, seem astonishingly durable. For one thing, the deep contradictions giving rise to oppositional forces are not about to disappear. For another, the harsh "shock therapy" of capitalist economics following the disintegration of command systems in the former USSR and elsewhere has already bred, in a few short years, its own powerful counterreaction—evident, for example, in the resurgence of socialist and other leftist currents in Eastern Europe by 1993. Further, the *dispersion* or even impotence of anti-system movements should not be confused with their presumed obsolescence. Whatever its defects and failures, socialism may indeed experience a renewal here and there, but it will probably follow rather different patterns (with more innovative modes of action, strategies, and visions) than in the past. The present interregnum could well turn out to be more a transitional phase in the evolution of a novel (and not yet concretely defined) post-Marxist radicalism than any permanent triumph of global capitalism. Predictions grounded in 1980s-style conservatism cannot be expected to stand the test of future developments. If the socialist tradition has reached its apogee as a universal, morally superior alternative to capitalism, its ideological legacy nonetheless survives in countless ways. And these residues will no doubt help reshape the new terrain of popular struggles at the turn of the century and beyond.

In many ways this book has its origins in my graduate student days at the University of California, Berkeley, where I began work first on the deradicalization of Italian communism and then on the political thought of

Antonio Gramsci. The motivations of that period remain just as strong today as then, more than two decades ago: to understand the contours of radical-democratic change, especially in the industrialized countries; to explore the relationship between Marxist theory, strategy, and politics; to analyze the multiple dimensions of an always complex and shifting oppositional politics; and, more broadly, to bring into view the dialectic between ideas and material forces in the flow of history. If the views of Marxian socialism presented here are more pessimistic than what informed my previous work, this simply reflects an intellectual evolution regarding the particular fate of conventional socialist politics rather than a negative judgment concerning prospects for radical change in the larger sense. The very decline of socialism may in fact open up new possibilities, anticipated in part by the growth of new social movements since the 1960s, that could allow for a full reconceptualization of radical politics.

This broad theme was already sketched in my *Social Movements and Political Power* and, more tangentially, in the more recent *Intellectuals and the Crisis of Modernity*, where I argue for a post-Marxist radicalism incorporating elements of Marxist theory but simultaneously going far beyond it. The interpretation of the socialist tradition set forth in the following pages builds upon this and much of my earlier work, notably *The Impasse of European Communism*, which analyzed the paralysis of established Marxist strategies in the European setting. Chapter five of the present book (on Eurosocialism) is an extensively adapted and updated version of chapter three in my *Social Movements* book. The epilogue is a revision of an article published in *Society and Nature* (1:5, 1994), entitled "The New World Order and Social Movements."

I wish particularly to thank Roger Gottlieb, who first encouraged me to undertake this project, for his patience and support over the past few years. A good many friends were present when I needed them: Darrell Hamamoto, Allan Hess, Gary Hudson, Jan Jocoy, Mary Jo Johnson, Lee Meihls, Tom Pollard, Randye Sandel, Hal Sarf, Bob Spivey, and David Steinman, among others. I was also blessed with abundant help in research and manuscript preparation, for which I would like to thank Jane Bock, Mika Manty, John-Paul Cherry, Connie Tasch, and Theresa Webb. Finally, my editor at Routledge, Cecelia Cancellaro, has helped to make what has been a long and sometimes challenging process a very special and rewarding one as well.

1

INTRODUCTION
Socialism, Democracy, and the Dilemmas of Power

IN HIS CLASSIC VOLUME *The Dilemma of Democratic Socialism*, PETER GAY wrote that "a democratic socialist movement that attempts to transform a capitalist into a socialist order is necessarily faced with a choice between incompatibles—principles and power". On the one hand, a "democratic socialist movement that remains faithful to its principles may never achieve power;" leaders who decide to "cling to democratic procedures under all circumstances may doom the party to continual political impotence." At the same time, there is every temptation to seize power by any means available, including violence, thereby violating and ultimately destroying the very democratic content of socialism which, following Marx, was always the *sine qua non* of a socialist order.[1] Gay concluded his study by observing that if the predicament of democratic socialism at the turn of the century, and later, revolved around the perpetual quandary of power, then the new (postwar) dilemma "appears to be one of impotence."[2]

Written in 1961, Gay's perceptive analysis identifies a pressing set of concerns that have shaped the contours of socialist politics well into the 1980s. By the 1990s, however, the dilemma seems to have been reduced to one of its polarities— impotence—as the socialist tradition moves rapidly from the familiar state of crisis to one of historical *decline* on a global scale. Power has indeed been won, ostensibly on behalf of socialist goals, in one country after another—East, West, and South—in the postwar years, but the result has been uniformly one where "principles" have been largely abandoned, whether in the guise of Leninism or social democracy, or a "third" alternative. The irresistible logic of power has led inexorably to either regime collapse (Eastern Europe) or profound deradicalization of parties both in and out of government (Western Europe.) In every case, the historical outcome has been essentially the same: full-scale retreat from the socialist vision. Meanwhile, socialist movements and parties in opposition have been reduced to their own dynamic of impotence and marginalization.

The modern socialist legacy that began in the nineteenth century was propelled by a spirit of boundless hope and optimism: Out of the ashes of self-destroying capitalism a new universe would come into being, replacing the Hobbesian world of brutish self-interest, exploitation, and violence with an order defined by the French revolutionary ideals of *liberté*, *egalité*, and *fraternité*. The limits of the bourgeois revolution—and liberal democracy—would be overcome within a transformative process leading to a classless and stateless society where, finally, the social division of labor would be abolished. The ethos of Enlightenment rationality, with its emphasis on human progress made possible by technological innovation, industrial growth, and material abundance, was expected to produce a convergence of democracy and socialism as an outgrowth of class struggle. By the 1890s movements, unions, cooperatives, and parties had established a presence on the European continent, setting in motion an era of oppositional politics that would not be exhausted until at least a century later. In a world of ever-expanding corporate-state domination, the best elements of the socialist tradition have upheld the vision of a truly democratic, egalitarian order grounded in an emancipatory conception of human action and potential.

But the dreams of countless Marxists and socialists, working in countless organizations and political arenas, have never come close to fulfillment; worse, by the early 1990s, realization of the dream appears to be more remote than ever. There has been no ongoing transformative process—East, West, or South. The very image of a unified proletariat evolving, through its own heroic self-activity, into a majority force for revolutionary socialism has turned out to be a tragic myth. Governments ostensibly dedicated to socialism have translated the ideal into a sad caricature of itself, while modern capitalism has become far more adaptive, coordinated, and dynamic than classical Marxism, with its nearly chiliastic notion of historical inevitability, ever imagined. In the twentieth century, the twin Marxist political legacies of Leninism and social democracy have had to negotiate a labyrinthine maze of obstacles: the bureaucratic state, fascism, and Stalinism, not to mention omnipresent global capitalism and, in the post World War II years, U.S. economic, political, and military hegemony. It is within this overpowering reality that the distortions, defeats, and even monstrosities of the socialist legacy must be measured and analyzed. At the same time, by the 1990s it was no longer clear what "socialism" had come to represent or even what remained on its agenda—or indeed what had died in the ruins of Eastern Europe or the dismal experiments in France, Spain, Greece, and elsewhere.

Socialism: From Crisis to Decline

During the century since organized socialist movements and parties first appeared, the tradition has moved from crisis to crisis, struggling to maintain its political identity and strategic coherence while hoping to prevail against new challenges and obstacles. For the most part, "crisis" brought with it not only threat and risk but also new opportunities. With the collapse of communism in the Soviet orbit and the waning of socialism in the industrialized countries, however, the tradition has entered a phase of decline from which it may never recover. Any reversal of fortune will probably have to occur within an entirely reconstructed ideological and organizational framework, as part of an emergent post-Marxist politics.

The decline of what remains of the Marxist tradition leaves an enormous political void that, since the late 1980s, has transformed the very terrain of discourse and conflict on a world scale. Jean-Paul Sartre's familiar claim that "Marxism represents the philosophy of our epoch" seems, finally, to have been drained of its historical validity even as the theory itself retains much of its original conceptual value. Change in the 1990s proceeds at an increasingly rapid pace; the collapse of communist regimes, end of the Cold War, European integration, globalization of the economy, the mounting ecological crisis—all of these events and developments give rise to a shifting paradigm of world politics. Rather than democratic insurgencies filling this void, we have witnessed nothing short of chaos produced by the return of fierce ethnic, religious, and national identities, most graphically illustrated by the bloody civil war in former Yugoslavia. In most regions of the world, the power of huge bureaucratic states and transnational corporations has atomized social and political resistance, undermining the very idea of socialism (or even democracy) as an organizing principle—a development exemplified by powerful centrifugal tendencies at work in Eastern Europe and

Russia. The erstwhile boundless faith in Marxian socialism shared by millions of people around the world seems to have finally dissipated. Radical subcultures tied to the industrial working class and Marxist intelligentsia have lost their capacity to generate counter-hegemonic alternatives to a neo-corporatist status quo even as that status quo breeds ever-wider popular alienation and resentment. The irrationalities of global capitalism have seemingly colonized the left opposition itself, especially in the advanced industrial world. Modernity emerges as a double-edged phenomenon: the very conditions that reproduce intense social contradictions (class polarization, economic stagnation, bureaucratic rule, ecological crisis) also undermine prospects for democratic socialism or its future equivalent.

The death of communism in the Soviet sphere meant that a highly flawed, bureaucratized concept of socialism came to a belated end. Indeed, the astonishingly rapid collapse of the Soviet Communist Party (CPSU) reflected not so much the overthrow of an existing state system as the final eclipse of Leninism on a world scale—the disintegration of a theory (and practice) born during the revolutionary tumult of early twentieth-century Europe. The discrediting of cherished Leninist principles (vanguard party, command economy, party-state, ideological universality) now seems an accomplished fact, despite the ongoing ideological struggles in Russia. The view that an authoritarian political order could somehow lead to social equality or a true community of interests, not to mention democracy, has apparently been put to rest (although radical voices were making precisely this point long ago, even before the failed Soviet experiment was launched). The fatal defects of bureaucratic centralism in the USSR, China, and elsewhere point to a general predicament of the Bolshevik model and not, as is so commonly believed, of "Stalinism" or "totalitarianism."[3] A vanguardist and essentially statist strategy was conceptualized by Lenin well before 1917 and was subsequently embraced (and refined and expanded) by *all* Soviet leaders, from Lenin and Trotsky through Stalin, Khrushchev, Brezhnev, and even (until the very end) Gorbachev. The primacy of the CPSU, enshrined in Article Six of the Soviet Constitution, was never even debated until 1990, and then only under the duress of events.

By the 1980s the ruling Soviet party had long since become a pale effigy of the dynamic Bolshevik original. Swelled with petty bureaucrats and careerists cut off from the everyday social life of the country, its bourgeois-style managerial leadership was bereft of ideological vitality; Marxist discourse was confined to the dusty textbooks of CPSU theory, which few took seriously. The centralized party-state required an instrumental rationality favoring narrow interest group politics, elite stratagems, and bureaucratic infighting. Gorbachev's policies of *glasnost* and *perestroika*, introduced in 1985 but implemented very unevenly, accepted this Byzantine reality even as they sought to transform (or rationalize) the state system and economy from within. In the end, the CPSU, like the ruling parties of Eastern Europe, was so bankrupt that it could not be saved even by the most extreme reform measures. The unintended effect of Gorbachev's initiatives was to provide space within which the coordinator economy and party-state would be radically challenged and overturned.

Leaving aside the dramatic 1989 upheavals in Eastern Europe, which were catalyzed by the Polish Solidarity movement, the final stage of dissolution actually goes back to February 1990, when Gorbachev asked the CPSU Central Committee to abandon its monopoly of power, which it did by a lopsided vote. But Gorbachev ultimately had no alternative vision to the one he inherited, no realistic plan of action. As Dusko Doder and Louise Branson argue in their book *Gorbachev*, the innovative Soviet reformer was in fact beholden to those very institutional interests that he was trying (in fits and starts) to subvert.[4] The writer Yuri Bondarev observed that Gorbachev was like an airplane pilot "who had taken off but does not know where he is going to land."

The October Revolution was made possible by Lenin's great organizational and strategic genius that found its expression in the Jacobin party, which viewed liberal democracy with nothing short of contempt: the bourgeois state was to be smashed and overthrown, not conquered. That such a party could mobilize great masses of people, seize power, and build a new state system is beyond doubt, at least in underdeveloped settings like Russia of 1917. Whether it could ever lay the groundwork for a socialist, or *democratic* socialist, order is yet another matter. The legacy of Bolshevism has been a combination of authoritarian command and mass passivity, fetishism of material growth and grossly uneven development. With industrial and technological modernization, with the spread of urban life and the maturing of civil society, social orders established on a foundation of Leninism were sooner or later bound to unravel. Modernity eventually undermines both the dictatorial ambitions of vanguard elites and the smooth functioning of central hierarchies. This is why the Communist parties of Western Europe jettisoned their Leninism (sooner in practice than in theory) long ago, and why some parties (for example, the Italian) chose to discard the Communist label altogether.

The erosion of Leninism is thus tied to the collapse of an entire theoretical and political edifice.[5] The trauma of Soviet society in the 1980s was rooted in the disappearance of legitimating mechanisms that once rather effectively governed all areas of social life. As supreme confidence in Marxist-Leninist ideology vanished, its sense of universality gave way to the turbulence of a decentered, fragmented public sphere where new parochial identities were being sought after, defined, and protected. The resurgence of localism, ethnicity, religion, and nationality—identities long suppressed by Leninism—today gives expression to a chaotic world turned upside-down.

If departure of the Soviet model left an ideological vacuum, there is in neither Eastern Europe nor the Commonwealth of Independent States an infrastructure in place that can supplant the old, delegitimated forms of central planning and control. Alternative designs consist of little more than speculative hopes and visions, while rhetorical allusions to "democracy" and the "free market" possess no concrete institutional or political content. The familiar dogma of a "classless society" produced by "world revolution" has simply been replaced by a new, even more nebulous form of propagandistic discourse. In this milieu, the celebrated rebirth of civil society signifies nothing other than a Hobbesian war of one provincial group against another, one set of interests against another, all lacking coherent ideological guideposts. At this point it is necessary to ask: What can democratization mean in such a political universe?

With the Communist bureaucratic apparatus dismantled in all East European countries, beginning with Poland, a return to Stalinist forms of oppression seems inconceivable. In Russia, on the other hand, the old party-state elites manage to cling to positions of authority while also retaining some popular support. Obsessed with institutional stability and maintaining their own privileged interests, they would like to turn the clock back to Brezhnev (not Stalin). The timidity of the August 1991 attempted coup against Gorbachev suggests that a reversion to Stalinist-type coercion, even if possible, was rather far from the minds of the organizers. Although comfortable with some degree of liberalization from above, the *apparat* still holds to the generic Leninist view of democracy—namely, that the party-state is by definition democratic since it represents the historical interests of the "great mass of the Soviet working people."

Gorbachev's alternative to Brezhnev's technocratic managerialism was, from the outset, something akin to Kadar-type "liberalism" introduced in Hungary during the early 1960s: political opening from above, with economic restructuring (decentralization) accompanied by the relaxation of social and cultural controls. Gorbachev added a new twist to the Kadar model by initiating, on a still limited scale, bolder forms of democratic experimentation. Confronting head-on the crisis of bureaucratic centralism, Gorbachev set out to reform the power structure—making it more flexible and bringing it closer to daily life—without sacrificing its authoritarian features. But Kadarism, in the USSR as in Eastern Europe, was doomed insofar as such broadening of the public sphere, once legitimated, was bound to generate radical changes and demands that would ultimately pull the old order down: the changes unleashed by Gorbachev could not for long be confined within a bureaucratic-centralist model. Hence the tumultuous movement toward autonomy of most of the Republics, the economic chaos, the breakdown of old political norms—and Gorbachev's reluctant decision, in early 1990, to abandon the sacred principle of CPSU hegemony. As in Eastern Europe (notably Hungary and Poland), Kadarism turned out to be not the savior but the death knell of Leninism.

The eclipse of social democracy, too, followed a deep, tortuous, long-term historical process shaped by a convergence of factors, many of them already visible at the turn of the century. The European-centered tradition, from the orthodox writings of Karl Kautsky before World War I to the more pragmatic initiatives of French Socialist François Mitterand in the 1980s, was always motivated by a search for an alternative to both capitalism and authoritarian socialism. Its historic ideals depended upon a fusion of Marxian socialism and liberal democracy, which, from a strategic viewpoint, signaled a departure from the polar extremes of vanguardist intervention ("putschism") and anarchist insurgency—neither regarded by the social democrats as compatible with the Kautskian "democratic road." Socialism demanded not an overturning or supersession of the bourgeois state but rather its democratic transformation leading to a new equilibrium of class forces. At least until World War I, the distinction between "reforms" and "revolution" made little sense to most social democrats.

In the seventy-five years since the German Social Democrats (SPD) first won governmental power after World War I, no less than fifteen parties broadly linked to this tradition—most of them in advanced capitalist societies—have followed suit. As in the case of rival parties, their electoral fortunes and their programmatic achievements have oscillated greatly. Both the British Labor Party, which first came to power in 1924, and the Swedish Social Democrats, which followed in 1932, were able to remain in power for long stretches of time; so, too, were the Austrian, German, Danish, and French parties. Their common agenda, allowing for certain national peculiarities, was readily identifiable up to the 1980s: strategic emphasis on elections and parliamentary action; democratization of the state within the confines of pluralist liberalism, public control over the economy by means of nationalizations, joint holding companies, and regulatory policies; a welfare state guaranteeing universal social services and full employment; and progressive social and cultural change (for example, separation of church and state, legalization of abortion, educational reform).

The post World War II successes of social democracy have been remarkable in many European countries, most notably in Sweden, which in the 1990s still lives on as something akin to a "model" welfare state replete with near full-employment and a wide range of viable (if increasingly fragile) social programs. But nowhere has anything resembling a "transition to socialism" been made possible by a series of accumulated reforms; nowhere has social democratic power led to a fundamental break with the capitalist system. On the contrary, long periods of governance (and in some cases opposition) have given rise first to a crisis of political identity and then, ultimately, to deradicalization and abandonment of social goals. Obsessed with modernization, growth, efficiency, and stability as core values, social democratic elites wound up accepting the parameters of capitalist democracy and eventually became indistinguishable from competing party elites. They constructed a *Volkspartei*, or "catchall party," hoping to duplicate the electoral triumphs of their liberal and conservative counterparts. After several decades a pattern was set: Without exception, the parties became institutionalized fixtures within the orbit of political power, no longer capable of taking popular initiatives. Despite its brief Mediterranean "renewal" in the 1980s, social democracy today has retreated from asserting even a strong *reformist* presence in European politics.[6]

The recurrent impasse, and eventual decline, of European social democracy cannot be attributed to any single factor (for instance, Robert Michels' famous "iron law of oligarchy"), despite longstanding efforts to do so since the turn of the century.[7] Michels's analysis of the conservative tendencies inherent in the processes of internal party bureaucratization can hardly be ignored. Neither can the role of electoral politics, which ensnares parties in a web of political and institutional commitments that always seem to block radical goals. More recently other factors have entered into the picture: collapse of the growth-driven Keynesian welfare state model after the 1970s; decline of the manufacturing sectors and with it the shrinking of traditional working-class culture; the enormous mobility of capital made possible by the spread of transnational corporations and the shift toward European integration; competitive pressures unleashed by the world market; post-sixties challenges from the new social movements and Greens; and the media-induced political spectacle in which parties emerge as superficial vote-getting machines. Whatever the combined influence of such features, social-democratic deradicalization stems as much from the conscious *strategic* decision of leaders to operate strictly according to liberal-democratic rules of the game as from external pressures.[8] Social democrats have always set for themselves a contradictory task: managing the corporate-state order and at the same time seeking to fundamentally alter it. Hence, the predicament goes much deeper than leadership betrayals or limits imposed by historical conditions. The decline of vision, therefore, has been neither conjunctural nor accidental: much like the fall of communism, there have been momentous structural and ideological changes over time that, by the 1990s, are probably irreversible.

In the Third World, where social democracy has been a marginal factor, bureaucratic centralism has had a greater resiliency and staying power than elsewhere. The persistence of a Leninist mystique is traceable to the postwar successes of Maoist revolution in China and Vietnam, and to the seductions of a command economy designed to foster rapid modernization. Following the Soviet pattern, Leninist regimes in Asia, Africa, and Latin America were able to achieve some degree of national independence and economic development, along with extensive reforms here and there, but in no country did these regimes achieve much momentum toward equality or democracy. On the contrary, new power structures and class systems were brought into being that often deepened social cleavages.

With perhaps the single exception of China, Leninism in the Third World rarely embraced any clear articulation of socialist goals. The simple themes of independence and modernization seemed appropriate in a setting dominated by immense poverty, huge foreign debts, uneven development, and the legacy of colonialism. Anti-system movements, parties, and governments, hoping to avoid the pitfalls of Western capitalist democracy, opted for radical-nationalist mobilization that adopted many, if not all, of the features of Soviet communism. Legitimacy was built on a foundation of three discourses: nationalism, modernization, and the mystique of socialism. Under such circumstances there could be no real movement in the direction of democratic socialism. Once Leninist or quasi-Leninist governments were firmly established (as in China, Vietnam, North Korea, Cuba, and Angola), the "socialist" component of legitimation was soon obliterated by the other two principles. The outcome was shaped by a fixation on distinctly *modernizing* goals—growth, efficiency, expansion of state and military power, enhanced leverage in the world economy. Although many Third World regimes still cling to bureaucratic centralism—with a few scattered anti-system movements (for example, in the Philippines) wanting to emulate it— the logic of *decline* in the Soviet sphere has long been at work here as well. If Marxism-Leninism once offered a hopeful alternative to global capitalism, at least for poor Southern countries, today it promises little beyond a strategic model that failed. Paradoxically, the very process of modernization set in motion by Leninist party-states also gives rise to a dynamic of adaptation and integration within the powerful machinations of the capitalist system. Future Third World regimes are therefore likely to evolve toward some variant of state capitalism (China) or, following the examples of Romania and Albania, wind up being overthrown by popular upheaval. In neither outcome is democratic socialism of any variety likely to flourish.

As for the United States, economic and political development from the outset has followed its own rather unique path; there is abundant truth to Werner Sombart's thesis of American "exceptionalism."[9] Thus, given the peculiar hegemony of capitalist democracy throughout U.S. history, to refer to the "decline" of socialism is quite meaningless, insofar as socialism achieved only a limited mass presence and never posed a serious threat to the status quo. Despite brief moments of rapid growth before and during World War I, the Socialist Party could never establish a foothold in the political system. The deeply entrenched two-party structure was defined by a legacy of liberal capitalism that easily absorbed or blunted the relatively timid advances of socialists and communists between the 1890s and 1950s. Class consciousness did exist, but rarely was it translated into European-style socialist politics. Even during the Depression years, with massive poverty and unemployment, the great majority of workers refused to go against capitalist values and priorities. Racial, ethnic, and regional cleavages divided workers, leading to a more fragmented proletariat than was characteristic of the European pattern analyzed by Marx. The undeniable material achievements of U.S. capitalism, along with the peculiar workings of Lockian individualism, reinforced this atomizing tendency. In the postwar years other factors compounded the situation: widespread affluence and consumerism, social and geographical mobility, mass culture, and the integrating role of politics tied to patronage and spectacle. In this setting, a Marxist presence, although revitalized as an intellectual phenomenon in the 1970s and 1980s, was inevitably confined to the universities and limited sectors of the new middle strata; the corporatist public sphere remained as narrow as ever, closing off genuine anti-system alternatives.

Ironically, this closure actually brings the U.S. more in line with the global deradicalizing trends mentioned above, in effect nullifying the traditional importance of American exceptionalism; common world patterns now serve to obscure historical differences.[10] Today the narrow, superficial, integrative features of American politics, which at best reduce socialism to a marginal ideology, could define the norm for Europe, Russia, and other regions where modernity transforms the political culture. From this viewpoint, the worldwide Americanization of politics is simply another expression of the secular decline of socialism. Whether such a pattern can survive for long, given the severe contradictions generated by modernity, is another matter.

If the twentieth century began with a nearly messianic optimism about socialist possibilities, it is closing amid a pervasive sense of defeat and demoralization. The very *idea* of revolutionary change has become submerged beneath the postmodern disorder of the 1990s: social and cultural fragmentation, local retreat, resurgence of market values, political conservatism. Even where socialists have won power their ideals have been compromised and distorted beyond recognition. At one level this phenomenon can be seen as part of a narrowing public discourse symptomatic of bureaucratic rationality and expanded state-corporate power. At yet another level it stems from relentless economic, political, and military pressures brought to bear by the world capitalist system, imposing constraints upon anti-system struggles East, West, and South. Where oppositional challenges were not crushed or derailed (Chile, France) they were typically forced into an authoritarian mold (USSR, Cuba). At still another level it is impossible to ignore some fundamental defects of Marxian socialist theory: economic determinism, fetishism of the industrial proletariat, absence of a thorough democratic critique of bureaucratic or statist domination, inadequate conceptualization of issues related to race, ethnicity, gender, and ecology. The overall decline of socialism cannot be analyzed without taking into account a combination of factors both external and internal to the tradition itself.

Liberal Hegemony or World Disorder?

For ruling elites, along with their theorists and propagandists, the collapse of communism and Soviet power on the world scene has inspired a return to Daniel Bell's famous (but highly misleading) "end of ideology" thesis.[11] For observers taking their cue from Francis Fukuyama, the ideological void left by a departed communism has been amply filled by liberal democracy, which finally, after an era of bitter, protracted battles, has been able to "conquer" all other ideologies.[12] Liberalism, in both economics and politics, now spans immensely diverse nations, regimes, and cultures—thanks mainly to the powerful influence of the world capitalist market—with far less difficulty than before. Liberal hegemony is strengthened on a global scale by sustained economic growth, prosperity, political freedoms, and the modernizing requirements of science and technology. Competing ideologies no longer pose a truly universal challenge, for if history (following Hegel) embodies progress to higher levels of rationality then unquestionably "liberalism is the superior form."[13] According to Fukuyama, history has been shaped by two parallel processes—the logic of science and the logic of human recognition, or freedom—and "both conveniently culminated in the same end point, capitalist liberal democracy."[14]

This argument rests upon several interrelated assumptions. First, that dictatorships of whatever ideological stripe have lost their viability with the impact of modernity. Second, that the global market has expanded to the point where it can effectively integrate human activity on a world scale, not only economically but ideologically. Third, that hegemonic liberal institutions and practices are most compatible with the universal strivings for freedom, democracy, and affluence. Fourth, that popular struggles for change traditionally associated with leftist politics will increasingly be posed, and take shape, within this liberal public sphere; autonomous radical movements can make headway here and there, but they cannot be sustained for long in such an unfriendly environment. One corollary that follows from this is that anything resembling revolutionary socialism has finally, after a century of futile efforts, become totally obsolete.

In the wake of the tumultuous revolutions in Eastern Europe and the collapse of Soviet power, this analysis—speculative as it is—has a certain seductive appeal. The spread of the global marketplace, dominated by transnational corporate power, enhanced mobility of capital, and celebrations of the "free market," seems more invulnerable than ever. Local power, including that of most nation-states, has been undermined in an era of economic, media, and even cultural internationalization. The very notion of planning and regulation, not to mention transformation, of institutions on a global level seems hopelessly beyond reach: grassroots citizens' actions appear to have lost their capacity to win new positions of institutional power. The critical question today is: How can profoundly post-liberal ideals of socialist egalitarianism flourish in this type of environment?

The problem with this argument is that it ignores too much social reality to be persuasive: socialist decline does not itself guarantee unchallenged ascendancy of a new capitalist order, despite the propagandistic claims of its proponents. For one thing, the historic *conflict* between the economic and political sides of liberalism, between capitalism and democracy, can be expected to intensify as huge corporations and financial institutions extend their predatory and authoritarian domains. The global impact of capitalism is certain to bring more of the same problems that have accompanied modernization in the absence of powerful counterweights: massive poverty; class polarization; debt-ridden Third World economies; megacities overcome by unemployment, crime, and violence; growing differences between North and South; ecological devastation. Put bluntly, the *economic* side of liberalism (not to be confused with the "free market," which exists nowhere) can only work against political democracy and institutional stability; it is scarcely a design for substantial harmony or equilibrium required by the "end of history" argument. Reflecting on "the Leninist extinction", Ken Jowitt observes that disorder and crises are likely to be the legacy of the new global shift—one reason being the failure of liberalism, given its obsession with individual self-interest and material values, to offer a true source of personal identity and collective solidarity.[15] Contra Fukuyama, the permanence and solidarity of liberal capitalism on a world scale cannot be predicted on the basis of prevailing trends.

The prospects for international liberal consensus are further undermined by the mounting rivalry among capitalist powers (the European Community, U.S., Japan) and the emergence of newly-competing nations (Brazil, South Korea, Taiwan, Mexico, Indonesia) in a post-Cold War milieu where the "rules of the game" have significantly changed. Surface unity of the new world order barely conceals a subterranean economic and political fragility. Although a powerful and unifying world market does exist, the reality is that most capital resources are still linked to particular states that are forced to compete with other states in a framework of "trans-state capitalism." Since there is no transnational state—the United Nations remains a tool of the leading G-7 powers—bitter and prolonged trade wars and other forms of economic rivalry can easily disrupt the smooth functioning of a new world order.[16]

Disruption and even chaos could result from yet another set of conditions: the global ecological crisis. Understandably, this challenge to order and consensus does not figure in the neat constructs offered by "end of history" theorists. Yet the destructive legacy of both capitalist and communist industrialism already calls into question the growth-driven forms of production and consumption that prevailed for at least two centuries. Ecological decay is reflected in the massive depletion of natural resources; deforestation; thinning of the ozone layer; radiation fallout; disruptive worldwide climate changes; poisoning of the air, water, soil, and food; and growing population pressures—all of which threaten to permanently destabilize the biosphere. And what assaults the biosphere is also bound to assault the dominant order of things. Among sources of this crisis are a world capitalist system with its growth mania, emphasis on market over social values, fossil fuel driven economics, harmful technologies, consumerism, spread of military weaponry, and sharpened Northern exploitation of the South (and East). The severity of the crisis is such that, unless drastic measures are taken to alter these patterns within the next generation or so, it could be too late to preserve a fully inhabitable planet. And such measures will not, and probably cannot, be implemented in a world dominated by transnational corporations.[17]

The irony is that the decline of socialism parallels a similar decline of *liberalism.* Indeed, the socialist tradition has always developed within the orbit of liberalism, as part of an Enlightenment rationality linked to faith in science, technology, and industrial expansion. Modernity itself has turned out to be a double-edged phenomenon. The expectation that authentic citizenship, or democratic participation, would be fully achieved within a bourgeois framework of universal suffrage, free elections, and multiparty systems has been badly tarnished. The liberal-capitalist revolution begun in England, France, and America has never fulfilled its grandiose promises; alongside undeniable material and social advances have come far more poverty, inequality, and social atomization than its first architects ever imagined. The dark side of the bourgeois revolution has been imperialism, shrunken forms of democracy, ecological crisis, and growing social polarization on a world scale. But it has simultaneously generated, especially since the 1960s, significant anti-system social movements, mostly in the West but also, and increasingly, in the East and South.[18] These movements—labor, urban protest, indigenous, environmental, feminist—although generally fragmented and localist, reflect the persistence of strong crisis-tendencies in the world system and the fallacy of a liberal consensus-equilibrium model.

The Demise of Marxism?

Surveying the wreckage of socialist politics in the 1990s, it is necessary to move beyond the familiar themes of crisis and dilemma. Despite heroic moments and periodic accomplishments, the tradition can now be judged as anything but a success. The main organized socialist currents—social democracy, communism, Eurocommunism, Eurosocialism, Third World liberation movements—have run aground. While the global crisis of capitalism has actually intensified, and while anti-system opposition continues along its disparate paths, the very idea of a totalizing or unifying framework that could point toward something akin to the "transition to socialism" seems to have been overwhelmed by the flow of history. Indeed, the deepening tensions and contradictions of modernity point toward a post-liberal and post-socialist political framework.

If Marxism as theory and practice was grounded in historical forces tied to nineteenth- and early twentieth-century industrialism, then the appropriate question is: What is left today? What elements of Marxian socialism remain valid in the contemporary world? To what extent can the tradition be reconstituted to take into account new material and ideological conditions? In what *context* can the theory emerge as anything more than a speculative ideal—a moral outlook that, although superior to the possessive individualism of the capitalist market, can offer little guide to political strategy? Does "socialism" now signify anything more than a broad popular struggle for equality and democracy, a kind of radicalized populism?

Clearly the intellectual and moral attraction of Marxism, however understood, remains strong: it is still the single most important source of vision, analysis, and critique of the dominant order. Marxism remains very much part of a general *Zeitgeist*, or worldview, even if it can no longer inspire strategies and methods of political action. In the final analysis, however, the decline of socialism as a political phenomenon is inseparable from the crisis of Marxism as a theoretical legacy. Historically, Marxism has often embraced a straightforward dialectic of labor struggling against capital, wresting power from the bourgeoisie, and then establishing a classless society. It was a dialectic that invariably moved through the sphere of production, shaped by the discourse of economic rationality. But in highly industrialized capitalism this logic no longer holds in the same way but rather extends far beyond the concerns of workplace and production to what André Gorz refers to as "the growing conflict between the bureaucratic-industrial-military machine and the general population."[19] The decline of socialism is rooted in compelling historical changes that force a basic rethinking of issues related to conflict and change in the transformed setting. The crisis of modernity, collapse of the Keynesian welfare state synthesis, proliferation of new social movements, and diffusion of postmodern cultural and intellectual trends are particular signs of this shift.

Some key elements of the capitalist system first observed by Marx still persist: the idea that such a mode of production gives rise to its own social contradictions, that it naturally generates antagonistic class divisions, and that it is responsible for human alienation in every area of life. Despite major structural and ideological changes within capitalism over the past century, this system remains the source of intractable social problems. But the notion that socialism will grow almost mechanically out of objective historical conditions, that class struggle is the only driving force of emancipatory change, is no longer tenable. Indeed, the very concept of historical necessity, with its pseudo-scientific certitudes, can now be viewed as nothing other than sheer myth. The era of single agencies of revolutionary transformation—vanguard classes, parties, and elites—has finally come to an end, along with the eschatological idea of capitalist breakdown leading to mass insurrection. If socialism lives on today in any sense, it probably connotes nothing more, or less, than a process of ongoing democratization in the spheres of the economy, politics, and everyday life.[20] As for Marxism, it is already giving way to different variants of a post-Marxist synthesis that combines in diverse ways a number of distinct theoretical currents: Western Marxism, cultural radicalism, ecology, and feminism, among others. The eclecticism and indeterminacy of this framework corresponds to a world of increasingly dispersed conflicts and movements—and to the eclipse of a "pure" socialist ideal.

The continued irrationality of global capitalism prompts many Marxists to look ahead to the next wave of socialist struggles that will, somehow, overturn the distortions and misapplications of earlier "waves" that had to confront insuperable obstacles.[21] The twin failures of "revisionism" and "Stalinism" can be surmounted by drawing the appropriate lessons from a painful history. In the view of such Marxists, a system that revolves around markets, profits, and unbridled growth can only be replaced by a *socialist* order anchored to fully democratic structures and priorities. But the problem, as I have argued, runs much deeper than the presence of temporary detours and roadblocks; it goes to the very core of Marxian socialist theory. Moreover, the contemporary impasses leave us with nothing that can serve as future revolutionary models. Although many leftists still romanticize traditional labor struggles, the reality is that a distinct class consciousness no longer has the power to unite and mobilize large masses of people—if it ever did. It should be noted that, contrary to much received wisdom, traditional social democratic and Leninist strategies were *always* multiclass in nature.

For this and other reasons the "transition to socialism" has never been conceived in terms of a strictly class politics, informed by the vision of a proletarian majority taking power. If this generalization holds, then the vast complexity and diversity of anti-system movements today more than ever will require a wholesale reassessment of cherished premises.

The Democratic Imperative

If the socialist legacy has gone from crisis to decline, then what of democracy? Do the fates of the two greatest political ideals of the twentieth century remain intertwined? A striking feature of the social landscape in the West since the 1960s has been the rebirth of widespread citizen participation outside the realm of normal politics. The growth of local movements and popular protest has fostered an evolving paradigm of new radicalism defined by direct action, grassroots democracy, post-materialist concerns, and a redefinition of citizenship. It has been fueled by a broad distrust of elites and alienation from centralized state power that is commonly seen as bureaucratic, patronage ridden, and corrupt.[22] In many countries (Germany, Brazil, France, Italy, Sweden) Green movements and parties have established a subversive presence in this oppositional climate; their hope, in a transformed political culture, is to broaden the public sphere and challenge the traditional left for hegemony.

The degree to which the political culture in any of these societies has been altered significantly, however, remains open to debate. Social movements have established a durable presence in the West, but their democratizing potential has often been negated by institutional and ideological closure of the public sphere. Aside from a few notable exceptions (for example, Germany), Green and other post-materialist initiatives have been confined to civil society.[23] Popular struggles for local sovereignty and autonomy, extending individual and group rights, have their modern origins in the great European bourgeois revolutions and the spread of liberalism, from the time of Locke and later Paine, Jefferson, and Bentham, through the early anarchist and Marxist traditions and, in the twentieth century, syndicalism, democratic socialism, the new left, and the Greens. Visions and strategies have differed, but the democratic promise has been kept alive within the orbit of social movements that opposed dictatorial regimes and other forms of domination: state bureaucracy, corporate control, militarism, patriarchy, and racism. These recurrent struggles have produced an historic democratic shift toward liberal-pluralist politics defined by regular elections, constitutional rule, a framework of basic human rights, and multiparty competition. But today liberalism, no less than socialism, has emerged as a cloak for massive elite power and privilege. Indeed, the neo-corporatist public sphere that hovers over modern democratic initiatives may be even less malleable than what the early liberals faced two centuries and more ago.

Historically, capitalism and democracy have always been in conflict.[24] The very discourse of autonomy, participation, and citizen action finds little resonance in a productivist ethos of accumulation, economic self-interest, and possessive individualism. The separation of economics and politics in earlier phases of capitalist development encouraged a truncated, partial view of democracy that never extended beyond narrow state-institutional boundaries. The fear of untrammeled tyranny was balanced by an equally strong aversion to mass entry into the public arena that was commonly referred to as "mob rule." Liberal theory itself typically lacked a vocabulary of class, exploitation, and popular struggle, molded as it was by the force of property and market relations. But there is no way to avoid the critical question: What social and economic forms are most compatible with democracy? A strictly procedural emphasis favored by classical liberalism, and recycled for the modern context by Schumpeter and Dahl,[25] resolutely sidesteps this issue. Twentieth-century liberal capitalism conforms to what C. B. Macpherson calls the "equilibrium" model—a pluralist-elitist framework where participation is reduced to occasional choices among competing elites and citizen access to power is severely limited.[26] This paradigm subordinates even the more visionary liberal impulses of thinkers like Locke, Rousseau, Jefferson, and J.S. Mill to the authoritarian morass of modern state, corporate, and military power.

With the decline of liberal democracy, there is the further question of whether, and to what extent, capitalism can be effectively challenged within a liberal-capitalist framework. As mentioned previously, throughout the twentieth century—particularly since the 1950s—a convergence of liberal and socialist traditions has been taking place within European political culture. In the protracted legacy of parliamentary socialism that spans from Karl Kautsky to Palmiro Togliatti and the modern Euroleft, one finds a powerful leftist defense of exactly those procedural aspects of democracy that today appear so atrophied and so inimical to far-reaching social change.[27] Norberto Bobbio, for example, insists that the complexity and scope of modern society requires an elaborate system of democratic forms and procedures that inevitably limits the efficacy of direct action and popular assemblies; even socialism must depend upon a liberal foundation. Yet, as Perry Anderson suggests, any merger of these two traditions will probably foreclose prospects for any real "democratic road" to socialism, given the massive political and economic constraints at work. From a *political* standpoint, pluralist democracy is organically tied to the growth of huge corporations, the extension of state and military power, elections as media spectacle, and an atomized, depoliticized citizenry. In economic terms, struggles to overturn capitalism within strictly liberal-democratic parameters are bound to fail insofar as " the space for radical reform [in the system] is closed by the very properties of the economic order that call out for it."[28]

Today, perhaps more than ever, the very meaning of democracy needs to be clarified—its institutional norms and practices, its social and material conditions, its human and political tranformative potential. If a truly radical-democratic model is possible, then movements for change will have to expand the boundaries of both liberalism and socialism that, to this point, have bequeathed to us a common heritage of statism and social hierarchy.[29] Basic to such change is recovery of a sense of citizenship—elaborated first by the Greeks and later by such theorists as Rousseau, Jefferson, and Kropotkin—that long ago was corrupted by a an elitist, economistic, and individualistic version of democracy. As Sheldon Wolin observes, the advanced industrial countries have all the formal properties of democracy but none of the grassroots, participatory underpinnings; the discourse of citizenship itself is abandoned in favor of an abstract language of "rights" and "obligations."[30] In this context, politics is normally seen as an alien realm where fear, distrust, and cynicism hold sway over norms of citizen engagement that ought to shape democratic ideals. This demeaning of citizenship is linked to a weighty mood of powerlessness, a reluctant acceptance of state and corporate power even at a time of debilitating societal problems. According to Wolin, a strategy for democratization will have to renounce the outmoded "state paradigm" while building new forms of collective life largely *outside* the institutionalized corporate-state sphere.[31]

The democratic imperative thus entails a whittling away of concentrated power that ultimately depends upon a revitalization of civil society. As John Keane puts it, "[C]ivil society should become a permanent thorn in the side of political power."[32] To this might be added other forms of power. The historic task of broadening the foundations of democracy —resisted by liberalism and abandoned by socialism—begins to approximate what democratic socialism might mean in the modern world, even as the worn labels are questioned and eventually discarded.

Political Strategy and Social Change

Twentieth century politics has witnessed the failure of both socialism and democracy to fulfill radical promises. To some extent this failure may be understood as one of blocked convergence: socialism in its ideal conception always meant some form of *democratic* socialism (proletarian self-emancipation, workers' control, et cetera), but its actual legacy has been one of statism. However, the achievement of popular democracy required the breakdown of class and social divisions (an end to capitalism) —something that no country has yet experienced. Ideological labels (communism, socialism, even liberal democracy) have been compromised and discredited; the old claims are regarded with deep suspicion. Yet the ideals as such retain their validity in a world beset with human misery and powerlessness. Any future convergence of these ideals, however, will necessitate a fundamental rethinking of history, politics, agencies, even goals—not to mention the very ideological labels that define such ideals. The dilemmas of power identified by Gay at the outset of this chapter are simultaneously, and more deeply, rooted in the interplay between social vision and historical possibilities. And, following the pattern of turn-of-the-century socialism, they remain manifestly dilemmas of political strategy.

In a period of highly dispersed sites of conflict and opposition, there are clearly no easy resolutions of these questions. At the same time, if radical-democratic change has any future potential it will require a far more focused understanding of state governance in capitalist society than what has informed Leninism, social democracy, and even "third road" efforts in the past. This means that *strategic* thinking, grounded in a fusion of vision and analysis, planning and action, will have to engage the evolving post-liberal, post-socialist environment in creative ways. New strategies can only be effective if they accept a reality of shifting conditions, discourses, and methods.[33]

The theoretical resources needed to advance radical-democratic change include elements of both Marxism and liberalism—the Leninist idea of "smashing" the bourgeois state was rendered obsolete long ago—not to mention elements of communitarian anarchism, Western Marxism, critical theory, feminism, and ecology. The familiar hackneyed themes of "revolution" and "transition to socialism" do not begin to capture the more complex and diversified process of democratization that must incorporate every region of social and political life. If the state cannot simply be overturned, to be replaced by an entirely new political order, neither can it be ignored, as if civil society were all that matters; either extreme is a recipe for authoritarian rule. The state system will have to be confronted, reformed, and democratized in a way that coincides with parallel changes in civil society tied to grassroots social movements and forms of local democracy. Centralized power cannot be broken down and democratized unless the old insurrectionary and party-based models are finally jettisoned. The familiar bureaucratic distortions of Leninism and social democracy, along with the impotence of classical radical schemas, can be summed up in the crude one-dimensionality of those strategies: either vanguardism/statism or anti-statist localism. And such strategies, often burdened by a labor-centered dialectic, are incapable of confronting the *multiple* forms of domination — capitalism, bureaucracy, patriarchy, and so on—that characterize modern society.

It follows that any future post-Marxist strategy will have to approach the liberal-democratic state not as a fortress to be assaulted or conquered but as a shifting balance of forces that can, through radical intervention, be pushed gradually in a popular democratic direction.[34] The state in capitalist society is neither a monolithic apparatus superimposed upon civil society (posited by Leninism) nor a truly open, pluralistic, accessible political system that can be transformed strictly from within (assumed by social democracy). Nor is it the type of structure that can be expected to crumble from the cumulative assaults of popular movements (as conceived by the radical left). As Antonio Gramsci argued, the state in advanced capitalist society is organically tied to civil society and its labyrinthine web of social and authority relations, to a whole "*ensemble* of relations" touching the furthest reaches of daily life. More recently, Ernesto Laclau and Chantal Mouffe restated this concept as follows: "[T]he state is not a homogeneous medium, separated from civil society by a ditch, but an uneven set of branches and functions, only relatively integrated by the hegemonic practices which take place within it."[35] In strategic terms, a transformative politics is unthinkable without democratization of all spheres of public life, including the state, workplace, and community. The main problem for the left today, which also corresponds to the suppressed legacy of democratic socialism, is that such a strategic model does not exist and perhaps cannot exist (or at least prevail) in a universe of rapidly shifting political discourses and actions.

2

THE MARXIST ORIGINS
From Theory to Politics

THE MODERN CONCEPTS OF DEMOCRACY AND SOCIALISM HAVE THEIR ORIGINS IN
the late-eighteenth- and nineteenth-century discourses of classical liberalism, utopianism, and early Marxism. As an outgrowth of the French and
American Revolutions, along with the industrial and technological transformations sweeping Europe and North America, democracy and socialism
symbolized a break with the past: the *ancien régime*, feudalism, Church
hegemony, rigid social hierarchies. Yet the ideals and visions that grew out
of this historic process—freedom, equality, community, rights—were
scarcely the product of any emerging consensus. On the contrary, they
became very much part of a contested terrain shaped by rival interests, ideologies, and movements that accompanied the great bourgeois revolutions,
the popular upheavals of 1848, the Paris Commune and, finally, the rise of
labor unions and parties in the 1870s. Within this profound shift of social
and authority relations the fate of democracy and socialism was deeply, and
seemingly forever, intertwined.

As Macpherson correctly suggests, even within the liberal tradition there
was little consensus about the meaning of democracy, beyond the vague
notion that governments should in some way rest upon a foundation of con-
sent and obligation.[1] Issues regarding social class, the state, legality, and
modes of participation led to sharp debates. In its original phase, going back
to the time of Locke, liberal democracy could be understood as simply one

dimension of the capitalist revolution, with its emphasis on private property, market relations, and the strivings of *homo economicus* within civil society to achieve a full measure of citizenship. Clearly such market assumptions about human behavior and *social development*—restated in different ways by Adam Smith, Jeremy Bentham, and James Mill—have permeated liberalism up to the present. The utilitarians, who viewed human beings as maximizers of (economic) self-interest, hoped to base democratic principles upon a foundation of classical political economy, which, in the end, could sustain only the most limited forms of popular influence. Madison and other early American liberals seemed to agree that the main idea of representative government was to promote a free market and guarantee property rights within an institutional framework that not only protected ordinary citizens from tyrannical rule but also insulated elites from the turbulence of mass action (or "mob rule"). The market oriented liberals always postulated an organic connection between capitalism and democracy.[2]

Other liberals, however, saw this relationship as far more problematic; their view of participation was more cultural and political than economic. Thus Rousseau, affirming the key importance of equality and community for realization of democracy, questioned whether a system grounded in private property and material expansion would ever be compatible with genuine democratic practice. Paine called for an ethic of political responsibility that celebrated militant popular action in the service of revolutionary change. Jefferson insisted that democracy be grounded less in fancy slogans and paeans to the capitalist market than in commitments to the economic independence of *all* citizens. And J.S. Mill, rejecting his father's narrow utilitarianism, argued for a broad, visionary conception of democracy that entailed cultural and intellectual—not just economic—development of human beings liberated from the dead weight of feudalism. For Mill and others, liberal politics was not to be reduced to the laws of capitalist production. Such views, although still confined to the parameters of liberal ideology, were more emancipatory insofar as they combined what Macpherson calls the "developmental" and "participatory" strains of the tradition.[3] At the same time, with the notable exception of Rousseau, the market mechanism and class structure of capitalism remained unchallenged.

Of course, the utopian socialists, anarchists, and other radicals of the period had entirely different intentions: Their search for a genuine (egalitarian, communal) democracy forced them to reject the harsh realities of class society. If the fullest development of the human personality was an ultimate goal, then the capitalist division of labor, with its various hierarchies, would have to be eliminated to make room for more socialized modes of activity. Since liberalism failed to confront class and power divisions, it was regarded as little more than a deceitful sham. Most liberals adhered to the Enlightenment belief that a new era of democracy would arise from a confluence of factors: collapse of feudal authority, emergence of the market, diffusion of science and technology, and the accumulated effects of popular suffrage, rights, and freedoms. In contrast, the radicals proposed a deeper transformation of civil society leading to breakdown of the social division of labor as a true measure of democracy; liberal ideals appeared as mere abstractions when material conditions were left out of the equation. It was in this ideological context, and based upon these political sensibilities, that Marxism first established its roots in the 1860s and 1870s. Indeed, the whole theme of democracy was fully restated by Marx and Engels—a restatement that proposed, for the first time, a systematic convergence of the two epic projects: democracy and socialism.

Classical Marxism: State, Revolution, Democracy

Any discussion of Marxian politics inevitably starts with the ambitious, systematic critique of capitalism undertaken by Marx and Engels in the nineteenth century. The source of an entirely new, and increasingly complex, social division of labor, capitalism embodied not only a specific mode of production (a break with the feudal past) but an entirely new civilization in the making, with its own distinct culture, politics, laws, and ways of life. With the emergence of a new class system, pitting the ruling bourgeoisie against oppressed workers, the capitalist order was rooted in a logic of maximizing profits, exploitation, and, sooner or later, class polarization. Marx and Engels anticipated that this polarization would be hastened by explosive social contradictions of the system and worsening conditions of proletarian life: alienation, poverty, disempowerment. Driven by the imperatives of capital accumulation, the bourgeoisie would be unable to significantly ameliorate the conditions of polarization. The predictable result, as the *Communist Manifesto* affirmed confidently, would be proletarian revolutionary overthrow of capitalism leading to the abolition of classes and the eventual rise of socialism.[4]

Marx and Engels saw the bourgeoisie as a dynamic, predatory force bent on manipulating Enlightenment values of economic and scientific rationality in order to support its own interests. Progress meant the unleashing of human productive capacities on a new scale, tapping the potential for creativity, innovation, growth—and of course material self-aggrandizement. As capitalism brought new wealth and technology, it also brought enormous misery to workers and groups that were pushed to the margins of society. Despite its dynamic historical role—and its grandiose promises of freedom, democracy, and prosperity—the ruling class in fact *blocked* the potential for general human progress. From a classical Marxist standpoint, therefore, liberal-democratic claims resting upon a foundation of constitutions, laws, procedures, and formal rights were empty abstractions, since they flew in the face of harsh economic realities; the vast majority of workers and poor were excluded from the benefits of Adam Smith's "invisible hand," the Hobbesian "social contract," and Hegelian notions of a universal will.

As a theory of radical change based upon proletarian self-emancipation, early Marxism (if such a label makes sense) sought to assert its conceptual supremacy not only over liberalism but over (right) Hegelian philosophy, the utopians, and anarchism. Each of these rival theories lacked an adequate grounding in historical conditions and class forces. For Marx and Engels, there could be no unitary notion of democracy that ignored the social context of individual or group choices; capitalism by its very nature subverts participatory, collective alternatives. To be genuine, democracy would have to tap the depths of human self-activity within civil society, as part of an historic *struggle* to overcome burdensome scarcity and alienation. And such a process, of course, could only be the work of subordinate *classes* fighting to transcend their status as objectified entities and force a break with the logic of capitalist rationality.

In certain respects, Marx and Engels tended to equate democracy with mass struggles—for example, the European uprisings of 1848 and the Paris Commune of 1870–71, temporary as these were. In a more profound sense, however, the unfolding of democracy was viewed as a transformative *process* requiring much more than constitutions and legal procedures. If capitalism brought exploitation and misery to the proletariat, the system would eventually also generate class consciousness among enough workers to produce a massive revolutionary force. Acting as an organized universal class, workers would fulfill their democratizing mission, transcending the distortions and illusions of liberal democracy at the same time.

The Marxian concept of the state must be understood in this context. In contrast to the liberal view of state power as more or less the expression of common, public, and universal values, Marx adopted a more dialectical theory: the state is a product of historical and social development, a manifestation of class formations and class struggle. As Marx and Engels put it in *The German Ideology* and elsewhere, the modern state in capitalist society is dominated by the bourgeoisie; indeed, its primary function is to reproduce the conditions of capital accumulation. A key element of bourgeois domination, the state operates as an ideological and repressive apparatus needed to sustain orderly and stable rule. From this standpoint, even the most liberal-democratic state perpetuates its existence as alienated power. Only by means of its transcendence and abolition, as proletarian social and political power begins to erode its oppressive and coercive functions within civil society, does the state lose this essential class character. So long as the state exists as a mechanism imposed on civil society, the very possibility of democracy—of generalized popular rule—is negated.

Was liberal democracy, therefore, nothing but a sham, a false arrangement to deceive and tame the masses? Sometimes Marx and Engels appear to take this position—for example, in their famous reference in the *Manifesto* that "the state is nothing but the executive committee of the bourgeoisie"—but on the whole their critique was more modulated. On the one hand, the bourgeois state does rest upon various fictions: liberty and citizenship for all, the common good, universal ideals. And it does clearly embody the alienation of the mass of citizens from politics, which they experience as either coercive (governmental decisions) or inconsequential (popular input). Yet the actual evolution of states is obviously more complex, an outgrowth of powerful tensions between the particular and the universal, form and substance, domination and autonomy. In fact, unchallenged monolithic rule has been rare. It turns out that liberal democracy, with all of its flaws, does allow a modicum of space for class contestation. While capitalism needs bureaucratic and even coercive power to preserve its stability, where universal suffrage and other rights have been won the state constitutes a terrain upon which the masses can achieve limited but nevertheless empowering reforms.

Classical Marxism actually never formulated a coherent theory of the capitalist state. In general, Marx and Engels sought to ground their view of politics in the materialist conception of history or, more specifically, in the logic of capitalist development: this was basically the analysis contained in Marx's *Capital* and Engels's *Origins of the Family, Private Property and the State*. Pushed to extremes, this scheme tends to reduce state functions—indeed all politics—to underlying economic factors. But neither theorist was content with such a mechanistic formulation: class struggle was too explosive, and state power far too variable, for reductionism of this sort to make political sense.

What required analysis was the relationship between class and state power, especially under conditions of liberal democracy. Of course, the state typically served bourgeois interests in myriad ways—safeguarding the accumulation process, intervening at moments of crisis, legitimating the capitalist order, et cetera. Economic power was paramount, and the ruling class was able to establish the rules of politics in virtually every case. Still, that was hardly the end of the story: the state may possess varying degrees of autonomy (a phenomenon never fully explored by Marx), and thus is not simply and *always* a direct instrument of capitalist rule. Clearly the bourgeoisie utilizes democratic forms (elections and parliaments) as a technique of manipulation and control, insofar as they serve to mystify or conceal the *real* sources of (economic) power. But class power is never uniformly translated into state power, and liberalism in particular introduced a whole new range of mediating pressures and contradictions. For one thing, popular struggles give bourgeois-democratic forms new content by pushing those forms to new limits, reshaping in the process the contours of political activity and reconstituting the state as contested terrain.[5] Neither Marx nor Engels, however, managed to theorize this problem very clearly—a lacuna that would later have far-reaching strategic implications.

If democracy in the discourse of classical Marxism suggested a critique and transcendence of both capitalism and liberalism, then the outlines of an alternative democracy should have been visible enough. In fact, Marx and Engels devoted little attention to this problem. Marx did take up the question of *socialist* democracy briefly, in *The Civil War in France*, where he analyzed the legacy of the ill-fated Paris Commune. In its valiant attempt to transform Paris into a popular democracy, the Commune seemed to Marx to represent the embryo of a new revolutionary order, despite its catastrophic tactical mistakes. On the one hand, by seizing power so boldly in the French capital, the proletariat acknowledged its "imperious duty" to render itself "the masters of its own destiny." On the other, the inevitable collapse of communal power revealed a bitter truth: The working class could not simply conquer the ready-made state machinery (that is, the bourgeois state) and wield it to its own purposes.[6]

The Commune was set up as a working body comprised of various executive and legislative functions. Its key significance for Marx was the truly *popular* character of its governmental system: municipal councilors were chosen by universal suffrage in the various wards of Paris, and all offices were revocable at short terms. The first decree of the Commune abolished the standing army and replaced it by the armed people; the police were stripped of their political power; church privileges were abrogated; public service was to be done at workers' wages; and every public servant, including magistrates and judges, were to be elected. In sum, all political initiatives were taken from the central government and put in the hands of the general electorate. The Commune, as Marx saw it, was a model of "self-government of the producers," based upon *mandat imperatif* and held together by local assemblies. It was a true break with the past—an overthrow of centralized state power that had been a "parasitic excrescence on the nation."[7] Marx saw in the Commune a "thoroughly expansive political form, while all previous forms of government had been emphatically repressive."[8] The first working-class-defined political system in history, "the Commune was...to serve as a lever for uprooting the economic foundations upon which rests the existence of classes and therefore class rule."[9] By taking matters into its own hands, by infringing upon the prerogatives of the "natural superiors," the Commune demonstrated that the working class was the only force capable of transformative social action.

In reality, the Parisian *coup* never came close to being socialist, or the "glorious harbinger of a new society"—nor could it have done so. For one thing, the notion that the Commune was a proletarian affair was a myth; workers made up only a small minority of the movement and government, and they were not the leaders. For another, the political methods behind the conquest of power were far more Jacobin or Blanquist (that is, vanguardist) than Marx seemed willing to admit. The Commune, inspired by the efforts of Parisian radical intellectuals and cut off from the rest of France, was in part the product of romantic delusions of revolutionary change. Still, Marx's commentary on this episode reveals, more than elsewhere in his writings, a keen sense of the dialectical relationship between politics and economics and, in his vision of the future, an attachment to the ideal of local self-government that resembled Proudhon's quasi-anarchistic federalism more than anything else.

Marx's reflections on the Paris Commune pose yet another range of questions concerning the role of the state—in this case involving the relationship between socialism and democracy during the transitional process. Quite obviously, what happens during the transition from capitalism to socialism (or full communism in Marx's terms) will have an enormous bearing upon future social and authority relations. This is one reason why the issue of political strategy looms so large in the Marxist tradition. A major difficulty with classical Marxism, however, was the absence of any coherent basis of strategic thinking. Indeed, it is possible to locate at least "three tactics" in

Marx, as Stanley Moore, argues[10], but even this does not exhaust the complex debates that extend from Marx to those concerned with the challenges of twentieth-century politics.

At the most general level, Marx believed that capitalism would give rise to the conditions of its own supersession, owing to deep, intensifying contradictions that, in the end, could not be suppressed. The system was doomed on the basis of its own inherent developmental logic: capitalism laid the foundations of revolutionary change by virtue of its thoroughgoing transformation of social existence, with an exploitative mode of production giving way to more rational forms. The transition to socialism would require a gradual process during which the old order more or less exhausts its potential, exposing the heightened contradictions. This coincides with Marx's emphasis, in *Capital* and elsewhere, on the processes of accumulation and class formation in the long-term development of capitalist society. Here Marx looked mainly to the English model, with its gradual shift from feudalism to capitalism and the slow emergence, within civil society, of a majority proletariat prepared culturally and politically to seize the initiative.

Marx largely avoided strategic discussions, on the grounds that the precise conditions of transitional politics could never be predicted; the revolutionary overthrow of state power would be the final act in a long historical drama. Where the English model held sway, the main agenda of socialists would be to build a strong, independent, majoritarian working-class movement by means of education, union and party organizing, and the incessant struggle for reforms—as Marx advocated in the *Manifesto*. The proletariat can become a new dominant force only where, as a majority, it effectively advances democratic struggles in both civil society and the state. Where revolution is the work of a small Jacobin elite it is inevitably a *false* revolution imposed upon a civil society not yet ready for socialist transformation. Only when increasing misery, class polarization, and anti-capitalist consciousness pose an imminent threat to the system does a revolutionary overthrow make sense. Implicit in Marx's general outlook was a strategic flexibility allowing for socialist participation in the bourgeois state, incrementally and peacefully—at least up to the moment of a fundamental shift in power relations. But the nature of that shift itself was never defined. Presumably it would not be engineered by a Jacobin vanguard, for that would subvert the claim of a broad proletarian movement struggling democratically to transform civil society.

By the 1880s and 1890s, with the rise of strong parliaments, universal suffrage, and mass parties in Europe, Marx and Engels came to endorse, without much equivocation, participation in the bourgeois state as a viable instrument of class struggle. Engels's co-authorship of the Erfurt Program for German Social Democracy in 1891 solidified this strategic turn, even as it retained the familiar critique of liberal democracy as a sham[11]; Engels understood, as before, the bourgeois state to be a form of alienated politics where people are able to exercise little real control over their lives. Early Marxism adhered to the idea that winning power ultimately meant the overthrow of capitalism, which was simultaneously an economic and political fact: It meant nothing less than the full expression of proletarian self-activity.

Electoral politics, of course, had enormous *tactical* utility: It could help to educate, organize, and mobilize workers for change; it could secure meaningful reforms. And it could even bring some measure of institutional power. Marx and Engels understood fully that winning elections would never be tantamount to winning class power, but they did believe—from all indications—that it could pave the way by empowering the disenfranchised majority. Yet if universal suffrage offered the proletariat new opportunities, there were serious limits and pitfalls. Could an insurgent movement or party resist the compelling logic of parliamentarism? As Marx cogently observed in *The Civil War in France*, the proletariat could not simply hope to conquer the existing state machinery as a stepping stone to revolution; instead, its goal must be to create entirely new state forms consonant with a socialist mode of production. More than that, the ultimate vision would necessitate a radical abolition of politics—a transcendence of coercive state power in any form—made possible by the emergence of a classless society. If class divisions gave rise to the state forms as an instrument of domination, then the shift toward a classless society was something akin to a "withering away of the state"—the precise features of which neither Marx nor Engels ever specified. Genuine *socialist* democracy was premised on a complete dismantling of the state system including, presumably, the various accoutrements of *liberal* democracy. After a necessary transitional period, popular socialist initiatives would create the foundations of local self-government consistent with the "free association of producers." Participation in the bourgeois state was apparently meant to be *tactical*, in the sense that liberal forms were not expected to carry into the revolutionary future.

Democracy: A Marxist Predicament

For Marx and Engels, the ideal of socialism meant public ownership of the means of production, abolition of inequality and exploitation, breakdown of the old social divisions—and democracy. It is hard to doubt the democratic sensibilities and intentions of classical Marxism: if capitalism signified oligarchy and domination by its very logic, then socialism was inherently democratic, since the state was no longer a coercive domain of professional bureaucrats, the military, and the police. Inspired by the Paris Commune uprising and the growth of labor movements in Europe, Marx and Engels were strongly optimistic about the future.

This optimism, however, was never informed by any clear articulation of either political strategy or post-capitalist revolutionary forms that were expected to define the new egalitarian order. Although this is understandable in the context of classical Marxism, which focused on the dynamics of capitalist development, it did lend ambiguity and confusion to later Marxist struggles around issues related to democracy. As noted above, Marx's only extended discussion of a post-revolutionary state was contained in his account of the Commune in *The Civil War in France*, where he referred to the radical democratization of public life in glowing terms, citing its break with the oppressive past: the end of coercion and terror, deprofessionalization of administrative tasks, establishment of a peoples' militia, opening up of free expression, and so on. It was an enviable model, but the Commune was eventually turned into a debacle when the French Army crushed it, killing about 14,000 citizens and deporting another 10,000 in the process. What was patiently built over several months was brutally destroyed in only a few days, with little effective resistance. Unfortunately, the larger political implications of this disaster—and its relevance to Marx's overall theoretical structure—never received much attention. Nor did such analysis enter into Marx's deliberations elsewhere. Thus, from the standpoint of classical Marxism, a truly viable and *democratic* politics of class struggle remained shrouded in ambiguity.

Marx's overwhelming emphasis on economics, on the dynamics of capitalist development, left the precise institutions of political power that were to shape the larger process of social transformation unaddressed. What is the relationship between social and state power? What popular agencies of change were to engineer the revolution? What were the mechanisms of proletarian consciousness formation? Of organizational leadership? Of strategic intervention? Even more relevant to the issue of democracy: How was the bourgeois state to be reconstituted or, if necessary, overthrown? What were the structures of democratic participation, both during the transition and in the post-revolutionary setting? On these vital questions classical

Marxism was virtually silent or so vague that it was impossible to draw firm political conclusions.

The familiar dilemmas concerning strategies for winning state power clearly illustrate this problem. For example, we have seen how the general theoretical outlook of classical Marxism—visible in the *Grundrisse* and *Capital*—supported the idea of a majoritarian revolution grounded in work-ers' self-activity and the gradual (but fundamental) transformation of civil society. State power would be confronted at the very end of a long historical process, which, however, was never clearly outlined. Stanley Moore refers to this model as the "majority revolution."[12] Marx's abiding fear of Jacobinism was evident in this outlook. Yet, as Moore correctly argues, the Marx-Engels inclination between 1844 and 1850 was something altogether different: in their writings of that period, they assigned the decisive role to a small cadre of dedicated elites who would carry out an insurrectionary overthrow of bourgeois power, a strategy influenced by the French radicals (Babeuf, Blanqui) and the vanguardist Communist League. According to this vision, sometimes referred to as "permanent revolution," the proletariat would seize the initiative from the capitalists as part of a continuous transformative process defined by radical leaders. Moore's term for this model is "minority revolution."[13] Finally, there was the strategic view, apparently favored by Marx and Engels beginning in the 1870s, that a gradual reformism carried out within the institutions of bourgeois democracy could lead to socialism in advanced countries (for example, the U.S. and Holland) where liberalism was deeply entrenched. New opportunities provided by universal suffrage, along with the growth of trade unions and mass parties, might allow for a relatively peaceful, evolutionary transitional process. Moore calls this approach the "competing systems" strategy.[14] In later years the Marxian clas-sics were cited in support of each political choice—Kautsky's "orthodoxy," Lenin's vanguardism, and Eduard Bernstein's reformism. It can further be argued, based in part upon Marx's understanding of the Paris Commune, that a *fourth* tendency associated with radical insurgency and workers self-management (later pursued by syndicalists and council communists) might be located in the Marx-Engels texts.

In no instance, however, did the classics elaborate the foundations of a democratic socialism: this absence of a *political* theory of the transitional process was one of the most striking features of early Marxism, with pro-found consequences for twentieth century socialist politics. Beyond vague notions of popular control that were expected to supersede class-based sys-tems of state power, no framework of a post-capitalist democracy was ever suggested. This predicament goes to the very core of Marx's theoretical vision, for it dramatizes a lack of concrete political mediations linking long-range goals and immediate popular struggles.

Such an imposing void cannot be attributed to historical contingency, ambiguities in the texts, or flaws in strategic reasoning. The problem runs much deeper: the theory lacked from the outset any systematic political foundations, and thus any articulation of uniquely socialist forms of authority that would supersede the old forms of domination.[15] This void within early Marxism has several explanations, the first and most obvious being that Marx and Engels (along with many subsequent theorists) thought that communism on a world scale would arise organically and also quite rapidly. Issues of power, democracy, and strategy were never regarded as pressing or urgent insofar as the flow of history would somehow "resolve" them without the need for political formulas and strategic blueprints (which, in any case, were seen as "utopian"). Marx apparently believed that socialist transformation would resemble the transition from feudalism to capitalism (roughly following the English model), at least to the extent that changes in civil society would necessarily precede, and anticipate, the actual transfer of political power—but he never conceptualized this process in relation to the problem of strategy.[16]

A second—and tightly connected—source of difficulty is that Marx's most significant opus, *Capital*, was largely a critique of political economy, a theory of the workings of the capitalist system that in many respects remained confined to the very historical paradigm it sought to transcend. The framework, imposing in its brilliance, nonetheless tends to undercut creative political vision since its categories (wage, price, profits) were so thoroughly imbued with bourgeois categories. Moreover, although Marx himself never reduced politics to an "underlying" economic structure, he did supply Engels and the orthodox Marxists of the Second International with a theoretical arsenal sufficient to sustain their own devaluation of politics.

The rigid materialism and scientistic objectivism of these early Marxists collapsed the role of political strategy—indeed, every aspect of human subjective intervention—into an all-engulfing apparatus of production that constituted the driving force of history. Their imputed laws or mechanics of capitalist development undermined the need for a conscious, well conceived scheme of transition grounded in the ongoing struggle for a democratic socialist order. The familiar scenario of crisis and breakdown of the capitalist economy amounted to a fatalistic, even metaphysical, conception of history, which propelled Marxism toward the most naive, almost apolitical, faith in progress made possible by the fullest expansion of market forces. If capitalism was expected to disintegrate from its own internal contradictions (the falling rate of profit, crises of overproduction, immiseration of the proletariat), then the transitional phase, however defined, was never really viewed as problematic. The ends and means of revolution were understood as immanent in the logic of capitalism itself, more or less automatic responses that rendered superfluous any concerted effort to *build* new social and authority relations through all stages of historical change. Engels and Plekhanov, even more than Marx, insisted that the *real* objective was a new system of production, an entirely new material base upon which a rational, egalitarian order could be constructed. The notion of defining *in advance* the actual character of socialist transformation was ridiculed as an exercise in abstract speculation; after all, change was seen as a process born more out of dialectical "necessity" than of conscious political intervention.

Yet another element of this predicament stems from Marx's ontological view of history—and with it his understanding of how human identities are forged—as shaped by material processes: laws of economic motion, labor process, class relations, and so forth. These were clearly central features to any socialist outlook, but Marx allowed them to obliterate other aspects of the social totality, including divisions (and identities) forged around race, ethnicity, gender, nationality, religion—and politics. An otherwise dialectical theory ignored the rich and complex interplay between material factors and these multiple divisions embedded deeply in human history. It also ignored the powerful role of ideology and culture in shaping or mediating class and power relations, and in molding personality structures at least partly independent of economic forces.[17] The guiding assumption that a rational, socialized economy controlled by the proletariat would naturally generate transformations elsewhere was consonant with a one-dimensional (and profoundly undemocratic) politics.

The limits of classical Marxism became all the more obvious by the 1890s, when theory entered into the sphere of movements, parties, and, later, governments. Abstract concepts like "dictatorship of the proletariat" and "withering away of the state"—even the conquest of power itself—were scarcely useful in the day-to-day political battles that consumed Marxian socialists. The very ideal of socialism was quite often deferred to a remote (and typically indecipherable) future. Meanwhile, with no *socialist* political theory to guide them, European trade unions and labor parties found themselves engulfed by, and often attached to, liberal-democratic institutions, virtually by default. The result was that prevailing (bourgeois) definitions of power and democracy quickly became the operational code of social democratic elites in practice. In both its orthodox (Kautsky) and reformist (Bernstein) variants, social democracy appeared as the culmination of the bourgeois revolution precisely to the extent it integrated the proletariat into the liberal-democratic public sphere. In overcoming this impasse, the Leninist vanguard model set out to "smash" the bourgeois state and seize power on behalf of the workers and peasants, establishing a centralized proletarian "dictatorship" that, by its very *raison d'être*, would represent the (imputed) democratic interests of the masses. But, aside from its glib references to the soviets, which in Russia were eventually colonized by the party-state, vanguardism suffered the same fate as social democracy: absence of a democratic-socialist theory and strategy.

Not that such outcomes could be attributed to a theoretical void in the classical texts alone. It would be unrealistic to expect a full-blown theory of the capitalist state or democratic self-management from socialists whose formative concepts were developed in the mid-nineteenth century. The point is not so much that the work of Marx and Engels was unfinished (especially as it applied to the state), but rather that their major contributions preceded the era of parliamentary democracy and mass socialist parties. Engels lived long enough to witness the origins of German social democracy as a mass-based electoral party, but the German Social-Democratic Party (SPD) was only in its infancy when he died in 1895, thus ruling out the possibility of his reflective historical analysis and judgment. Neither Marx nor Engels had any real experience with liberal forms, and, moreover, there is little in their writings that anticipates the great transformations of the modern state system. This left the door wide open for subsequent theorists and movements to articulate political strategies more or less *de novo* in the fluid and explosive period between 1895 and the mid-1920s, as they struggled to come to grips with the legacy of classical Marxism in the context of new political challenges.

After Marx: The Quest For Political Strategy

Out of the debates, factional schisms, and popular struggles of this period evolved four identifiable Marxist tendencies: the orthodox or "centrist" (the Kautsky-Bebel prewar influence within the SPD, Austro-Marxism), the reformist-evolutionary (Bernstein, Turati, most of the trade union leadership), the vanguardist-insurrectionary (Lenin, Bordiga, the early

Comintern), and the radical left (Luxemburg, the council tendency). Each represented an often coherent, sometimes chaotic groping for political solutions during a time of social turbulence, war, and new conflicts posed by imperialism and the Bolshevik Revolution. And each operated, often implicitly, from a distinct set of premises concerning the nature of the state, the overall assessment of capitalist development and imperialism, the problem of democracy, and sources of class consciousness. Of course, attitudes toward parliamentary democracy (at that time a novel phenomenon in many countries) varied greatly, even if these attitudes did not always produce concrete strategies and tactics.[18]

If the fight for socialism involved a common dedication to values of equality, a rational-secular culture, and internationalism, this implicitly meant a struggle for democracy. But democracy—much like these other values—was the object of widely diverse meanings, interpretations, and definitions, just as the ideal of socialism was the focus of competing strategies. Hence the creative synthesis of classical Marxism, which aspired to a kind of systemic totality, produced its own inner tensions and ambiguities after the turn of the century.

Marxism achieved its first widespread organized political expression in the Second International, spanning the period from 1889 to World War I. The main function of the International was to coordinate the activities of the increasingly large number of socialist formations concentrated in Europe. Leszek Kolakowski has referred to this period as the "golden age of Marxism," insofar as the theory at that time constituted a recognizable school of thought but was not yet codified into any system of a dogmatic orthodoxy.[19] In fact, the major parties—German, British, French, Belgian, Italian, Polish, Russian—were influenced to varying degrees by both Marxist and non-Marxist ideas. British socialism, for example, was shaped as much by the utopians, progressive liberals, and, later, the Fabians as by Marxism. The Italian Socialist Party (PSI) was the product of syndicalism as well as Marxism. Moreover, party leaderships were divided into rival factions, so that unity and consensus were norms typically honored only at the level of ideological ritual.

The leading party of the Second International was the SPD, which had its roots in the German Social Democratic Workers Party founded in 1869 under the leadership of August Bebel and Karl Liebknecht. The most dynamic socialist organization in Europe until the War, it fought for labor unionization, universal suffrage, social reforms—as well as an end to Bismarck's repressive state, which, among other things, imposed harshly restrictive laws against the SPD. Despite these laws the party grew during the 1870s and 1880s, winning 1.5 million votes and returning thirty five deputies to the Reichstag in 1890. The SPD's Erfurt Program of 1891 outlined a comprehensive and optimistic vision of socialist revolution grounded in mass struggles for labor reforms, parliamentary action, capitalist regulation, anti-militarism, women's rights, broadening of public health care, and universal education. Many of the proposals contained in the *Communist Manifesto* could be found in Erfurt more than forty years later. Party leaders shared the view that reforms would help push capitalism headlong toward crisis and collapse—toward its rendezvous with history. The SPD skillfully built upon its popular, forward-looking image to win three million votes in 1912 (giving it one-third of the total and making it the largest party in Germany). Political success was based upon three pillars: electoral strength, trade unions, and community-based organizations like cooperatives. This tripartite strategy was also pursued by other parties in Europe, to varying degrees.

Kautsky, who co-authored the Erfurt Program with Bernstein and Engels, was not only the theoretical leader of the SPD but the guiding "orthodox" figure of the Second International. The conception of Marxism that Kautsky adopted early in his political career was hardly modest—that of a unified, self-contained system of thought embracing the totality of social existence. If Marxism could stand as a coherent scientific theory grounded in naturalistic principles, then its power of vision and analysis required no enrichment from outside sources. Kautsky viewed socialism as an historical necessity rooted in the laws of motion of capitalism, which would generate anarchy, economic breakdown, class polarization, and, ultimately, a revolutionary assault on the system. In this schema, the realm of ideas, culture, and consciousness was decisively shaped by unfolding material forces; the growth of proletarian class consciousness was seen as a natural response to these forces. Following Marx, Kautsky believed that socialism was possible only once capitalism had reached its most advanced stages.

In *The Class Struggle* and other writings, Kautsky emerged as the original architect of what later became known as the parliamentary road to socialism.[20] Whatever the nuances of his strategic outlook or changes in his views after 1914, he never wavered from his commitment to liberal-democratic forms as the main arena of political action. The economic and social complexity of advanced countries (Britain, Germany, the U.S.), along with new opportunities provided by the growth of suffrage, mass working-class parties, trade unions, and legislative bodies, made insurrection outdated.

Kautsky argued that since the gradual expansion of proletarian organizations and culture made possible by capitalism gave socialists new levels of ideological and political strength, the state as it was constituted by the bourgeoisie could be used for anti-capitalist ends.[21] Of course, the powerful German state was still a class apparatus—one controlled by the ruling capitalists in pursuit of their own interests—but this relationship could be turned around once the process of democratization opened up new spaces for frontal struggles against the system. Parliamentary activity, by crystallizing and legitimizing socialist goals, would accelerate this process by hastening the breakdown of capitalism, which could not indefinitely sustain more efficient and socially equitable forms of production. At least until 1914 Kautsky believed that socialism would never arrive without a revolutionary *rupture* involving seizure of political power by the organized proletariat.

Leaving aside controversy over the mythical "fifty one percent" working-class support needed for a transition to socialism, the advantages of a parliamentary-based strategy were for Kautsky quite clear. It would introduce the masses to norms of democratic participation, help forge class solidarity and a sense of political empowerment, and minimize the need for violence—while presumably curbing the authoritarian power of the military and state bureaucracy.[22] Above all, it would help socialists gradually establish control of political institutions, which he thought could be wrested from controlling bourgeois interests. Kautsky abandoned the simple instrumental approach to the state as a tool of ruling-class domination in favor of a more *dialectical* view: Class struggles eventually determine the character of political institutions.

Although Kautsky's concept of the transition assumed a complete overturning of the capitalist economy, it did not anticipate the kind of automatic collapse or catastrophic break with the past that is commonly read into his theory. True, the Erfurt Program did endorse the breakdown scenario—without, however, drawing out the strategic implications of such a scenario. The theory he adhered to throughout all the twists and turns of social-democratic politics was that of a series of economic crises building toward class confrontation and a break with the outmoded structure of capitalist production.[23] In other words, the economy was seen as the locus of sharpening contradictions generated by objective historical forces, while the political system (that is, bourgeois democracy) was viewed as a stable, durable form persisting through all stages of socialist transformation.[24] But here Kautsky remained frustratingly imprecise about how and through what mechanisms the break was expected to occur—no doubt a lingering residue of his Marxist "orthodoxy."

If Kautsky consistently pressed for a merging of socialism and democracy, it was typically *parliamentary* democracy that he had in mind; one does not encounter a discussion of *socialist* democracy, or even a systematic critique of the liberal state (including bureaucracy), anywhere in his work.[25] At times he seemed to rely strictly on electoral-legislative activity as the basis for advancing working-class interests and socialist politics.[26] He was implacably hostile to all types of extra-parliamentary struggle (for instance, "direct legislation," mass strikes, popular assemblies), the more so after 1914 when his famous debates with Lenin came into the open. He regarded local, anti-institutional forms as a heritage of pre-industrial, syndicalist politics, appropriate to the adventurism and irrationality of romantic sectors of the peasantry and petty bourgeoisie. As for ongoing management of the state and economy, Kautsky had little patience for such high-sounding but ambiguous ideals as popular self-management and workers' control. The requirements of planning and coordination in a complex society essentially closed off any alternative to centralized administration, even under socialism.[27] Although the "parliamentary road" stood opposed to arbitrary state rule, authoritarian social controls, and the oppression of minorities, it appeared comfortable with the workings of normal legislative and bureaucratic routines.

Kautskian strategy presented itself as the legitimate heir to the Marxist classics, resting its case upon premises (especially the breakdown thesis) that seemed less and less relevant to the European historical situation and the real opportunities it furnished. In contrast, Bernstein's political evolutionism corresponded more directly to the immediate practical interests of the SPD's trade union and parliamentary leadership and reflected, moreover, the party's actual strategic location. Bernstein shared Kautsky's fixation on parliamentarism and the idea that socialism, to be truly democratic, must inherit and *expand*, rather than overturn, liberal institutions and practices.[28] But he diverged sharply from the conventional Marxist belief—identified with the late Engels, Bebel, and Kautsky—that capitalism would give rise to unresolvable contradictions, propelling it toward crisis and class polarization and leading eventually to a basic rupture in the old social relations of production. Bernstein viewed capitalism in the advanced European countries as stable and adaptable enough to contain imminent crises. An expanded public sphere, the vitality of electoral politics, a flourishing trade union movement, and increased prosperity all indicated the possibility of a reconstituted capitalism that, as it became progressively democratized, might evolve peacefully toward socialism. Although he presented his theory as a critique of the breakdown scenario, it was really something else—a complete rejection of the notion that capitalism cannot survive its own internal crises, and that the transition to socialism requires a qualitative break with the past.[29]

If Bernstein shared Kautsky's hostility to insurrectionary politics, the former went much further in his theorization of a unilinear, relatively harmonious, and crisis-free transition to socialism. For Bernstein, whose volume *Evolutionary Socialism* precipitated explosive debates after 1900, the ultimate goal would be realized on the basis of new opportunities presented by a dynamic capitalism rather than the unfolding of historical laws leading to class warfare. From this viewpoint, the bourgeois state was more than a simple organ of class domination; its expanding democratic forms constituted a public sphere within which socialists could enhance their economic and political power. *Economic* strength would derive not only from the growth of labor organizations and social reforms but also from the greater prosperity that capitalism brought even to workers (or at least the most skilled and privileged sectors, which Engels referred to as the "aristocracy of labor"). *Political* strength would derive from the numerical growth of the proletariat and, with it, broadening membership and popular support of socialist parties.

According to Bernstein, when socialists managed to carve out new positions of electoral and institutional power within the existing political system, as the SPD had done, they could bolster their capacity to win genuine reforms that might whittle away capitalist domination and generate a new balance of forces.[30] Instead of an explosive rupture, capitalism would gradually give way to its negation—to socialism. In the optimistic environment of the SPD, Bernstein thought that the *ends* of socialism were nothing more than the actual reform process itself, which had little to do with the outworn revolutionary phraseology of Marxist theorists. Thus, he asked, "But is social democracy today anything beyond a party that strives after the socialist transformation of society by means of democratic and economic reforms?"[31] The pillars of reform were unions, cooperatives, and municipalities, as well as parliament itself. Here Bernstein departed from Kautsky, who insisted that reforms were worth winning only to the degree they solidified and empowered the working-class movement as it moved toward its ultimate goal of socialism.

Bernstein flatly rejected the classical Marxist emphasis on historical laws, class polarization, and capitalist breakdown scenarios. For him there was no single logic of capitalist development; the system varied enormously from one setting to another. His evolutionary thesis favored an "ethical socialism" over dialectical necessity, empirical observations of social reality over teleological assumptions about the future. Since future vision was dismissed as abstract, utopian, and metaphysical, the struggle for incremental reforms assumed the status of an ultimate goal; socialism was simply one of many possible outcomes.

Bernstein went far beyond Kautsky in his view that liberal democracy represents the *sine qua non* of modern political institutions: it has permanence, allows for genuine popular participation, and must be a decisive feature in the struggle for reforms. Indeed, socialism is the "legitimate heir" of liberalism, insofar as the broad aims of both are the "development and securing of a free personality."[32] Talk of democratic socialism was regarded by Bernstein and the SPD right-wing as "romantic nonsense." References to classical schemes like proletarian self-emancipation and "the withering away of the state" were seen, predictably, as lacking political substance. Like Kautsky, he accepted the centralized state with its various hierarchies as an unchangeable feature of complex modern society, and he defined suffrage as the most important form of political engagement. Given their agreement on such basic premises, it is hardly surprising that earlier theoretical differences between Kautsky and Bernstein narrowed (and eventually collapsed into the Bernsteinian evolutionary schema) in the 1920s, with the Jacobin fears spread by the Bolshevik Revolution and the rise of a more democratized Weimar Republic.[33]

Bolshevism: A Jacobin Response

There was an enduring consensus among theorists and leaders of the Second International that socialism required centrally coordinated forms of production and state administration, that the old anarchist (and syndicalist) vision of a stateless order governed by small, local, self-contained communities was hopelessly utopian. It was assumed that, with the socialization of the economy, the state would be transformed into an organ for the social administration of things rather than of people. At the same time, Marxists in the advanced European countries uniformly insisted that socialism would be nothing without democracy: universal suffrage, party competition, freedom of cultural and political expression, the right of assembly. Indeed, democracy was generally regarded as an automatic feature of socialist transformation—however limited that democracy might have been conceived. Both Kautsky and Bernstein, for example, recognized that various democratic freedoms—products of both bourgeois revolutions and working-class struggles—had become fixed elements of European politics, central to the very idea of progress. From this standpoint, the idea of a vanguard revolution was unacceptable, since it would lead inevitably to the imposition of state authority on civil society and the subversion of democratic practices.

The Second International consensus that socialism demanded high levels of capitalist development and liberal democracy was countered by Lenin's Jacobin model (first outlined in 1902) and the Russian Revolution, which more or less followed its prescription. The pre-revolutionary Russian context that provided the backdrop of Leninist theory and Bolshevik practice, of course, lacked even the bourgeois-democratic trappings of the Wilhelminian state in Germany. Oppositional politics was denied legitimacy under tsarism, forcing popular movements to conduct their struggles underground in an atmosphere of repression and quasi-military combat. Lenin's theory and strategy drew more or less exclusively from this experience. He was familiar with European parliamentary systems and even commented at length on how Marxists should approach the relatively open sphere of elections, legislatures, and trade unions (as in "Left-Wing Communism"), but his concern was always more tactical than theoretical.[34] Hence Lenin's theory of the state, along with the political strategy it inspired, was largely a theory of the authoritarian *tsarist* state even though Lenin employed the term "bourgeois state" quite loosely in his writings.

Understandably, therefore, Lenin defined the state that the Bolsheviks had to confront after 1903 as a repressive apparatus built strictly for the reproduction and defense of ruling-class interests. Insofar as "the state is the product of the irreconcilability of class antagonisms" and constitutes "an organ for the oppression of one class by another,"[35] it stood as an alienated structure above civil society, detached from mass struggles and from the interests of the vast majority of the people. The core element of the state, bourgeois or otherwise, was the central bureaucracy—the main locus of class rule even where parliamentary forms existed. Although Lenin thought that within capitalist development the bourgeoisie would allow, and possibly thrive on, limited democratization, he was also convinced that the bureaucratic side of the state would reassert itself and close off this space in response to economic crisis, war, and the thrust of oppositional movements. He viewed bourgeois democracy as simultaneously illusory and fragile—illusory because during stable times it would be manipulated by the ruling class to instill in the masses a false sense of participation, fragile because it was not likely to survive the advanced stages of imperialism and war. In Russia, the frail beginnings of democratization (the dumas, constituent assemblies, and so on) were cut short when the regime of Nicholas II tried desperately to maintain its hegemony in the midst of crisis and popular upheaval.[36]

Lenin harshly attacked the thesis (supported in Russia by the Mensheviks) that existing state forms, no matter how "democratic" they appeared, could be internally restructured and taken over for socialist purposes. Efforts to route the struggle primarily within and through the state would sooner or later run up against powerful business interests and the bureaucratic Leviathan, reducing any "democratic" strategy to a sad illusion. The only viable solution was one of frontal assault channeled through mass mobilization outside the institutions of state power and directed toward their dismantling. The only rationale for participating in those institutions (for example, the duma in Russia) was tactical and propagandistic, to prepare for their overthrow on the path to socialism. In their place would be erected new mass, proletarian forms of power, the nucleus of a new state (dictatorship of the proletariat) that would give new meaning to democracy. Although these forms would initially require some hierarchy and centralization, their class content rendered them far more democratic than any preceding system because they embraced the historical interests of the vast majority. Lenin argued that constitutions and legal procedures (so vital to *liberalism*) mattered little, since they only conceal the more significant elements of class power and coercion: the key question is always which class exercises domination.[37]

At this point, Lenin's thinking moved in two directions. There was the Lenin who argued for direct democracy in *State and Revolution*, who called for "dual power" and "all power to the soviets" during the revolutionary events of 1917 and in his final months expressed great anxiety over the party-state bureaucracy that was already getting out of control. And there was Lenin the architect of the vanguard party, the believer in firm political and economic discipline, and the worshipper of capitalist forms of technology and administration.[38] In the course of history the second Lenin readily prevailed over the first: the dictates of revolution itself, the Civil War, and global isolation favored centralization of power, while "democracy" (both within the Bolshevik party and Russian society as a whole) came to be viewed as a "petty-bourgeois illusion." Embryonic structures of self-management, including soviets and factory committees, were destroyed or disappeared within a few short years after the October Revolution; by 1921, after Lenin's ban on internal factions, the struggle for party democracy was resolved on the side of the centralists. Thus, the dictatorship of the proletariat already contained the seeds of bureaucratic centralism that were later to find such fertile soil under Stalin.[39]

The key to understanding Lenin's centralist impulses lies in his theory of the vanguard party, which lent continuity to his strategic outlook after 1902 and most closely corresponded to Bolshevik practice. From the outset Leninism stressed the dangers of "economism" and "spontaneity" (equated with narrow trade unionism and anarchism) and called for a unified, centralized, and flexible revolutionary organization that would be more effective than the open, disaggregated parties of the Second International.[40] Such a party was designed less for the supposed ordeal of underground battle (a theme commonly overplayed) than for the task of carrying out a Jacobin-style revolution. Two important conditions shaped this strategy: a small proletariat coexisting with a huge peasantry in an overwhelmingly pre-industrial society, and a weak state with precarious ideological support and subject to extreme crises of legitimacy.[41] All of the celebrated features of the classical vanguard party—quasi-military command structure, the professional cadre, power orientation, ideological unity—make sense in this context.

For Lenin, in contrast to Kautsky and Bernstein, everything hinged on the immediacy of the revolutionary struggle for power. As Lukács observed, Lenin succeeded in refuting the "laws" of capitalist development and injected a sense of urgent political action into Marxism; the strategy was one of *Realpolitik*.[42] The pressing agenda was not socialism—that remained in the distant future—but the seizure of state power in order to establish the *preconditions* for socialism. Leninism thus advanced the subjective element but tied it to instrumentalist concerns about methods and techniques. The state itself, through the intervention of the militant party, was seen as the primary weapon of class struggle. After the manner of Machiavelli's *Prince*, the party-state emerged as the agent of political rejuvenation and the embodiment of a new collective will. Since the dictatorship of the proletariat (embracing interests of the oppressed majority) was a qualitative advance beyond the dictatorship of the bourgeoisie or the *ancien régime*, domination was not considered a problem by the Bolsheviks: what counted were the *purposes* for which power was used. Nor did the vaguely anarchistic vision of participatory democracy that Lenin sketched in *State and Revolution* define the actual transition to socialism.[43] Form and content would have their own separate realities. Bureaucratic centralism and statism were thus built into

the Leninist model from the outset, confined as that model was to the theoretical and political limitations of the Russian context.

If Lenin's Jacobinism meant conquest of state power as the first priority,
with socialist development to follow, then the party-state was inevitably
superimposed upon an amorphous and even hostile population. Mediating
structures (soviets, factory councils, local organizations) that could help
democratize the revolutionary process had little space to flourish, and were
ultimately either obliterated or transformed into "transmission belts" of
party policy. A shift in social and authority relations was the main responsibility of the vanguard, whose contradictory task could only perpetuate the
gap between state and civil society historically typical of Russia.[44] The logic
of this situation was clear: An ideologically enclosed stratum of professional revolutionaries became the exclusive theoretical and political bearer of
socialist aims, which produced two separate levels of discourse, two realms
of activity—one expressed through the radical culture and language of
intellectual activists, the other through the manipulated responses of the
popular strata.[45]

As early as *What Is to Be Done?* (1902), Lenin carved out the rudiments
of a theory that would lead to such a division of labor. Following Kautsky's
famous *Neue Zeit* essays, he argued that Marxism was the product of an
intellectual rather than working-class tradition and would have to be
brought to the proletariat from outside the class struggle, through the initiative of the (vanguard) "external element." (Kautsky's paternalism, of
course, assumed a much different form than Lenin's.) Spontaneous mass
action would forever be unable to break free of bourgeois ideology because
such action, trapped in its social immediacy, could never adequately grasp
the *totality* of relations that would move it to a higher plane. Lenin wrote:
"Class consciousness can be brought to the workers *only from without*, that
is, only from outside the economic struggle, from outside the sphere of
relations between workers and employers. The sphere from which alone it is
possible to obtain this knowledge is the sphere of relationships of *all* classes
and strata to the state and the government, the sphere of the interrelations
between *all* classes."[46] For Lenin, then, the notion that only revolutionary
elites can possess scientific knowledge (Marxism) informed his concept of
the vanguard party as the repository of the historical interests of the proletariat.

Although Lenin was no Blanquist—he explicitly rejected the idea that revolution could be the handiwork of a small clique of conspirators—his outlook was always that of a vanguardist hoping to seize power at the right

moment. In this strategic context, the visionary anti-statism of his *State and Revolution* could produce no effective anti-statist politics, no real concept of socialist democracy grounded in new forms of authority. His uneasiness with the authoritarian excesses of the young Soviet regime could generate no serious critique of bureaucracy.[47] And his commitment to soviet power and workers' control of industry did not preclude his introduction of "one-man management" and the borrowing of capitalist methods of organization.[48] All this made perfectly good sense given the weight of a political strategy designed to overthrow the autocratic tsarist state and consolidate Bolshevik power under harsh conditions.

The Radical-Left Alternative

In the years preceding World War I, the European socialist tradition was riding a great crest of optimism: after significant leaps in popular support and electoral success in a number of countries, socialism appeared to be on the verge of dramatic political victories that would seem to confirm Marx's vision. Capitalism appeared to be entering a phase of crisis and upheaval. The industrial proletariat had grown rapidly in both numbers and class consciousness. The future seemed to belong to a socialist movement that was regarded as the true heir of Enlightenment and democratic values. With the onset of war, however, most social-democratic parties wound up endorsing the military policies of their own governments, thus abdicating their commitment to proletarian internationalism; many lost their ideological identity in the midst of chaos and confusion. And none of the parties were strategically prepared to seize revolutionary opportunities that came during and after the war. Social democracy had reached a political limit, lacking the capacity to intervene in part because of the debilitating bureaucratic flaws earlier identified by Michels.[49]

The Bolshevik Revolution broke this impasse, bringing to power the world's first "socialist" government and restoring—at least for a time—a global sense of Marxist ideological fervor. The European left had experienced a momentous triumph. The validation of Lenin's strategy was simultaneously a powerful blow against the Kautsky-Bernstein vision of a parliamentary road to socialism: the SPD, among other parties, emerged from the war electorally strong but lacking ideological direction. After 1919, with the formation of the Comintern, nascent Leninist parties mounted serious challenges to the social democrats in several European countries. Yet the

Bolshevik success was hardly an unqualified one. Isolated in the wake of failed revolutions elsewhere, the Soviet model gave rise to strong authoritarian practices, which, already by the early 1920s, crushed the very local democratic forms that had propelled the Bolsheviks to power. The seeds of bureaucratic centralism, as we have seen, were planted by Lenin as far back as 1902, when he outlined his theory of the vanguard party.

These flaws in both social democracy and Bolshevism were rather visible to broad groupings of European radicals, within and outside Marxism, who believed that the historic leftist commitment to democracy, equality, and community had given way to facile compromise with the bureaucratic state. The sources of radical-left critique, which affirmed local self-management against hierarchical control, date back to the utopian socialist, anarchist, and syndicalist traditions of the nineteenth century. Strong in southern and central Europe, as well as in Russia and England, these traditions were an enormous catalyst to working-class mobilization from 1890 through the 1930s. They also constituted the ideological basis for a fourth strategic alternative within Marxist debates of the period—one that was identified mainly with the German-Dutch radical left. In the aftermath of the abortive 1905 revolution in Russia, prominent figures like Rosa Luxemburg, Anton Pannekoek, Herman Gorter, and Henriette Roland-Holst organized a small nucleus of radicals who were prepared to challenge the narrow parliamentarism of the Second International. Rejecting the strategic alternatives offered by Kautsky and Bernstein, they looked to spheres of struggle beyond routine party and trade union activity: the mass strike, popular insurrection, factory committees, workers' councils. Their vision of democracy, consonant with Marx's theme of proletarian self-emancipation, emphasized local revolutionary forms and processes transcending the limits of the bourgeois state, as well as (later) the Leninist system of "proletarian democracy" in Russia.

Georges Sorel's revolutionary syndicalism was perhaps the most militant radical voice at this time. Sorel mounted a wholesale assault on social democracy, while attempting to recover an ethos of class warfare and proletarian independence that was lost in mainstream socialism. Influenced by Nietzsche and Bergson, Sorel, whose major ideas were contained in *Reflections on Violence*,[50] emphasized psychological factors—notably the role of "myth"—in the development of class consciousness which he believed was more significant than the "objective" factors stressed by Marx, Engels, and Kautsky. In fact, Sorel turned away from Marxism *tout court*, dismissing the theory as excessively abstract, pseudo-scientific, and a less-than-useful guide to action. In contrast, Sorel upheld the principle of spontaneity tied to direct, unmediated mass insurgency—to the heroic proletarian seizure of power at the point of production. The defining features of Second International orthodoxy, including all-embracing theoretical schemas, historical laws, and elite intervention, were a deadly recipe for workers' passivity. For Sorel, revolution would be a total, apocalyptic, even violent event led by the workers themselves rather than party and trade-union leaders or intellectual vanguards. The end result would be nothing short of direct self-management by the associated producers. His brilliant insights into the failures of Marxist orthodoxy, influential in the later development of Western Marxism, could not be ignored.[51] The alternative proposed by Sorel, however, was yet another matter: Although clearly popular and democratic in spirit, his embrace of unbridled spontaneity and glorification of class warfare allowed for no concrete institutional definition of revolutionary process compatible with democratic ideals.

For Luxemburg, the democratic pronouncements of SPD and Bolshevik leaders were equally devoid of content. Democratization for her involved more than programmatic statements, efforts to "broaden" liberal structures, or promises of equality and popular rule to be introduced by benevolent, tutelary elites at some later stage. She viewed it as a deeper process of social transformation firmly rooted in mass self-activity. Within the SPD, Luxemburg fought against elitism, bureaucracy, and authoritarian manipulation that was typically justified by appeals to "scientific" Marxism; against this she argued for the more or less unmediated subjectivity of the proletariat, which she fully expected to produce a revolutionary democracy characterized by "self-administration of the masses." In contrast to most in the SPD hierarchy, she was always vigilant in the search for new political opportunities, new avenues of struggle, new forms of popular initiative. She found her inspiration, as did Sorel, in the explosive mass strike based upon the volcanic (but ultimately futile) 1905 Russian upheavals.[52]

The foundation of Luxemburg's strategic orientation—and for the radical left in general—was the imminent crisis of capitalism, which for her (contra Kautsky) ruled out prospects for internal transformation of the bourgeois state. With advancing crisis, popular upheavals would force the bourgeoisie into an authoritarian posture to defend its threatened class interests; electoral victories would turn out to be hollow, and social reforms (where possible) would only help to stabilize a faltering capitalist system. The parliamentary road was a myth, since it never challenged the real centers of bourgeois power nor looked to the masses as the actual protagonists of democratic socialism.[53] In opposition to Bernstein, Luxemburg insisted that no concept of transition was possible without a theory of crisis based on the social contradictions permeating capitalist development. And,she argued, in opposition to both Bernstein and Kautsky, democratization involves proletarian control of production as well as the state. Her conclusion: The leading SPD strategists had become hopelessly trapped within a liberal conception of democracy.[54]

As for Lenin, she shared only his views that capitalism was in the throes of global crisis, that parliamentary systems were little more than adornments of bourgeois power—and that the controlling state apparatus would have to be overthrown, destroyed, and replaced by a revolutionary system of power. (Here, of course, Luxemburg's focus was the prewar German state.) But they differed fundamentally over the essence of the new state, as well as over the political methods for achieving it. Luxemburg maintained that the vanguard party was bound to trample upon norms of democracy in the name of organizational efficiency, inevitably reabsorbing the masses into a new bureaucratic order. She was convinced, rightly as it turned out, that Lenin's authoritarian means would subvert his proclaimed emancipatory ends. The problem with vanguardist politics lies in its obsession with a power-oriented leadership, which emerges as a substitute for mass activity and social struggle. True, the mobilization of popular support is necessary for the revolutionary conquest of power, but the active, leading, decisive component remains the party.[55] Lenin hoped to sidestep this problem in two ways— through a definitional startagem (dictatorship of the proletariat equals democracy) and by deferring the issue to a future stage (when the withering away of the state would accompany the full realization of communism).

Luxemburg was the first important Marxist theorist to pose the question of socialist democracy. Yet, unlike Kautsky, Bernstein, and Lenin, she never formulated an integrated political strategy that could produce concrete tendencies within the mass struggles of the time. Rejecting the twin extremes of parliamentarism and vanguardism, she found refuge in the "masses," in much the same fashion as Sorel, as she struggled to counter the powerful anti-democratic currents at work within Marxism. But her vision of a mass strike—and her call for a "dialectic" between leaders and followers—furnished no tangible solution to the problem of building a sustained democratic socialist movement. Her uncompromising faith in the mass strike resembled, more than anything else, a Sorelian myth that enabled her to avoid the intricate questions of democracy in their concreteness, as part of the struggle to create radical economic and political institutions.

The task of identifying the constituent elements of democratic-socialist strategy was left to Antonie Pannekoek and the council communists, whose main premises (imminent crisis, proletarian self-management, direct mass action, and so on) were close to Luxemburg's. Not content with the diffuse spontaneism of the mass strike scenario, they were more attracted to the *organizational* development of local democratic forms (soviets, factory committees, workers' councils) that appeared in 1905 Russia and later grew into sizable movements not only in Russia but in Italy, Germany, Hungary, the Netherlands, and elsewhere. They saw in the council form the embryo of a revolutionary order more collective and transformative than anything envisioned by the social democrats or Lenin.

Pannekoek's analysis of the SPD situated the party within early phases of capitalist development: once having achieved an institutional presence within the political system, the SPD adopted the logic of bourgeois politics. Social democracy came to embody not the subversion of bourgeois society but its rationalization, insofar as it stabilized the state apparatus by reinforcing methods of formal democracy, initiating limited social reforms, and integrating large sectors of the working class into the system. Thus, "In Germany, the development of the party form was subject to the particular conditions of the bourgeois revolution and served, through its Marxist imagery, to achieve for the emergent proletariat a secure place within capitalism."[56] The growth of imperialism, which fostered a militant nationalism within growing strata of the working class, further encouraged this tendency. By 1908—at about the same time Luxemburg, Michels, Sorel, and Gustav Landauer were refining their own critiques of German social democracy—Pannekoek had concluded that the historical task of the SPD was to "reorganize capitalism on a new foundation," on the assumption that the working class, through its parliamentary and trade union strength, could eventually conquer the state machinery. The reality, however, would be a new system of domination (state capitalism) erected behind the "facade of socialism."[57]

Pursuing this line of thought, Pannekoek found himself engaged in a head-on theoretical clash with Kautsky in 1912. Writing in *Neue Zeit*, Kautsky chastised the radical left for its seeming anarchistic indulgence of undisciplined mob politics and its lack of organizational focus—surely a valid critique when applied to some radical currents. Pannekoek responded that Kautsky's single-minded parliamentarism, not to mention his equation of socialism with nationalization and state planning, led him into a theoretical and strategic cul-de-sac: preservation of the existing state system at all costs. For Pannekoek, this was more than a question of Kautsky's failure of imagination: "It is simply that our perspectives correspond to different stages in the development of organization, Kautsky's to the organization in its first flowering, ours to a more mature level of development in which a variety of forms of action (insurrectionary as well as legal) could be integrated into a total revolutionary process, all leading to the dissolution of the capitalist state."[58] Kautsky was so preoccupied with organizational growth and survival of the SPD that virtually his entire theory and tactics served to shield the bureaucratic apparatus from the risks of social revolution."[59] The fatal defect of parliamentarism was that, whatever the disclaimers of its supporters, it saw electoral activity "not as a means of increasing proletarian power, but as the battle itself for this power," which sooner or later led to an institutionalized political division of labor within the movement. Wrote Pannekoek: "If one holds that political conflict should occur exclusively within parliament, then the parliamentarians are the only people called upon to wage it. It is not the working masses who are involved, but their representatives who fight on their behalf. The masses only figure at the ballot boxes…. The party deputies thus take up a vanguard position; they become a special class, the 'guides.'"[60]

The foundations of a new order, therefore, needed to be built outside the organized Marxist parties and trade unions, for the leadership of such organizations was too committed to preserving its bureaucratic status. The best strategy was ultimately what the workers fashioned themselves by means of their own activity. All other "solutions" that delivered mass initiatives over to representatives or delegates were illusory, for, in Pannekoek's words, "The real forces of revolution lie elsewhere than in the tactics of parties and the politics of governments."[61]

The institutional alternative to a party-centered socialism would be a federated system of local councils. In the highly charged atmosphere of postwar Europe, with capitalism in crisis and social democracy in shambles, the council radicals thought that the tremendous upsurge of proletarian militancy would organically and spontaneously generate a flowering of revolutionary organs at the point of production—a dream that was to be only partially and briefly fulfilled. Pannekoek was convinced that the emergent "soviet system" would in time uproot and abolish the state bureaucracy, transferring the management of production and society into the hands of the masses and laying the basis of a fully socialized state. This process was expected to mature through internal proletarian struggles, as a by-product of capitalist evolution rooted in the "natural groupings of workers in the process of production, the real basis of society."[62] Here Pannekoek and the council communists shared Luxemburg's critique of the Bolshevik Revolution, but he carried the analysis even further. He concluded that in Russia "Marxism" (or Leninism) became the modernizing ideology of a radical intelligentsia bent on mobilizing a small proletariat behind essentially state-capitalist objectives. The predictable result was a new system of production directed by a state bureaucracy and rationalized by a centralized planning apparatus—with the workers forming an exploited class.[63]

Pannekoek saw in local councils the primary agency of socialist transformation; they would constitute instruments of popular control at the workplace and in communities and provide mediating forms between proletarian self-activity and revolutionary goals. Councils would flourish particularly at times of crisis, accompanied by mass strikes, occupations of plants, and other modes of direct action. Like Gramsci in Italy, Pannekoek looked to the councils as mechanisms of struggle against ideological domination; the new system of authority had to rest upon *psychological* as well as structural foundations. Pannekoek located the failure of the Bolshevik Revolution in its inability to achieve this fundamental shift as the source of its early degeneration.[64]

The council movement soon collapsed of its own inertia and isolation, or was absorbed into the party and trade union spheres once the postwar upsurges subsided. It was in Italy that the councils produced their most dramatic successes—and failures. In the period 1918–20 hundreds of factory councils (*consigli di fabbrica*) sprung up at Fiat and other factories in Turin, transforming the city into a "Petrograd of Italy." Built around the *Ordine Nuovo* movement, councils became the catalyst for massive demonstrations, general strikes, factory occupations, and street actions. Gramsci, the leading theoretical force behind *Ordine Nuovo*, heralded the *consigli* as the beginning of a "new era of humanity"; he saw in them the bearers of a revolutionary momentum advancing "beneath the political institutions of bourgeois society" and against the inertia of the Socialist Party and trade unions.[65] By breaking down the old habits of obedience and passivity, creating new social relations at the point of production, the councils appeared as the nucleus of a new socialist state where centralized authority and hierarchy would become superfluous. Gramsci envisioned the councils, which in Turin were only embryonic forms of workers' control, as key agents of ideological struggle, helping to instill in the proletariat a "psychology of the producer" that would enable it, as a class, to overcome its sense of impotence. The councils would also be prefigurative, insofar as they could liberate that which is potentially socialist within capitalist society by realizing emancipatory values in the present.[66]

The historical reality of the Italian councils fell far short of this visionary Gramscian theory. For one thing, while the *consigli* upheld direct democracy and attacked the principle of "delegation," in practice they operated according to delegation and elected a small council of commissars to direct all activities. Further, coordination *between* councils was never effectively worked out. Beyond that, the council movement was almost totally cut off from the Socialist Party and the unions; isolated politically as well as geographically and economically, *Ordine Nuovo* was vulnerable to the armed might of the bourgeois state, which finally brought its power to bear during the factory occupations of April-May 1920 and resolutely crushed the council insurgency.[67] Although council communism was destroyed or eventually died out in Italy and Central Europe after World War I, the tradition lived on, to reappear again in new contexts: in Spain during the Civil War, in Italy again during the Resistance, and in many industrialized countries during the 1960s.

From the standpoint of democratic vision, the radical left opened up new theoretical and strategic territory within the Marxist tradition—and beyond. In fighting against the very notion of party-centered socialism, the left refused to succumb to the liberal conception of democracy or Lenin's conflation of vanguard party and general will. Moreover, since the workers were "innately" revolutionary they had no need for leaders to teach and organize them; mass insurgency generated its own local discourse that was neither scientific nor esoteric. Yet the radical-left framework, too, was riddled with ambiguities and contradictions. A theory of self-conscious proletarian struggle, it lapsed at times into a rigid economic determinism; an effective critique of statism, it failed to develop an alternative concept of the state upon which a viable political strategy could be built; a compelling theory of democratic transformation, it expressed an extreme productivism that gave rise to a narrow workerism—with it faith in a heroic unitary proletariat—that precluded any notion of *generalized* self-management or social revolution outside the workplace.

As for the council movement itself, insofar as its strength depended upon extreme crisis, its trajectory was bound to be unstable and ephemeral. Unable to understand this limitation, Pannekoek and the council theorists never came to grips with the incapacity of the postwar insurgency—including the one he experienced firsthand in Germany—to survive as a democratizing force.[68] (Gramsci did come to grips with this obstacle, and left behind the legacy of the *Prison Notebooks* in his effort to synthesize the radical-left and Leninist approaches.[69]) Ironically, the productivism and localist impotence of the council movement arose from the same mechanical separation of politics and economics that was a major flaw in social democracy, with the order of emphasis now reversed.[70]

The Triumph of Statism?

The fate of European Marxist parties and movements in the twentieth century has been decisively influenced by these early struggles and debates, which seem to reappear in each new setting. It is noteworthy that each major current placed great emphasis on democracy as an integral part of socialist transformation, consistent with Marx's original vision, but none actually developed a comprehensive theory of *socialist* democracy. Each was therefore partial, having failed to put forward even those objectives necessary for democratization: generalized self-management, reconstitution of social life, overturning of the capitalist division of labor. Problems involving the critical issue of state power in the transitional process were never worked out—in fact, were never adequately *confronted*.[71] And not coincidentally, each downplayed or ignored the role of popular consciousness—that is, the sphere of active, subjective intervention in everyday life vital to the unfolding of self-emancipating human personalities and social relations. The privileging of "scientific" over "ideological" discourse, a major legacy of classical Marxism, reproduced a division between elites and masses that in the end was bound to devalue popular self-activity.

For Kautsky and Bernstein, the problem was a theory confined to the very assumptions of liberal politics, including their failure to extend even a limited understanding of democracy into the sphere of civil society. The radical left was able to overcome this problem, with its emphasis on direct, non-bureaucratic forms of struggle, but ended up without a *political* strategy that could give shape to such forms; it either dismissed the role of organizational mediations altogether (Luxemburg), or lapsed into a strict production-centered schema that turned the entire bourgeois society into an immense factory (the council communists, early Gramsci). Finally, Lenin's Jacobin preoccupation with vanguardist solutions (later shared in modified form by Gramsci) simply deferred the question of democracy: Statist methods of mobilization and control were the natural outgrowth of the Leninist instrumental drive toward state power forged in conditions of harsh struggle and global isolation.[72]

Despite their differences, what all of these currents shared was a mechanistic conception of the state that detached politics from the economy, indeed from the whole realm of civil society.[73] What they lacked was a vision (and strategy) pointing toward transformations in each sphere of bourgeois society. Of course, these theories were products of an earlier (competitive) phase of capitalism, when the state was much less developed and less organically enmeshed within the broader system; political institutions were not yet involved on any large scale in accumulation or legitimation functions. Under such conditions, a relatively feeble and isolated state apparatus appeared more vulnerable, either to a simple process of internal democratization or to direct overthrow from outside. The anticipation of massive crisis and upheaval, shared by all in this period except Bernstein (who abandoned any revolutionary pretensions), reinforced this rather cavalier attitude toward the state. Like Marx in the 1840s, these currents embraced a triumphal stance that looked to the impending dissolution of capitalism and rapid march toward socialism. This helps to account for the exceptionally vague discussion of transitional forms during this period (again, with the qualified exception of Bernstein). It also explains the simplistic dichotomies that characterized strategic debates of the time: parliamentarism versus insurrection, reform versus revolution, internal democratization versus vanguard organization.

The failure of the European radical left to break out of its insularity and generate a sustained movement beyond the postwar crisis meant that the Marxist legacy would be appropriated by social democracy and Leninism (or its Stalinized variant) until at least the 1960s. In both cases, the theory eventually served as the legitimating worldview of political elites and cadres, industrial managers and planners, parliamentarians and trade-union bureaucrats—all of whom, whatever their motivations, would use their power to maintain a privileged status over the "masses" they claimed to represent.[74] Although social democracy and Leninism pursued different roads to power (especially once the latter became a model for Third World revolutions), the result was that both strategies led to the same anti-democratic politics: extension of bureaucracy in both the state and economy, political division of labor within the movement, suppression of social revolution and local forms of self-management. By the late 1920s, and emphatically by the 1930s, the idea of socialism had become inseparably connected with the reality of authoritarian politics.

3

AFTER LENIN
The Defeat of Democratic Socialism

OUR REFLECTION ON THE EARLY MARXIST TRADITION ILLUMINATES A SERIES OF intense debates around leadership, organization, and political strategy that were never resolved. Yet the post-World War I historical context—the Bolshevik Revolution, failed insurrections in Europe, the rise of fascism and Stalinism—ultimately forced certain outcomes of those debates. Among other things, the fast pace of events undermined and then obliterated the teleological dimension of socialist politics: popular self-emancipation, social equality, democracy. Marxist theory, increasingly assimilated into bureaucratic social-democratic and communist parties, became so detached from its origins as to be unrecognizable. In the period 1920 to 1945 these parties, much like European politics in general, gave rise to an authoritarian and statist legacy that would continue for decades.

The defeat of democratic socialism in the 1920s, however, was not strictly a matter of historical conditions: the trend toward authoritarianism was reinforced by theoretical and strategic flaws carried forward within the Marxist tradition itself. Above all, none of the prewar strategies—social democracy, Leninism, the radical left—were able to produce a conceptual framework of the transition from capitalism to socialism adequate to a truly democratic agenda. The best that could be achieved was a replication of the liberal democratic formula confined to the limits of elitist pluralism. None were able to give full articulation to the conditions under which the capitalist division of labor might finally be overcome, including the *political forms* of a democratic-socialist state. In the end these approaches led either to institutionalized absorption into the bourgeois state (social democracy), bureaucratic centralism tied to the party-state (Leninism), or retreat from effective political engagement altogether (the radical left).

In the absence of a comprehensive theory of *socialist* authority relations, these strategic models either paved the way for new systems of domination or wound up adapting to the existing ones—or simply vacated the political field entirely. In one way or another, they fed into the familiar "statist myth of socialism," which has persisted throughout the twentieth century.[1] The classic ideal of merging socialism and democracy—or, more accurately, establishing the basis of a uniquely democratic socialism—was now reduced to an abstracted and ritualized discourse that had little to do with a genuine shift in social and authority relations. Socialism was redefined to satisfy the instrumental needs of party elites for the moment as they struggled to win power, whether by electoral or insurrectionary means. Within Marxism, such a predicament dramatizes the significance of mediating structures that could link immediate popular struggles with long-term, transformative goals. In any event, the triumph of statism was never a function simply of "revisionism" or "Stalinism"—not to mention the leadership's "betrayal" of the masses—but had deep roots in both the historical conditions and strategic outlooks of the time.

Eclipse of the Radical Left

A persistent quandary for socialist politics, therefore, was how to create a revolutionary strategy that could be simultaneously effective and democratic, that could overturn the old power structure without duplicating its repressive features under a different ideological guise. The outlook most sensitive to this problem—and most visionary in its politics—was always that of the radical left (especially council communism), which actually owed more to the anarchist and syndicalist traditions than to Marxism itself.[2]

The first principle upheld by all radical-left currents was uncompromising hostility to statism: the goal was to *replace* the centralized political apparatus with popular organs, not to "smash," conquer, or even transform it. Anti-statism embraced three fundamental concerns: aversion to *all* forms of social and political hierarchy; discomfort with large-scale parties and trade unions that independently perpetuate bureaucracy, oligarchical control, and the split between leaders and masses; and the ideal of prefigurative struggle within local organizations (workers' councils, soviets, action committees) that anticipate a future liberated society and "state" in the present. The radical left sought a dialectical unity of ends and means, goals and methods. The council movement rejected vanguardist notions of the dictatorship of the proletariat as well as the Bernsteinian stratagem of structural reforms, insisting that the outcome in both cases was destined to be a government of bureaucratic elites. There could be no anticipation of the future in the context of present struggles: egalitarian, democratic processes are inevitably suppressed by the contradictory (instrumental, power-oriented) methods used to achieve them.

The radical left struggled to forge a theory (and practice) of socialist democracy that was nowhere to be found either in social democracy and Bolshevism, aside from a few abstract formulations that bore little relationship to the actual strategies pursued. As we have seen, Pannekoek and Gramsci, for example, were preoccupied with small, face-to-face collective institutions of popular control designed to reinvigorate and democratize class struggle at the point of production; they stressed the self-activating principle against the "external element." Closer to everyday life, this strategy could more effectively address issues of popular consciousness; it could also give support to a leadership that was part of the collective life of the community and more or less directly accountable to it. From this standpoint—the idea of proletarian self-activity—the radical left could pose the question of bureaucracy and hope to challenge the capitalist division of labor. By refusing to compress the immense realm of social and authority relations into the material "base," or sphere of production, it could incorporate a much wider range of needs and demands in the political agenda. The factory councils that proliferated in many European countries before 1920 embodied much of this democratic spirit.[3]

Unfortunately, the radical left advanced only one side of the dialectic: Avoiding politics, it was unable to arrive at a complete theory of socialist transformation—or popular democracy. For socialists, the dilemma remained unresolved: how to combine local, prefigurative, democratic concerns with essentially authoritarian norms required in the struggle for state power. Thus, the council movement typically wound up trapped in its own spontaneism, relinquishing its capacity to solidify and concretize its objectives. Its partial character reduced its strategic ability to fight for transformative aims: where failure did not result from spontaneist impotence (as in Italy), it came from either absorption into normal politics (Germany) or outright destruction by force (Russia). The historical lessons are clear: any strictly local, prefigurative approach will predictably be overwhelmed by massive organizational forces that surround it, sometimes including vanguard parties of the left. The legacy of classical anarchism, syndicalism, and council communism is one of political futility. Clearly, revolutionary success depends upon society-wide organizational coordination and strategic planning of some sort. The radicals assumed that a lengthy period of ideological contestation rooted in popular struggles would generate new forms of consciousness and daily practice that subvert the capitalist order. But the mechanisms for transforming consciousness and effecting the transition to a new society always remained vague. Moreover, as historical experience shows, the difficulty of maintaining local bastions of popular control in a generally hostile and repressive environment is probably insurmountable.

From the famous Marx-Bakunin debates of the late 1860s until World War I, the European left followed a course of intense polarized conflict: organization versus spontaneity, leadership versus self-activity, centralism versus localism, and so forth. In some respects, this polarization was sharpened after the Bolshevik Revolution, when Jacobin success forced radicals into retreat everywhere—including Russia, where Kronstadt anarchist sailors, factory committees, the Left Opposition, and Ukrainian peasant anarchists under the leadership of Nestor Makhno eventually lost their battles against the nascent Soviet leadership.[4] In Italy, the revolutionary council movement of 1918–1920 spread throughout the north and seemed ready to gain political momentum, only to be defeated by a combination of its own lack of strategic coherence and the national militia. Similar, but more localized, insurgencies in Germany met a similar fate. A Soviet government established in Hungary in 1919 lasted less than a year. When the popular upsurges that swept crisis-ridden postwar Europe collapsed, so too did the radical left; local democratic forms vanished almost overnight, giving way to bureaucratic party, trade union, and state institutions. By 1921 the social-democratic and communist parties, surrounded by auxiliary organizations and "transmission belts," had effectively asserted their domination of the European left.

The wide divisions that characterized twentieth century socialism were already visible in the European Marxist debates going back to the 1890s. They were mirrored in the 1903 Russian Social Democratic Labor Party (RSDLP) split, which gave rise to the Bolsheviks and Mensheviks. They were intensified in Russia and the rest of Europe after 1914, when the social democrats almost uniformly took national chauvinist positions in response to the war, and then after 1917 with the explosive impact of the Bolshevik

Revolution. By the 1920s the idea of worldwide socialist unity was reduced to a myth. The ascension of a Leninist party-state in the Soviet Union, along with the establishment of the Comintern in more than a dozen countries, defined theoretical and strategic issues for the labor movement in the sharpest of terms. In those early days the conflict between social democrats and communists was framed in starkly polarized language: reform versus revolution, electoral politics versus insurrection, domestic priorities versus proletarian internationalism. The reformist moderates (Kautsky, Turati, Jaures) stood opposed to the vanguardist militants (Lenin, Trotsky, Bordiga). Social democrats rallied around the banner of anti-communism, upholding ideals of the Enlightenment, including a secular liberalism that strongly downplayed the teleological element of Marxism. Communists, for their part, defended a Jacobin version of socialism centered in Moscow as the source of a new revolutionary civilization—one that held European liberal-capitalist values in total contempt.

The resulting sectarian hostility made leftist collaboration virtually impossible—at least until the short-lived Popular Front experiments in France and Spain during the mid-1930s—contributing in no small part to the rise of fascism in Italy and Germany. Although popular support for the left grew in the 1920s, such support was never translated into political success: Schism led to strategic standoff, which in turn ruled out any conquest of political power. Thus, while social democrats and communists in Germany could amass nearly sixty percent of the vote at their peak, mutual antagonism blocked unified anti-capitalist politics. The irony was that, despite an enormous ideological gulf separating them, party elites in both camps were able to build their own networks of bureaucratic privilege "above" the mundane world of popular struggles.

Perhaps nowhere was this ideological gulf more pronounced than around the question of liberal democracy. The social democrats inherited Bernstein's evolutionary model, which, by the 1920s, amounted to a defense of liberal institutions at all costs—what would turn out to be an enduring legacy. In contrast, the communists endorsed Lenin's uncompromising disdain for bourgeois democracy as little more than a debating society cut off from the real centers of power; except for tactical and propagandistic maneuvers (as in running candidates for office), electoral politics was regarded as a sad illusion.[5] After the Bolsheviks consolidated power in Russia, some countries (Germany, England) experienced brief phases of social-democratic governance. It is probably safe to say that in all countries where Social Democracy expanded its presence it became deradicalized to the point where it bore little relationship to the visionary image of socialist politics identified with the early Marxist tradition. As ideological discourse narrowed, parties turned into agencies of class accommodation and popular demobilization—just as Michels predicted they would.[6] Reflecting upon the Italian situation, Gramsci commented that the Socialist Party of Italy (PSI) leadership, unable to take political initiative at a moment of great crisis, behaved as if it were nothing more than a helpless "spectator of the events."[7]

Fearful of too much mass mobilization, social democratic elites preferred stability, labor peace, and compromise—an outlook consonant with their desire to solidify institutional positions within the liberal-democratic state. Social reforms were made possible in exchange for adherence to the dominant order: bargaining instead of disruption, bureaucratic give-and-take, deference to governmental authority. Thus, social democracy had already come to represent a pale version of socialism that amounted to a reformist extension of capitalist liberalism, even while its leaders continued to proclaim the goal of revolution held over from the 1890s.

Communist elites, for their part, fought incessant and sometimes ruthless ideological battles against the "renegade" social democrats, who were regarded as agents of class collaboration and imperialism with their base in the skilled, privileged "aristocracy of labor." The very success of the Bolshevik Revolution dictated the validity of Leninist insurgency politics, the vanguard party, and preeminence of the USSR in carrying out worldwide proletarian struggles. In defense of the centralized party-state, CPSU leaders—from Lenin to Bukharin, from Trotsky to Stalin—proclaimed the Soviet dictatorship of the proletariat to be a thousand times more democratic than any bourgeois "dictatorship," with its sham parliaments designed to obscure the oppressive reality of capitalist financial and industrial power. All of this merely gave new meaning to Lenin's imputed conception of democracy: representing the historical mission of the workers, Bolshevik power was by *definition* democratic.[8]

If revolutionary ideology had a diminishing presence in European labor movements and electoral politics after 1923, the communist parties sought to fill this void by means of aggressive Comintern policies designed to win over social-democratic supporters. The communists made dramatic gains in Germany, Italy, and France as well as China, insisting upon the "actuality of the revolution," even though the phase of crisis had seemingly passed. While social democrats nervously pushed for moderation, communists prepared to mobilize for radical action—witness the disastrous Chinese insurrection of 1927. At this point, of course, Soviet leaders were desperate to escape the isolation growing out of their unique predicament: ruling a "socialist" country surrounded by hostile capitalist states. Yet this became the harsh reality, and with Stalin's rise to power in the late 1920s the system became more rigidly centralized, more stridently nationalist. Thus, while the social democrats moved inexorably away from Marx's vision of proletarian self-emancipation in their quest for electoral victories, so too, in quite different ways, did the communists with their fetishism of bureaucratic command in all realms of social life. Instrumental concerns (power, efficiency, control) prevailed over teleological goals (including democracy) as both formations struggled to build centers of power in their own fashion.

Although European post-revolutionary socialist discourse was fragmented beyond recognition, the consequences in each instance proved a crushing blow to the radical left. Social democrats became so attached to parliamentarism that any mass mobilization or civic disruption was to be avoided under any circumstances; desiring legitimacy, they opted for stability. Communists, on the other hand, turned their attention to the Soviet party-state, which was immersed in the twin goals of rapid modernization and consolidation of power in a relatively underdeveloped country with a huge peasantry. Stalin, like Lenin, was anxious to duplicate the feats of economic and administrative efficiency accomplished by the capitalist West.[9] By the mid-1930s Stalin had erected a bureaucratic-centralist system based upon firm elite control, a command economy, and social conservatism. In this scheme of things, there was no room for autonomous soviets, factory committees, and popular organizations that were so vital to the Bolshevik success; they were either disbanded, crushed, or transformed into instruments of party-state rule.

The Soviet Union emerged as a bureaucratically integrated class system in which popular democratic forms would ultimately become "dysfunctional." Although statism in the USSR took on entirely different characteristics than the statism of European social democracy, the outcome for the radical left was essentially the same: dispersion and defeat. In both cases the potential for collective self-activity and deep changes in civil society needed for socialist transformation was negated by highly instrumental politics. The radical left, of course, sought to transcend the logic of statism but lacked the political resources necessary to compete with larger organizational forms. It could not build upon the great revolutionary upsurges of 1914–1923, when democratic socialism appeared to be on the agenda. This historic failure ultimately stemmed from the failure to achieve a synthesis incorporating both popular spontaneity and the external (or vanguard) element, prefigurative concerns and the struggle for state power—precisely that synthesis required for a viable democratic socialism.

Social Democracy: Triumph and Failure

At its inception in the 1890s, social-democratic theory—filtered mainly through the SPD and the tutelary influence of Kautsky—defined its mission as one of socialist transformation. It was Marxist and resolutely anti-capitalist, even if its chosen political methods would give rise to intractable compromises. Serious ideological disagreements among the leading theoretical and political figures were blurred by a common attachment to parliamentarism as the main locus of efforts to merge socialism and democracy. Later, even when virtually all social-democratic parties became institutionalized fixtures within the capitalist state system, practicing ideological moderation and interest group politics, the ultimate (Marxist) objective of socialist revolution was often loudly proclaimed. After the Bolshevik Revolution most social-democratic parties, compromised by their political impotence during and after the war, gravitated toward a fierce anti-communism that would forever stamp their development. By the 1930s mass-based socialist parties of the Second International took root in several European countries, exercising various degrees of hegemony on the left and winning positions of institutional power. With the notable exception of Spain, their commitment to electoralism and gradualism seemed to fit the mood of popular constituencies in the period after 1923; civil insurrection was no longer a real possibility. Simultaneously anti-fascist and anti-Stalinist, their social-democratic tradition was the main bearer of Enlightenment values between the wars, still upholding the ideal of a socialist order more or less inspired by classical Marxism.[10]

The social-democratic road to power was premised on the formation of a parliamentary majority with largely working-class support; unions and cooperatives figured in this strategy, but electoral politics was always key. If enough votes could be amassed, then institutional power could be won and social policy could be enacted favoring proletarian interests. Whether this would lead to socialism—to a radical break with capitalism—was a hotly debated matter, as we have seen. What was rather obvious, as Robert Michels observed just after the turn of the century, was the widening gulf between theory and practice in the social-democratic experience: the image of radical proletarian unity coexisted with an elitist party increasingly assimilated within the structures of capitalist democracy. In the post-World War II period this tension was resolved in favor of the "practical" side of party politics. Marxist theory was explicitly and officially abandoned by one party after another, starting with the SPD's Bad Godesberg declaration in 1959.

By the early 1950s the newly created Socialist International (SI) was composed of thirty-nine member parties, the majority of them in Western Europe. The number grew to fifty-four parties with fifteen million members in 1970. Increasingly removed from the communist orbit, the postwar socialist current evolved into a moderate, even centrist force during the 1950s and 1960s—a trend that was reinforced when several parties (in France, Sweden, Austria, and Norway) were voted into power. These parties presided over a continuous expansion of the Keynesian welfare state, but they generally did not propose (much less implement) any broad anti-capitalist reforms. The very idea of a proletarian revolution, or indeed any kind of transition to socialism, within the conditions of advanced capitalism was dismissed as utopian.[11]

Yet the long-term transformation of social democracy was far more complex. The problem was that an incremental, parliamentarist strategy was incompatible with a systematic attack on the centers of capitalist economic and political power. Integration into the dominant structures was inevitable, given the overriding logic of winning and maintaining power as a matter of normal politics: obsession with immediate results, vague appeals and programs designed to offend no one, balancing of diverse interests, institutional stability, and catering to large capital as a source of new investment. Such logic typically conflicted with the imperatives of popular mobilization.[12] Never really a proletarian movement, social democracy took on the character of a catchall party—a *Volkspartei* in the German context—in which coalitions and alliances were shaped strictly by the dictates of electoral politics. In the end parliamentarism created a distance between the party apparatus and mass constituencies, reproducing class fragmentation rather than class unity and solidarity.[13] Lenin's original critique of the Second International seemed to be confirmed: entry into the bourgeois public sphere obscures class politics and revolutionary possibilities insofar as it blocks, rather than enhances, formation of class consciousness.[14]

The political consequences were predictable enough: postwar social-democratic governance in several European countries in effect allowed for the expansion of domestic capital, multinational corporations, and an EEC (European Economic Community) based in the monopolies, not to mention a strengthening of the NATO alliance as part of the Cold War defense of U.S. global interests. A renovated welfare structure did improve the quality of life for most workers and poor people in these countries, and Keynesian mechanisms adopted even before World War II did soften the worst features of the capitalist cycle. But these economies were still controlled by private capital, income distribution was scarcely altered,[15] and the bureaucratic side of the state grew. The historical role of social democracy was to manage the crisis tendencies of capitalism, administer the economy and state more efficiently, and rationalize the accumulation process by means of state planning, fiscal controls, and technological innovation. In this way, the social-democratic parties became instruments of bureaucratic order, technological rationality, and the mixed economy—an outcome quite distant from what Kautsky and even Bernstein envisioned at the turn of the century. Their ideologies were closer to liberal pluralism than to socialist egalitarianism. Their fear of losing electoral support was matched only by a fear of civil upheaval (or a return of fascism) that might force them to break with the imperatives of capital in order to preserve their "socialist" image.

The prototype of social-democratic integration was the West German party, which governed from 1969 to 1982 in coalition with the Free Democrats. During the period when the SPD was carrying out extensive reforms, it further bolstered its position as a statist, modernizing, Cold War party committed to preserving capitalist class and power relations. Even before its stunning defeat in the 1983 general elections, the SPD was an exhausted and depleted party incapable of presenting a real alternative to the Christian Democrats, a predicament that went much deeper than Helmut Schmidt's particular brand of cautious managerial leadership.

During the period of coalition rule, the SPD presided over an authoritarian "security state" that, among other initiatives, enacted measures barring leftists from public employment (*Berufsverbot*). The West German state apparatus, always a powerful ally of big capital, was bolstered by a renewed social contract involving government, business, and unions designed to guarantee growth oriented production on the basis of regulated class collaboration.[16] The security state essentially functioned to mediate group interests while setting limits to popular participation within the established public sphere. Economically, the SPD-engineered *Modell Deutschland* followed three lines of development: stimulation of a private market with the export sector playing a decisive role, technological restructuring of industry, and expansion of trade with the Soviet-bloc countries. Only a broad range of social reforms, implemented mainly in the early 1970s, distinguished the German accumulation model from more strictly capitalist configurations that existed elsewhere; even so, the main beneficiary of these reforms was the middle class.[17] All of this was designed to bolster the already privileged position of West Germany in a period of sharpening global economic competition. In foreign policy the SPD energetically followed the U.S. lead and endorsed conventional Cold War assumptions and policies: a stronger NATO, U.S. missile supremacy over the Soviets, deployment of the Euromissiles, and so on.[18] Even Willy Brandt's earlier *Ostpolitik*, or "opening to the East," was intended to fit the American preoccupation with detente at that time. Moreover, SPD criticisms of U.S. intervention in the Third World were generally timid and lacking in conviction.

By the late 1970s the SPD encountered its own celebrated crisis of identity, which was less a "crisis" than the actual loss of identity as an oppositional force in German society.[19] With Marxism formally jettisoned in 1959, even vague pretenses of socialist commitment that party elites clung to after Bad Godesberg could no longer be taken seriously. Now a pluralist electoral party with only electoral ties to its popular base, the SPD drifted away from even the minimally cohesive leftist culture that sustained it throughout the 1950s and 1960s. This reality, along with an old-style managerial politics rooted in technological pragmatism—part of the longstanding *Parteienstaat* culture—ensured that the SPD would be unable to make contact with emergent social currents sweeping Germany during this period.[20] Shifting cleavages of the post-Fordist order, characterized by the decline of traditional labor and growth of the new middle strata, gave rise to a new political atmosphere. As post-materialist conflicts around urban, quality-of-life, and environmental concerns led to the proliferation of Citizen Initiative groups and new social movements with an extensive grassroots presence, party leadership simply failed to respond. There were significant overtures to affluent elements of the middle strata but, despite pressures from the small leftist faction (*Jusos*), the SPD retreated from these new grassroots challenges. Catchall electoralism made strategic flexibility *in this direction* all but impossible. The logic of this predicament became more debilitating with the emergence of the Greens as a serious radical challenge in the 1980s.[21]

At the same time, as SPD programs and policies became less distinguishable from those of the Christian Democrats, the likelihood that they could offer solutions to the mounting economic crisis (reflected by double-digit unemployment rates in the 1980s) had become distant. Neither the party leadership nor the labor movement seemed capable of, or interested in, overcoming a long-ingrained corporatism; defense of the social contract took precedence over any vision of social change. Lacking any transformative ideology or commitments, or even any desire to broaden the confines of pluralist democracy, the SPD could only fall back upon platitudinous slogans and manipulative *Realpolitik*, which did pay electoral dividends until the early 1980s. As one commentator noted, "[C]ategories such as class struggle, exploitation, and classless society are gone for good, and are openly replaced by the postulate of Christianity and morality." Beneath this, the SPD, "when considered as an electoral party, in terms of party structure, in terms of the social composition of its leading bodies and congresses, is a party of clerks and public servants."[22]

Here, the SPD paid a heavy price for its unyielding attachment to ecumenical politics and to the *Parteienstaat*. Efforts to transcend a primarily working-class identity ultimately moved the party to the *right*, not the left. An aging membership and popular support compounded the party's strategic rigidity in the 1980s. The rapid upsurge of Green politics dramatized an obvious reality: the SPD had lost even its *image* of a change-oriented party.[23] The leadership (whether under Helmut Schmidt or Hans-Jochen Vogel) was drawn largely from technocratic ranks. The Greens, on the other hand, derived their strength from a youthful urban radicalism, commitment to a "new politics" of local empowerment, and a solid base in the new social movements galvanized by issues of peace, ecology, feminism, and grassroots democracy.

After winning ten percent of the vote or more in most large urban areas, the Greens were able to stun the SPD in the 1983 and 1987 general elections, blocking any possibility of the SPD entering national governments and laying the groundwork for "red-green" coalitions in some regions (for example, Hesse in 1987). While the Greens' social base was neither large nor stable, the ideological challenge posed by a radical force of such vitality forced the SPD leadership to make "Green" cosmetic changes in its electoral appeals. But the SPD was never able to reconstitute itself in forward looking (not to mention "socialist" or "Green") directions.[24]

In the final analysis, SPD success always depended upon the viability of a German economy rooted in Keynesian inspired growth policies that held sway from the 1950s to the 1970s. It required institutionalized labor-management cooperation, labor discipline, public investment, and a refined welfare system. Social corporatism of this type, which also shaped development in other European countries,[25] was made possible by a lengthy period of expansion and prosperity, as well as the relative absence of grassroots movements. The German model collapsed in the 1980s, however, giving way to an economic downturn reflected in massive unemployment, drastic social cutbacks, and civil strife (on both the left and right). The decline was exacerbated by the process of German reunification in the early 1990s, when the burdensome costs of assimilating the former East Germany—along with new waves of immigrants from Eastern Europe—were thrown into the equation.

After reunification, the SPD did manage to hold the allegiance of roughly one-third of the German electorate, despite its failure to make expected inroads into the eastern regions. The goal of national governance was not completely beyond reach. Yet, by the early 1990s, the SPD was obviously bereft of anything resembling a political direction; "socialism" became an embarrassing topic of discussion, to be avoided if possible, at party forums. The mass organizations had withered, labor was in decline, and local activism was no longer a part of the SPD *modus operandi.* In retreat, SPD elites counted on the Green phenomenon and its supporting context of new social movements to be short-lived. In any case, it appeared that the historic antagonism between elites and masses within the SPD had finally been resolved in favor of a broad mainstream consensus built mainly around restoring German unity and power, around reinvigorating the old growth model.[26] If Michels turned out to be mistaken on this point, he was emphatically correct in yet another part of his thesis: the famous concept of "embourgeoisement," applied originally to the early SPD, was surely more valid than ever in the German setting.

A second social-democratic model is represented by the Italian Socialists (PSI), who have served as junior partners in a national governing coalition for roughly the past three decades. If the SPD was the classical mass-based integrative party, the PSI can be understood as a mediating power broker within the postwar Byzantine maze of Italian political groupings. A party much smaller than the SPD or the Swedish Social Democratic SAP—with a peak of 14.3 percent of the vote in 1987—the PSI has typically been able to achieve a moderate "balance" between right and left, between Christian Democrats (DC) and (until recently) Communists. To this end, particularly under the modernizing leadership of Bettino Craxi, it stressed the need for large-scale "grand reforms" that would give the Socialists identity and leverage vis-à-vis the Christian Democrats, while simultaneously neutralizing the Communists or at least undercutting their claim to a role in government.[27] For Craxi, who served as prime minister from 1983 to 1987, the ideal was a "complex equilibrium" of political forces within which the PSI could play a leading or at least influential role.[28] In reality, however, the PSI was for twenty years more or less absorbed within the ruling coalition dominated by the DC. Thus, its effectiveness in pressing for real social reforms, beginning with the *apertura alla sinistra* ("opening to the left") in the early 1960s, was extremely limited. (Despite an abundance of local and regional Socialist-Communist governing coalitions, the two parties were never able to revive the short-lived Popular Front experiment of 1947 on a national level.)

In the nearly fifty years since Pietro Nenni engineered a split with the PCI, the Socialists have failed to recapture their strong pre-1921 presence in Italian society: aside from their relatively small electoral base, they have never arrived at any clear political identity or ideological direction. In this respect the PSI was, until the mid-1980s, devoid of even the rationalizing coherence found in the German socialist party. After being named PSI secretary-general in 1976, Craxi frequently pointed to the SPD as a model for the Italian party. (Of course, the SPD had, until the rise of the Greens, no competition on the left, whereas the PSI was always in the shadow of the more powerful Communists.) Like the SPD, the PSI long ago abandoned Marxism, but in contrast to the northern European parties it never fully embraced the shift toward capitalist modernization—although once Craxi took power in 1983 the party made gestures in that direction.[29]

Craxi's ascension to the Italian leadership brought the PSI to levels of political respectability not attained since the late 1940s; the party managed to reverse more than three decades of steady decline. In 1946 the Socialist vote was about twenty percent, but dropped off to barely thirteen percent in the 1950s, and then to less than ten percent in the 1960s and 1970s, before returning to better than fourteen percent in 1987. More significantly, Craxi injected a new sense of political morale and activism into the organization, reviving its long-submerged quest for identity. The PSI now presented the image of a modern, technocratic, reformist party more in touch with changing economic and political conditions: it would strive to overcome the archaic residues of traditionalism, capitalist inefficiency, and right-wing ideology (all still widespread in Italy). With the Christian Democrats and Communists both in the midst of internal crises, the Socialists were able to occupy new terrain. The Craxi "renewal," however, abandoned all pretenses of challenging the status quo, bringing the formal PSI outlook more in line with deeply ingrained practices. One source of its conservatism was that through years of both local and national governance, the PSI managed to construct a huge patronage network, especially in the South.

Weakened by charges of ineptitude and corruption, and suffering loss of support at the polls, the Italian Socialists could not build upon the momentum generated by Craxi, remaining in the early 1990s very much a party with no long-range strategy or vision. The PSI, now closer to an electoral machine than before, offers no program critical of monopoly capital or the multinationals; its concept of democracy, or decentralization, lacks specificity; and it stands behind labor discipline and austerity, having in 1984 weakened the mechanism of the wage index (the *scala mobile*) that stood as a symbol of trade union gains in the 1970s. It adheres to a stridently pro-U.S. foreign policy that previously included enthusiastic support of NATO Euromissile deployment when Italian public opinion (in 1983) was strongly opposed. A party dominated by civil servants, teachers, and technical and cultural workers, the PSI has remained as aloof from new social movements and the issues they engage as the more labor-centered SPD. This paradox is explained by the party's continued role as broker and its *clientelismo*, along with a peculiar brand of technocratic liberalism inherited more from U.S. experience than from Marxist theory—all of which favor an instrumental politics quite at odds with the thrust of popular struggles and democratic empowerment associated historically with socialism..

If the SPD was the quintessential expression of classical social democracy, the Swedish Socialist party (SAP) has, since its first ascent to power in 1932, been identified with a more progressive, dynamic image of the modern welfare state. In Gosta Esping-Anderson's words, "Social Democracy offers to the world one of the most durable and successful labor movements anywhere, and Scandinavian social democracy stands as the international model."[30] For the better part of the past sixty years the Swedish model provided a beacon not only of stability and efficiency but also of social equity. The SAP was commonly drawn to the radical side of social democracy, with its emphasis on broad welfare reforms, workers' participation, and extension of "social" citizenship (beyond mere voting) to all parts of society—within the framework of capitalism and the state system. Swedish party leaders, like their cohorts elsewhere in Scandinavia, sought to build popular strength on a foundation of unions, co-ops, and parliament, hoping to chip away at capitalist power and privilege and shift the balance of social forces in order to give more political leverage to labor, farmers, and other subordinate groups. For this strategy to work, however, an SAP-led coalition had to use state power as a planning and regulating mechanism, with the goal of pushing the capitalist system to its maximum human and technical potential.

The Swedish model was therefore constructed around a dialectic of politics against markets, characterized by an unceasing effort to decommodify
both labor and social services.[31] From the outset the SAP grounded its oppositional identity in a social bloc extending beyond the industrial proletariat
itself. This strategy has worked admirably: since the 1930s, the SAP has been
the dominant political force in Swedish society, winning several elections
and governing the country, mainly in coalitions, for a total of about forty
years. Over time social democracy has taken on the character of a party, government, and political culture deeply embedded in the very fabric of both
the Swedish state and civil society.[32]

At the same time, SAP success meant that it would most likely follow the
time-honored European social democratic pattern: a corporatist partnership of government, business, and unions. In Sweden this arrangement dates
back to the Keynesian revolution of the 1930s, although its more developed
features took shape in the 1950s and 1960s when capitalist growth could
accommodate far-reaching reforms. The aim was to stretch democratic participation and social equality to their limits—that is, within the matrix of
capitalist accumulation and hierarchy. During postwar expansion the SAP,
when it functioned as a ruling party, was able to contain the crisis tendencies of capitalism in part by erecting a refined welfare state edifice.

The material and cultural accomplishments of the Swedish model since
the 1930s have been impressive: the harsh effects of industrial expansion,
class differences, and urban hardship were ameliorated as nowhere else. In
part, this was made possible by the very strength and continuity of social
democracy; in part, by the very smallness, homogeneity, and affluence of the
country. The accomplishments have been many: nearly full employment,
abolition of poverty, the most efficient *and* accessible system of health care in
the world, a generous family policy, vast public infrastructure, relative gender equality, and a democratized economy with extensive worker participation in large firms. Under SAP hegemony roughly eighty-five percent of the
workforce has been unionized. The health care network is generally considered to be the most developed part of the Swedish welfare state; publicly
financed and compulsory, it is run by twenty-three county councils and
three large municipalities, with generally open access. Since the system is
managed at the local level, the remote and impersonal technocratic features
taken for granted elsewhere have been minimized.[33] Such an extensive program requires not only a challenge to market priorities, like those that have
driven the commodification of health care in the U.S., but also a rejection of
state-bureaucratic practices that define Soviet-type systems. The system

could only function effectively, of course, where a highly progressive tax structure funds an expanded public sector, which, in turn, depends upon steady economic growth rates of the sort that prevailed in Sweden from the 1940s to the 1970s.

SAP achievements were built on a foundation of an expanded economy and public sector, as well as a powerful labor movement and culture virtually unique among advanced industrial countries. At its peak, more than eighty percent of Swedish workers belonged to trade unions. The political culture has long been steeped in the discourse of universal claims, cooperation, and labor solidarity, affirming an ethic of collective sharing against the possessive individualism of market society. A majority of the Swedish population has viewed the SAP as representing the general interests of society around the broad ideals of "socialist democracy." Beyond their obvious material or sectoral gains, SAP-engineered reforms were seen as empowering, a step along the path of social transformation; this was no simple "welfare state." A key question has been: how far would this vision of social transformation extend? Would it have anti-capitalist implications?

Olaf Palme, a leading figure of Swedish social democracy and prime minister from 1969 to 1976, insisted that the core element of SAP ideology should be the broadest possible democratization of the state and economy. Whereas the SPD model stressed a more narrow version of wage struggles and workers' participation (co-determination), Palme emphasized worker and citizen involvement at all levels of decision-making, including the power to shape investment priorities, hoping this would permit a grassroots challenge to the power of capital.[34] A crucial ingredient of this scheme was the famous "Meidner Plan," first introduced in the early 1950s, which was designed to set up wage-earner investment funds that gradually turned over ownership to the workers themselves—going far beyond profit-sharing or co-determination plans that left the structure and social relations of capitalism intact.[35] Economic democracy programs of this sort had been outlined and even partially introduced by other northern European social-democratic parties, but they were never intended to carry out radical changes: Capital remained firmly hegemonic. In the end, however, the same would be true of Sweden. While Sweden introduced the most radical plan in the world with the Co-Determination Act of 1977, giving workers significant power at the shop floor, company administration, and general management, the high expectations of SAP and trade union leaders were never met. In fact, little changed as big companies went about their business as if no actual reforms had been introduced—mainly because the issue of ownership was never even posed.[36]

The legacy of Swedish social democracy has therefore been a decidedly mixed one. With no truly competing force on the left to challenge its progressive claim to rule, the SAP was able to have a decisive influence on the country's postwar development. And, for the most part, its social policies represented a standard against which other industrialized societies could be judged. With an electoral support consistently over thirty five percent, it had a peak membership of 1.3 million and a skilled and pragmatic leadership with a vision of social transformation. However, that vision of social transformation did not go beyond the parameters of capitalism or, for that matter, the bureaucratic state.

A powerful appeal of the postwar Swedish model was that it offered a viable alternative to both the harsh, individualistic capitalism of the West and the bureaucratic centralism of the Soviet bloc: social reforms were genuine, and they made life much better for the great majority of people. By the early 1990s, however, this model had completely unraveled and the SAP found itself out of power. A system in which about eighty percent of the economy remained in private hands was, of course, dependent upon continuous growth and prosperity in strictly capitalist terms. So long as dynamic accumulation fueled profits, investments, and jobs it also facilitated the kind of class harmony and social reforms, not to mention full employment and workers' participation, that defined the Swedish model. But once the growth syndrome evaporated the rest of the social-democratic agenda began to disintegrate. As an export driven economy Sweden was at the mercy of the world market, and when the global system went into crisis Swedish capital lost its dynamism and hence its customary room to maneuver. Austerity, layoffs, and social cutbacks were the order of the day, as in most of the rest of the world. Sweden was hit harder, however, given the enormous size of its public sector and the historic commitment of the SAP to massive social programs and corporatist stability; in outgrowing its own earlier political framework, capitalism left the SAP behind. The degree to which the SAP and unions were dependent upon the imperatives of the banking system and the caprice of the world market was such that the social democrats could no longer deliver on their longstanding promises.[37] The result was that the peculiar mix of ingredients that made the Swedish model viable could apparently no longer be sustained.

Yet the fate of the SAP—or the SPD and PSI—was scarcely a unique one but rather part of a general historical trend that sharpened the contradictions always present in social-democratic strategy. Since 1945 the progressive role of these parties has been associated with a continuous phase of capitalist prosperity, increased state planning, and expanded social services. It was a period, too, of strengthened working-class economic and political power.[38] By the late 1970s, however, this tradition had reached its historical limits, not merely as a source of oppositional politics but as a form of governance within capitalist society. The Keynesian welfare state, buttressed by a corporatist social contract designed to reconcile class differences, began to disintegrate in the midst of global crisis and revitalization of social forces outside the state system; it could no longer maintain its simultaneous expansionary and reformist legitimation. One response to the decline of social-democratic integration was a return to an anti-Keynesian conservatism (monetarism, supply-side economics, reprivatization), which explains the rise of politicians like Thatcher, Reagan, and Kohl.

Beneath this historic shift lies a pattern of development both continuous and predictable. The social-democratic version of structural reforms, at least in its postwar incarnation, was never meant to challenge or overturn the capitalist mode of production or create new forms of authority. On the contrary, it was conceived from the outset as a means of rationalizing this system in order to alleviate its crisis tendencies, introduce new social priorities, and improve general living standards. Steady electoral growth of many European social-democratic parties was achieved on this basis.[39]

As we have seen, this project was centered on several interrelated elements: a rejuvenated welfare system, social planning, technological modernization, and fiscal and monetary controls—all meant to eliminate obstacles to steady accumulation and growth within a mixed economy. At the same time, it relied upon investing all political resources in the existing public sphere (elections, parliamentary activity, bureaucratic influence). In most cases, the end product was a party of corporatist assimilation, cut off from any process of mass mobilization when out of power and a responsible, cautious partner in the task of crisis management when in power. (Social democrats were better prepared than conservative parties to satisfy those imperatives, given their base of support in the labor movement and their enlightened rationalizing ideology.) This phenomenon was hardly new or unexpected; it was built into the original Kautsky-Bernstein convergence that took shape after World War I, which meant that the embourgeoisement of social-democratic parties was only a matter of time.[40] In this context, the "decline" of social democracy must be understood as a long-term shift in political goals and values grounded in deep historical experience, including institutionalization, rather than a simple loss of electoral support (which has *not* typically occurred).[41]

The modern social-democratic predicament stems largely from the collapse of the Keynesian synthesis initially forged in the 1930s; prospects of an organized state capitalism rooted in class conciliation seemed far less promising by the 1980s. Several factors have contributed to this historical shift. First, because of the dramatic slowdown of economic growth in the advanced countries, overall demand for public services could no longer be met at the old levels, undermining a key programmatic linchpin of social democracy. As Keynesian thinking confronted the fiscal crisis of the state, it became impossible to devise methods for sustaining both social programs and the prevailing tax structure, full employment and balanced budgets, wage increases and dynamic investment policies. Second, environmental pressures made capital accumulation (Keynesian or otherwise) more difficult. The dysfunctions of poorly planned industrialism and urbanization—blighted cities, depleted land and water, polluted air, toxic wastes, global climate changes—imposed new obstacles to further economic expansion. Moreover, the diminished supply of natural resources (or at least the added expense of obtaining them) meant that sustained development was now more problematic than in the preceding era of "economic miracles."

In yet another realm, Keynesian solutions brought more governmental intervention and, with it, bureaucratization of social life that eventually gave rise to popular resistance in the form of grassroots movements. With the state replacing or complementing the market as a distributive-regulatory mechanism and thus being forced to solve a wider range of problems, it began to absorb systemic contradictions to the extent that state power became more fragile.[42] Further, growing numbers of workers refused to accept labor discipline and austerity policies imposed by governing social-democratic parties in the desperate search for international advantage. The social contract made less and less sense, especially once it became clear that corporate restructuring programs were throwing large numbers of workers out of jobs (notably in the manufacturing sector). Finally, this entire impasse was aggravated by the increased mobility of capital and structural fragmentation of the global economy. In the absence of a rational system of coordination beyond the nation-state (or regional groupings of states like the EEC), the cyclical and anarchic tendencies of international capital inherent in a competitive market easily get out of control.[43] The lack of any "Keynesian" mechanism on a world scale means, for example, that multinational corporations and banks pursue their interests largely outside the fiscal and monetary structures of particular governments. It also means there can be no rational planning instrument for shaping investment policies or counteracting the dysfunctions of uneven development. At the same time, working-class or anti-capitalist intervention in economic decision-making face even greater impediments than before.

Hence, the European social-democratic model that seemed to operate so smoothly through the postwar growth period was destined to fall under the weight of its own heavy contradictions. Responding to intensifying pressures of the global economy, it had little alternative but to adapt to the priorities of capitalist accumulation: profits, productivity, austerity, export-driven growth. In such circumstances, Keynesianism could barely move beyond the parameters of market competition, whatever social goals it might project or ideological attachment to welfare state democracy it might have.[44] From this viewpoint it would have been difficult to imagine, within the European setting, a real turn toward socialized forms of investment, popular control of the state and economy, and egalitarian class and social relations.

The process of social-democratic decline was further hastened by a range of social and *political* trends at work since the 1960s. One such trend: the class identity of these parties (such as it was), eroded further as the labor sector—defined broadly as blue-collar manual work—shriveled on average to less than twenty-five percent of the general population. The proliferation of job categories and dramatic growth of the new middle strata created a more fragmented work force, eroding solidarity while reinforcing individualism, privatized lifestyles, and depoliticization. The effects of modernity (technocracy, the mass media, social and geographical mobility, et cetera), along with the electoral process itself, pushed this trend along even further. A key underpinning of the early socialist tradition—development of a large, relatively unitary, and class-conscious proletariat—was now decisively overturned.[45] A deradicalizing logic was not built into this loss of class identity, but the inability of party leaders to adapt to new conditions and opportunities gave rise to much anxiety and disorientation about future directions. The boundary between social-democratic and non-social-democratic identities was now scarcely visible: the parties had lost their moorings, as well as what remained of their oppositional status.

Perhaps an even more devastating outgrowth of modernization was the decline of party systems as agencies of popular mobilization and social change. Parties of every ideological label became institutionalized fixtures within the corporatist public sphere, especially where electoral politics had been established for several decades or more.[46] For social democrats the result was not only bureaucratic stagnation and *embourgeoisement* but also strategic inflexibility that seemed to trap the parties in a rigid *modus operandi*. This narrowing of electoral politics reflected the catchall status of large parties and led, by the 1970s, to a closing of the state system that forced oppositional activity to the margins of the dominant public sphere. What occurred in most industrialized countries was a surge in local grass-roots struggles challenging the legitimacy of mainstream parties (including both communists and social democrats): the new left, extra-parliamentary opposition, new social movements, and the Greens. For their part, the social democrats distanced themselves from such post-materialist and democratizing currents, viewing them as a threat to their power and privilege. This power and privilege, of course, had nothing to do with socialism. No doubt Claus Offe was correct when he observed that, while socialism cannot be built without state power, neither apparently can it be built *on* state power.[47]

Given this intersection of social-democratic strategy, institutionalization, and the conditions of modernity, then, it would be miraculous had any of these parties been able to carry forward an ideological discourse roughly true to their socialist origins. In reality, social democracy became a repository of liberal (or neo-liberal) ideology, with its emphasis on markets, individualism, competition, and social mobility, and its push for corporatist integration. In most cases, even a moderate reform image was too much to sustain, although some socialist parties (especially in Southern Europe) would experience revitalization in the 1980s as they began to engage the new social forces. For most, catch-all electoralism and ordinary liberal politics seemed to be an inescapable legacy. As Jan Sundberg puts it, "The Social-Democratic parties of today [1992] resemble the liberal parties in their organizational functions as well as their ideology."[48] After roughly a century of experience, the illusion that mass-based social-democratic parties with a claim to governmental power could set in motion a transition to democratic socialism, whatever their limits and contradictions, was finally put to rest.

Communism: The Soviet Model Implodes

The Bolshevik Revolution presented to the world an image of the first socialist project that managed to win state power. Marxism was indeed the legitimating ideology of the nascent Soviet government, which, in theory, derived its claim to rule from the great majority of workers and peasants that formed the core of the insurgency. In 1917 and 1918 the new leadership announced a series of decrees intended to lay the groundwork for "socialist construction": nationalization of large enterprises and banks, far-reaching land reform, creation of a peoples' militia, abolition of the dreaded *okhrana* (secret police), curbing of orthodox church powers, liberalization of social and family policies, and so forth. Optimism that a new emancipatory order was about to be built in Russia, within limits imposed by the global economy and politics, was rather contagious at the time, especially among the European radical intelligentsia. This would be the first salvo in a worldwide revolutionary process. And the regime, despite its obvious authoritarian trappings that coincided with Lenin's own vanguardist theories, was viewed by most Marxists of the period as a herculean step toward (proletarian) democracy.

But neither Lenin's strategy nor historical conditions would prove to be favorable to socialist development. From the earliest days of the post-revolutionary period, the Bolshevik party-state had two main interrelated thrusts: on the one side, administrative centralization and rationalization, on the other (rapid) industrialization. In order to consolidate power and develop economically, the Soviet leadership was forced to move rapidly and make compromises; time was of the essence. Its overriding preoccupations were those of productivity, efficiency, and control—ambitious goals requiring a new emphasis on science and technology in a relatively underdeveloped country destroyed by war and civil strife. Lenin's view of revolution as a two-stage process made sense in this context: Only with the full expansion of the forces of production could transformation of the "superstructure" (social and authority relations, culture, et cetera) become a recognizable goal. To reach this second stage, all human and technical resources have to be mobilized as part of the drive toward political control and economic growth. Here Lenin favored adoption of various capitalist techniques, including Taylorism, assembly-line production, "one-man management," and material incentives that Marxists always believed would undermine working-class solidarity. Such presumably "neutral" devices, implemented to pave the way toward full-scale communism, actually wound up subverting those ends while pushing Soviet development toward bureaucratic centralism. In fact, this outcome was consistent with the premises of Leninist strategy and the dictates of the historical setting. Authoritarian and productivist methods that ultimately extended the social (and political) division of labor were introduced in the early years of the Bolshevik regime and, while they forced a good many retreats from espoused aims, were consistent with the major tenets of Leninism.[49]

Bureaucratic centralism in the USSR was thus neither an historical aberration nor a Stalinist imposition; although it did constitute a new type of social system, it was the logical outgrowth of Jacobin strategy. The impetus toward "modernization" and the administered society was set in motion once the original (Leninist) path was chosen. Emphasis on the state as a vehicle of "socialist construction" in an economically backward society where the regime commanded only minimal support guaranteed future statist development—assuming that the regime survived. While Bolshevik leaders counted heavily upon insurgency abroad, Jacobinism also presupposed a strong element of risk and even isolation. Post-revolutionary conditions—economic chaos, civil war, left opposition—reinforced centralizing tendencies but did not *cause* them, since the strategic approach was designed to anticipate and confront such conditions. And the historical situation was not inconsistent with the assumptions of Leninist politics.[50]

With the Soviet regime largely cut off from the countryside, resting upon a narrow social and ideological foundation and facing popular opposition from both left and right, democratization was an unthinkable and impossible goal. Thus, in the period 1918–1920, the Bolsheviks already moved to eliminate opposition within the party (culminating in the ban on factions at the tenth Party Congress in March 1921) and managed to subordinate or destroy the hundreds of mass organizations that provided the backbone of revolutionary struggle in 1917. The local Soviets became auxiliaries of the party and quickly lost their democratic political content; trade unions were reduced to the status of "transmission belts," the workers' opposition was eliminated, factory committees succumbed to the logic of autocratic management; radical critics were driven from the party and finally subdued by military force at Kronstadt and in the Ukraine.[51] Conflict and crisis in Russian society strengthened the Jacobin tendency toward harsh restoration of order, cutting short experimentation with new popular forms of authority. "Unity" became the rallying banner of the centrist leadership. In the absence of an effective counter-force within civil society, the party-state emerged as the unchallenged locus of all initiatives and policy decisions.

Centralization did not go unopposed within the party. The Left Communists, including even Bolshevik luminaries such as Osinsky, Radek, Shliapnikov, Smirnov, and Kollontai, whose main public voice was the journal *Kommunist*, argued against the primacy of the party and for a return to power of the local assemblies.[52] Many in this group believed that bureaucracy itself was the main enemy of socialism and argued that revolutionary ideals (including those laid out in Lenin's *State and Revolution*) had already been forgotten—an argument that Trotsky would make *later*, in the 1930s. They stressed issues of workers' control, local autonomy, and open debate within the party. Lenin's consistent response (which was also Trotsky's and Stalin's) was to defend hierarchy, centralized planning, and labor discipline against such "utopian" and "syndicalist" critiques. The debate between Left Communists and Leninists continued through 1921, but the leftists had too little organizational leverage to mount an effective attack. Moreover, one of their guiding premises—that revolutionary initiative should be taken away from the party and "returned to the class"—was clearly unrealistic given the small, weak, and isolated proletariat in Russia, not to mention the obvious historical pressures. Instrumentalism readily prevailed over teleological goals, including democracy.

In the period of his active leadership, Lenin scolded the Left Opposition for its "purism" and for advancing "unreal demands." Here it should be emphasized that Lenin did not primarily defend centralized power on grounds of temporary expediency, although this argument did come into play. On the contrary, he viewed the dictatorship of the proletariat as a transitional democratic structure, since it expressed the historical interests not of a small ruling class (as under capitalism) but of the vast majority, that is, the working class. Lenin equated workers' power with the actuality of Bolshevik rule, mocking the "petty bourgeois illusions" of leftists who clamored for greater democratic participation. After 1921, "democratic centralism" gave way to bureaucratic centralism, the principles of command and subordination took root, and an elitist corps of *apparatchiki* gained control of the party. These organizational features were later extended to new dictatorial heights under Stalin, but the architect of "socialism in one country" hardly created them *de novo* after he took power in the late 1920s.[53]

This classical predicament, one that was repeated in subsequent communist revolutions, reflects the absence within the Bolshevik tradition of principles that could give shape to a democratic-socialist alternative. The predominant vision one finds in Lenin is that which was actually followed *in practice*—a kind of adaptive, flexible tactical outlook that guaranteed by default a reliance on vanguardist or statist strategy. It was a political pragmatism that neatly accommodated Lenin's unwavering instrumentalism and scorn for the local, prefigurative side of politics. The impotence of the Left Communist attack, despite its lofty anti-authoritarianism, becomes all the more intelligible: with no theoretical alternative beyond the generalized spontaneist slogans of the soviets, and with Russia in the throes of crisis, its critique appeared shallow, moralistic, and devoid of strategic content. In this way it mirrored the flaws of the European radical left in general.

Looking at the larger context of Bolshevik theory and practice after 1903, the vanguard party clearly emerged as the lever of politics, and, after 1917, the centralized party-state. Given this reality, party leaders did not—and *could* not—raise the issue of genuine democratic participation. What organizational forms, authority relations, and social practices could give substance to the transitional period and to the Marxian promise of a classless and stateless society? What *political* mediations could pave the way toward the "withering away of the state," where political institutions would finally lose their repressive functions and popular self-management would be realized? These questions generated yet another, more intractable one: Could authoritarian forms that so naturally emanated from Jacobinism ever be transformed internally to give way to a more emancipatory, democratic phase of transformation?

These and kindred questions were never taken up within the Bolshevik tradition. Not surprisingly, Lenin never outlined the *structural* features of the dictatorship of the proletariat. His demand for "all power to the soviets" was more slogan than theory: the local assemblies were treated as mere stepping stones to the party's conquest of power—not ends in themselves or the nucleus of a new socialist state.[54] The party always took precedence over the soviets and, in reality, strove to deny their autonomy. Consistent with Lenin's emphasis on administrative rationality, the Bolshevik view of socialism appeared to be anchored in large-scale organization.[55] Even in the quasi-anarchistic *State and Revolution* he argued that popular control was impossible under conditions of production in advanced industrial society, that "complex technical units" such as factories, railways, and banks could not operate without "ordered cooperation" and subordination.[56] This, in combination with Lenin's willingness to have the party-state take over the rationalized work process, "ready-made from capitalism," helps to explain his fascination with state capitalism as a necessary stage in the transition to full communism. Implementation of workers' control, self-management, and other "syndicalist" schemes would not be congruent with this hierarchical agenda.

As A.J. Polan writes, Lenin wound up "smashing" the authoritarian state only to recreate a new one in its place.[57] The democratic prescriptions of *State and Revolution* were so nonspecific and devoid of structural properties that they could never be integrated into real political practice; they remained "beyond" politics, outside history. A major problem here, as noted, was Lenin's narrow class determined conception of state—a view passed on to subsequent Soviet theorists and leaders. He believed that, once the old ruling class was evicted from seats of power, the state, under the aegis of the revolutionary party, would more or less naturally become a vehicle of the proletarian majority rather than the bourgeois minority. Given this predetermined outcome, all coercive and authoritarian political functions were expected to disappear. In other words, both the vanguard party and the dictatorship of the proletariat were, *by definition*, democratic instruments for advancing the class struggle. Lenin's theory *and* practice inevitably undermined any self-conscious, comprehensive, or democratic elaboration of the transitional process. In fact, it would not be long before the "proletarian" party-state evolved into a new type of Leviathan.

Less than a decade after Lenin departed, Stalin would argue as follows: "We are in favor of the state dying out, and at the same time we stand for the strengthening of the dictatorship of the proletariat, which represents the most powerful and mighty authority of all forms of state which have existed up to the present day. The highest possible development of the power of the state, with the object of preparing the conditions of the dying out of the state—that is the Marxist formula."[58] This "dialectical" style is clearly Stalin's, as is the strong embellishment of state authority, but its extreme Jacobinism is hardly a radical or mystical departure from the political theory that preceded it.

Although classical Marxism itself was in many respects an anti-statist theory, Soviet development after Lenin reproduced what Stojanovic calls the "statist myth of socialism."[59] Within the Jacobin tradition, "socialism" became inseparable from the idea of state activity: control, ownership, planning, capital accumulation, employment of the work force. And the state emerged, on a foundation of Marxist-Leninist discourse, as the main instrument of legitimation. The Stalinist mobilization system, designed to further consolidate Bolshevik power and modernize Russia as quickly as possible, was fully in place by the mid-1930s. Rapid industrialization from above depended upon a command economy, a series of Five-Year Plans set by the party, and extensive collectivization of agriculture. This approach won out over Bukharin's alternative outlined during the "industrialization debates" of the late 1920s. Bukharin argued for a more evolutionary pattern of development allowing for a mixed economy, greater local autonomy, and more modest (and presumably less repressive) forms of state planning.[60] Stalin's famous "socialism in one country" amounted to a strategic reorientation in the aftermath of the failed European revolutions: ultimate (socialist) goals would have to be deferred while the material and technological basis of a new order was being forged by the party-state. Historical pressures required a *stronger* governmental pressence, material incentives, bureaucratic expertise, income differences, and a return to traditional cultural values (nationalism, religion, the family). Marxian ideals of social equality and popular self-management were dismissed as "childish leftist illusions."

The Stalinist system, galvanized by a sense of urgency, isolation, and simple paranoia concerning enemies both internal and external, persisted well into the postwar years—its residues continuing into the Khrushchev, Brezhnev, and even Gorbachev reigns. Its syndrome included unchallenged single party rule, a single official ideology, strict cultural and intellectual controls, an apparatus of terror, cult of the all-powerful leader, and subordination of mass organizations to party dictates. State domination over civil society was buttressed by a resurgent nationalism and militarism. The economy was run by state ministers and managers in Moscow. Foreign policy, while never as expansionist as Cold War propagandists would have it, at times bordered on the xenophobic. By the time of Stalin's death in 1953, a new ruling class of party elites, state bureaucrats, industrial managers, and military leaders had been firmly established.[61] Although this reality was a clear departure from Lenin's vision, it had deep roots in his Jacobin model of revolution.

After World War II, this same model spread to other parts of the world: China, Vietnam, North Korea, Cuba, and, of course, the East European countries. In some cases (notably China), the revolution was more broadly nationalist—carrying with it more popular legitimacy than in Russia—while elsewhere (in most of Eastern Europe) Leninist regimes were imposed by Moscow and thus were unable to establish any congruence between state and civil society. Muscovite governments created after World War II in Poland, East Germany, Hungary, Romania, Bulgaria, and Czechoslovakia could never escape their initial antagonistic relationship to domestic social forces: peasants, Church, intellectuals, professionals. Nationalism worked *against* Communist stability, against perpetual efforts to solidify bureaucratic-centralist rule. While these regimes served as a security zone for the USSR, their capacity to mobilize popular support except in the very troubled case of Romania, was practically nil. The end result was a highly modified version of Leninism. It produced a tense standoff between regime and population that was destined to unravel over time—as it did in 1956 Hungary, 1968 Czechoslovakia, 1979–1981 Poland, and, finally, the explosive upheavals of 1989 that overthrew the entire Muscovite order.

If bureaucratic centralism turned out to be more fragile than either its proponents or detractors imagined, its historical impact was still more or less uniform: state domination over civil society, command economy with centralized forms of ownership and planning, obliteration of local democratic structures, an administered order that sought to transform people into passive objects.[62] In this context, the very idea of a transition to socialism took on a nearly mystical quality. Apparently the modes of consciousness, social relations, and political practices needed to constitute an egalitarian society in the future would spring up out of nowhere, with no prior lengthy and organic process of transformation *within civil society* to generate them. Meanwhile the bureaucratic penetration of civil society in Soviet-type systems ultimately reduced the notions of "advanced democracy," "state of the whole people," and "withering away of the state" to illusory, ritualized dogmas.[63] While statism of this sort was most fully developed in the USSR under Stalin, the impact of Jacobin politics in all other countries where it succeeded was an *extension* of the same (however fragile) system of domination. The label "state socialism" was always a contradiction in terms.[64]

Thus bureaucratic centralism contained its own seeds of decline and, eventually, collapse. The command system that appeared so relevant to predominantly agrarian countries because it could stimulate rapid economic development through state initiative lost its effectiveness with advancing levels of industrialization. A system that so completely emphasized the priorities of heavy industry over consumer goods, rigid ideological controls, decision-making at the center, militarism, and an ethos of combat with the rest of the world could not persist indefinitely. Indeed, the disintegration of Soviet and East European Communist power that began in the late 1980s actually has its origins in earlier phases of development (including Stalinism itself). The Jacobin model received its first major blow with Khrushchev's efforts to demystify the vanguard party, criticize Stalin's rule, and permit "different roads to socialism" in the 1950s. As Ken Jowitt argues, this "Leninist extinction" (if Leninism was still the appropriate label for the USSR) signified the erosion of an entire "international political order."[65] Despite the brevity of his reign, Khrushchev emerged as an important architect of this historical process in his struggle—not altogether successful—to reconstruct the Soviet party-state on a more open, democratized footing. At this point it was left to the Maoists in China, Vietnam, and elsewhere to carry forward the banner of Leninist revolution appropriate to an agrarian setting.

The seemingly invulnerable system of bureaucratic centralism—built by Lenin, consolidated by Stalin, and managed by the post-Stalin hierarchy—

served Soviet modernizing elites well in their program of rapid industrialization. A new society was constructed, but—after several decades of creating vast new urban areas, a huge state apparatus, modern factories, collective and state farms, and networks of communication, transportation and education—those in command had weakened the very foundations of that system. At a certain point (surely by the late 1950s), increased centralized control only retarded economic growth and technological innovation; the command model became a fetter upon efficiency and development. Statist power and privilege stood in direct opposition to modernizing trends favoring a scientific-technological ethos, managerial, professional, and working-class autonomy—and broader political participation.

With mounting systemic crisis in the 1960s, the Brezhnev regime tried valiantly to contain those pressures and defer genuine structural change. Retreating from Khrushchev's more experimental (and risky) initiatives, the Brezhnev model was inherently conservative, insofar as it was designed to contain powerful centrifugal forces in a society beset with growing conflicts. The hallmark of Brezhnevism was its further refinement of the bureaucratic system; its goal was a slightly more open, pluralist, and *efficient* political economy within the framework of party-state hegemony. To achieve this, Soviet elites introduced modest economic reforms aimed at decentralization, outlined a shift toward consumer interests (in the Ninth and Tenth Five-Year Plans), and stressed technological development as the basis of increased productivity. In the end, as we shall see, these moves to restructure the system were too feeble and indecisive (in contrast to similar reforms in China during the 1980s), too compromised by the power ambitions of those same leaders. By the 1980s Brezhnevism outlived its usefulness as a post-Stalin transitional form, having sustained uneven development at the expense of Soviet workers, managers, professionals, and consumers.

One major dilemma for Soviet elites since the 1930s was that the command economy was always geared to the interests of a huge military-industrial complex. The USSR built the world's largest military force to protect the world's longest international borders, maintain internal security, and deter other countries from launching war. A further dilemma revolved around the absence of genuine democratic participation, which also meant the lack of self-correcting mechanisms to ensure the adequate flow of information for purposes of decision-making and planning. Since the party-state channeled interest articulation into a relatively insular bureaucratic realm, Soviet politics was bound to lead to the disenfranchisement of workers, the rural population, national minorities, and even professionals, giving rise to a political culture of alienation, cynicism, and distrust. Statist rule actually *depoliticized* the Soviet masses by blunting the expression of nonconformist ideas, critical thinking, and oppositional politics. The nearly total absence of an authentic public sphere, where open discourse and legitimate articulation of interests was possible, set the USSR apart from the less centralized and insulated regimes of Eastern Europe. In any event, the repression of local autonomy was a basic source of irreconcilable conflict within the system—conflict that was bound to explode sooner or later.[66]

One such source of conflict was that effective utilization of technology, expertise, and skilled labor was prevented by the absence of democratic input. Another was that popular legitimacy was inevitably weakened where local autonomy and participation was denied. The struggle for democratization in the USSR and Eastern Europe became visible, on a small scale, in the 1950s and 1960s and later intensified during the 1970s and 1980s. Groups outside the party-state apparatus began to push for reforms: for a shift toward greater control over wages and working conditions by labor, for expanded managerial authority and decentralized planning by the technocratic intelligentsia, for increased ownership of land by rural producers, for broader political and cultural freedoms by the creative intelligentsia,[67] and for greater availability and variety of consumer goods by the general population. The Czech movement under Alexander Dubcek in 1968 (pushing for technocratic reforms from within the managerial and skilled working-class sectors) and the more explosive Polish Solidarity struggles of 1979–1981 (popular movements for an independent trade union and grassroots democracy) were the two most dramatic expressions of this trend after 1956. Soviet elites were able to contain such challenges to bureaucratic centralism, but not indefinitely.

The durability of Communist rule cannot be understood strictly or even primarily as a function of state coercion and terror; the role of ideology as a source of popular consensus was probably more decisive, especially in the USSR and China. The Soviet party-state was able to legitimate itself among broad social strata attached to the goals of national renewal and material betterment that fell under the heading "socialist construction." It's stability was ensured by rapid industrialization. However, by the 1980s, a crisis of legitimation was visible not only in Eastern Europe (where nationalist symbols persistently rallied opposition to stagnant Muscovite regimes) but in the USSR itself. Traditional modes of hegemony—official state Marxist ideology and Soviet nationalism—worked reasonably well during the long, harsh periods of sacrifice that accompanied "capitalist encirclement," rapid industrialization, World War II, and postwar reconstruction. But the ideological requirements of a more rationalized system seeking integration into the world market were at odds with the Soviet brand of "Marxism" mixed with patriotism, which ultimately lost its mobilizing appeal.

After many years of depoliticization, the hegemonic (Marxist-Leninist) values of Soviet society had few defenders outside the esoteric realm of the ruling apparatus. Alienation from political orthodoxy was a pervasive cultural motif among workers, youth, intellectuals, and national minorities. Evidence of a mounting crisis of legitimation could be found everywhere: a dramatic increase in alcoholism, decline of worker productivity, cynicism toward any form of authority, a trend toward privatized lifestyles, and spread of "hooliganism" among youth. Having implicitly conceded the end of Marxism as a single repository of truth and meaning, the Brezhnev leadership moved to achieve ideological reconsolidation on the basis of imported codes—namely, technological rationality and consumerism. More precisely, Brezhnevism from the mid-1960s to the mid-1980s represented a Sisyphean effort to combine what remained of Marxism with technological rationality and modern consumerism within a new ideological synthesis.

But this effort was probably doomed from the start. First, as we have seen, popular indifference toward the official, ritualized Soviet version of Marxism-Leninism had been deepening for some time; state ideology had lost its persuasive appeal. Second, whereas technological rationality had become the preferred worldview of Soviet modernizers, it erected new obstacles and challenges to the system of domination. Above all, it reinforced the ascendant role of the technocratic intelligentsia against embattled party-state elites, calling into question not only the dominant role of the Communist party but also the guiding motif of bureaucratic integration itself. By the 1980s this internal dialectic—along with pressures stemming from the international market—were so formidable that the contradiction could no longer be deflected. A further difficulty was built into the logic of technological rationality, since it furnished, in the USSR as elsewhere, a much too narrow, instrumental basis of legitimation for a system desperately in need of broader, more compelling social and political values.[68] Finally, expanded consumerism could be used to promote domestic stability for brief periods, but a fundamental shift in consumption patterns (and general material well-being) required a break with traditional priorities shaped by heavy industry and the military sector. Such a break could never occur without reversing chronic uneven development—that is, without overturning the Soviet model itself. Further, for both technological rationality and consumerism to serve as effective legitimating codes they would have to be associated with tangible material benefits made possible by sustained economic growth. Yet the very limits of bureaucratic centralism rendered such prospects highly unlikely.

Once popular consensus at the level of everyday life began to unravel, it fed into a cycle of decay and instability that would never be reversed.[69] Obstacles created by a closed public sphere,[70] the identification of Marxism with an authoritarian state, and the growing incorporation of the economy into the world market all suggested that Soviet leaders would be hard put to find renewed legitimating symbols for bureaucratic centralism—or any statist regime that might replace it. The highly administered character of the Brezhnev regime closed off struggles for political revitalization, especially from below, thus ensuring a perpetual crisis of legitimation.

The ascendancy of a strong liberalizing reformer in the person of Gorbachev thus made sense under such pressing historical conditions. Gorbachev took over the CPSU leadership in March 1985, emerging as a savior of the Soviet model at a time of severe problems, both economic and ideological. Gorbachev's mission was to restructure the system from above while retaining most of its basic historical features: the party-state, Communist ideology, the centrally planned economy. At the outset it was not clear to anyone, including Gorbachev, how far *perestroika* would have to be extended. But Gorbachev's "new thinking" introduced a powerful element into Soviet politics—recognition that the Brezhnev managerial model had failed, even on its own terms. Modernity in its diverse expressions (economic complexity, technology, urbanism, increased levels of education) had finally destroyed the firmaments of the post-Stalinist order and now threatened to undermine Communist rule in any form. Gorbachev's solution was to steer the system toward a reconstituted party-state that would be more open and decentralized, more grounded in popular sentiment, and more rational in its foreign policy.[71] This strategy alone would permit the USSR to avoid the twin dangers of reaction (Stalinist restoration) and political chaos.

Gorbachev's vision depended upon an uncertain mixture of reforms: internal party and general societal democratization (within limits), relaxation of party controls over cultural and intellectual life, a shift toward ideological moderation and relativism; managerial decentralization, and renewed emphasis on technology. This convergence of *perestroika* and *glasnost* was to be nothing short of a cultural revolution from above, designed in large part to meet the imperatives of modern society. It could not work, however, without a full reorientation of Soviet foreign policy, involving first and foremost withdrawal from the East-West confrontation that had shaped world politics since the late 1940s. Gorbachev's domestic and foreign initiatives were fully set in motion by 1987-88.[72]

The question of whether Gorbachev's bold agenda could be carried out in a way that might salvage some residue of socialism was never answered. Forced to pursue a balancing act between the entrenched party-state elites and impatient Westernizing reformers like Yeltsin, Gorbachev stumbled and then ultimately lost his footing. His far-reaching initiatives, designed to preserve the core of the system, quickly unleashed explosive forces—both "left" and "right," above and below, domestic and foreign—that could no longer be tamed by the power structure, which crumbled sooner than anyone could have predicted. Instead of revitalization, the new changes produced economic stagnation and political chaos, making Gorbachev's agenda unworkable. Of course, the collapse of Communist rule in the USSR and Eastern Europe was hastened by forces set in motion by the liberalizing reforms instituted after 1985, but the collapse itself was unavoidable. Mounting social conflict and popular revolt occurred in a period when the central mechanisms of power and coordination were breaking down, leading to the epochal upheavals of 1989–90. Having lost its legitimacy, even a renovated centralized bureaucratic structure could not endure for long. By 1990 the Gorbachev leadership had exhausted its range of solutions to the crisis, both within and outside the socialist tradition. Gorbachev engineered the demise of the old system but did not, and could not, lay the foundations of a new one.

Roughly three-quarters of a decade after the Russian Revolution, the Bolshevik tradition that had so influenced twentieth-century politics appeared to be dead. Just one year before the 1917 revolution Lenin's theory of imperialism attempted to explain how world capitalism was destined to collapse because of its own contradictions. The Bolshevik seizure of power would be the first salvo in that process. The upheavals of 1989–90, however, gave expression to a completely opposite reality: it was actually communism, a system that emerged as a global alternative to capitalism, that ended up imploding from its own internal conflicts and dysfunctions. Popular revolutions in every East European country, the disintegration of Soviet power, and evolution of the Chinese system toward what is best described as state capitalism all validated this historical phenomenon. Ironically, the end came as bureaucratic-centralist systems were becoming exposed to those very "Western" forces and ideas that communism was originally supposed to subvert: nationalism, liberalism, religion, consumerism, cultural trends, the blandishments of capital and technology.

The growth of oppositional tendencies in the Soviet bloc over time, penetrating the illusory facade of "totalitarianism," ultimately revealed the hollowness of Marxist-Leninist orthodoxy. (Of course, by the 1980s this system was "Leninist" in name only, having degenerated into a conservative party-state based upon bureaucratic social relations and traditional political culture.[73]) Those oppositional forces were galvanized from both above and below—above from a technocratic and critical intelligentsia fed up with party controls, below from workers and consumers demanding a higher standard of living as well as greater personal freedoms. Communist party-states were in an advanced stage of decay precisely to the extent that the command system failed to adapt to the requirements of modernity.

At the same time, struggles for social and political change, no matter how radical, were hardly motivated by any systemic ideological alternative to bureaucratic centralism. Years of depoliticization had undercut this prospect. A new vision framed in socialist or Marxist language was generally ruled out insofar as it was associated with the very hegemonic ideology used to prop up centralized power; even something along lines of the Swedish model, which Gorbachev seemed to embrace at moments, was out of the question. Vague images of liberal democracy, populism, and the "free market" floated about the scene, but they had no strategic relevance to actual possibilities. Many elites looked to a liberalized Brezhnevism (essentially the more open Kadar model in Hungary), but, as we have seen, this choice was blocked by the mounting crises of bureaucratic centralism in the 1980s. The Chinese model—a gradual shift toward state capitalism—might have offered the most promising route (for stability, at least), but it seems never to have been seriously considered.

The period leading up to collapse was largely one of "anti-politics"—a flight from "utopias" and global visions of change—that corresponded partially to the fashionable postmodern ethos in the West.[74] Prospects for social planning that could lead beyond bureaucratic centralism while avoiding total dissolution or chaos were thereby negated. The intellectuals, for their part, tended to renounce a public sphere that was contaminated by the old discourse. Even in the relatively open institutional matrix of Poland and Hungary, opposition meant transcending the limits of what Miklos Haraszti called the "velvet prison." Intellectuals of all stripes rebelled against the symbols and norms of an authoritarian system, which helped to precipitate the collapse of Communist legitimacy.[75] Organizations like KOR and Solidarity in Poland, the Civic Forum and Charter 77 in Czechoslovakia, and myriad ad hoc intellectual and cultural groups throughout East Europe rushed to fill the growing void. New public space opened up, but for the most part what filled it was a bizarre mixture of ideas old and new that scarcely added up to a viable alternative. The experience of the Vaclav Havel regime in Czechoslovakia, which turned away from communism but could find no viable alternative to pursue, reflected this predicament.

From the disasters of capitalist "shock therapy" in Poland to civil war in Yugoslavia to the explosion of centrifugal social forces in the USSR itself, the flight from politics clearly engendered catastrophic results. The breakdown of centralized rule everywhere gave rise not to class conflict but to ethnic, religious, and national conflicts that, in a few short years, took an enormous toll in chaos and violence. For both elites and masses what often dominated public discourse was a nostalgia for the past mixed with grandiose myths about enormous benefits to be derived from Western capitalism and liberal democracy. The erstwhile Soviet bloc appeared, at least for the short term, to have exhausted its historical options.

The revival of "civil society" in Eastern Europe and the USSR thus represented only a partial surge toward democratization at best. Single party rule gave way to open elections and broader freedoms, Marxist-Leninist ideology lost its privileged status, and there was a renaissance of intellectual and cultural activity. In 1989 the Berlin Wall came down, symbolizing an end to decades of communist domination. But the new setting brought a return of elite power in a different guise as many leading party-state *apparatchiki* became high rolling capitalists and speculators. It also brought widespread social strife and political instability that made democratic practices virtually impossible to institutionalize. And it brought economic stagnation and disruption accompanied by unemployment, erosion of social services, increased debt, and overall decline of living standards. These trends were most visible in Poland, but no former communist society has been immune to them since the late 1980s. Under such conditions the transition to self-organization within civil society anticipated by many radicals has little space to flourish. The eclipse of Jacobinism has not yet allowed for a process of repoliticization or a move toward democratic socialism, even of the Swedish type. On the contrary, it provoked massive confusion and even powerful currents of reaction—witness the failed neo-Stalinist coup attempt of August 1991. In the end, more than anything else, the collapse of communism forced a deep reassessment not only of the obsolete Soviet model but of the entire Marxian socialist tradition as well.[76]

Statism: Illusion of an Epoch?

The prolonged ascendancy of both social democracy and communism firmly established the main contours of twentieth-century Marxist politics: since the 1920s "socialism" has been inseparably linked to a statist legacy, while the radical left wound up submerged except for brief moments of outburst (Italy 1918–1920, Spain 1936–1939, Hungary 1956, France 1968, Poland 1979–1981). These two hegemonic strategies originated as challengers to capitalism, yet each succumbed to rationalizing pressures of the world capitalist system. They won power in their separate national contexts, yet they eventually became victims of their own political flaws and contradictions that, in turn, grew out of a certain theoretical void within Marxism itself— above all the absence of any *democratic* framework for the transition to socialism.[77] Statist illusions were never a matter of leadership myopia or betrayal but a function, in both cases, of the complex interaction between strategic choices and historical processes. The "triumph" of party-centered socialism ultimately turned into disillusionment and then defeat.

Social democracy from the time of the Erfurt Programme emphasized the centrality of a "democratic road" to socialism, but efforts to internally transform the capitalist state either collapsed in the midst of crisis (Germany) or brought "working-class" parties into power, or a share of power, where they could administer a rationalized state capitalism (Sweden). Nowhere did social democracy seriously attack the exploitative features of bourgeois society—the class system, social hierarchy, the market economy. The expansion of parliamentary democracy only masked the essence of a social order where centralized state power coexisted with an atomized and disempowered populace. And the social democrats more or less went along with this deception. In the course of Soviet development, on the other hand, Leninism signalled the institutionalization of "proletarian democracy" in the form of a single party state. It also manufactured a popular democratic mythology—the vanguard party as bearer of the historical will of the masses—in order to conceal the brutal actuality of bureaucratic centralism. Under this banner victorious revolutions were carried out in China, Vietnam, Yugoslavia, Cuba, and elsewhere. In the case of both social democracy and communism the democratic-socialist ideal amounted to little more than a mystifying facade, despite the sometimes impressive material accomplishments of these traditions. The ideal was either distorted by the imperatives of capitalist production or overwhelmed by the awesome power of an authoritarian state. As the public sphere narrowed, the space for local organizational forms, workers' control, and popular initiative was severely eroded where it did not vanish altogether.

From this standpoint, "successful" Marxist strategies embellished three defining elements—statist politics, commitment to economic rationalization, and the hegemonic role of technocratic intellectuals—each incompatible with sustained democratization. *Statism* concentrated power within a governmental apparatus responsible for both accumulation and legitimation functions, reproducing a public sphere that was anything but open and democratic. Paradoxically, just as the lower classes were integrated into state, party, and interest group structures for the first time, the actual opening for expanded democratic participation narrowed. *Rationalization* was directed toward eliminating residues of traditionalism—the institutional and ideological barriers to economic growth—that would make possible an administered system of planning, technological development, and labor discipline. In this sense "socialism" emerged as yet another rationale for the capitalist division of labor, carrying forward the old forms of domination (class, bureaucratic, even racial and patriarchal) in a new context.[78] The vehicle of change was a modernizing stratum that mobilized intellectual capital (knowledge, communication skills, technical expertise, et cetera) to create a new power bloc incorporating the working class. Ideologically committed to advancing proletarian interests, in time this stratum (especially where it came to power) emerged as a dominant technocratic force over that very class.[79]

For European social democracy, the main goal was restructuring capitalism within a multiparty framework, permitting the freer development of "social capital." In Soviet-type regimes, the single party state used its controlling presence to enact a range of modernizing aims dependent upon central planning, state ownership, and rapid industrialization. In both cases the historical outcome was similar: ascendance of a rationalizing instrument that, beneath its dedication to egalitarian and democratic goals, would fulfill (in an extended and even progressive way) the familiar tasks of the bourgeois revolution where capitalism itself itself was too weak or otherwise incapable of organizing the economy and winning support of the working class.

If the ideological erosion of social democracy and the political collapse of communism signified more a global *decline* than a crisis of the Marxian socialist tradition, by the 1990s this predicament was met by a seeming worldwide rush to embrace neo-liberal formulas. The turn toward "free market" schemes, austerity programs, and traditional values was accompanied by a flight away from grand visions of social transformation. That such a turn could be so readily accepted following decades of leftist governance only revealed that socialist political culture was never grounded in the rich diversity of civil society. This obvious fact was connected with another: there had been no real democratization of either the state or society as a whole, no process giving expression to a basic shift in social and authority relations.[80] The socialist tradition was confined to the realm of *haute politique*, namely, the arena of parties, leaders, governments, and contestations for state power. When politics takes on this one-dimensional character, it is quickly reduced to the art of fraud, manipulation, and control; the ordinary citizen is excluded from access to power, rendering democratic ideals unrecognizable. Whether this historic failure of social democracy and communism, visible as early as the 1950s, reflected the end of Marxian socialism as such or was merely a matter of bankrupt *strategies*, or flaws in the model of a party-centered socialism, would remain a conundrum for history to resolve.

4

THE THIRD ROAD I
From Vanguardism to Eurocommunism

ALTHOUGH THE IDEAS COMMONLY REFERRED TO AS EUROCOMMUNISM DID NOT
gain currency until Italian Communist leader Enrico Berlinguer outlined his
famous "theses" in 1973–74, as a broad strategic outlook its beginnings actually go back to the late 1940s—even to some themes introduced by the
Austro-Marxists decades earlier. The essence of Eurocommunism was a
vision of socialist transformation that looked beyond the limits of both
social democracy and communism while appropriating the best elements of
each. It upheld the possibility of a "third road" that would restore the
promise of democratic socialism obliterated by decades of fascism,
Stalinism, and Keynesian welfare state capitalism. And it hoped to revitalize
the European left at a time when fresh theories and strategies were being
desperately sought.

The Break with Jacobin Politics

Perhaps the most far-reaching historical significance of Eurocommunism
was its direct assault on, and final break with, its increasingly remote
Bolshevik origins; its full flowering in the mid-1970s signaled the eclipse of
Leninism in the West. No Bolshevik-style vanguard party achieved much
success in the advanced capitalist societies: there was nothing close to a revolutionary seizure of power in any European country after 1920. Such par-

ties either shriveled into small isolated sects or gradually evolved into derad-icalized mass formations with a distinct new identity. The Mediterranean Communist parties on the whole fit the second pattern: large, innovative, and relatively popular, they underwent periodic bursts of transformation after the 1920s, resulting in strategic and tactical adaptations that in time pulled them away from the Soviet model (in practice more that in theory) and opening the path to mainly national commitments within their orbits of political activity. Foremost among those commitments was the one to parliamentary democracy—to defend and strengthen it where it already existed (France), to help restore and revitalize it where it had been smoth-ered by fascism (Italy and Spain).

Non-ruling Communist parties around the world were born of the clas-sic split within the international socialist movement—a split that was defined more sharply in the wake of the Russian Revolution. Bolsheviks and Mensheviks, communists and social democrats became implacable enemies, not only in Russia and Europe but in every country where they vied for hegemony. The Comintern's famous "twenty one points" establishing crite-ria for membership in a truly Marxist-Leninist combat party erased all ambiguity concerning this division, which would profoundly shape world politics from the 1920s to the 1980s. There were moments of common alliance and collaboration, including the ill-fated Popular Front govern-ments in France and Spain of the mid-1930s, but such moments were brief and tense. As a rule the communists waged dedicated struggles against the social democrats, who at varying times were contemptuously dismissed as "social fascists," as a fulcrum of imperialist reaction, or as the simple con-duit of (modernizing) capitalist interests.[1]

Before long, the ruling Soviet Communist party degenerated into bureaucratic centralism while European social democrats, both governing and oppositional, became thoroughly enmeshed in the liberal-capitalist sys-tem. If this process was clearly visible by the 1960s, powerful trends in that direction were identified by insightful observers as early as the 1930s.[2] Further, many radical leftists had been arguing all along that Marxian socialist ideals would inevitably be smothered by the fundamentally elitist and bureaucratic features of communism and social democracy alike. They concluded that an entirely new theory of the transition would have to be formulated, inspired largely by icons from the radical left: Pannekoek, Sorel, Luxemburg, Korsch, Lukács, Gramsci, and Reich. Both Cornelius Castoriadis in the 1950s and André Gorz in the 1960s emphasized the need to break with the dominant authoritarian and economistic models of socialism, arguing that it was necessary to go beyond the false choice between insurrectionary politics and old-fashioned reformism.[3] The complexities of modern society would demand a much more sophisticated understanding of socialist objectives *and* the methods for achieving them: ends and means were inseparably connected.

Social democracy, whatever its flaws, did at least converge with important elements of the European liberal tradition: parliamentarism, a reformist ethos, an open political style that respected diversity and conflict. But Leninist vanguardism was another matter. Communist parties in power claimed to be the single source of authority and legitimacy, ruling over a complex network that subordinated local and international forms of activity to party control. Guided by a "scientific" Marxism and allegiance to the international proletarian movement, those parties—heirs to the Jacobin legacy—were "democratic" precisely insofar as they "represented" the totality of interests in the governed society. The social realm was completely obliterated by a political apparatus that over time became increasingly bureaucratic and intrusive into everyday life. The hegemonic Marxist-Leninist ideology became so ritualized that it eventually produced a numbing, depoliticizing effect on the great mass of people, reducing the very idea of participation to a charade. To the degree that leaders of *non*-governing Communist parties were expected to follow this Soviet model, they were sooner or later confronted with a painful choice: either continue along the path of electoral decline, or break with their Leninist heritage.

One problem with Leninist parties operating in a liberal-democratic setting was their profoundly authoritarian cast: in effect they reproduced within their own sphere of action the bourgeois division of labor, embracing Soviet-style the all-powerful role of professional cadres. The historic Jacobin preoccupation with ideological correctness, organizational discipline, and seizure of state power stood opposed to the complexities of political life in advanced capitalist countries—not to mention the democratizing thrust of modern social movements. This separation of the political and social realms coincided with an instrumentalism that, over the course of time, came to devalue the rhythm and flow of local struggles. A fatal defect of Leninism was that a single party possessing a monolithic ideology cannot ideally represent the interests and goals of immensely diverse social constituencies or movements in highly-developed societies. From a democratic-socialist standpoint, any "meta-discourse" that aspires toward global unification of oppositional struggles is neither desirable nor possible.[4] Where the vanguardist mode achieved its aims—most often in preindustrial countries—the prospects for genuine democratic representation were typically held in check. Regardless (or perhaps because) of their modernizing accomplishments, Leninist regimes typically extended the network of domination while narrowing the articulation of popular interests and movements within civil society.

After the late 1940s Leninism in fact became an increasingly marginal force in Western Europe and North America. Prospects for repeating Bolshevik-style insurrections in the postwar West, where most countries combined a long phase of economic growth with relatively stable liberal-democratic institutions, seemed virtually nil. The painfully difficult choice for the Marxist left was: Either discard the Leninist model with its authoritarian illusions or risk degeneration into tiny, isolated political sects. The latter path was actually the destiny of Marxist-Leninist (or Maoist) groups in every capitalist society where they had any significant presence. By the early 1990s such groups lived on in only a few countries (Italy, France), but even their influence was almost exclusively intellectual.

At the outset, of course, Communist parties in the West emerged as bureaucratic instruments of Soviet foreign policy; strictly indigenous, domestic concerns were subordinated to the dictates of "proletarian internationalism," while strategic debates were cut short by elite appeals to the victorious Soviet experience. In the aftermath of World War II, however, it was possible to see the beginnings of a Communist shift toward emphasis on primarily local or *national* conditions—inspired by the successes of the Yugoslav and Chinese revolutions, as well as huge partisan movements in Italy, France, Greece, Czechoslovakia, and elsewhere. The crucial theme here was the political adaptability and strategic flexibility of parties hoping, gradually and furtively, to escape the CPSU straightjacket held tight by Stalin. Although rarely outlined in theory, the move toward greater innovation was at first most visible in Western Europe where mass-based Communist parties appeared in several countries during the immediate postwar years (notably in Italy, France, and Finland). Already in 1945 Italian Communist leader Palmiro Togliatti, at the PCI's (Italian Communist Party) Fifth Congress, strongly urged a *via nazionale* that would abandon, once and for all, the concept of violent revolutionary seizure of power as outmoded.[5] At the level of non-ruling Communist *practice* this shift was accelerated in the 1950s and 1960s, with the death of Stalin, the increasing bureaucratization of the USSR that discredited it as a viable model, and upheavals in Poland and East Germany (1953), Hungary (1956), and Czechoslovakia (1968). Gradually but emphatically, Communist parties adopted a *modus operandi* that accepted the permanence of parliamentary democracy and rejected in practice (if not theory) the viability of Leninist politics for the West.

Togliatti's early vision of a distinctly *national* and *popular* communism—one that would point the way toward a *terza via*, or "third road," between social democracy and Soviet communism—held sway in Italy even as strong residues of Leninism persisted. (The myth that Communist parties in every setting were "Leninist" continued as official dogma well into the 1970s). The phase of "duplicity," as Italians called it, lasted until the Eurocommunist shift when, through the initiatives of PCI leader Berlinguer and Spanish Communist leader Santiago Carrillo, the last vestiges of old-style Comintern politics were officially discarded. Now largely independent of Soviet foreign policy priorities and preoccupied with electoral politics, Eurocommunist parties in Italy, France, Spain, and Greece became more and more sensitive to domestic pressures and the logic of liberal-democratic politics. The very notion of "smashing" the bourgeois state and establishing a dictatorship of the proletariat was no longer taken seriously except by dwindling old guard factions desperate to retain the symbols and hopes of an earlier revolutionary period. By the 1970s, therefore, the Communist label no longer offered meaningful clues to actual political behavior.[6]

From Togliatti to Eurocommunism

In their formative years (from the early 1920s to the mid-1930s) European non-ruling Communist parties were, as disciplined Comintern affiliates, thoroughly attached to the Leninist worldview. Having departed the Second International out of frustration with the paralysis and fatalism of social democracy, their leaders adopted the "twenty one principles," which included adherence to the vanguard party, democratic centralism, dictatorship of the proletariat, and the priorities of Soviet foreign policy. Ostensibly dedicated to the insurrectionary overthrow of the bourgeois state, they rejected the use of electoral politics for strategic purposes (as a method for actually gaining power) in accordance with Leninist theory and Bolshevik practice. The Russian events, understood as the first successful socialist revolution in history, were looked to with reverence—even if European Marxists often had little familiarity with early Soviet history. The specific (and vastly different) social and political conditions in the West had virtually no strategic importance during this period. Communist parties in France, Italy, and Spain, for example, upheld the Leninist insurrectionary model with a sense of enormous pride and certitude.[7]

Roughly a half century later, these same parties had come full circle: taking a page from Kautsky and Bernstein—early implacable foes of Bolshevism—they ardently celebrated the positive features of the liberal tradition and pluralist democracy. In a March 1977 meeting in Madrid, the three general secretaries (Georges Marchais of the PCF, Berlinguer of the PCI, and Carrillo of the PCE) issued a joint statement "respecting the pluralism of political and social forces and the guarantee ... of all individual and collective freedoms: freedom of thought and expression, of the press, of association, of assembly and demonstration, of the free circulation of people inside their country and abroad, trade union freedom ... the inviolability of private life, respect for universal suffrage and the possibility of democratic alternation of majorities, religious freedom, freedom of culture, freedom of expression of the various philosophical, cultural, and artistic currents and opinions." The declaration concluded: "This determination to build *socialism in democracy and freedom* inspires the conception elaborated in full autonomy by each of the parties."[8] One detects scarcely a trace of Leninism here, although party leaders did insist upon retaining the "spirit of Lenin." This departure, however, took place gradually and unevenly, in response to a series of domestic and international conditions and events.

For the French and Italian parties, the third road model had its origins in the antifascist struggles of the Popular Front and especially the Resistance years of the late 1930s and early 1940s, from which the parties emerged as patriotic mass organizations committed to electoral politics and postwar "democratic reconstruction." This development led to short-lived participation in ruling governmental coalitions in 1947, which collapsed with the onset of the Cold War and the widening schism between Communists and Socialists. What began as essentially a defensive maneuver evolved into an institutionalized postwar strategy of "structural reforms" once the parties adapted to their parliamentary systems. After the failure of European Resistance movements to generate a revolutionary breakthrough in any developed country, the long-cherished hopes of insurrection were abandoned even though they continued to be routinely mentioned in official party statements. Not only in France and Italy, but in many other European countries—Greece, Denmark, Austria, Norway, Belgium, Luxemburg, Finland, and Iceland—Communist parties entered national governments after the war, moving into opposition only when East-West tensions made continued collaboration with rival parties impossible. Many of these parties maintained an extensive presence in local governments, and some returned to share national power (as in Finland) once the Cold War softened in the 1960s. Even in opposition, however, Communist parties abided strictly by the norms and practices of bourgeois democracy; not only did they shy away from activities involving class confrontation, their entire political outlook shifted toward reformist moderation.[9]

During the immediate postwar years, some Communist parties were trapped in a politics of duplicity, suspended between Leninist ideological identity and everyday parliamentarism. In the PCI, this strategic ambivalence was concretely resolved in 1953 in favor of Togliatti's concept of structural reforms, which the party later openly championed in the wake of the 1956 events: initial stirrings of de-Stalinization in the USSR (including tentative approval of "different" or "national" paths to socialism); the Hungarian uprising; and the first appearance of polycentrism in the world Communist movement, which Togliatti outlined at the Eighth PCI Congress in 1956.[10] In the PCF under Maurice Thorez, dual politics continued into the 1970s, its contradictions mystified and repressed by a residual Jacobin ideology, a heavy-handed organizational centralism, and a sense of embattled political isolation (explained by the party's failure to build popular support beyond its early postwar peak). Although it had engaged in frontist and electoral politics since the mid-1930s, only after 1964—and then halfheartedly—did the PCF begin to present a strategic self-conception in tune with this history and critical of the insurrectionary model. Even so, it took the leadership another decade to abandon the pretense that Leninism and the democratic road were somehow compatible.[11]

Once the PCI and PCF moved to reassess their identities openly and systematically, once their domestic entanglements took precedence over Soviet internationalism, their adoption of policies tied to structural reform became more uncompromising and irreversible. The strategy of democratization, however limited, was less a matter of choice than a requirement of political success, or even survival; it was, above all, geared to a phase of capitalist development in which the rule of a single party seemed no longer plausible. This process advanced more rapidly in the PCI than in other Communist parties, largely because of its size (offering greater chances of electoral success) and the influence of Togliatti. It was accelerated by the internal triumph of the PCI's right wing in the late 1960s, culminating in the expulsion of the leftist *Il manifesto* group in 1969. The arguments of the right—that "neocapitalist" conditions allowed for and required a reformist insertion of the party into the bourgeois state—coincided with the PCI's expanded role in Italian society, notably its strong presence in local and regional governing coalitions.[12]

Events of the late 1960s and early 1970s added to the momentum favoring this Communist definition of the democratic road. These included the decline of Gaullism in France and *immobilism* of the center-left coalition in Italy; the Soviet invasion of Czechoslovakia; the challenge of the new left (dating from the May 1968 events in France and the "hot autumn" in Italy); the dramatic leftist defeats in Chile and Portugal, revealing the need for broad popular alliances going beyond the proletariat; a mellowing of the historic Socialist antagonism toward the Communists; the consistent electoral gains of the PCI, which for the first time won more than one-third of the vote in the 1975 (regional) and 1976 (national) balloting, carrying it to the threshold of national power.[13]

Beneath this were four significant long-term factors: the erosion of Catholicism in Italy and France, detente between the U.S. and the Soviet Union, the Sino-Soviet split and the onset of pluralism within world Communism, and, perhaps most crucial, the long-term involvement of the two parties in liberal-democratic institutions. All of this contributed to legitimation of the parties domestically—reflected in the manifest decline of anti-Communism—and to their innovative flexibility on questions related to the USSR and the Marxist tradition in general. The PCI was far in advance of other non-ruling Communist parties in moving along this path.

The PCE's transformation, on the other hand, occurred later but more abruptly. After nearly four decades of clandestine activity under the Franco dictatorship, PCE leaders were anxious to shed their "outlaw" status and switch to legal methods of struggle. Underground politics took its toll, not only physically but ideologically: the PCE grew more and more insulated and detached from social reality during the harsh and repressive decades following the Civil War. Especially before 1956, the PCE's Leninism signified a rigid attachment to Bolshevik strategy and passive subservience to the CPSU line and Soviet foreign policy. Throughout this period a highly centralized apparatus remained intact.

The first signs of change appeared in the mid-1960s with the Franco regime's decreased public support and the PCE's growing participation in the new workers' commissions (*comisiones obreras*), which in regions like Catalonia had established bargaining relationships with management. Then, in 1968, Carrillo stepped forward as a vocal critic of Soviet intervention in Czechoslovakia, seizing this moment to attack Soviet bureaucratic centralism and, by extension, the concept of the dictatorship of the proletariat, which he argued was outmoded and incompatible with the ideal of democratic socialism. From this standpoint, and with the expectation that the decaying Franco dictatorship would soon crumble and give way to bourgeois democracy, the PCE embraced the "democratic road." However, it was not until 1977—after Franco's death, legalization of the PCE, and the holding of Spain's first national elections since 1936—that the party could implement this strategy in practice.

What distinguished the situation of the PCE from that of the PCI and PCF, of course, was that parliamentary structures had not yet fully appeared in Spain. Even during the 1970s the imperatives of anti-fascist struggle still weighed heavily on the Spanish left. That reality permeated every dimension of the PCE's program and strategy and was reflected in Carrillo's books, interviews, and statements.[14] It also defined the two-stage conception of the transition advanced by Carrillo: First destroy the remnants of fascism and secure liberal democracy; then begin the process of socialist transformation. In Carrillo's words: "The great thing today is to smash the forced integration constituted by fascism. In order to do this, what is needed is a coalition government which will restore liberties. Tomorrow the advance to socialism will be posed."[15] This is not to deny that the PCI and PCF were also preoccupied with fascism and the threat of reaction, but merely to indicate that Spain in the 1970s was at a different level of political development from either Italy or France. More than anything the PCE sought to play an integral role in the pluralist reconstitution of Spanish society while staking out its own claim to legal opposition.

With the strategic outlook of the three Mediterranean Communist parties changing drastically, new theoretical formulations (for example, on the state, concept of the party, class forces, nature of the transition) were bound to follow. Interestingly enough, it was the theoretical codification of already established organizational practices—a step coinciding with the *political* birth of Eurocommunism—that provoked so much controversy and triggered the initial Soviet response.[16] The Eurocommunist position, no longer considered particularly heretical, was strongly affirmed and defended (notably by Carrillo and Berlinguer) at the June 1976 meeting of twenty seven Communist parties in East Berlin. Although criticisms of the Soviet model were muted, CPSU leaders were forced to yield on every major issue.[17] In this case, as in others, the conflict revolved around Lenin—or at least what passed for Leninism within the communist tradition.

What Eurocommunist parties had to confront and reject, was the sacred notion of the dictatorship of the proletariat. For, although Leninism never took hold as a concrete strategy in the West, its lingering mystique and symbolic imagery did have political consequences for an entire range of party activities. The official break did not occur until the 1975–1978 period, although the implications for such a departure were already present in Togliatti's postwar writings on the *via italiana*, which he tried to square with ideological convention by employing the innovative concept of the "democratic dictatorship of the proletariat."[18] Togliatti's notion of "progressive democracy," sketched in 1944–1946, necessarily required for its actualization a non-vanguardist party—a mass, nonsectarian organization representing the working class and allied strata within the framework of pluralist competition. At this time the PCI set for itself the primary goal of consolidating liberal democracy in the continuing struggle against fascism; the transition to socialism would be delayed until domestic and international power relations became more favorable. Immediate politics was largely tactical, directed toward broadening space within the existing institutional spheres. The impetus for this departure came not only from the Resistance, which transformed the Communist party from a small sect into a heterogeneous mass party, but from the frontist policy of interclass alliances laid down at the Seventh Comintern Congress in 1935.[19]

In Togliatti's view, the PCI was but one part of the state and society existing alongside other parties and forces; no single party could assert an exclusive moral claim to rule, and no Marxism possessed absolute scientific authority. A *democratic* transition would require the PCI's continuous institutional presence in what party literature reffered to as a "secular, nonideological, and pluralistic" state. Togliatti accurately observed that the dictatorship of the proletariat was always a vague concept in classical Marxism and that its only historical embodiment (in the USSR) was not something that the vast majority of Italians, with memories of Mussolini's authoritarian state still fresh, wanted to duplicate. Yet, despite the obvious contradictions between the *via italiana* and Bolshevik strategy, Togliatti, owing to his long and deep attachment to the USSR, could never break with the party's official Leninism.

An important Comintern figure for eighteen years, Togliatti internalized the outlook of the Soviet leadership—its perception of world politics, its sense of priorities, its strategic and tactical orientation. His attachment to the CPSU was unqualified. In the 1930s Togliatti's influence encouraged the spread of Popular Front attitudes among PCI leaders that carried over into the Resistance and postwar years. By 1944–45, the war and partisan mobilization appeared to present new revolutionary opportunities: the power structure was in shambles, councils and other local forms of participation had spread throughout northern and central Italy, and the PCI had grown rapidly into a thriving "national popular" party. But such opportunities were never actually pursued. On his return from Moscow in 1944, Togliatti steered the party toward a frontist and defensive "new course" strategy. The PCI spurned insurrection, turned away from local democratic forms, induced the partisans to surrender their arms, and moved toward collaboration with status quo parties around immediate priorities of "reconstruction," enacting a Republican constitution, and building a government of "national unity." In this vein, the PCI entered every Italian cabinet between April 1944 and May 1947, hoping to solidify institutionally a popular antifascist coalition. At the time such tactics corresponded perfectly to the Soviet premise of "capitalist stabilization" and the decline of the proletariat as a revolutionary agent in the West.[20] In any case, the PCI (and the USSR) did operate as an instrument of postwar Communist moderation.

Togliatti's genius—both in terms of his party leadership and theoretical guidance—lay in his shrewd application of Resistance themes and concepts derived from PCI founder Antonio Gramsci, within a frontist orientation, to the challenges and pressures of the postwar situation. For example, Togliatti quickly appropriated Gramsci's seminal ideas of national popular struggle, social bloc, and ideological hegemony, but translated them into a framework of electoral mobilization, elite alliances, and structural reform of the existing state system. The Gramscian vision of revolutionary change aimed at subverting bourgeois class and power relations was largely abandoned. The "party of a new type" envisaged by Togliatti was a mass-based national formation, but one that would help create an "expanded democracy" within the political framework of the reborn Italian Republic. Togliatti's famous editorials in the party journal *Rinasita* during the late 1940s and early 1950s ceaselessly hammered away at this departure from pre-1935 PCI strategy, all the while legitimating it by means of explicitly Gramscian (and even Leninist) symbols. Of course, the Comintern's Popular Front policies originated as a strictly *tactical* maneuver, and this was surely the definition given to them by the PCI during and immediately after the Resistance. In retrospect, however, this frontism can be understood as the genesis of *via italian*, as an institutionalized tactic that evolved into the later structural reformist (Eurocommunist) strategy.[21]

It was only after 1956, as we have seen, that the PCI was able to launch the *via italiana* in earnest. Togliatti now began to spell out theoretically the premises of a *strategy* charted within and through the parliamentary system: instead of being overthrown from below and replaced by a new proletarian state, the power structure would be internally democratized as part of a lengthy transitional process. This perspective dismissed the familiar Leninist warning against utilizing the bourgeois state as a *primary* mechanism for advancing socialism. Togliatti noted the "complexity" and increasingly popular character of modern liberal democracy and concluded that the state could be transformed from an instrument of capitalist domination into a sphere of open contestation within which a working-class (and socialist) presence could be extended. In PCI parlance, the idea of a "secular, nonideological" state would supplant the outmoded Marxist concept of an "instrumental" state.[22] Thus, with each new social reform, with each new institutional position conquered, the PCI, in alliance with other "democratic anti-monopoly" forces, could set in motion a shift of power away from the large corporations and favoring the working class. In the language of Gramscian strategy, it could hope to achieve socialist hegemony within a reconstituted state that was no longer controlled by a single monolithic ruling class. Since the boundary separating state and civil society in "neo-capitalism" was more diffuse than in early capitalism, the system was seen as more vulnerable to incursions of all sorts.[23]

These were the strategic assumptions, linked to an evolutionary, peaceful, and more or less stable transition, that paved the way toward the Eurocommunism of Berlinguer, Carrillo, and Marchais a decade after Togliatti's death. While introducing no real theoretical originality, Eurocommunism, like the *via italiana* that preceded and informed it, carried forward a refinement of traditional social-democratic and Popular Front agendas. It reflected not so much an extension of Gramsci's Marxism—for Gramsci, the democratic road defined in this way was nothing but a massive deception—but used it to legitimate clearly non-revolutionary goals.[24] The reintroduction of Gramscian concepts barely concealed an underlying strategic outlook that was actually closer to Bernstein that to Gramsci.

Filtered through Togliatti, the PCI's "Gramscian Marxism" thus allowed the party to occupy a new (parliamentary) strategic position while retaining its nominal Leninism.[25] Despite strong pressure from the most militant electoralist faction led by Giorgio Amendola, however, the leadership under Luigi Longo somehow clung to its "Leninism" throughout the 1960s. These pretensions were abandoned only in the aftermath of the Thirteenth Congress in 1972, when Berlinguer introduced the *compromesso storico* (historical compromise) tactics calling for political collaboration between Communists and Christian Democrats. Fueled by electoral successes and the decline of DC strength, the PCI could now realistically focus its sights on national power. Under such conditions, it would have to avoid the pitfalls of building power upon a social foundation too narrow to sustain long-term success—a lesson adopted from the overthrow of the Allende regime in Chile. It would also have to escape the authoritarian legacy of Leninism, which enabled opponents to raise the bogey of Soviet dictatorship. The PCI's strategy now differed more explicitly and fundamentally from Lenin's: liberal democracy was seen as integral to all phases of socialist transformation, while time-honored commitments to nationalization of industries and central planning were sharply revised. Yet even the most profound changes were presented as an affirmation of continuity from Leninism through Togliatti's "new course" to Berlinguer's *compromesso* policy of the 1970s.[26]

In this situation, the PCI had to struggle to overcome its dualism of the early postwar years—the surface persistence of Leninism as a source of organizational identity alongside the electoralism and trade unionism of its everyday practice. As late as 1979 Berlinguer could say, "It is not our intention to fuel petty polemics or partisan controversies over 'Leninism.' At the same time, we have no intention of disowning or minimizing our party's historical ties with the October Revolution and Lenin's work."[27] In any case, the theoretical innovations that grew out of the Thirteenth Congress hastened the PCI's liberation from past myths, justifying in unambiguous terms its strategic adaptation to representative democracy and prefiguring the rise of Eurocommunism.[28]

Both the PCE and the PCF, on the other hand, experienced a later and much briefer process of internal debate over Leninism, but once the process was under way (in the early 1970s), party leaders resolutely swept aside orthodox symbols in their eagerness to demonstrate their Eurocommunist credentials. They wasted little time in getting rid of the dictatorship of the proletariat concept, which, as in the case of the PCI, imposed a tremendous ideological burden upon those organizations engaged in electoral activity or committed to the revitalization of bourgeois democracy. Carrillo argued that Leninist strategy had lost its rationale for Spain: Not only armed insurrection, but the vanguard party (and single party state) were obsolete owing to the diversification of social forces and the complexity of political structures. The formal rights and liberties produced by the bourgeois revolution, far from simply reflecting capitalist needs, must be deepened and carried forward under socialist development. Hence Carrillo could "easily imagine a socialist regime governed jointly or even alternatively by Communists, Socialists, and Christians who are in favor of socialism: a socialist state with a plurality of parties."[29]

Since Spanish fascism was still very much alive in the 1970s, Carrillo's preoccupation with liberal democracy made sense as part of a transitional program that, once carried out, would finally enable the PCE and other radical groups to pose the question of socialism. The irony here was obvious: although Spain lacked any longstanding representative tradition, the positions staked out by the PCE at the Ninth Congress in 1978 expressed the deepest commitment to pluralist democracy of any Communist party in history.[30]

The PCF was neither so critical of the CPSU nor so devoted to pluralist forms as the PCE and PCI. At the Twenty-second Congress in 1976, Marchais concluded that the terms "dictatorship" and "proletariat" were negative symbols that isolated the Communist party—the former conjuring up images of Hitler, Mussolini, and Franco (and presumably Stalin), the latter suggesting a restricted working-class rather than a "mass" base. In the new phase of struggle, characterized by the crisis of monopoly capitalism, radicalization of the middle strata, and "peaceful coexistence," socialism could be advanced without civil war or an overturning of bourgeois state power—assuming, of course, that the PCF could mobilize a broad anti-monopoly social bloc.[31] At the same time, the PCF leadership was less willing to question its avowed vanguardism, manifest in the idea that the party alone is the judge of Marxist theory and strategy, must exercise control over mass organizations, and is the sole representative of the working class. It was equally reluctant to part with democratic centralism.[32]

In debates over these basic departures from orthodoxy within international communism, the CPSU presented itself as the guardian of Leninist virtue. The Soviets accepted in principle the concept of differing roads to socialism after 1956, but they continued to stress the "leading role" of the vanguard party as a cardinal precept of revolutionary politics. In fact, CPSU theorists did not reject the strategic use of parliamentary forms in advanced capitalism, or even the possibility of a peaceful transition; the problem with Eurocommunism, in their view, was the "opportunistic" extremes to which the parties had gone in practice. Thus, the abandonment of Leninism was viewed not merely as a theoretical deformation but as a further step toward the parties' subordination to the bourgeois state apparatus and the market economy. In Soviet terms, Eurocommunists simply forgot that endemic crises of monopoly capitalism inevitably point toward rupture and transcendence of the existing order, even where parliamentary structures are utilized to prepare the way.[33] Soviet renunciation of pluralist socialism was really at the heart of the matter, since the Eurocommunist model constitut-ed a direct challenge to bureaucratic centralism and the facile equation of democracy with dictatorship of the proletariat.[34] CPSU leaders had every reason, therefore, to defend "Leninism" against the bold incursions of Carrillo, Berlinguer, and Marchais.

The stripping away of Leninist strategic language, even where old organi-zational principles lingered, was thus the hallmark of Eurocommunism in the 1970s. It would be easy to analyze this profound shift as merely symbol-ic, as nothing more that the delayed recognition of routinized political prac-tices. But that would be only half true; the break with Leninism also cleared away obstacles to change within the parties, allowing them to glimpse a more comprehensive democratic theory of transition. Contradictions nat-urally remained, but the foundations of a novel structural reformism in the spirit of Togliatti's *terza via* were more solidly established.

The Theory of Structural Reformism

Within international communism during the 1970s, the emergence of more than a dozen parties adhering to a reconstituted democratic road strategy gave rise to tremendous diversity—in levels of political development, orga-nizational strength, social composition, international ties, and even ideo-logical outlook. Each party, too, was shaped by a unique national history and culture. Moreover, the party leaderships were factionally divided into "left," "right," and "center" tendencies despite sometimes tortured efforts to convey a public image of unity. The myth of a homogeneous and united world com-munist movement was finally exploded once and for all. Still, for Eurocommunist parties a common strategy suffused all the differences and idiosyncracies, one that could be defined as structural reformist. In the case of the Mediterranean parties, this commonality was enhanced by shared geographical and cultural bonds, as well as by a shared history facilitating political linkages. The constituent elements of structural reformism, while never codified in any single document, were embedded in the theory and practice of these parties spanning three decades.

Eurocommunism looked to the institutions of bourgeois democracy—elections, parliament, local government, interest groups—as the fundamen-tal means of achieving a transfer of power. Whereas Lenin had emphasized the *tactical* importance of parliamentary activity, Eurocommunists turned to it as the locus of a long-range *strategy* for dismantling capitalist power and moving toward socialism. Liberal democracy would be retained as a matter of principle, echoing Togliatti's "new course" celebration of pluralist forms. In Togliatti's words: "We are democrats because we move in the framework of the Constitution, within democratic traditions and legality, and we expect from everyone all due respect for this legality and the application of all constitutional norms.... We have conquered the terrain of democracy in order to advance beyond it, toward socialism. It would therefore be absurd to negate it. On the contrary, we defend it. In fact, the urgency of socialist renewal...allows us to see in the norms of democratic and constitutional life not an obstacle, but a positive force for the constitution of socialism."[35] Insofar as objective conditions exist within capitalism for democratization of the state apparatus, no forcible destruction of that apparatus would be necessary. The postwar Italian, French, and Spanish Communist parties followed this prescription faithfully, committing the bulk of their resources to electoral politics while avoiding, under all conditions, any direct assault on state power.

The theory of structural reforms assumes that workers and other popular strata will achieve a steadily more powerful voice, sense of citizenship, and political strength with each electoral advance and institutional gain. As new positions are captured within the state, more space is created within which the left can subvert bourgeois hegemony and begin to extend its control over major sectors of the economy and society. The PCI and, to a lesser extent, the PCE advertised this strategy as a modern Gramscian "war of position" capable of generating an authentic mass party with new levels of collective participation. Such a "modification of structures"—one that brings the working class to power and supersedes the narrow, formal definition of politics typical of the liberal state—is required for democracy to be "completed."[36] The PCF conceptualized this approach as a "transition from a state of the monopolies to the state of the working people in which advanced democracy is a step toward socialism."[37]

Eurocommunist theory defended constitutional rights and liberties, including those of political opposition, through the transitional period and into socialism itself. As Togliatti stressed, pluralist democracy—whatever its flaws and limits—is more compatible with egalitarian social aims than Soviet-style centralization, whatever economic arguments might be made on behalf of the latter. This indissoluble connection between democracy and socialism meant, according to PCI theorist Luciano Gruppi, that "the struggle for human liberty, for parliamentary democracy, does not constitute a tactical moment, but is an essential part of the struggle for socialism as an ultimate goal."[38] Gruppi added that not only does parliament ideally play an active, decisive role in the transition, it is the "political system most appropriate to socialism."[39] Thus, Eurocommunist leaders viewed the state as an arena of contestation, where diverse social forces struggle for hegemony, rather than as an instrument of class or political domination; political solutions to the crisis of capitalism demand inputs from many sources—Marxist and non-Marxist, public and private, secular and religious.[40] This kind of socialist pluralism goes well beyond what even Kautsky had in mind. It is true that the main currents of the Second International accepted the linkage of socialism and democracy, but their vision of post-capitalist politics remained hazy, bound as it was to the incompatible concepts of the withering away of the state and dictatorship of the proletariat.

Along these lines, structural reformism meant that the entire array of premises associated with vanguardism would have to be eliminated. Carrillo's firm position, adopted at the Ninth PCE Congress, was that genuine pluralism compels any Communist party to abandon its scientific claim to be sole bearer of working-class interests; he saw the PCE as part of an unfolding "new political formation," in which other parties and mass organizations can play equal roles, in which party and state are not identical.[41] Carrillo's model, like Gruppi's, also abolished the Leninist "transmission belt" concept of party control over popular movements, such as workers' commissions, trade unions, and other local forms. According to PCI leader Pietro Ingrao, the Marxist party would remain a "leading" force insofar as it must shape state institutions and social processes, but it cannot become totally submerged in the state.[42] The PCF, for its part, had by the 1970s departed very little from its entrenched vanguardism and centralism, but that would change later with mounting domestic and international pressures.[43]

Well before the official shift toward Eurocommunism, postwar structural reformism signified an alliance politics tied to an expanding middle strata (civil servants, professionals, technicians, et cetera), broadening the definition of "social bloc" to include all social forces (potentially) opposed to the monopolies while encouraging electoral and governing coalitions with rival parties. Superficially resembling the Popular Front, this strategy differed from the earlier Popular Front approach insofar as it was essentially anti-capitalist rather than anti-fascist and ostensibly directed toward socialist objectives instead of defensive maneuvers designed to protect liberal democracy. The PCI's skillful use of alliance politics—it was always basically a multiclass party—was vital to its mobilization of a large, heterogeneous popular base and extensive local power network throughout Italy. It was rooted in what the PCI saw as a convergence of urban social forces growing out of the conditions of advanced capitalism—industrial workers squeezed by economic crisis, the middle strata radicalized by their loss of job control and social issues, the petty bourgeoisie suffocated by the expanded power of monopolies.[44] The PCF and PCE later adopted the strategy of a broadening social bloc built around incremental electoral gains, mainly because they were more fearful of party coalitions, but by the late 1970s their *modus operandi* fully converged with that of the PCI.

Structural reformism further insisted upon a process of institutional "renewal" at all levels of state activity: professionalization of the civil service, including elimination of huge patronage networks, nepotism, and corruption, along with a simplification of governmental ministries and agencies.[45] The overriding goal was to make the public sector more accountable to the general population, first by undermining monopoly and "parasitic" influences through greater parliamentary control; second by democratizing the police, military, and court systems; and third by decentralizing state power. The PCE and PCF managed to establish this strategy in practice—the PCE in the workers' commissions, mass organizations, and neighborhood groups; the PCI in municipal and provincial governments. In cities like Bologna, where Communist administration went back to 1945, the PCI moved to create "new norms of public life," meaning alternative approaches to urban management and planning that maximize local participation (for instance, in the neighborhood councils) and abolition of *clientelismo*.[46] This involved the gradual emergence of a "democratically planned economy," with a mixture of state and small-scale private enterprises.[47] Although the PCF agreed with this in theory, its local involvement was always relatively weak and so its centralism tended to prevail by default.

To be viable in its political context, Eurocommunism had to advocate internal party democratization characterized by a shift from hierarchical, disciplined, cell-based units toward more participatory forms allowing for a freer exchange of ideas and influences. The impact of the new left and social movements beginning in the 1960s forced the parties to confront new issues and adapt to a more open, less centralist style. Further, a series of volatile internal debates took place around the many issues posed by rather far-reaching challenges—for example, in the PCF and PCE over the break with Leninism, in the PCF following the dissolution of the Common Program and the left's electoral setback in March 1978, in the PCI around whether to pursue the *compromesso storico*. When party elites could no longer prevent those debates from moving into the open and perhaps taking a mass character, the old Leninist fiction of unity and secrecy—not to mention vanguardist leadership—could no longer be sustained.

The break with Leninism naturally dictated independence from the CPSU and the Soviet model, which had long since lost its appeal for most of the West European left. New spheres of autonomy were encouraged by de-Stalinization within the USSR and, later, by the diversity made possible by the Sino-Soviet conflict. The difficulties Western European Communist leaders encountered in trying to reconcile their domestic priorities with the bureaucratic centralism of "actually existing socialism" fed the drive toward indigenous models. For most parties, the 1968 Soviet overthrow of the reformist Dubcek regime in Czechoslovakia represented the last straw. The PCI after 1956 had already affirmed the right of parties to autonomy within international communism (Togliatti's famous "polycentrism")—a direction implicit in the *via italiana* strategy. In the early 1970s Berlinguer stated that autonomy for the PCI meant not only the freedom to carve out a distinctly "national" strategy (an issue resolved earlier) but also the pursuit of an independent global communist presence outside the two major blocs.[48] Carrillo's firm defense of these positions, both in *Eurocommunism and the State* and in various party statements, were equally compelling: He rejected the legitimacy of a "directing center" and the viability of the Soviet model, especially for advanced industrial countries.[49] The PCF, for its part, did endorse the principle of "national roads," but generally yielded to Soviet foreign policy initiatives.

Finally, the geographical proximity and cultural similarity of the Mediterranean parties encouraged formation of a common regional or European-based perspective, not only on matters of political strategy but also international politics. Contacts among West European Communist parties became more regular and intimate in the late 1960s, to the extent that by 1973 regular conferences were being held. A loose alliance among the PCI, PCE, and PCF was quickly forged, leading to a joint Italian-Spanish declaration in July 1975, an Italian-French statement in November 1975, and the common declaration of all three in Madrid in March 1977. The parties soon moderated their long-standing hostility to NATO and the EEC—as well as to the parties of the Socialist International.[50] The PCI sent its first delegation to the European parliament in 1969, after which several Communist parties announced their support of European federal structures; some parties worked to strengthen the parliament by introducing popular elections, which first took place in April 1979. By establishing a strong minority representation within this body, the PCI and PCF hoped to form a broad left coalition incorporating the German SPD, the French Socialists, and the British Labor Party. The PCE supported Spanish entry into the EEC as a crucial step toward confirming "European" status for both Spain and the Communists. The overall strategic basis for Eurocommunist regionalism was essentially an expanded version of the theory of structural reforms: enter and democratize the European parliament (and trade union federations) with the aim of creating a left majority that could attack monopoly power, lay the foundations of economic cooperation, and catalyze a European-wide transition to socialism.[51]

These constituent elements of a communist third road were never actually synthesized into a theoretical framework; they added up to a cautious and uneven search for a political strategy grounded in the conditions of advanced capitalism rather than any fixed model. Interestingly enough, party theorists rarely discussed this project in terms of the transition to socialism, preferring instead to view it as an opening in that direction made possible by the discarding of past myths and obstacles. This point is crucial, since it indicates the degree to which Eurocommunist departures were shaped by reaction against the Soviet model rather than a definitive vision of socialist transformation. While "left" Eurocommunists (for example, Fernando Claudin, Lucio Magri, Rossana Rossanda, and Nicos Poulantzas) tried to fill this void with theoretical initiatives independently of the organized parties, in the 1970s it was the "right" that held actual power and thus remained in control of political strategy.

If none of these revisions taken separately were completely original, as an *ensemble* they pointed toward a reconstituted Marxist theory of the state and party appropriate to evolving forms of conflict and struggle in modern capitalism. Leninism assumed that the bourgeois state rests primarily upon its coercive mechanisms (central bureaucracy, military, police), that it functions primarily as an agent of class domination, and that even the most "liberal" states are but thinly veiled repressive organs immune to real democratic transformation. Under conditions of an ineffective parliament subservient to a monolithic state apparatus, the only conceivable strategy is revolutionary overthrow of the entire system by means of vanguard party intervention. Rejecting this approach, Eurocommunists argued that the political forms of advanced capitalism are more complex and filled with greater contradictions than Lenin (and most traditional Marxists) theorized, their strength based less upon institutional force than ideological consensus, or bourgeois hegemony in Gramscian terms.[52] They held that Leninist concepts are outmoded precisely because their reference points—tsarist Russia, the early phases of European capitalism—are remote from conditions of postwar industrialized capitalism. The very discourse of a state-centered politics, with its emphasis on scientific theory, party-guided insurrection, military discipline, and heroic sacrifice, has little resonance in modern society.[53]

Eurocommunists held that liberal democracy comprises a vast and complex matrix of institutions and social forces that cannot be reduced to a single instrument of bourgeios domination; while that aspect of the state persists, the entire political system is partly the outgrowth of mass struggles that achieved reforms opposed by the ruling elites. The idea of a unified and impregnable state apparatus, controlled by a cohesive ruling class, turns out to be a myth. In the first place, a good many state functions—welfare, education, basic social services—do more than serve the accumulation and legitimation needs of capital; they also signify real advances for workers, the poor, and others. Second, the state itself (including even the military) is increasingly composed of diverse personnel recruited from a variety of groups. Third, the relationship between parliament (or electoral politics in general) and the state bureaucracy is more refracted and complex than it was during Lenin's time. In sum, the state in advanced capitalism should be seen as an arena of class struggle, not simply class domination; the old separation between politics and civil society has become blurred, with power taking on the character of an institutional network of relations between social forces.[54] At certain historical junctures, contestation permeates every sphere of state activity, thus sharply restricting the leverage of dominant groups.

Instead of moving to overthrow the bourgeois state, as Leninist strategy dictated, the Eurocommunist parties strove for a process of ongoing *internal* democratization, guided by the view that representative forms could be gradually infused with popular and socialist content. In this schema, the state becomes a continuous structural element in the transition to socialism; relatively autonomous from ruling-class control, it must be seen as a potential strategic tool of popular forces and movements seeking to alter established class and power arrangements.

Following their interpretations of Gramsci, Eurocommunist leaders pointed toward a marked shift of social and ideological blocs within the state orbit—a changing equilibrium of class forces rooted in an expanding socialist consensus and leading to an incremental modification of structures that Ingrao defined as an emergent "hegemony in pluralism."[55] The transition appears as a long series of steps toward democratization, where a single Marxist party does not actually prefigure the state but develops alongside it, functioning as a "mediator" between the state and mass constituencies.[56] As Carrillo noted, a breakdown of the postwar class equilibrium in Europe had been underway for some time—as reflected by the demise of Francoism in Spain, the erosion of Gaullism in France, and the crisis of the Christian Democrats and Catholicism in Italy. This shift would presumably enable the left to insert itself into the public sphere more effectively, to "turn around the ideological apparatus" and employ it against monopoly capital.[57] The greater the popular involvement in parliamentary structures the more intensified becomes the conflict between democracy and capitalism. Carrillo's analysis can be put differently: with each stage of democratization, with each socialist advance through the forms of liberal democracy, one can anticipate mounting legitimation crises around the state.

Implicit in Eurocommunist theory was an understanding of liberal democracy as both form and content: it constitutes an indivisible value in itself to the extent it fosters democratic participation, limits the exercise of arbitrary rule, guarantees basic freedoms and rights, and ensures a stable legality within which popular struggles can be advanced. All of these features exist *independently* of the particular balance of class forces. From this standpoint, the idea of liberal democracy emerges as an integral part of the new definition of socialism—a momentous break with the Marxist past that was opened up by Togliatti and refined by structural reform theorists in the 1970s and 1980s.[58]

As conceived by Togliatti and his many heirs in the PCI and elsewhere, the Eurocommunist version of a third road appeared more coherent and visionary than the rationalist schema of classical (Kautskian) social democracy. Although it shared the same commitment to electoral politics, modern structural reformism was less inclined to accept a scenario of catastrophic crisis leading to socialism and thus rejected a crude two-stage theory of revolutionary change—a pre-cataclysmic (adaptive, fatalist) period followed by a post-crisis (utopian, indeterminate) phase of transformation. In contrast to the orthodox "before" and "after" model, it presupposed an organic, evolutionary transformation in which bourgeois democracy shades gradually into socialist democracy. A theory of process rather than rupture, it denied the likelihood of capitalist collapse leading to insurrectionary upheaval.[59] Carrillo suggested, for example, that "economic and political catastrophes are difficult to imagine in the developed countries (including even Spain)."[60] Eurocommunism proclaimed its faith in class struggle but foresaw no intense or prolonged stage of popular mobilization in the West. In effect it ruled out the possibility of any conventional revolutionary situation.[61]

Although this strategic outlook incorporated some elements of 1930s-style frontism, as we have seen, it also offered an image of radical change that departed from the primarily *defensive* maneuvers of the Popular Front. This image of radical change was derived in great part from the powerful revolutionary legacy of Gramsci in Italy; indeed the link between Gramsci and Togliatti was long established in PCI lore. But Gramsci's revolutionary Marxism bore only a superficial resemblance to postwar structural reformism, the *via italiana*, and Eurocommunism. Key Gramscian concepts—war of position, ideological hegemony, social bloc, democratization—were systematically distorted and misused by Eurocommunist leaders. Ideas were translated into a political framework that emptied them of their earlier (critical, transformative) meaning. As a "Western" Marxist Gramsci did articulate philosophical, cultural, and political themes that have deep roots in Italian and European history[62]—themes modern Communist parties were anxious to coopt.

The PCI's fetishism of the "war of position" concept perhaps most clearly reflected this misappropriation of Gramsci's theory. For Gramsci, the war of position was only one side of a complex dualistic strategy that also integrated the "war of maneuver" within the contestation for state power. Whereas the former applied to the "organic" phase of ideological-cultural and social changes within civil society, the latter involved the "conjunctural" element of political-military struggles for institutional control. Gramsci's *doppia prospettiva* thus assimilated both the consensual and coercive dimensions of the transitional process: reconstitution of everyday life and the overturning of bourgeois structures within a setting of crisis, class polarization, and popular upheavals.[63] The Eurocommunists, however, completely rejected the second dimension—the war of maneuver—thus abandoning the possibility of rupture, or revolutionary break, that was always central to Communist politics.[64] If democratic road strategists allowed space for the unfolding of economic crisis, they surely did not expect it to lead to intensified class struggle and popular mobilization, as Gramsci did. And if they foresaw a legitimation crisis, they did not see it as explosive enough to challenge the structural basis of class power.

Beyond this, the war of position itself was radically reconceptualized by Eurocommunists. Instead of broadening the terrain of conflict to encompass new spheres of social life within civil society, it effectively narrowed contestation to the bourgeois political-institutional realm. The PCI, for example, pursued the *via italiana* in order to extend the party's parliamentary room to maneuver and (especially during the period of the *compromes-*

so storico) with hopes of gaining a share of national governmental power. It sought to consolidate positions of strength within institutions that have, at best, a peripheral connection to struggles at the workplace and in the community. From Togliatti to Berlinguer, the PCI accentuated the political over the social and favored efforts to penetrate and colonize the bourgeois state over attempts to establish a grassroots presence.[65] And this strategy achieved considerable success on its own terms, owing to the great electoral results it produced. At the same time, however, the *via italiana* failed to present an alternative to rationalized state capitalism and even stood as an obstacle to the growth of social movements that emerged in Italy after the mid-1960s. The contrast with Gramsci's ideal of a counter-hegemonic revolutionary process rooted in civil society could hardly be more striking.[66]

What did evolve instead was a renovated theory of structural reformism that recalls the guiding logic if not the full essence of Bernsteinian social democracy—notably its assumption of a linear, incremental process defined by gradual democratization of the bourgeois state. In both cases, the explosiveness of class contradictions was downplayed if not ignored, while anticipation of a new kind of state grounded in popular forms of control faded away. What also disappeared was the time-honored Marxian idea of a class-conscious proletariat as revolutionary subject, as maker of history. At the same time, Eurocommunism amounted to far more that a recycled Bernsteinian evolutionary socialism: a range of diverse influences could be detected, including frontism, neo-Marxism, the new left, and even residues of Leninism.[67]

A thread connecting these influences was the continuing Eurocommunist reliance upon a powerful labor movement that could pursue reforms which, regarded as a whole, would contribute to the progressive socialization of capital. This schema, of course, was at the core of classical (and in some case, modern) social democracy.[68] But Eurocommunism set for itself tasks and objectives—at least in theory—that social democracy virtually ignored: democratic process, social and cultural struggles, feminism, and *autogestion* (self-management). If the transformative potential of such tasks and objectives was limited by efforts of party leaders to channel them into the electoral arena, the very fact that they were championed meant new space for oppositional politics. In any case, Eurocommunist parties ultimately paid a heavy strategic price for their obsession with electoral politics: if their vision of socialism lacked coherence and specificity, it was even further deflected and submerged by the corrosive instrumental demands of pluralist bargaining. This predicament was further reflected by the frequent use of almost meaningless concepts like "renewal," "advanced democracy," and "democratic planning," and by a hazy strategic plan in which "elements of socialism" were somehow expected to gain ascendance without direct class confrontation.[69] Even if this vision could be eventually converted into Eurocommunist political successes and institutional power, a more questionable assumption remained—namely, that the unyielding commitment to economic and administrative rationalization could be satisfied without undermining the norms of democratization vital to the third road strategy.

Eurocommunism in Decline

In the mid-1970s Eurocommunism occupied what had been a strategic vacuum for the European left: the debacle of Stalinism, the declining appeal of the Soviet model, paralysis of social democracy, and collapse of the radical left opened up a new space for the revival of Communist parties long considered political relics. Previously stagnant parties in France, Spain, Greece, and Finland saw ideological renewal in the promise of an alternative route to socialism that could avoid the pitfalls of social democracy and bureaucratic centralism. In the Mediterranean, both the French and Italian Communist parties had already achieved success on a foundation of strong electoral support, huge and disciplined mass organizations, a controlling role in the trade unions, local government and co-ops, and open, flexible ideologies. In 1976, after winning 34.6 percent of the vote, the PCI seemed to be at the doorstep of national governmental power, which, it was hoped, would finally give the party leverage to decisively influence Italian politics. Historical conditions appeared ripe for a Eurocommunist breakthrough— but the breakthrough never came. With the onset of the 1980s the Western parties, in one fashion or another, all ran into a political impasse as Eurocommunism—a journalistic catchphrase less than a decade before— now was seen as obsolete, as just another failed Marxist strategy.

In Italy the simultaneous success and failure of Eurocommunism could be measured by the fact that, to a great extent, it had become deeply embedded in the mainstream political culture. After the PCI's dramatic gains in the 1975 (regional) and 1976 (national) elections, its oppositional role yielded to a semi-governing one—although its *local* governing position, generally in coalition with the Socialists, was established as early as 1945.[70] The importance of this national shift, however nuanced, was that it gave the PCI the kind of legitimacy it had been lacking, which of course was precisely the design of Berlinguer's *compromesso storico* policy. After 1976 the Christian Democrats were finally compelled to work, on a limited basis, with the PCI, and in March 1978 the Communists joined a parliamentary majority that supported the fragile five party coalition government. The PCI's Pietro Ingrao was elected as chair of the Chamber of Deputies. With a new stake in the routine functioning of the parliamentary system, the PCI helped to engineer a moderate reformist consensus that turned out to be perfectly acceptable to the DC and Catholic elites who were hoping to co-opt the Eurocommunist challenge. The long period of PCI "anti-system" status had apparently come to an end.

But the PCI could never develop its political momentum any further: although its electoral support eventually matched that of the long-dominant DC, it was never able to win real governmental power. More significantly, the price of obtaining legitimacy was a reformist politics so watered down that the party's "Communist" label became meaningless, impossible to distinguish from the archenemy social democrats. In the late 1970s PCI strategists developed an image of the party as a "force for government and a force for opposition," but in fact it was neither, stranded as it was between two modes of identity. The reality was that the Italian Communists had lost their transformative capacity and could function only as an *institutionalized* opposition much along the lines of the British Labor Party. Instead of fulfilling Togliatti's vision of a "party of a new type," the PCI wound up as a party very much like the others, even as it refused to discard its Marxist vocabulary.

In its continuous search for popular credibility and institutional presence, the PCI inevitably gravitated toward a modernizing liberal agenda: acceptance of the multinationals, a mixed economy, NATO and the EEC, bureaucractic organization, parliamentarism, and so forth. Beneath its everyday defense of elitist pluralism the PCI maintained an official attachment to the socialist tradition, the labor movement, and "renewal" of Italian society; it even sought out those modern social movements (feminist, peace, ecology, urban protest) that were challenging traditional Marxist politics. At the party's Sixteenth Congress in 1979 the *terza via* was indeed reconfirmed, but new debates around the centrality of Marxism entered the discourse, resulting in a decision to eliminate a belief in Marxism as a necessary criterion for PCI membership (recalling the SPD's Bad Godesberg shift in 1959). When the Communist vote fell to 30.4 percent in 1979, the party resolved its tense dualism by moving back into opposition, where it remained throughout the 1980s without much hope of surpassing the threshold of national governance.

With no clear identity setting it apart from the major parties, aside from its Marxist origins and its isolated subversive moments in history, the PCI continued its downward slide in the 1980s: both membership and electoral support declined, along with the party's once powerful role in local government. When the PCI suffered a defeat on the *scala mobile* referendum in 1985—a measure that would have guaranteed wage-indexing for workers to protect against inflation—its leftist credibility was eroded even further.[71] More or less silent on such crucial issues as governmental austerity programs, the PCI retreated to a vacuous "democratic alternative" formula which entertained no reforms that would threaten the power structure. Meanwhile, the Socialists under the dynamic stewardship of Bettino Craxi steadily gained electoral strength at the expense of the Communists, assisted by the economic upturn in Italy.

By 1989 the new PCI leader, Achille Ochetto, sought to restore party identity with his vision of a new course tied to *reformismo forte*, or "strong reformism," designed to shake up the PCI's bland politics. However, the fast pace of events in Eastern Europe and the USSR undercut this tactical change by revealing, more clearly than ever, the bankruptcy of the Communist label. The PCI leadership quickly slipped back into its *moderate* reformist pattern that made it hard to distinguish from social democracy. In the period 1989–90 the PCI developed close ties with the Socialist International, after making decade-long overtures to several of its parties (notably the French, German, and Swedish). Upon initiating a name change to the Party of Democratic Unity (PDS) in 1990, the majority of communist leaders decided to join the revived SI with hopes of rebuilding some political momentum. But electoral strength continued to ebb, with a drop of yet another five percent in the 1990 local balloting. The PDS wound up with roughly half the total PCI membership (700,000), winning less than twenty percent of the vote in the 1992 national elections, while the breakaway *Rifondazione Comunista* came away with about 300,000 members and only six percent of the vote. Intense debates on future strategic directions surfaced in the early 1990s as the PDS divided into three rather distinct camps: conservative (Giorgio Napolitano and the heirs of Amendola), moderate and centrist (Ochetto), and left (Ingrao, Lucio Magri, Luciana Castellina).[72]

What was once a dynamic political force—the largest and most innovative non-ruling Communist party in the world—was now in a relative state of decomposition, seemingly incapable of recovering its lost sense of mission.[73] Constituencies that were historically inclined to support the PCI in large numbers—workers, youth, intellectuals—now often looked elsewhere (to the Socialists, Radicals, or Greens) as the very idea of Communist inspired change lost even more of its appeal. While the PDS entered the 1990s as a stong mass party, capable of reaching more that one-fifth of Italian electorate, it was clearly no longer a mobilizing vehicle at any level; it would scarcely be recognized by Togliatti, much less by Gramsci.

One dimension of the Eurocommunist decline was its failure to engage the widespread local activism of new social movements during the 1970s and 1980s: elements of the party leadership were ideologically prepared to do this, but traditional barriers—partly theoretical, partly organizational, but mainly electoral—blocked this path. The PCI, operating from a position of institutional and ideological leverage in the 1970s—and with some presence in the new middle strata—did seek to incorporate the energies of such movements (especially feminism and ecology). But it did so with the aim of integrating these struggles into a rather unbending framework of electoral politics that, were it to succeed, would only blunt popular initiatives from below while narrowing general objectives.[74] The relationship between the PCI and new movements was always therefore a tense and ambivalent one. Movement activists, for their part, were tempted to look to the Communists for tangible political results in a context of extreme localism and futility. And by actively proselytizing among these movements the PCI sought to assimilate their constituencies and themes, hence stemming popular insurgency from the left as well as the challenge of rival parties. At the same time it could also hope to revitalize its own popular base.

Yet this approach gave rise to its own dilemmas, since PCI elites were willing to yield only so far as to integrate the more visionary interests and priorities of new movements.[75] Such interests and priorities would be taken seriously only to the point where they would not alienate more supporters (for example, Catholics, blue-collar workers, old line militants) than they might attract with a full-scale reorientation of party strategy. In this vein, the PCI during the early 1980s championed peace and opposed deployment of Pershing II missiles in Sicily but remained lukewarm toward the peace movement itself and was very careful not to extend its criticism of this U.S. policy to the whole of NATO or the EEC. And while it took up the "woman question" directly in the mid-1970s and fought for progressive divorce and abortion legislation (though not without much prodding from below), it strongly resisted taking up the broader range of feminist concerns, which it argued would be divisive for party members and supporters.[76] Of course the PCI could always hold out the promise of such immediate political gains as expanded female participation; but feminist issues like child care, birth control, more liberal abortion laws, consumer and health care services, and the quality of neighborhood life were either dropped or squeezed into an acceptable cultural matrix.[77] Finally, the PCI proclaimed its commitment to local democratic forms (neighborhood councils, the *comitati di base*) that had grown out of the extra-parliamentary left, but the party simply absorbed them into its hierarchical structure and subverted most of their transformative content. For the PCI, as for other Eurocommunist parties, "democracy" had little meaning beyond *pluralist* democracy. Indeed, as we have seen, the party never really formulated a theory of democratic socialism that transcended the old political boundaries. This was predictable enough, given the degree to which it had become institutionalized.[78]

In the end, the PCI chose to assimilate social movements because its rather conventional *modus operandi* could not possibly accommodate the radical side of these movements. Having long ago abandoned Leninism and the Soviet model, Italian Communism evolved—fitfully to be sure—in the direction of northern European social democracy. Once in power, the PCI would probably have set out to rationalize the economy and political system within a state capitalist matrix, hoping to overturn traditional barriers to growth that chronically plagued Mediterranean countries.[79] At the same time, as a mature electoral machine the PCI could hardly afford to ignore or reject the new movements, especially since they would provide a pole of attraction for social forces that, out of a sense of frustration and powerlessness, might turn to the Communist party as the best hope for winning *some* political gains.

If the PCI carried structural reformism to such extremes that modern communism was no longer distinguishable from social democracy, the PCF actually moved in reverse: it *retreated* from Eurocommunist positions in the period after 1978. Still dedicated to the third road in theory, the French party—confronted with its own mounting identity crisis—rapidly fell back upon a more familiar pattern: organizational centralism and discipline, old-fashioned workerism, a pro-Soviet stance, social and cultural conservatism (especially around themes pertinent to the new movements). This retreat only served to insulate the PCF from the feminist, ecology, and other movements at a time when labor, squeezed by "restructuring" and austerity measures, was in a state of decline.

In France events revealed that the strategy of structural reformism was only partially and ambivalently internalized by the PCF leadership: in other words, its Eurocommunism was rather incomplete. Even while the party decided to abandon its official Leninism it was still wedded to traditional forms of organization and strongly resisted any genuine internal democratization. Though overtly critical of the Soviet model, it continued to identify with the general aims of Soviet foreign policy (endorsing, for example, the military intervention in Afghanistan). More to the point, it held to an *ouvrierisme* (workerism) that severely inhibited its capacity to build new bases of electoral strength within the new middle strata. Old theoretical biases held sway.[80] At a time when the manufacturing sectors were beginning to decline, the PCF clung to a heroic vision of the proletariat standing face-to-face with capital that was more appropriate to an earlier capitalist period. Immersed in working-class culture, the party upheld traditional virtues linked to religion, family, hard work, and clean living. This social location in French politics explains why the PCF could so energetically support traditional growth oriented programs (including nuclear power) while self-consciously distancing itself from new movement themes.[81]

The PCF was nonetheless more committed than ever to electoral politics and pluralist democracy as a matter of principle. It was stranded somewhere between a deep Leninist vanguard instinct and a social democratic mission it hoped to preserve under changing historical conditions, much like the Italian party of the 1950s and 1960s. For this uneasy dualism and wavering the French Communists were to pay a heavy electoral price. In the 1981 national elections, won by the revived Socialists in a smashing victory, the PCF vote dropped to fifteen percent (from a consistent postwar level of more than twenty percent) and forty-eight seats in the National Assembly, by far its worst showing since 1936. The decline continued through the 1983 municipal elections, with the Communists barely able to hold their strength at ten percent, precipitating a new crisis of morale among party members. Alienated more and more from intellectuals, youth, and progressive elements of the new middle strata, the PCF suffered membership loss as well as electoral decline throughout the 1980s.

This downward spiral was basically set in motion during the period 1979–1981, when the French Communists had opposed a unfied left alliance—similar to the failed Common Program—which the Socialists favored. At the Twenty-third Congress in 1979 the PCF in fact defined itself as a "revolutionary party" distinct from the social-democratic tradition, insisting upon a full rupture with the capitalist system and a return to themes of class struggle. As these deliberations illustrated, the PCF leadership had never made its peace with the earlier Eurocommunist shift.

But the PCF "revolutionary" turn did not obstruct its entry into the

French national government in 1981, when the Communists became a junior partner with the Socialists. The party's relationship with Mitterrand, however, was tense and conflicted, resulting in a break in 1984 over austerity and other issues after the PSF began moving dramatically to the right. Once removed from the cabinet, the Communists resumed their futile efforts to carve out a firm oppositional identity to the left of the Socialists that could win broad popular support. In or out of government, the downward trajectory continued: the PCF vote fell to 9.7 percent in 1986 and then 6.7 percent in 1988. The eventual collapse of communism in Eastern Europe and the USSR accelerated this development insofar as the PCF continued to be viewed by most of the French electorate as a Jacobin party incapable of fully breaking away from the Soviet model—at least until the events of 1989–90 forced it to do so. Under these circumstances, the third road model was easily co-opted by the Socialists.

The postwar alignment that transformed the PCF into the largest, best organized, and most influential force on the French left was thus finally shattered. In part, this can be interpreted as the delayed consequences of the May 1968 events, when the party hierarchy fiercely opposed the mass mobilization of popular groups, insisting that the moment for social upheaval was not "objectively" ripe and that direct action would lead only to misguided adventurism and, very likely, to the growth of reaction. Informed by this outlook, the leadership tried to sabotage the May insurgency, toward which end it worked (successfully) with the Gaullist regime to transfer the center of political activity from the streets and barricades into parliament. Whatever the immediate wisdom of that policy, the long-term result would be a chasm between the PCF and new social forces that persisted into the 1980s. Explosive new left themes that were given impetus by the May Events—efficacy of direct action, *autogestion*, feminism, ecology, cultural radicalism—were forced outside and against the party organization.[82] This was politically crippling, since even if the new social movements were not able to sustain a concrete presence in French society after the early 1970s, the demands they advanced were pervasive throughout the middle strata. Hence, while the PCF was busy attempting to discredit the Socialists as just another bourgeois party, it was they rather than the Communists who emerged as the beneficiary of middle strata support in the early 1980s.[83] By the early 1990s French Communism stood essentially as a political relic, a conservative bureaucratic machine cut off from the social forces around it, with its base reduced mainly to the "red belt" industrial areas around Paris and in the north.

As the PCI evolved toward an increasingly timid structural reformism and the PCF retreated to a quasi-Leninism, the Spanish Communists were quickly sapped of their political strength and became, in the early 1980s, a marginal force overwhelmed by the far more innovative Socialists. In contrast to the PCF, the PCE—less developed and more confined to the periphery than its French counterpart—looked expansively in the direction of the new movements from the outset, hoping to appropriate their energy as a means of building a mass party.[84] During the 1970s a broad range of popular forces emerged from long repression under Franco's dictatorship: workers' commissions, local neighborhood organizations, feminist groups, the student left, and movements for regional autonomy (for instance, in the Basque Country). The PCE saw in these forces powerful movements that would reshape prospects for democratization, and eventually pave the way toward resurgence of the Spanish left. In the first elections after Franco's death, in 1977, the Center-Right was swept into power, leaving the PCE on the periphery of political life (with only nine percent of the vote and twenty parliamentary deputies). From the standpoint of the general electorate, the PCE despite its new-found strategic flexibility, was still much too associated with its Stalinist past and its ambiguous Civil War legacy.

By the late 1970s, nonetheless, the PCE was moving steadily in a Eurocommunist direction under the stewardship of Carrillo: Hoping to build a progressive social bloc, it set out to implement a PCI-style alliance politics. It had become perhaps the most adaptive and "liberal" of all non-ruling Communist parties even with the resistance of a sizable old guard. The PCE's Ninth Congress was open and participatory to an extent unprecedented for Communist parties. Spain thus appeared as a major testing ground for Eurocommunist strategy, which sought to integrate the best of the Marxist tradition, liberalism, and the social movements. Yet within a few short years this hope collapsed amidst the stunning Socialist triumph in 1982 which gave the PSOE (Spanish Workers' Party) not only a clear majority but uncontested hegemony on the Spanish left. The PCE came out of the debacle with only 3.6 percent of the vote and thirteen deputies in the Cortes—a disastrous outcome from which it was not likely to recover.

Carrillo, who was replaced by Gerardo Iglesias as PCE leader in the aftermath of the defeat, blamed the outcome on "external" factors such as the attempted military coup preceding the elections. But the PCE's problem went much deeper. The party leadership, aging and cut off from the most dynamic social forces in Spanish society, was still tied to the past in ideological if not organizational terms: its conservative style alienated many voters, especially young people who were put off by the party's cultural tradition-alism and patronizing attitude. In this context, a far more youthful and cul-turally adaptive PSOE leadership could step into the void, made even larger by the collapse of the right, and appeal to new constituencies without having to explain away historical anachronisms. The PSOE skillfully played on the themes of local self-government, anti-militarism, feminism, and cultural renewal. For its part, the PCE tried valiantly to appropriate these themes but in the end did so in a less than convincing manner.[85]

In late 1982, when Iglesias took over from Carrillo, the PCE was a demor-alized organization with virtually no capacity to restore its membership and electoral base. The strong pro-Soviet faction finally broke away in 1983, leav-ing the party even weaker and more disaggregated. Throughout the 1980s the PCE lived on as a pale replica of its more vital past—a victim of its own internal flaws, the collapse of the Soviet bloc, and the remarkable successes of the PSOE. Periodic efforts to revitalize Spanish Communism after 1983 made little headway, and the party simply continued its descent into oblivion.

The experience of all three Mediterranean parties reflects the failure of Eurocommunism to chart the hoped for third path to socialism. The reality is that Eurocommunism constituted not so much a fundamentally new strategy as a transitional phase in the European left, between an outmoded Leninism and the rise of new oppositional forms. Structural reformism embodied the tense merger of two contradictory elements: a Marxist (or even Leninist) theory and an eminently social-democratic practice. Efforts to resist the logic of deradicalization in favor of old commitments, as in the case of the PCF, only led to further isolation and powerlessness. Both the PCI and PCE seemed ready to adapt to this logic, but only the PCI was strong enough (and perhaps tactically wise enough) to effectively pursue it and thereby allow for a partial opening to the social movements. In none of these experiences, however, was it possible to speak of a new oppositional form that departed significantly from the past.

The Logic of Deradicalization

By 1990 Eurocommunism no longer existed as a vehicle of social change in the Mediterranean or anywhere else, much less as the fruition of grandiose visions entertained by many Marxists in the 1970s. The collapse of com-munism in the East, of course, only hastened the demise not only of the Soviet model and Leninism but of anything resembling an authoritarian socialism: *any variant* of the original Bolshevik ideal seemed moribund, especially in the industrialized countries where modernity negated the very premises of vanguardism and insurrection. Virtually all non-ruling Communist parties have become marginalized fossils within their political cultures, including the PCF and PCE. As for the PCI, it alone made the transition from a Leninist to a mass reformist party, in the process taking on a new label and identity close to the social democratic tradition it had always excoriated. In reality, only the PDS in Italy emerged within the new setting as a strong party with any realistic aspirations for governance, but those aspirations, as we have seen, were purchased at a steep ideological price. The PDS, like all non-ruling Communist parties, has become thoroughly deradicalized.

The Togliattian theory of structural reforms, with its seductive promise of a third road to socialism, in the end wound up recycling the Bernstein-Kautsky synthesis that dominated the Second International.[86] By the 1980s, at a time of intensifying global economic and ecological crisis, this model could be viewed in a more critical light—as a stratagem for containing the crisis in European capitalist societies by means of rationalizing both the capitalist economy and liberal-democratic state.[87] The PCI/PDS strategy in fact always embraced a "left" approach to rationalization that stressed social and welfare reforms, decentralization, and greater working-class involvement within the political system more in alignment with the "state-capitalist" (northern European) rather than bureaucratic-centralist (Soviet) model of modernized development. The Eurocommunist project involved stabilization of capitalism on a new footing, namely, by disposing of barriers to economic expansion such as parasitism, inefficiency, corruption, and chronic uneven development between north and south. This historic task was never accomplished by the bourgeoisie, nor by the center-left governments of the 1960s and 1970s. Postwar Christian Democratic hegemony, with its familiar reliance upon the Church, traditional values, and *clientelismo*, merely obstructed the move toward rationalization; the PCI was quite anxious to take up this challenge.

The Eurocommunist program of the 1970s, revived in modified form under PDS auspices in the 1990s, had a rationalizing coherence that went beyond vague references to "renewal." With Italy caught in the midst of a debilitating vicious cycle involving economic stagnation, political immobilism, and terrorism, the PCI leadership was preoccupied with finding intermediate measures that could reverse these crisis tendencies and revitalize the economy within the priorities of domestic and international capitalism.

Initial steps were defined as organically linked to socialist values insofar as they would presumably lay the groundwork for the transition. By the 1980s, however, it was the capitalist "present" that came to overwhelm the socialist "future" in PCI thinking: The very logic of a modernizing strategy dictated this outcome.[88]

The PCI's extraordinary shift of positions on issues of European integration, NATO, the capitalist market, and even the role of multinational corporations should be understood in this context. Beginning in the late 1970s the role of multinationals was fully redefined within Eurocommunist literature: they were no longer viewed as the simple agents of international monopoly capital but as potentially constructive forces in bringing to less developed areas of Europe (and the world?) the virtues of science, technology, planning, expertise—and of course, capital. PCI ideology distinguished between "good" and "bad" multinationals, with the "good" ones assigned a modernizing role in agricultural mechanization, industrial restructuring, and overall technological expansion. From this standpoint the PCI (and later the PDS) rejected the "ritual condemnation" of multinationals as the embodiment of absolute evil, suggesting instead that they were really the most productive and unifying sector of advanced capitalism.[89] As Eurocommunist theorist Luciano Libertini wrote, "We do not believe that the multinational corporations are the creation of the devil. On the contrary, they are an essential structure of capitalism in its present phase of development," particularly insofar as they contribute to the "unification of world markets."[90] But although the PCI urged the multinationals to invest more capital in Italy, their regulation still remained critical. Hence, there should be a uniform code of operations for the EEC, curtailing the exploitative excesses of the multinationals by making it more difficult for them to evade taxes or move without impediment from one area or country to another.

The various components of rationalized development—institutional renewal, "democratic" planning, social investment, technological innovation, agricultural modernization—coincided neatly with the larger Eurocommunist political impulse; they are the hallmark of modern structural reformism. Taken together, they represent the vision of a stabilized system of production and administration built upon a matrix of state and private initiative in a setting, like the Mediterranean, where tradition-bound capitalism had become unworkable. Whether or not the PCI/PDS could ever achieve national power, from a socialist viewpoint this project appears to be as contradictory as those it superseded. Such a mode of accumulation (and legitimation) would surely sweep away the main archaic features of Mediterranean capitalism—and indeed much of this was accomplished during the revived center-left governance of the 1980s—but its very dynamics can only reproduce the social hierarchies of a class-based society. The same could be said of the Eurocommunist *political* strategy, which from the time of Togliatti revolved almost exclusively around parliament, local government, and the trade unions. In these areas, the parties—above all the PCI—won some degree of power, but not without reliving the dilemma encountered by classical (and modern) social democracy and rooted in the nearly obsessive pursuit of electoral politics and the threat of institutionalization that this sooner or later poses. After roughly four decades of stable Communist involvement in the structures of pluralist democracy, it is necessary to ask how much, and in what ways, a deeply ingrained parliamentarism has stifled the parties' capacity to mobilize workers and other strata toward fundamental social change.

The PCI best exemplified this predicament. Since 1945 the Italian Communists were able to achieve consistent electoral successes throughout most of the country, which they were able to translate into a powerful (but never hegemonic) institutional presence in the cities, provinces, regions, and even national political life.[91] As the PCI became a fixture within the system, moreover, the general political culture was transformed in a way that legitimated a Communist opposition or subculture—an unprecedented development for any European country. What it gained in the way of power and legitimacy was more than counterbalanced by a pervasive institutionization that carried through all spheres and levels of party activity. This process signified two basic developments: organizational merger with and absorption into the dominant political system, and accommodation with the structures of monopoly capitalism. Over time patterns of action became fully immersed in the surrounding social and political environment, reducing the PCI's scope of flexibility and local initiative so that it became, as we have seen, a party lacking any clear ideological identity.

Institutionalization dramatized the underlying contradictions of structural reformism, calling attention to what earlier Marxists referred to as the "illusion of bourgeois democracy." A central problem was that the Eurocommunist struggle for democratization, whatever its expanded or "advanced" character, was always limited in both theory and practice to the boundaries of *pluralist liberal* democracy. Surely this public sphere was, and continues to be, open enough for genuine representation of interests, political contestation, and social reform—but how open? The key question is: Can far-reaching change, achieved through popular anti-capitalist movements, be carried out strictly or even primarily within such a public sphere? Could Eurocommunist parliamentarism be compatible with efforts to dismantle the bureaucratic and repressive side of the capitalist state apparatus, to create specifically new forms of community and workplace democracy? Having rejected Leninist centralism, the PCI and other non-ruling parties failed to arrive at any distinctly socialist conception of democracy or the state. Indeed, to do so, even in theoretical terms, would be to make vulnerable their entrenched institutional position. In effect, "democracy" amounted to celebration (and further embellishment) of liberal values and practices: universal suffrage, civil and political freedoms, the multiparty system, representation of interests, bargaining, and so forth. Except for some attempts within the PCI and PCE,[92] party theorists have offered few critiques of bourgeois democracy (or bureaucracy) and made even fewer attempts to outline new principles of collective participation.

Because parliamentary democracy favors a complex network of bargaining and exchange based upon interest group politics—and since legislative action is so easily blocked by the extra-parliamentary power of capital, and state bureaucracy,—oppositional parties in bourgeois governments have always faced huge obstacles to the introduction of radical programs. Capital flight, administrative obstructions, the vast weight of privileged interests, and of course (where all of this fails) military intervention can be insurmountable problems facing any governing socialist party. (The failure of every Popular Front government, from Spain to France, from Italy to Chile, to sustain its ruling presence reflects this predicament.) Claus Offe's observation on this point is worth citing: "The pluralistic system of organized interests excludes from the process concerned with consensus formation all articulations of demands that are *general* in nature and not associated with any status groups."[93]

Both the logic of pluralism and the historical experience of structural reformist parties suggests that parliamentarism, whatever its obvious advantages over a classical Leninist strategy, functions to impede radical change: it favors a compromised, diffuse, and minimalist politics.[94] If liberal democracy as a formal arena of rules and mediations works against rapid or systemic alteration of class or power relations, those forces standing outside the parliamentary arena remain even more formidable. And the Eurocommunist parties had no real strategy for confronting the massive power of multinational capital, the state apparatus, or the military. This void was all the more critical since, in a period of expanding international monopoly capital, authoritarian tendencies within each of these spheres have overtaken parliaments and party systems, reducing their participatory side. In the late 1970s Poulantzas argued that the bureaucratized state "represents the new 'democratic' form of the bourgeois republic in the current phase of capitalism."[95] Since then this observation has only taken on added force. As capital becomes more concentrated, as pressures toward economic and political rationalization increase, the state correspondingly loses much of its "popular" character.

The implications of all this for any "democratic road" strategy are simply that the participatory side of the liberal state—the very terrain upon which the transition is supposed to unfold—is in serious decline. The drive to exercise democratic control over monopolies, the state bureaucracy, the military, or the judicial system from inside the legislative sphere runs up against huge barriers: mechanisms enabling such intervention are simply weak or absent. A related problem is that oppositional parties can gain access to those realms only if they are willing to yield most of their political autonomy. In this context the PCI, for example, was swept up in the symbiotic relationship between parliament and the executive, thus immersing itself (at the elite level) in all of the patronage, *clientelismo*, and influence peddling this produces.[96] Parties like the PCI and even the PCF, with their long history of parliamentarism, became far more integrated into this bourgeois public sphere than Eurocommunist theorists would ever have been prepared to concede.[97] The conclusion to be drawn here is obvious: although electoral politics was the overriding focus of Eurocommunist strategy, the shrinkage of that realm compared to other realms of power forced the parties to cultivate the bureaucratic sector, which the PCI had long been doing at the local level.[98] And this was perfectly congruent with the parties' rationalizing impulses. This predicament is even more sharply posed once leftist parties win national governmental power (as we shall see in Chapter 5).

The decision-making powers of legislatures have atrophied while leftist parties, where they develop a mass presence, have become integrated into the pluralist-democratic system. The organic relationship between mass parties and the state that accompanies institutionalization reflects the erosion of the party system as an agency of popular mobilization at the very moment that the bureaucratic leverage of parties may increase. Eurocommunism, like social democracy before it, reproduced this pattern. It may be that, as the mobilizing functions of leftist parties shrink, those parties' main role is one of *legitimation* to the extent they reinforce popular commitment to orderly, routinized, and stable political activity.[99] Of course, *some* mobilization may occur, but it is almost always dictated by—and restricted to—electoral calculations. Direct grassroots struggles that threaten class privilege or institutional stability are fiercely opposed, for they are bound to conflict with the logic of institutionalization.

This phenomenon had two major consequences for Eurocommunism: it reinforced alienated politics at the mass level and facilitated consensus at the elite level. For the PCI, obsession with becoming a *partito di governo* by electoral means led to the detachment of power concerns from social life, where the masses who are "represented" within parliament are kept distant from the sphere of power conflicts and bureaucratic maneuvers. The PCI's style of electoralism was graphically described by Maria A. Macciocchi on the basis of her own campaign as a Communist parliamentary candidate in Naples. Her critique explored the PCI's inability, within the electoral arena, to carry out ideological struggle and build durable ties with its constituents. Preoccupied with winning votes, party candidates were forced to stick with an approach emphasizing minimal reforms (for example, better sanitation) and abstract generalities (peace, renewal) while avoiding themes of popular struggle. Macciocchi wrote that campaigns degenerated into a "spectacle" involving "oratorical contests" between leaders who indulged the passivity of their supporters. The PCI, which nervously avoided references to class politics or socialism, differed little from other Italian parties in its overall political style—an ideological superficiality that Macciocchi attributed mainly to the legacy of frontism.[100] The subsequent Eurocommunist decline in the 1980s must be understood against this backdrop.

As the PCI invested more and more resources in electoral politics, the vitality of its mass organizational life suffered accordingly. Despite its huge membership, efforts to sustain ideological enthusiasm at the base only rarely succeeded after the 1960s. Communist presence in the 1970s and 1980s remained quite extensive, but it assumed a political-representational instead of a social-mobilizational character.[101] Electoral work was linked primarily to winning votes, not to the expectation of transforming social life in the community or merging immediate demands with general socialist objectives.

The weight of the evidence here seems rather conclusive: in strategic and programmatic terms, Eurocommunism represents a fitful and halting return to social democracy.[102] Party leaders, of course, always strongly rejected any suggestion that their own brand of structural reformism had much in common with that of classical social democracy. They insisted that, whatever the two traditions may have shared, the differences were always more fundamental, and they abhorred any association with the theories of Bernstein and Kautsky, any identification with the politics of the Second (later Socialist) International. And they were partly correct to the extent that non-ruling Communist parties did evolve within the Bolshevik and Soviet tradition inspired by Lenin.

Togliatti, the chief architect of postwar structural reformism, always emphasized the uniqueness of Italian Communism. He objected not so much to the particular methods and tactics of the social democrats, which after all were not too different from those employed by the PCI, but rather to their abandonment of socialism as the final goal. He argued that while in many countries social democracy had been able to retain its hold over large sections of the working class, its historical mission was to administer capitalism more effectively, not transform it.[103] Later Eurocommunist theorists reiterated this theme: Communists, unlike social democrats, remained partisans of the dialectical methodology of Marxism, the leading role of the working class, and the historic project of socialist transformation. From this standpoint, socialism meant a fundamental critique and transcendence of capitalism, a full break with an irrational and exploitative system favoring profits and growth over human needs. The social democrats, on the other hand, lacked any real Marxist identity; they long ago degenerated into opportunistic mediators between labor and capital.[104]

For decades the persistence of Leninist symbols constituted an impenetrable barrier between communism and social democracy; with the onset of Eurocommunism, however, this barrier was largely swept away, permitting convergence of the two strategies. And this is precisely what began to take place in the 1970s. In the case of parties like the PCI—and to a lesser extent other non-ruling parties—immediate political calculations and institutional imperatives came to decisively influence strategic direction. The distance between Togliatti and Kautsky was narrowed beyond recognition.

In fact, the Eurocommunist theory of transition was always compatible with the Kautsky-Bernstein notion that socialism must develop out of the enlargement of liberal-democratic norms and practices. Its prospects rested upon a growing public sector, entrenched pluralist traditions, the rise in educational levels and political consciousness of the working class, and the progressive role of the new middle strata. Its foundation was an expanded Keynesian steering of organized capitalism—with a socialist twist. Structural crisis might be viewed as an inevitable feature of capitalist development, but the system's collapse was ruled out. The assumption was that any catastrophic upheaval, any real social disturbance would jeopardize working-class gains and possibly open the door to fascism, a stance that required a

politics of compromise, order, and manipulation. Eurocommunism anticipated a gradual, linear, non-conflictual ascent to power that minimizes the
scope of direct action and grassroots democracy—not to mention popular
mobilization against capital. This rejection of the familiar Marxist crisis theory was congruent with the evolutionism of both Bernstein and the late
Kautsky, whose differences collapsed in the aftermath of the Russian
Revolution. At the outset, no Eurocommunist leader or theorist would
openly concede this parallel, hoping, no doubt, to avoid being tarnished
with the social democrats' historical record of failure. By the early 1980s this
reticence faded as the PCI began to court parties of the Socialist
International, setting the stage for collaboration and ideological convergence
during the coming decade. Any by the early 1990s these two erstwhile hostile
traditions had become virtually indistinguishable in practice, rendering the
"Communist" label meaningless and giving rise to a broader "Euroleft" tendency in several countries.[105] Meanwhile, Italian (and European) capitalist
power was restabilized following the turbulence of the 1960s and 1970s—
with the PCI and other leftist parties helping that process along.[106]

All of this was the product of a certain debilitating logic: Where nominally communist parties like the PCI managed to exert leverage within the state
system, their rationalizing commitments and their institutionalization over
time turned out to be incompatible with the very *possibility* of socialist
transformation, even though the old Marxist (and even Leninist) symbols
survived longer. And this strategic retreat was too pervasive, too embedded
in history, to be reversed by any leadership decision. It follows that the very
concept of a viable *Communist* party, in the historical definition of that term,
had long been meaningless—well before the fatal East European events of
1989–90. Aside from the irreversible phenomenon of deradicalization, the
old-fashioned statist, productivist, and workerist ideologies that reflected
Bolshevik and early capitalist experiences simply lack resonance in modern
society. In their adaptation to this reality the Eurocommunists, instead of
reclaiming the *radical* tradition, opted for a structural reformism that
seemed at the time to make sense.

The transition to a more rational social order, however, demands *at some
point* a fundamental break with the old forms of domination, a break that is
nowhere indicated in structural reformist theory. Indeed, such a break
would run contrary to the whole range of premises (and institutional attachments) underlying the Eurocommunist model. Historical experience suggests that it is crisis and polarization, not evolutionism and the pluralist
balancing of interests, that generates new opportunities, creates space for

popular struggles, and challenges institutionalized patterns sufficiently to allow for the expression of radical opposition. In this respect, Luxemburg's critique of Bernstein remains valid—namely, that far from being more "realistic," the idea of a stable, non-confrontational path to socialism is actually quite utopian.[107]

5

THE THIRD ROAD II
The Rise and Decline of Eurosocialism

IN ITS FUTILE QUEST FOR A THIRD ROAD TO SOCIALISM, EUROCOMMUNISM WAS
already in the process of dying by the late 1970s: its peak moment, after years
of steady advances, was the Italian Communists' brief entry into the governing apparatus during 1976–1978, after which neither they nor any other
non-ruling Communist party would come close to exercising national
power.[1] The most valiant efforts to sustain a political identity located somewhere between Bernsteinian reformism and Leninist vanguardism did not
work in any setting. This historical predicament, viewed in the context of a
thoroughly deradicalized social democracy in northern Europe, seemed to
offer few hopes that a Marxian socialist politics could be revived in any highly organized corporatist system where political parties had lost their capacity to mobilize. In short, throughout Europe there was a growing sense of
disillusionment with any kind of socialism—among workers, the new middle strata, intellectuals, and youth. And the waning of Eurocommunism—
always primarily a Mediterranean phenomenon in any case—only
intensified the disappointment.

This predicament was less a matter of political strategy as such than of historical circumstances combined with the lack of theoretical imagination
within an increasingly depleted Marxist legacy. If the teleological dimension
of Marxism had waned, did this mean that the traditional idea of popular
control over economic, social, and political life that had always defined
socialism was no longer viable, or even thinkable? Had "one-dimensionali-

ty" taken hold in the advanced capitalist countries, negating prospects for a mass-based political opposition? These were the sorts of questions posed not only by the obsolescence of both social democracy and communism but also by the visible decline of class identities and class conflict on a world scale, reinforced in Europe by the process of corporatist integration.[2]

Yet there would be the opportunity for still another furtive—and probably final—socialist embrace of the third road at a time when Eurocommunism had not been fully put to rest. The setting was once again the Mediterranean, where Socialist parties in one country after another received a new infusion political life, emerging as an ideological pole of attraction for elements of both the mainstream and radical left. In 1981 and 1982 alone, rejuvenated Socialist parties won dramatic electoral victories in France, Greece, and Spain; by 1984 not only these countries, but Italy and Portugal as well, were governed by Socialists either alone or in coalition. The Eurosocialist alternative was born.

The Mediterranean Socialists gathered strength at a unique point in postwar history. If corporatist integration prevailed in northern Europe, a convergence of economic, political, and ideological forces seemed peculiarly advantageous to new radical initiatives in the south, and indeed outside the state system of the northern countries too. Industrialized societies were approaching an end to ceaseless economic growth in a period of energy crises, spiralling military costs, and fierce struggles for competitive advantage in the world market. The consequences—massive unemployment, balance-of-payments deficits, fiscal crisis, decline of social services—were exacerbated by the failure of statist Keynesian mechanisms to reverse the downward spiral. In southern Europe, these conditions were further sharpened by chronic technological dependency upon the developed countries (the U.S., Japan, England, West Germany). At the same time, there was a gradual but pronounced transformation of the class and social structure resulting from erosion of new sectors tied to the public and service domains, technology and communications, culture and the "knowledge industry." This occurred, moreover, in a period of mounting popular disenchantment with bureaucratic structures that, in countries like Spain, Portugal, and Greece, produced an intensive assault on authoritarian states connected for years to fascist or right-wing military rule.

As far as political strategy was concerned, the Eurosocialists found themselves in a position to step into the ideological vacuum created by the eclipse of Marxist (and Leninist) models on the one hand and the decline of organized labor on the other. Earlier fascination with Soviet, Chinese, and various Third World models had been exhausted, and Eurocommunism, as we have seen, was unable to fulfill its promise. In this fluid situation, the search for alternative vehicles of change, for new strategies of social transformation, was both possible and necessary, although it would have to proceed against the grain of Marxist inertia. It was the Socialists, unencumbered by outmoded ideological and organizational formulas, who now began to occupy this terrain. The Eurosocialists, by all appearance, had become legitimate heirs to the European radical tradition or, put in different terms, the locus of a refurbished post-Marxist dialectic.

A major source of Socialist revitalization was the growth of new social movements in the preceding decade or so. The movements of feminists, ecologists, peace activists, youth, and urban protest groups, whatever their particular ebbs and flows, established a political momentum in the 1970s that helped rekindle a democratic political culture, largely outside the party systems, that could be recuperated by a non-communist left. In this setting Eurosocialism held out hope for a new kind of radicalism, or democratic socialism, attuned to broad social and participatory concerns of the new movements, rooted in diverse constituencies, and intent upon exercising governmental power in a new way. Such a departure would presumably amount to far more than a recycling of Keynesian welfare state politics; it would chart a strategic alternative to socialist transformation, beyond social democracy and Leninism.

The Socialist Revival

The rejuvenated Mediterranean Socialist parties were expressions of both continuity and rupture with the familiar social-democratic pattern: continuity insofar as they originated and developed as parties of the Socialist International, rupture to the extent that they offered an image of ideological rebirth and dynamism in contrast to the German model of welfare state politics. The Eurosocialist upsurge of the early 1980s actually had its origins in the 1960s, in the new left and extra-parliamentary struggles embodied in the May 1968 events, the 1969 "hot autumn" in Italy, and the later proliferation of grassroots social movements throughout Europe and North America. It signaled a fresh start toward deep structural change that had eluded the social democrats and communists—and seemed beyond the capacity of the new left, for reasons more fully elaborated in the next chapter. A "new" socialism, it held out an eclectic and imaginative ideology, an open and non-bureaucratic style of leadership and organization, a populist style of politics, and a youthful membership in touch with new constituencies, new ideas, new possibilities. Eurosocialism was post-Marxist insofar as it rejected the singular dialectic of class struggle, viewed history as a relatively open field of forces, questioned the primacy of material conditions, and dismissed prospects of an economic crisis leading to cataclysmic revolution.

In certain respects, this phenomenon represented a fusion of two rather distinct leftist currents: one working-class, the other the progressive side of the new middle strata. This historically novel synthesis produced new concepts to meet new demands posed by rapid technological changes on the one hand and insurgent popular movements on the other. It also produced a complex, non-sectarian ideology attuned to issues of grassroots empowerment, workers' control, and general democratization of state functions; decommodification of public life characterized by a broadening of universalist social programs and services at the expense of the market; cultural renewal directed against the stifling forces of traditionalism, Church hegemony, and monopoly domination; and reshaping of international politics aimed at subverting the bloc system (NATO and the Warsaw Pact) while striving for greater balance between the industrial powers and the Third World. To achieve this, Eurosocialism promised not a dramatic leap to socialism but rather a gradual, molecular process grounded in both state and civil society, national institutions and local communities. The historic dismantling of the old state, corporate, and military hierarchies would be accompanied by an unprecedented rebirth of the public spirit and citizen participation against two extremes of liberal individualism and state administered collectivism.[3]

At the same time, like Eurocommunism before it, Eurosocialism retained a conventional social-democratic faith in electoral politics (more broadly defined) and the parliamentary road to socialism. In a few short years the Eurosocialists did in fact expand the sphere of political discourse and action as well as the very definition of socialism. At issue was whether they could preserve and concretize their commitments while laying the basis of an alternative strategy for the future.

Among southern European Socialist parties, the French were clearly in the vanguard of this tendency. With the old SFIO (French Socialists) weakened and in disarray, and Gaullism still more or less hegemonic, the May events jolted the established political alignments. Beneath the post-1968 recuperation of the Fifth Republic came a pronounced social and political fluidity marked by a leftward shift of popular consciousness. One outgrowth of this unsettling process was a reborn French PSF that, in the period 1969–1971, experienced a definite but uneven radicalization from bottom to top. A massive influx of youth, feminists, environmental activists, young workers, and Christian militants (most of whom identified with Michel Rocard's PSU, or Unified Socialist Party) transformed the party from a stagnant bureaucratic institution into a dynamic activist organization more in touch with the social and cultural changes sweeping France.[4] In the wake of an ideological renewal stimulated by the involvement of *gauchistes* active in the May events, the PSU turned its back not only on its own social-democratic legacy but even more emphatically on the Communists, who were seen as hopelessly attached to an outmoded Stalinist apparatus and steeped in cultural conservatism. Galvanized by a new stratum of leftist intellectuals, who thought in terms of a "break with capitalism," the Socialists pressed for novel approaches and fresh solutions grounded in a radical critique of bourgeois society.

A crucial element of French Socialist growth and renewal in the 1970s was a creative, nonsectarian leadership drawn largely from the ranks of progressive sectors of the new middle strata (teachers, professionals, cultural workers, and some civil servants). Although moderate by party standards, François Mitterrand epitomized these leadership qualities; his organizational rebuilding program was simultaneously visionary and pragmatic, freed from past ideological formulas and cliches. Indeed, there seemed to be ample room within the party for coexistence of both old and new left, Marxists and non-Marxists.[5] Party membership grew from a low of 10,000 in 1969 to 40,000 in 1973, then skyrocketed to 165,000 in 1977 and nearly 200,000 in 1981. The PSF-affiliated trade union confederation, the CFDT (French Confederation of Labor), reached a level of one million members by 1980.[6] Moreover, at a time when the PCF was losing support despite its Eurocommunist turn, the Socialists were able to run up remarkable electoral gains, outpolling the PCF in 1978 by 22.6 percent to 20.6 percent only a decade after the SF10 had been left for dead. With the PCF still immersed in workerist politics, the Socialists were shrewdly constructing their own version of alliance strategy, or *fronte de classe,* designed to build a left majority that could win governmental power (ideally without the PCF).[7]

The surprising 1982 electoral victory of the Spanish Socialists symbolized revitalization of the Iberian left after several decades of fascist rule. Even before Franco's death in 1977 the beginnings of democratization were well underway, in part the result of popular reaction against an authoritarian model of industrial development (and political control) that had kept Spain on the margins of Western Europe. Already by the late 1960s, an expanded public sphere outside the dictatorial state made possible the rise of grass-roots movements—workers' commissions, neighborhood struggles, and a variety of new left, youth, and women's organizations. As in the French case, such popular mobilizations served to rejuvenate the long-dormant Socialists (and to a lesser extent the Communists) during the mid- and late-1970s. The PSOE emerged from the Franco period organizationally weak and ide-ologically compromised, its image one of order and traditionalism.[8] Its main political objective was the liberalization of Spanish society—a gradual and peaceful transition from fascism to bourgeois democracy within the con-fines of the monarchy. Beyond that it had no clear identity or mission.

After 1977, however, the PSOE experienced an uneven but steady process of radicalization. Transformed in great measure by the popular movements, which were fueled in turn by widespread anti-Franco sentiment and eco-nomic crisis (with fifteen percent unemployed), the Socialists were able to create a new leadership around the influx of thousands of young militants, a good number of whom had participated in assorted new left, anarchist, and Trotskyist groups. Their concerns went far beyond restoration of liberal democracy or Spanish entry into the European Community, encompassing a creative blend of economic, political, and social demands that challenged the centers of privileged interests. More populist than workerist, the PSOE appealed to diverse social groups but had no real presence in the trade union movement, a deficiency it tried to correct in 1977 by setting up its own labor confederation (the UGT or General Labor Union). In 1979 the party lead-ership, following the pattern of the French Socialists, turned to the dynamic Felipe Gonzales for new guidance and a fresh beginning. Gonzales, whose charismatic appeal did much to ensure the party's rapid growth, envisioned a distinctly progressive but non-Marxist course with the aim of putting the PSOE at the head of a majority social bloc. As the membership consensus at the Twenty-eighth Congress reaffirmed, such a departure would allow for innovative programs, enabling the Socialists to occupy a terrain distinct from both centrist Social Democrats and the PSOE.[9] What the PSOE did share with these tendencies, of course, was an abiding commitment to elec-toral politics.

This Socialist strategy produced results that surprised even the party's most dedicated supporters. From a tiny sect in the early 1970s it rapidly grew into a mass party ready to contend with the "center" and right for govern-mental power. The rise of the PSOE was accelerated by several conditions: widespread anti-Francoism, the economic crisis, fragmentation of the cen-ter-right (UDC, or Union of the Democratic Center), and the debilitating paralysis of the PCE. In the 1977 national election the Socialists won twenty-nine percent of the vote (compared to nine percent for the PCE), setting the stage for their astonishing breakthrough in 1982. Membership increased from less than 4,000 in 1975 to 200,000 in 1979, building steadily over the next few years.[10] Vigorous grassroots organizing activity was carried out in all parts of the country, with the result that by 1982 the Socialists were easily the largest and most dynamic political force in Spain—an impressive achievement in the span of barely a decade.

Like their French and Spanish counterparts, the Greek Socialists experienced rapid organizational growth and ideological renewal during the 1970s just as the old political alignments were being upset by emerging popular movements. And much like the Spanish party, the Greek PASOK (Panhellenic Socialist Movement) was an expression of strong democratizing tendencies impatient with years of right-wing authoritarian rule. But in contrast to the French and Spanish Socialists, the Greek party originated more or less *de novo*; its roots in the traditional left were tenuous at best.

Founded in 1974, PASOK built a grassroots presence by means of sustained populist activism, expanding its membership to 150,000 by 1977 and its electoral support to twenty-two percent of the vote and ninety-three parliamentary seats in the same year.[11] It too fed on popular hostility to the traditional power structure—to social forces that had kept Greece on the European periphery for so long: the military, church, multinationals, the EEC, and, of course, a repressive and corrupt Greek state. Much of this hostility was channeled into local (both urban and rural) citizens' movements and a variety of new left groups that eventually formed the backbone of PASOK. Party strength was quickly consolidated through the development of more than fifteen thousand branch and local committees in towns and villages around the country. Much like the French and Spanish parties, PASOK set out to construct a broad multiclass alliance with hopes of mobilizing an electoral majority. It emerged as a party not only of the middle strata (which were smaller numerically than elsewhere in Europe) but of the disenfranchised—urban workers, peasants, petty bourgeoisie, the poor. The result of these efforts was a stunning Socialist triumph over Karamanlis's fading conservative New Democracy forces in 1981.

The PASOK leader, Andreas Papandreou, epitomized the new type of Socialist leader represented by Mitterrand and Gonzales. As an intellectual from an academic background, he saw in PASOK a vital source of new ideas for Greek development—a party freed from conventional social-democratic attachment to Keynesian reformism, bureaucratic solutions, American hegemony, and Cold War ideology. One key to Papandreou's success was his ability to synthesize the concerns of democratic socialism and Greek nationalism. (Because of a closer identification with Third World views and interests, owing partly to the peripheral location of Greece itself, PASOK was less anxious than either the French or Spanish parties to disown Marxism entirely.) Thus Greece would be forced to break decisively with its dependent past and follow its own third road outside the dictates of the Socialist International, which PASOK saw as a tool of U.S. and European monopoly interests.[12] The absence of a strong social-democratic tradition in Greece, along with the division of the communist left into two small competing parties, would presumably make this task easier.

Therefore, after barely a decade of political revitalization the Eurosocialist moment arrived in the early 1980s, securing a Mediterranean outpost of resistance to the rising tide of conservatism in the West. First, in May 1981 the French Socialists won a lopsided victory over a demoralized and divided Gaullist right; the PSF's thirty-eight percent of the vote and 283 seats in the National Assembly ensured it an absolute working majority for five years, making France the first advanced capitalist country to elect a definitively leftist government to national power. Mitterrand became the new president with a promise to radically alter the political landscape of the country and, with it, to perhaps inspire changes elsewhere in Western Europe. As new social constellations came to the fore, the scope of discourse and struggle—the sense of what was historically possible—seemed to expand almost overnight. The PSF breakthrough instilled a mood of optimism and exhilaration—and even more astonishingly, a spirit of left unity—that was absent in France during the postwar years. Thus, while the Communists dropped from 20.9 to 15.4 percent of the vote and from eighty-six to four seats in the legislature, they entered the Mitterrand government and accepted four cabinet portfolios, although not without ambivalence. Overall, the obstacles to far-reaching structural change appeared very manageable.

Both the Greek and Spanish parties duplicated these results within the ensuing eighteen months. In October 1981 PASOK won a governing majority in parliament (172 out of 300 seats) and the presidency with forty-eight percent of the vote. The conservative New Democracy returned only 115 deputies while the two Communist parties were able to elect only fifteen. Papandreou characterized this turn of events, which ended a half-century of right-wing rule, as a critical historical shift that would permanently alter the face of Greek politics. PASOK followed its national success a year later with a string of local electoral victories that included 175 mayorships out of the 276 contested.

The PSOE followed suit in October 1982, winning fourty-eight percent of the vote (nearly double its showing of 1977), giving it 202 of 350 seats in the Cortes, control of the presidency, and complete supremacy over the debilitated UDC (now reduced to twenty-two percent of the vote and sixty-five deputies). The Socialist victory further ensured the downward slide of the Communists, who dropped to 3.8 percent of the vote and from twenty-three to five seats in the legislature. Gonzales's appearance in Madrid on election night was celebrated by a large tumultuous crowd that seemed to sense the historical meaning of the PSOE landslide: it was a moment symbolizing the final, dramatic break with Francoism and the legitimation of liberal democracy. Indeed, Socialist popularity no doubt grew in the wake of a failed military coup the preceding year and subsequent rumors of new attempts. The PSOE further solidified its national gains with new successes in the May 1983 municipal elections, where it won an absolute majority on sixty-five city councils representing urban areas of more than 100,000 population. As in France and Greece, the socialist ascent to power in Spain created large new areas of social and political space within which popular struggles could be articulated and concretized. The public sphere was broadened far beyond the limits of corporatist integration in northern Europe.[13]

A Break with Social Democracy

Just as the balance of power was shifting rightward in northern Europe and the U.S., newly revived Socialist parties were preparing to move against the historical grain in Mediterranean Europe: they would become ruling forces in France, Spain, Portugal, Greece, and even Italy. Eurosocialists in each setting benefitted profoundly from the inability of right-wing and center-right governments to satisfy burgeoning popular demands. With Marxism everywhere in decline, this leftward shift opened up space for a novel post-Marxist radicalism—an innovative search for democratic and egalitarian structures—that had never been seen before, at least not on such a broad scale. At a time of realigning social forces and constituencies throughout the industrialized world, Eurosocialism signified the restless struggle to arrive at new strategies, methods, and styles of political action that could mobilize the largest number of voters around *transformative* agendas. These agendas coincided with the trend toward a "new politics" grounded partly in the post-materialist themes of new social movements, partly in the growing role of the new middle strata. As Michael Harrington observed, such new possibilities corresponded to the familiar ideal of democratic socialization (as contrasted with *authoritarian,* Bolshevik-style socialization) in a context where genuine democratic outcomes could be much greater than, say, in 1917 Russia or 1949 China. In fact, the ascendancy of several Socialist parties to national power, in the same region and at roughly the same time, was historically unprecedented. Yet, if this ascendancy meant new triumphs for the left, it also brought new challenges and dilemmas.

Before analyzing the record of Eurosocialist parties in government, it may be useful to explore more fully the political outlook they shared. While the French, Spanish, and Greek Socialists each moved along separate trajectories, it was possible to identify at least four commonalities: democratization, non-Keynesian economic structuring, cultural and social reform, an independent foreign policy. Strategically, this would be accomplished through a multiclass social bloc that, once in power, would gradually transform the economy and state. Thus Eurosocialism represented a unique blend of novelty and tradition, new approaches and old commitments, radicalism and moderation, which turned out to be a source of both strength and weakness as reflected in the reappearance of some familiar predicaments.

The Mediterranean Socialist agenda in the early 1980s involved first and foremost a new phase in the long struggle for democratization that began with the bourgeois revolution: its slogan could well have been "democracy first, then socialism." Or, in Felipe Gonzales's words, "I'll tell you what a socialist society is, and everything else is a joke. To design a socialist society like a painting...is foolish.... There is no other definition of socialism than the deepening of democracy in every direction."[14] This project was an expression of three complex and interwoven dimensions: the historical context in which the parties came to power, their style of political mobilization, and their long-range ideological objectives. For the Spanish and Greek Socialists electoral victory symbolized the end of a long period of fascist dictatorship during which the left was suppressed and marginalized, whereas for the French it meant a return to left hegemony following more than two decades of Gaullist authoritarianism. In every case this break resulted in a rather sharp (and perhaps durable) realignment of political groupings built upon a popular wave of anti-authoritarianism, which, in itself, constituted an important step toward democratization. For each party, moreover, success depended upon a lengthy prior stage of grassroots organizing and popular initiatives by diverse groups and movements. The electoral breakthrough was essentially the culmination of democratizing changes within the political culture that went back to the 1960s. Finally, in opposition to both Leninism and social democracy, Eurosocialist parties were firmly committed to the ideal of democratic socialism—the concepts of self-management, workers' control, and local autonomy—in contrast to the bureaucratic model, which upheld the state (or party-state) as the decisive agent of change.

In the case of French Socialism, democratization meant overturning the entire legacy of statism, or *dirigisme*, that goes back to Napoleonic centralism at the time of the French Revolution. The PSF matured in the 1970s as a party of *autogestion*, as an expression of the new left participatory spirit it assimilated from the May events and carried forward into the 1980s. Its goal was to broaden the decision-making base of all French institutions: the welfare system, large industries, trade unions, education, and, of course, the state itself. To this end, the CFDT called for a new type of unionism centered around issues of "control" as well as broad social demands, although this emphasis receded after 1981. Decentralization of managerial functions would take the form of democratic planning, which would give regional and local bodies greater decision-making power against the corporate and technocratic strata. In this sense, the PSF would be the vehicle of a "capillary democracy" that filters up organically from below, ultimately transforming the state in the process.

For the Spanish party, on the other hand, the key task was to curb the immense power of the military, which had been a dominant force in the country since 1868 and remained a bastion of extreme reaction even after Franco's death. The PSOE promised to expand civilian control over the military, reduce its size and budget, and professionalize all of the branches (thus presumably undercutting the fascistic bent of the officer corps). The PSOE also campaigned on a platform attacking state bureaucracy, which would be replaced by a decentralized political system; they proposed overhauling the Francoist legal code and court system as well. The Greek Socialists emphasized more or less the same priorities. They declared their intention to reduce the power of the church, the military, and multinational corporations, although their first priority was the public sector, which they set out to "modernize" by eliminating the long-standard practice of *rousfeti*, or "corruption." PASOK also focused its attention on the spread of local committees and producers' cooperatives in both rural and urban regions of Greece, and on the regeneration of grassroots branch activity within the party itself.

The second Eurosocialist preoccupation—basic restructuring of the domestic economy—was both as ambitious and vague as the concept indicates. In general terms, each party outlined its long-term commitment to a socialized economy in which resources would be collectively owned and equally shared, class divisions would be abolished, and foreign dependencies would be severed. More immediately, Socialist programs were geared to economic modernization that (particularly for Spain and Greece) would enable the Mediterranean countries to overcome their poor competitive and semi-colonial position within the international market. Allowing for differences of emphasis and context, the programs identified three main tasks: public supports for technological development, democratic planning for social and economic reforms, the gradual breaking down of exploitative monopoly interests. On the basis of significant momentum in this direction, the intermediate result would be a post-Keynesian mixed economy, in which a non-bureaucratic public sector and market forces would combine in a dynamic, growth oriented, democratized system. Riding the crest of huge popular mandates, the Socialists planned to institute rather sweeping changes; the anti-capitalist substance of these changes, however, remained fuzzy.

The French Socialists came to power with a promise to restore industrial growth, combat unemployment, and initiate the transition to a more egalitarian economy. The first priority was massive new infusion of public funds into the high-technology sector (for example, electronics and computers) with the aim of boosting its profitability and competitive position in the global market. If this scheme turned out to be successful, the high-technology sector could become the accelerator for French industrial expansion in the 1980s and 1990s. The PSF was also prepared to carry out a new series of nationalizations in the leading industrial, banking, and commercial sectors, but within a more participatory framework (grounded in *autogestion*) than was previously the case. Technology-inspired growth, along with significant increases in public investment and control, was expected to generate new jobs, raise the overall standard of living, and lessen demands on the welfare system while reversing the always precarious balance-of-payments deficit. Ironically, these expectations depended upon a modified Keynesianism that shared a number of traditional social-democratic premises.

As for the Spanish and Greek parties, they too had become obsessed with growth and modernization. The PSOE counted on rapid technological progress to set in motion a rationalization of the country's archaic industrial sectors, which would finally permit integration of Spain into the European Community from which it could derive all the benefits of modernity. This was less a matter of creating super-competitive technology sectors as such than of applying technology to enhance productivity in all areas of the economy. In contrast to the PSF, the Spanish Socialists were reluctant to embark upon full-scale nationalization projects or otherwise expand state power. Modernization itself, with heavy emphasis on the market, was expected to produce a dynamic sequence of changes that, at the very least, would significantly reduce unemployment (which stood at sixteen percent in 1982). Once the economy was thus reinvigorated, the Gonzales government would likely be in a position to initiate more sweeping social reforms.

PASOK's designs to transform the Greek economy were similarly tied to technological rationalization, but perhaps with a greater sense of urgency, given the country's more peripheral status. A program of state directed technological research and development was intended to improve overall productivity, stimulate growth, and cut the balance-of-payments deficit, with the hope that this would ease the worst manifestations of the crisis. At the same time, PASOK adopted a more radical (and nationalist) position toward the internationally-based monopolies than either the French or Spanish parties. Although Greece had joined the EEC in 1979, when the Karamanlis regime was in power, PASOK wanted to reassess a relationship that, it argued, simply perpetuated Greek colonial status and economic backwardness relative to Western Europe and the U.S. Aside from strong encouragement for small businesses and producers' cooperatives, however, the actual means by which monopoly power would be effectively broken (or even curtailed) were never clearly defined. PASOK had no ambitious plans for further nationalizations (sixty percent of the economy was already state controlled), or for regulating the huge export trade sector exemplified by Greek shipping. Socialist leaders anticipated that such challenges—and probable confrontations—could be deferred.

In its desire to carve out a third road, Eurosocialism energetically pursued themes—feminism, the environment, culture—to a far greater extent and in different ways than had either social democracy or communism. The impact of new social movements was very much in evidence. Still, the parties' programmatic content was rather tentative and unspecified—in part because this was such novel terrain, in part because global competition forced the leadership to give first priority to economic issues. Further, insofar as the Socialists championed an ideology of secular modernity, there was a general belief that economic progress itself would trigger large-scale social and cultural changes that in turn would undermine traditional values. There was a consensus that efforts to impose such changes by means of state policy might end up being counterproductive.

In each country the most urgent area of social concern appeared to be women's issues, which entailed three layers of change: a call for reforms that had been central to feminism (liberalization of abortion and divorce laws), broader female participation in Socialist parties and governments, and the abolition of sexist practices at the workplace and in society as a whole. Environmental problems were less directly attacked, although the parties did outline general plans for developing solar power, fighting air and water pollution, and reversing urban blight. Because France was more highly industrialized than Spain or Greece, and possibly owing to earlier inroads made by the Ecologists, the PSF seemed more prepared than either the PSOE or PASOK to carry out immediate environmental reforms. The very appealing but poorly defined vision of "cultural renewal" was likewise taken up by each of the parties. Tied to a rekindling of economic and political nationalism, the aim of cultural revitalization meant above all expanded public subsidies of creative work in film, art, music, and literature, which, it was thought, would further strengthen those progressive indigenous traditions already predominant in Mediterranean culture. Finally, the Eurosocialists pushed for broad secular changes in the educational system (less church intervention) and the legal code (more liberal censorship laws), especially in Spain and Greece, where traditionalism persisted and even bourgeois rights and freedoms had long been denied.

Yet it was in the sphere of international politics that the Eurosocialists seem to have departed most from the traditional social-democratic pattern. The major social-democratic parties in postwar Europe were without exception pro-NATO and anti-Soviet: they viewed the Atlantic Alliance as a fulcrum of U.S. political and military strategy directed against the Soviet bloc. The new Socialist foreign policy taking shape in the early 1980s, however, began to resist the aspired domination of both superpowers and challenged the very legitimacy of bloc competition, which it saw as dangerously destabilizing—the source of an arms race that could precipitate nuclear war at any time. The French, Spanish, and Greek parties all expressed ambivalence (and even hostility) toward NATO to one degree or another. Hence they hoped to frame an independent foreign policy that could provide new political leverage for Western Europe, indeed the continent as a whole, in a realigned global structure. For the Third World, such policy initiatives meant creating an alternative to both U.S. imperial control and the Soviet developmental model—a "democratic socialism" that, given a progressive balance of forces, would receive support from the advanced countries. The strategic methods for implementing such a novel foreign policy, however, varied greatly from party to party.

For the French Socialists an independent role in world politics served to justify further solidification of the *force de frappe* (French nuclear deterrent) inherited from de Gaulle. Mitterrand's concept of balance between the two blocs suggested not so much reduction of military forces or disarmament but rather nuclear modernization that lent credibility to a deterrent force separate from NATO, the U.S., and England. While this stance distanced the French from NATO, it did not signify a policy of outright rejection; the goal was instead mutual coexistence within a shared anti-Soviet framework. The PSF was willing to live with a strengthened NATO, including deployment of Euromissiles, so long as this did not encroach upon French prerogatives. The Socialists came to power with the aim of increasing military spending and bolstering the French role in Europe, based upon a merger of left political vision and nationalist Realpolitik.[15] Neither Spain nor Greece possessed such a nuclear potential, however, so the Socialist fear of bloc politics in these countries gave rise to a more rejectionist attitude toward NATO and the continued U.S. military presence in southern Europe. Both the Gonzales and Papandreou governments spoke of terminating relations with NATO (the PSOE promising a national referendum on the issue) and closing down American bases in their countries, although this would necessarily be a gradual process. Each party supported grassroots peace initiatives—which at the time engaged millions of Europeans—and each opposed the U.S. decision to station new, more modern missile systems on the continent, even though neither Spain nor Greece was chosen as a nuclear site. Their foreign policy was inspired by the historic antagonism toward the industrialized powers, which infused it with a "Third World" dialectic of the periphery challenging the core while also seeking to emulate it in certain ways. For both parties there was also an obsession with curtailing the power of a military apparatus in which reactionary ambitions were still very much alive. Whatever the points of convergence within Eurosocialist foreign policy, therefore, the tensions produced by these critical differences were bound to surface as each Socialist government staked out its strategic perspective.

Whatever the evolving nature of this Eurosocialist "synthesis" in the 1970s and early 1980s, it clearly had much in common with social democracy while also departing from it in significant ways. It shared a firm commitment to parliamentarism, winning incremental reforms within the political system, and building multiclass alliances. It foresaw no total break with the corporations or state, that is, no fundamental social transformation leading to a new type of system. Insofar as it anticipated no epochal crisis or collapse of capitalism, it projected an evolutionary and relatively peaceful mode of change not too far removed from Bernstein's vision. But Eurosocialism differed from social democracy, not simply because of its ideological eclecticism and social diversity but also because of its more expanded political outlook. Whereas social-democratic parties were normally comfortable in their historical role as rationalizing agents of capitalism, the revitalized Eurosocialists presented an image of democratic socialism embracing a qualitatively new kind of society. Theirs was a vision of a fully democratized, egalitarian, and culturally renewed order that could not be achieved by merely turning the existing state apparatus around to accomplish socialist ends. The path to socialism would therefore be neither a direct overthrow of the power structure nor a smooth evolutionary process in which the old forms gradually yield to the new, along the lines of the Eurocommunist schema. It would ultimately involve a complete restructuring of the complex system of domination rather than yet another effort to administer that system more humanely and efficiently.

At the same time, Eurosocialist parties appeared as little more than faint echoes of their distant Marxist origins; their hallmark was a willingness to rethink old ideas, programs, strategies, and methods. They assigned no privileged status to the industrial working class or labor movements; they anticipated no explosive crisis of capitalism; they were suspicious of old-fashioned productivist solutions (whether Marxist or Keynesian) that rely upon the benefits of growth; and they viewed the sphere of ideology and politics—not the economy—as the main arena of social transformation.[16]

Yet in their strong desire to construct a wide electoral base the Socialists projected an image of moderation, caution, and reconciliation, to the extent that their programs were often infused with a vague and minimalist language reminiscent of social democracy. Leaders were wary of being perceived as too radical by mainstream voters, most of whom wanted *some* change but were not prepared to accept fundamental social or institutional transformation. During electoral campaigns the parties usually steered toward safe issues (peace, democracy) or nebulous promises (economic stability, growth) under the rubric of broad slogans: *por el cambia*, "for a change" in the case of the PSOE, *Megali Allaghi*, "Great Change" in the case of PASOK. They upheld a sense of optimism and progress tied to modernizing advances that, though understandable from the viewpoint of Mediterranean countries attempting to break the cycle of dependency and marginality, was bound to conflict with their radical, egalitarian side. Moreover, despite occasional references to socialism as an ultimate goal, party statements never clearly specified the methods required to carry out even intermediate objectives. Even before the Eurosocialist ascent to power, therefore, ideological limits to this peculiar brand of structural reformism seemed evident despite the grandiose claims of many leaders and supporters. But such ambiguities could not nullify an overriding historical fact: within a relatively brief time span the Mediterranean Socialist parties had become the largest and most successful ensemble of leftist formations in European history.

Eurosocialist victories brought a mood of popular euphoria to southern Europe, along with an expanded leftist institutional presence enabling the parties to set in motion long-delayed reforms. And in each country the Socialists introduced progressive measures that flowed from their structural reformist framework. Within a year of their electoral successes the parties swept away all outward appearances of conservative hegemony while enacting a flurry of reforms in virtually every area—the economy, the state, culture, family life, religion, the military. Only in foreign policy did they refrain from undertaking any significant new departures.

The French Socialists began as the most ambitious reformers, announcing in the period from spring 1981 to late 1982 one series of far-reaching measures after another. Nationalizations—previously a focal point of tensions between the PSF and Communists—were extended to about ninety percent of banking and credit enterprises and several key industrial sectors: electronics, computers, steel, glass, armaments, and aluminum. With public control of investment funds greatly expanded (to roughly thirty-five percent of the total), the state could stimulate and protect favored areas of growth (like electronics and computers) so as to bolster the French economy in the world market. Welfare and social security benefits were extended, the minimum wage was increased by ten percent, and unemployment was countered by means of greater public spending (including a large boost in the military budget). The Mitterrand government also moved to decentralize the power structure, that is, to reverse the long-standing tendency in France toward technocratic statism. In March 1982 the PSF announced a law "on the rights and liberties of communes, departments, and regions," giving new authority to local and regional bodies while curtailing the legendary authoritarian domain of the prefects. At about the same time the Auroux Laws were enacted to reinforce the bargaining rights of trade unions. In other areas the government established a ministry of women's affairs, embarked upon two large solar projects, doubled funding for French arts and culture, abolished the death penalty, and broadened occupational safety and health regulations. The Socialists were able to push through these and other changes with only minimal resistance from the right opposition and conservative managerial elites.[17]

If the Spanish and Greek Socialists achieved less during their first year or so on power, they nonetheless managed to generate the same atmosphere of change and dynamism; they projected an innovative leadership more open and willing to challenge established patterns. In February 1983 (just five months after taking office) the Gonzales government decided to nationalize the Rumasa conglomerate, Spain's largest business empire with a work force numbering 300,000, and close down eighteen banks. Although the PSOE conceded that this had more to do with restructuring inefficient or failing enterprises than with any move toward socialism, it did provide the government with new leverage over investment. Meanwhile, the Socialists introduced measures reducing the political influence of the Catholic Church and professionalizing the military (but stopping short of a full-scale purge of conservative senior officers). On social issues the government sanctioned divorce, legalized marijuana, and made serious (but still limited) efforts to bring more women into political life. Perhaps most important, the PSOE brought an energetic and youthful leadership to Spanish society that was dominated since the late 1930s by a closed fascist (or semi-fascist) hierarchy.

A similar pattern of events unfolded in Greece. Once in power, the Papandreou government embarked upon new projects with a fervor and optimism unprecedented in modern Greek political history. In 1981 the country was swept by a populist spirit. PASOK did not immediately nationalize large-scale industrial or financial enterprises, but it did act to overturn rigid monetarist policies that the Karamanlis regime introduced in 1979. At the same time, it also enacted a more progressive taxation scheme, expanded some welfare benefits, and permitted small businesses to secure loans under more favorable conditions. During their first year in power the Socialists granted wage increases keyed to the level of inflation, froze consumer prices, and broadened social security benefits. In the political sphere they pushed for a liberalization of trade union and labor laws, greater separation of church and state, and professionalization of the civil service— reforms that would take many years to fully carry out under even the best circumstances. In February 1983 the Greek parliament approved sweeping changes in family laws, which, among other things, gave women legal equality and made divorce easier. In early 1984 women were guaranteed equal pay for equal work. As in France, the Socialist government more than doubled the budgetary support for indigenous cultural and artistic programs.

Contrary to what many observers anticipated, the Eurosocialists refrained form initiating any profound shifts in foreign policy, a consequence largely of their preoccupation with domestic issues. The PSF, as we have seen, felt compelled to follow the lines of Gaullist nationalism; their only deviation was a modicum of support for some Third World anti-imperialist movements (as in Central America). The early foreign policy record of both the PSOE and PASOK might be summed up as one of loud words (directed against NATO, the EEC, and U.S. hegemony) accompanied by relatively little action. Unlike the PSF, however, the Spanish and Greek parties did oppose the Euromissile plan, even if Gonzales seemed to waver from time to time. But the PSOE delayed a promised referendum on Spanish participation in NATO, and PASOK stepped back from its earlier commitment to have U.S. military bases removed from the country and to reassess its EEC membership. By 1984 both the Gonzales and Papandreou governments seemed ready to coexist, however uneasily, with the controlling powers of NATO and the EEC, raising the question of whether Eurosocialism did in fact represent a final break with social democracy on international issues.

But this question could not be restricted to the realm of foreign policy, since within only three years of the historic Eurosocialist breakthrough even the most visionary domestic initiatives were engulfed by a wave of conservatism and retreat that sapped the momentum and, ultimately, the popularity of the parties. This development, moreover, was clearly more than a temporary setback or tactical maneuver; it could be traced to a particular set of ideological, strategic, and historical factors that in the end were destined to block Eurosocialist progress in the direction of a third road. These factors would impose a series of contradictions and dilemmas similar to those previously experienced by social democracy and Eurocommunism.

The Politics of Retreat

An emphatic turn toward political moderation and timidity, which by 1984 would dash the radical expectations of even the most optimistic partisans, could be observed in three broad areas: the economy, structure of state power, and foreign policy. In some cases (for example, the international policies of the French Socialists) this conservatism reflected not so much a shift or "retreat" as it did a simple continuity with previous goals and priorities. For the most part, however, this process involved a significant (if not altogether surprising) retrenchment in terms of earlier party commitments, and indeed even of reforms implemented during the triumphal first months of governance. Such a reversal could be understood above all as a response to external conditions or pressures emanating from the global economic situation. At the same time, the shift could be attributed to *internal* factors to the extent that the parties themselves failed to articulate or press for a comprehensive, radical, anti-capitalist solution to the crisis.

Once in power, Mediterranean Socialists became obsessed with economic matters and therefore chose to defer their qualitative social and political goals. The historical context dictated an approach calling for "development first, then socialism," as the Spaniards put it. The consensus among party leaders was that, in the absence of dynamic economic development, qualitative demands would ultimately be blocked or distorted. In fact, despite some very real changes, a good deal of initial reformist activity was largely expressive or symbolic. Broad programmatic options were narrowed in order to combat various manifestations of the crisis—a narrowing vortex that sooner or later would converge with the logic of capital accumulation.

If the Eurosocialists were driven to stabilize their respective national economies within the global capitalist division of labor—a task viewed as the first step toward socialist transformation—their efforts bore few immediate results. Of course, reform initiatives did allow the state broadened discretion for making investment decisions, but only to a limited extent. And party leaders were convinced that workers and the poor should no longer be forced to shoulder a preponderant burden of the crisis. Nonetheless, by the end of 1984 France, Spain, and Greece were beset with the same abiding problems: sluggish growth, high levels of unemployment (8.2, 19.5, and 10 percent, respectively), shrinking investment capital, growing budgetary deficits, unstable currencies. Only the decay of urban social services was slightly reversed. In reality these countries were essentially trapped within their peripheral relationship to the international market economy; much like Third World countries, they (at least Spain and Greece) were unable to break the vicious cycle of dependency and stagnation.[18] The prospects for genuine progressive reforms, whatever the theoretical inclinations or political intentions of Eurosocialist leaders, were by 1985 highly remote.

The economic dimension of this Eurosocialist reversal was tied to three interrelated elements: technological restructuring, austerity, and movement toward a neo-Keynesian market economy. From the viewpoint of party leaders, as we have seen, survival in an increasingly competitive world capitalist system called for a shift in the direction of high-technology production, to be subsidized and protected by the state. The manufacturing sector would have to be modernized if these countries hoped to compete effectively within the international market.

To this end the Mitterrand government heavily invested public funds in research and development for the strategically vital, but still limited, electronics and computer industries. In order to stimulate productivity throughout the economy it began an energetic rationalizing project that, in 1983–84, resulted in massive worker layoffs in the auto, steel, and shipyard sectors. Restructuring along these lines eliminated roughly 30,000 jobs in the steel industry alone.[19] In several cases plants that were unprofitable were simply shut down by the government. Those most harshly affected were poorly skilled, low paid African workers who had recently entered French basic industries in large numbers. In May 1983 a drastic anti-inflation program was carried out, including tax increases, wage limits, utility rate hikes, severe restrictions on the number of francs that could be spent abroad, and cutbacks in spending for some social services. This coincided with a modest Keynesian initiative—deficit spending accompanied by increased transfer payments—to help counter the worst effects of restructuring.[20] At the same time, in order to stimulate new investment the PSF looked more and more to the private sector, or at least to a partnership between government and business; fearing capital flight, it courted the involvement of multinationals. By 1984 the kind of entrepreneurial mood that was prevalent in Gaullist France returned with a vengeance.

Such efforts to insulate the French economy from the harmful vicissitudes of global crisis—always problematic from the standpoint of socialist objectives—eventually cut deep into the government's leftist base of support. Restructuring and austerity policies were met with militant resistance both from within the labor movement and the North African community, where the jobless rate climbed to forty percent. Protests by hundreds of workers at the Talbot auto plant in 1983 led to a series of confrontations with riot police.[21] Later in the same year a wave of protests, strikes, and even plant occupations swept Peugeot, which, with government approval, laid off some 2000 workers. In early 1984 more than 30,000 steelworkers marched through the streets of Paris to protest plant closings and layoffs, and millions of government workers staged a one-day protest strike in opposition to austerity and repressive wage policies. The PSF Minister of Industry, J.P. Chevenement, resigned his post out of exasperation with Mitterrand's economic programs. More significantly, the Communists, no longer interested in supporting these policies or enduring the consequences, exited from the governing coalition in June 1984, a split that did not seriously erode government stability (the PCF held only four cabinet posts) but further undermined Socialist credibility in the labor movement.[22]

By late 1984 Mitterrand's popular support dropped to a favorable rating of thirty-three percent in the public opinion polls.[23] Perhaps even more revealing was the party's terrible showing in the spring 1984 European parliamentary elections, where it received only twenty-one percent of the vote compared with 37.5 percent in the general election. Several months after this debacle, the Socialists, now on the defensive, finally abandoned their last piece of overtly progressive legislation—the educational reform bill—following a wave of massive right-wing demonstrations. A measure of further decline was the poor outcome of the March 1986 parliamentary elections, where the PSF won only 33.1 percent of the vote (212 seats), losing its legislative majority along with the premiership to the Conservative coalition.

The PSF embrace of austerity policies, or *plan de rigeur*, signaled abandonment of the idea of rupture with the capitalist system; the guidepost now was the neo-liberal ethos of a mixed economy.[24] Socialist goals as such were predictably devalued—not merely deferred—by most PSF leaders. As economic imperatives further tightened political constraints, the "climate of business confidence" assumed primary importance in a situation where the PSF had framed no coherent alternative strategy from the outset. Efforts to implement even moderate versions of *autogestion* were overwhelmed by this reality.[25] Familiar capitalist methods of governance exacerbated some recurring economic problems, resulting in greater unemployment, reduced purchasing power for workers and the poor, and cutbacks in social programs. Party leader Lionel Jospin spoke about the need to respect the "laws of capitalist economics" in order to arrive at realistic solutions, and Michel Rocard called for a reduction in state power so that free enterprise would have more space in which to flourish. Their sentiments were validated by the turn to the right at the Socialists' Toulouse Congress in October 1985. With the emergence of Laurent Fabius, a smooth, technocratic premier, the model increasingly upheld by the PSF was identical to that of the SPD, the British Labor Party, and the Swedish Social Democrats.[26]

Like the PSF, the Spanish and Greek Socialists sought to avoid any head-on confrontation with the centers of domestic and international capital: they too relied heavily on new infusions of private investment to reverse the downward spiral. For the PSOE, the private sector (with state involvement, to be sure) was the linchpin of technological rationalization and, by extension, of breaking down barriers to full participation in the EEC. The Gonzales government moved to close down unproductive enterprises and banks, establish wage ceilings, and pursue foreign capital. The idea was to create a high-technology infrastructure, enabling Spain to capture an expanded share of the global "post-industrial" market. In contrast to the French approach, however, this stratagem did not depend upon large-scale nationalizations. Even in the case of the Rumasa takeover by the state, within a year the PSOE decided to return the bulk of its assets to private groups and foreign investors. But in general the Spanish case fit the overall Eurosocialist pattern, with technological restructuring, austerity, and neo-Keynesian programs paving the way for a technocratic apparatus that effectively marginalized the left and trade unions while solving few economic problems. By 1985 the Socialists were still not able to revitalize the economy, even within the parameters of capitalism, so that unemployment hovered near seventeen percent, social services lagged, and budget deficits continued to grow. As a result, Gonzales too suffered a drop in popularity, which he later recuperated. Austerity policies and layoffs were protested by thousands of workers, who staged brief general strikes in the northwest and Basque Country. More than 20,000 shipbuilding workers were laid off in 1983, while the state-owned Altos Hornodel Mediterraneo steel plant was being phased out with a loss of 8,000 jobs.[27]

Restructuring made a shambles of Socialist promises to cut unemployment by nearly a million; between 1982 and 1985, on the contrary, about 700,000 jobs were lost in all, with youth joblessness rising to nearly fifty percent.[28] In economics, as elsewhere, the PSOE came to value pragmatism and flexibility over any specific programmatic objective. As one observer noted, "[T]he social democratization of the PSOE was so profound between 1982 and 1986 that the right was hard pressed to find fault with the Socialist government."[29] Indeed, PSOE economic policies differed little from those of Thatcher and Reagan.

The Greek situation followed more or less the same path. As in Spain, the PASOK-engineered marriage between the state and big business was arranged without even the pretense of a structural-reformist attack on monopolies and multinationals, except that in Greece far greater attention was devoted to the rejuvenation of small-scale enterprises and farms. Less than a year after the election that brought the Socialists to power, hostile references to the EEC, multinationals, and even U.S. hegemony were markedly toned down. Such a confrontational posture, after all, would disrupt even a modest start toward technological restructuring. In fact, the Greek project wound up more limited than either the French or Spanish for several reasons: a narrower resource base, a draining military budget that accounted for seven percent of GNP, a less developed industrial base, and a feeble state apparatus that itself was badly in need of modernization. Thus, efforts to redirect investment—for example, toward research and development, social services, subsidies to small businesses—did not go very far even where they were successful. As Papandreou's initially harsh attitude toward EEC abated and PASOK stepped up its appeals to private capital, the market became a legitimate vehicle for development in Socialist thinking.

In order to extricate itself from a position of semi-peripheral dependency, Greece under PASOK rule sought to stimulate new public and private investment that, ironically, included strong appeals to outside capital (both Western and Soviet bloc). Within the public sector PASOK was preoccupied with improving efficiency, professionalizing the civil service, and cutting labor costs. There was simultaneously a turn toward monetarism, labor discipline, and wage controls. Although some labor benefits were increased, on the whole workers were asked to tighten their belts for the sake of badly needed modernizing changes.[30] Public spending increased during 1984–85, but after 1985 PASOK decided to introduce rather steep austerity measures while also modifying the wage-indexing scheme it established after the election.[31]

Unfortunately, this path turned out to be no more fruitful for Greece than for France or Spain. After several years of "Great Change" politics the country's economic burdens persisted, with levels of unemployment, inflation, and fiscal deficit remaining about the same. Still, Papandreou initially lost little of the popularity he enjoyed in 1981, despite these economic problems and a series of labor demonstrations against austerity, which began in January 1983.[32] He had continued support because, in the context of recent Greek history, PASOK remained a dynamic symbol of democratization and national unity, whatever the limits of its domestic policies. Its continued strength was reflected in the June 1985 parliamentary elections: The Socialists won forty-six percent of the vote (161 seats) compared with forty-one percent for New Democracy and ten percent for the KKE (Communists of the Interior).[33]

The Eurosocialist restructuring project was designed, in effect, to integrate Mediterranean economies more fully into the regional EEC system and the international capitalist market. To some extent, this logic was rooted in deep historical trends operating independently of party ideology and goals, which consequently reduced "socialism" to an abstract concept. Because the crisis of modern capitalism further sharpens economic and technological competition, giving rise to a situation in which only a few countries can be "winners" and most are "losers," radical alternatives are easily blunted by ideological modernization and fear of mass disruption. Socialist theorists argued that, at the present historical juncture, the only realistic choice is detente with private capital. Should leftist governments deviate from this logic, they risk losing sources of investment, which means destabilization of the whole economy, thereby nullifying any restructuring plans upon which reform initiatives must ultimately rest. There can be no immediate break with the world system, no avoiding the imperatives of accumulation within the matrix of capitalism. By going along with this logic the Eurosocialists opted for a broadening of market forces alongside statist forms of social investment and planning—without which modernization would be inconceivable. This amounted to a kind of "local Keynesianism" designed to manage the crisis of regional capital.[34] As such, it signaled a fundamental retreat from the unique strategies for radical change originated by the French, Spanish, and Greek parties.

Under these conditions "socialist" goals became more and more remote within the political framework of Eurosocialism. Within a few years after electoral victory, party work began to cohere around a "pragmatic" center dominated by skillful and adaptive functionaries for whom "modernization" became the key ideological lodestar.[35] As the theoretical first stage of progressive social change, modernization took on the character of an instrumental final goal, with all future stages consigned to a distant utopia. As one close observer of the PSF concluded as early as 1984, "Socialism, in its original inspirational weaning, as a working-class movement to change society, is quite simply being liquidated in France."[36]

The central political issues, therefore, revolved not so much around Eurosocialist adaptation to global market pressures—which was to some extent inevitable—but rather the degree to which there occurred a full-scale, self-conscious withdrawal of the commitment to the transition to socialism. From this standpoint, it is possible to speak of both *external* (global economic) and *internal* (strategic) factors in accounting for Socialist retrenchment. Thus, if we reflect upon the dilemmas at work within the party organizations, a different side of the problem becomes visible: Theorists and leaders never really formulated an alternative economic model consonant with their (socialist) ideological aims. Not surprisingly, once in power they lost the capacity for political imagination that had won them so much electoral support prior to 1981.[37] And they offered no comprehensive framework within which specific policies might be justified or make sense to the broad base of party members and supporters. Perhaps their orientation toward the new middle strata—and the corresponding narrowness of their labor support—pushed them into the arms of private capital as they struggled to consolidate their governance.[38] Whatever the case, by 1985 the Eurosocialists were in full retreat from the image of oppositional politics they had constructed during 1979–1982.

In France, this retrenchment was painfully recognized within what remained of leftist currents in the PSF, especially those centered around the research group CERES, which attacked the leadership for its failure to develop a radical economic strategy adequate to the (transformative) tasks at hand. Without a strong anti-capitalist program or vision, the party found itself backpedaling toward a (more rationalized) mixed economy that implicitly looked to the Japanese model, with its emphasis on free enterprise restructuring combined with technocratic integration, near full employment, an extended welfare system, and strong labor discipline. For the Eurosocialists this shift amounted to a form of neo-liberalism with a thin leftist veneer.[39]

By the end of the 1980s the Eurosocialist developmental agenda could be judged as anything but transformative, much less radical: an emphasis on growth, stability, technological innovation, and balanced budgets over the time-honored socialist values of redistribution and popular control.[40] The turn toward austerity measures overwhelmed even the best structural-reformist designs to expand the public sector as a basis for more egalitarian programs. Popular hopes that Socialist governance would mean a significant improvement in overall living standards were never met, even where—as in Spain—the party remained in power for a full decade. Even in the area of unemployment, a traditional litmus test even for social democracy, the situation generally worsened.[41] None of this was accidental, but was rather the inevitable product of a technocratic developmental model wedded to neo-liberal ideology.

In *political* terms, therefore, this restructuring agenda augurs a new phase of corporatism based upon partnership between state and capital, with trade unions relegated to a lesser role than in either traditional or postwar social democracy.[42] Given the extent to which such corporatism is required by the Eurosocialist approach to economic modernization, the long-term impact of their hegemony could only favor mass demobilization over active politicization, and this indeed was the trend in the Mediterranean: A brief post-election period of triumphal popular enthusiasm was followed by extreme passivity and cynicism in the mid and late-1980s. As the politics of modernization, institutional stability, and class collaboration took hold, party leaders had little choice but to discourage militant struggles or grassroots politics.[43] The decline of new social movements in France, Spain, and Greece probably had as much to do with this dynamic—the ability of left governments to absorb and domesticate oppositional energy—as with any internal collapse of the movements themselves.

Economic retreat cannot be separated from the sphere of politics insofar as states and party systems are profoundly influenced by the same restructuring processes. As we have seen, the Mediterranean Socialist parties all shared a firm commitment to democratization or, in their more visionary moments, to democratic socialism. They concretized this goal in practice as they moved to consolidate liberal-democratic structures and values against the earlier legacy of authoritarian regimes (Gaullism, Francoism, the Greek colonels). In this respect, Socialist rule was constructed upon decidedly popular foundations.[44] But democratization quickly encountered severe limits, largely because the mode of capitalist rationalization being carried out by the parties demanded hierarchy and discipline within a corporatist framework. This was one way to streamline the accumulation process: in the form of planning, subsidies, taxation and fiscal policies, regulation, research and development, and labor controls. Further, the pull of technological efficiency and administrative stability soon outweighed that of popular decision-making, decentralization, and *autogestion*. In fact, the emancipatory elements of democratic politics that figured so prominently in Socialist platforms were largely dropped without much debate. The twin emphases on growth and normal politics submerged the democratizing themes that accompanied the Eurosocialist promise of a third road.

In France, for example, the initial burst of decentralizing activity was quickly negated by a return to traditional *dirigisme*, centered in a large and well-entrenched technocratic stratum that the Socialists cultivated for their restructuring plans. Lacking roots in any genuine process of mass mobilization, the Mitterrand government initiated its reform project mostly from above; political boundaries were established and protected by the state. The PSF set out to bring the state and economy together within a unified structure that extended even beyond the Gaullist technocracy, for the state was now able to steer development (within limits) while also constituting itself as the key forum for interest group mediation. In effect, the Socialists were cultivating a type of capitalist socialization that would, if successful, lay the groundwork for a more institutionalized system of industrial relations. In this vein Mark Kesselman commented (in 1985) that "a review of Socialist reforms shows that the government is serving as a midwife to ease the transition to a mode of pluralist and corporatist regulation long prevalent elsewhere."[45]

With the passing of time, the PSF leadership demonstrated less and less interest in supporting popular struggles from below, and indeed wound up *opposing* many of their goals (those of the Ecologists, for example). The ideal of *autogestion* was largely discarded even as it was paid abundant lip service; decentralizing reforms took on a formal administrative and even cosmetic character; and routinized bureaucratic politics increasingly typified Socialist governance after 1983.[46] The distinctively *electoral* nature of Mitterrand's victory, and with it the displacement of popular activity, was more apparent with each passing year.

This move away from democratization also fit the Spanish case. In Spain, too, statism was a long and deeply ingrained tradition, but without the parliamentary trappings. The restructuring policies of the PSOE, while less ambitious than those of the PSF, actually carried forward and refined many centralizing features associated with Francoism—state planning, regulation, labor controls, and so forth. At the same time, the parliamentary system itself—or, more accurately, the transition from authoritarianism to liberal democracy—was still rather fragile in Spain. For some observers the issue of bourgeois democracy (and basic civil liberties) versus Francoism or military rule remained unresolved even in the early 1980s.[47]

Of course, the Spanish Socialists helped to consolidate the embryonic parliamentary system with its fragile but nonetheless important protection of general political freedoms. They also initiated judicial reforms and, more significantly, undertook an ambitious program of reorganizing the armed forces with the purpose of undermining their anti-democratic potential. At the same time, the Gonzales government on occasion resorted to harsh police methods in handling mass protests and demonstrations, including those organized by the left. In 1983, after continuous prodding from the right, the Socialists enacted stringent anti-terrorist laws that could be applied to virtually any type of political action. Moreover, there was the always strong personal figure of Gonzales, who was able to set the agenda for discussion and action within both the party and government, especially during the first few years of PSOE rule. An effective power-oriented politician, Gonzales established himself as an unchallengeable leader who could shape policy, disarm opposition, and in general act as a counterweight to democraticing reforms, which in most cases were largely superficial. The PSOE molded a governing apparatus to fit the requirements of stability and moderation, vital not only to its modernizing ethos but also a function of its consuming fear of political disruption and class polarization (which in turn stemmed from justifiable anxieties concerning the return of fascism).

In Greece, on the other hand, the process of democratic transformation was firmer and deeper. Not only did the PASOK government enjoy a broader base of support than the French or Spanish, but reversion to right-wing dictatorship seemed unlikely during the 1980s. More to the point, the Socialists managed to introduce the spirit, and to some extent the form, of popular involvement that went far beyond parliamentarism, as part of their ambitious effort to decentralize the state. PASOK itself was built on a foundation of hundreds of local branches, many of them sustained by lively mass participation. Grassroots mobilization became a reality in small Greek towns and rural communities, where cooperative and local assemblies began to flourish on a new scale and with a new sense of "great change." Still, there were the familiar problems that beset Eurosocialism in general: Despite its anti-EEC and pro-small business outlook, PASOK remained closely tied to large corporate and financial interests, while its modernizing project depended upon a corporatist infrastructure that was always integral to Greek capitalism.[48] Moreover, the cult of a strong leader exerted an overwhelming influence in Greek politics. Before the late-1980s scandals that drove him from office, Papandreou was able to control the party and government far more effectively than either Mitterrand or Gonzales, owing in part to his more charismatic style.

In its strong desire to streamline the state bureaucracy, PASOK generated a new system of highly concentrated power. The struggle to replace archaic patronage networks gave rise not only to a more professionalized civil service but to a new stratum of Socialist bureaucrats, which sought firm control over both labor and social movements. "Participation" was therefore increasingly managed from above, just as it was under the aegis of northern European social democracy. Initial attempts to organize formal self-management councils were abandoned as the local forms gave way to government controlled "advisory councils."[49] As the party merged with the governmental structure during the 1980s, the divorce between PASOK's democratic-socialist ideology and its quasi-authoritarian practice became more visible and a source of alarm for many activists.

In terms of democratization, then, Eurosocialism represented a clear advance toward liberal forms of governance—no minor achievement—but its vision of democratic socialism was obscured to the point of being almost completely forgotten. Power was concentrated in elite strata both within the party and state; the participatory role of labor and social movements was blunted; democratic reforms were undercut by bureaucratic hostility or impasse; and patronage machines continued to function throughout the Mediterranean.[50] The renovated party systems made possible by emergent popular forces seemed to require for their functioning a political culture shaped less by activism and engagement than by passivity and detachment—except, ironically, for those labor protests directed against the Socialist governments. This peculiar relationship between economics and politics had two distinct but interrelated consequences: Just as "socialism" came to signify a regrouping of old centers of power around new rationalizing ideologies, popular movements themselves wound up absorbed by the hegemonic state or otherwise lost their momentum.[51]

When judging Eurosocialist foreign policies, no easy generalizations can be sustained. Indeed, one could detect (in the early 1980s) unique patterns for each of the parties: a strongly Atlanticist, anti-Soviet orientation (France), a resolutely anti-American, anti-NATO ideology (Greece), and a position best described as ambivalent but leaning toward the West (Spain). However, despite these variations in official political lines, the actual conduct of Socialist international politics eventually reflected similar loyalties and commitments, owing to strong pressures brought to bear by U.S.-dominated regional and global structures. The course of Eurosocialist foreign policies paralleled in many ways those of social democracy, which in the postwar years endorsed the ideal of balance between the superpowers but which in practice never strayed from the NATO orbit. It became obvious, too, that Socialist retreat on the domestic front was bound to have far-reaching implications for the parties' international behavior: The decline of radicalism in each sphere was mutually reinforcing. It must also be kept in mind that the Mediterranean setting (especially in Spain and Greece) bred a certain marginality, backwardness, and dependency relative to northern Europe, which fostered Europeanist attitudes stressing integration and entry into the EEC.[52]

The founding convention of the French Socialists at Epinay in 1971 actually departed little from conventional social-democratic premises: the PSF consensus was that the European left should locate itself between the major blocs, while, at the same time, the party elite insisted that progressive social change must be pursued within the West European alignment of forces, since immediate revolution was out of the question. From this standpoint, the PSF rejected any dramatic break with the U.S. or NATO, whatever its (largely nationalist) differences with American foreign policy.[53] In a formal sense the Socialists faithfully adhered to the principle of balance—a perspective reinforced by the Gaullist vision of an independent nuclear arsenal giving France, under any government, a more powerful role in European affairs. In reality, however, PSF loyalty to the U.S. and NATO was never in question, if for no other reason than its own intractable legacy of anti-Sovietism (stemming in part from its domestic competition with the Communists). It could even be argued that, since 1981, the Socialists turned out to be more pro-Western than their conservative predecessors.[54]

After winning power, the French Socialists moved steadily closer to the U.S. and West Germans, even while they adhered to the irrepressible *force de frappe*. Their hostility to the Soviet bloc, along with an ardent nationalism, generated a Cold-War ideology that had become muted long before in the discourse of most European countries. The centerpiece of Mitterrand's foreign policy was to enlarge and modernize the French military, above all its nuclear arsenal. Despite austerity programs, military spending was increased yearly by an average of eight percent through the mid-1980s, the largest growth rate for any advanced industrialized nation. For French political life this meant acceptance and even glorification of the country's military role. The logical corollary of PSF policy was a tendency to view cynically all arms control schemes (which, in effect, would make secondary powers like France even less consequential) as well as the European peace movement, which the Socialists vilified as a misguided assemblage of romantic pacifists. On the first point, the Mitterrand government was counted upon as perhaps the strongest defender of NATO's Euromissile deployment; as for the second, the PSF frequently sabotaged efforts to broaden the peace movement in France.[55] An example of the latter was visible at the Mannheim Conference in May–June 1984, where the PSF blocked agreement on every attempt to forge a common French-German agenda on peace politics.

As a long-time *Atlantiste*, Mitterrand steered French foreign policy in the direction of global priorities set by Reagan and Bush. As Diana Johnstone put it, the PSF "has served to forge a consensus and a new version of Gaullism subservient to American 'global security concepts.'"[56] In this sense, a distinctly French deterrent force, however loudly championed, had little practical significance for world politics, insofar as there was no way it could ever be effective. For the French Socialists, however, nuclear nationalism furnished the illusion of military strength and international credibility, which explains their understanding of the peace movement and "pacifism" as a tool of Moscow. The July 1985 bombing of the Greenpeace vessel *Rainbow Warrior* in New Zealand by French agents intent upon sabotaging protests against nuclear testing in the South Pacific revealed this nearly hysterical obsession with the nuclear *force de frappe*. And Mitterrand's later leadership in swinging United Nations support behind the U.S.-engineered attack on Iraq in 1991 showed the extent of French identification with Bush's "new world order."

The ambivalence of Spanish foreign policy under the PSOE grew out of two conflicting pressures: a longstanding skeptical attitude toward Atlanticism reinforced by the memory of U.S. support for Franco and continued fear of American hegemony, and the previously mentioned desire for entry into the EEC. With the Socialists' lack of progress toward a post-Franco foreign policy, they eventually fell back into the pro-NATO camp more or less by default. During the 1982 electoral campaign, for example, Gonzales promised a national referendum on Spain's involvement in NATO. After two years of delay, the government decided to go ahead with the referendum, but with the promise that the PSOE leadership was now in favor of continued NATO membership, since Spain must honor its obligations toward the "collective defense of the West."[57] The overriding fear was that, in the event the country withdrew from the alliance, its prospective EEC membership would be in question. Under these circumstances the Spaniards predictably enough yielded to pressures from the U.S., West Germany, and other West European governments to remain within the NATO military bloc. In March 1986 Spaniards voted overwhelmingly (by 8.8 to 6.7 million) to remain within the alliance. The outcome was clearly a personal victory for Gonzales, who campaigned vigorously and was credited with almost single-handedly turning around the strong anti-NATO (and anti-American) sentiment in the country. Indeed, the month preceding the referendum witnessed a series of large anti-NATO demonstrations in several Spanish cities, including one of 750,000 in Madrid, sponsored by more than 150 peace, ecology, and leftist organizations united within the Pro-Peace Committee. A poll in October 1985 showed that only nineteen percent of the populace was ready to endorse Spain's entry into NATO.

The notion that Spain could somehow detach itself from East-West politics was, given the magnitude of its economic crisis and its fervent desire to modernize, nothing more than self-deception. Thus PSOE ideology, too, evolved away from its early radicalism toward Cold War anti-Sovietism: its rationale for the Euromissiles, acceptance of U.S. military bases, increased military spending, and dismissal of the peace movement was premised on the need to combat "Soviet expansionism." By 1985 its foreign policy differed from that of the French Socialists only in being less stridently nationalistic. And, despite uncertainties about whether the referendum would pass, Spanish participation in NATO was solidified after the Socialist rise to power: Spain was represented on virtually every alliance body, including the Defense Planning Committee.[58] With full integration into NATO and the EEC (admission was granted in June 1985), Spain thus appeared to be well on the road to its long-cherished Europeanization—which has continued apace into the 1990s, as PSOE elites further cemented their relationship with European bankers and industrialists.[59] In this context, continued Socialist references to peace and disarmament—and to a reduction of the U.S. military presence in the country—seemed rather empty.

In contrast to the French and Spanish parties, the Greek Socialists upheld an (attenuated) anti-NATO and anti-imperialist position from the time of their founding in 1974 until the late 1980s. From the outset, PASOK called for Greece to disengage from international organizations and alliances that might compromise the country's independence, and reinforce its postwar status as an American colony. It rejected the idea of military blocs and called for a "federated Europe." From this viewpoint both the EEC and NATO were regarded as mere tools of U.S. hegemony, which PASOK argued was incompatible with Greek socialism or even modernization. In May 1984 Papandreou delivered a scathing attack on U.S. foreign policy, characterizing its designs as those of "expansionism and domination." Meanwhile, PASOK's relations with the Soviet bloc grew warmer, to the point where Papandreou could praise the Jaruszelski regime in Poland (becoming the only Socialist leader to oppose Solidarity). Before the 1981 election PASOK threatened to close down several U.S. military installations on Greek territory, and although the issue was settled in 1984 (in favor of keeping the bases), public opinion remained opposed to the American military presence. Earlier, Papandreou voiced strong opposition to the Euromissiles but wanted to compromise on a sixteen-month postponement, hoping that the Geneva arms control talks would reconvene and arrive at a solution (which never happened). Beginning in 1981 PASOK pushed for a nuclear free zone in the Balkans, making it one of the few parties in the Socialist International to endorse such a scheme.

The Greek Socialist approach to international politics was clearly unique. A key factor was PASOK's deep roots in the peace movement, which in Greece was composed of three relatively large and active organizations. In the early 1980s Athens was a center of perpetual rounds of demonstrations, meetings, and conferences in connection with the arms race, militarism, and Third World issues.[60] This ideological orientation was reinforced by the small size of the country and its peripheral location in Europe, which explains its identification with anti-colonial movements and regimes.

Equally important was NATO's special postwar relationship with Turkey—Greece's historical competitor in the Aegean—and its assistance to the Greek military dictatorships. Whatever the underlying factors, this radical consensus around foreign policy goals was a significant unifying force binding together PASOK's leading cadres, especially since nationalist ideology helps to legitimate party governance.[61]

Yet the Papandreou government never took any dramatic steps toward a break with the West. One observer suggested that Socialist foreign relations was governed by little more than a series of "symbolic empty gestures."[62] Thus, after several years of PASOK rule, Greece remained solidly within the EEC and NATO, although the Socialists did insist upon the right of "selective participation" in NATO field maneuvers. In 1984 Greece negotiated a five-year extension on four U.S. military bases (and about twenty minor installations), with the proviso that the arrangement could be terminated in 1988, although, predictably, it remained intact. PASOK leaders apparently felt that any real departure from the Western alliance would only benefit Turkey (militarily) and harm Greece (economically) by discouraging foreign investment. They insisted, much like the Eurocommunists, that the most effective tactics were to "struggle from within" regional European structures. This logic inevitably gave rise to a partial retreat on foreign policy, but within an ideological framework of anti-Atlanticism that rejected conventional bloc politics.

Despite its sometimes fierce sounding rhetoric, therefore, PASOK cultivated an image of pragmatism and conciliation that quickly extended from domestic to international affairs: The slide from socialism to populism would lead to a moderating shift in foreign policy as well. If the Socialists wanted to avoid confrontation with Greek corporate interests, they were even less inclined to take on multinationals based in the U.S. and Western Europe; theirs increasingly was a stance of *adaptation*. A strategy tied to electoral politics and economic restructuring, while also pursuing the illusory quest to reconcile populist appeals and the requirements of large capital, could not possibly have produced any kind of "socialist" or independent foreign policy.

The general problem for Eurosocialism was that it did not really formulate an alternative socialist conception of international relations or collective national security. Only the Greek Socialists made even tenuous moves in this direction. Lacking such an alternative, the parties soon reverted to the old patterns shaped mainly by U.S. interests. Moreover, the costs and sacrifices likely to accompany full disengagement from the EEC and NATO for

any Mediterranean country were bound to be formidable. The vast economic, political, and even military pressures brought to bear by the U.S.
through its decisive influence in the world capitalist system can be overwhelming, especially in southern Europe where crisis and dependency were
historically acute. Hence Eurosocialist moderation in foreign policy was
probably less a matter of support for U.S. strategic ambitions or strong anti-
Soviet feelings than simply adaptation to the imperatives of economic and
political modernization. This dynamic separated Eurosocialism—at least in
its first few years—from postwar social democracy, which thoroughly
embraced U.S. interests in Western Europe.[63]

The Impasse of Parliamentary Socialism

The dramatic rise to power of rejuvenated Mediterranean Socialist parties
in the early 1980s occurred in something of an ideological vacuum: not only
liberalism but Keynesian social democracy seemed to have exhausted its
potential, Leninism and the Soviet model were discredited, and the promise
of Eurocommunism never materialized. In this setting Eurosocialism
appeared as the best hope, finally, for pursuit of the elusive third road strategy—meaning that France, Spain, and Greece would constitute the arena
where a new dialectic of change would unfold. Not only were the Socialists
able to assimilate the energy of the new social movements, they also enjoyed
the legacy of a renewed structural reformism, with its immense optimism
regarding electoral politics and prospects for a broad social bloc espousing
tranformative goals. As we have seen, in its initial phase the Socialist triumph was accompanied by widespread political activism that helped to revitalize the public sphere; the space for progressive advances was vastly
enlarged. But the subsequent retreat showed that the Eurosocialists were
ultimately unprepared to fill this vacuum and seize upon the opportunities it
furnished. More than a decade after its series of stunning electoral victories,
the Eurosocialist phenomenon can be judged rather harshly: it represents
not so much the subversion as the *consolidation* of bourgeois hegemony in
countries where it exercised power over time.[64]

Of course, this is a familiar criticism of European social democracy, except
that in the postwar years those parties never pretended to challenge the
power structure, never claimed to pursue democratic socialism or a third
road politics. The governing legacy of social democracy was unambiguous:
capitalist rationalization in the economic sphere, welfare state reformism in

the area of social programs, corporatism alongside an expanded pluralist democracy in the political system, and defense of U.S. and NATO strategic interests in foreign policy. In the end, social democracy served to reproduce and legitimate while also humanizing the structures of bourgeois domination. Put simply, Eurosocialism seems to have become reabsorbed into this traditional framework. It offered a new image and spoke a new language, but the underlying premises and attachments turned out to be roughly the same.

The dynamics of Socialist retrenchment can be located on two levels— productivism in the realm of the economy, corporatism and parliamentarism in the political arena. First, industrial restructuring brought with it an adaptation to immediate economic pressures dictated by the needs of capital accumulation and rationalization; ultimate goals were lost along the way. Certainly, it is true that most governments are forced to borrow money to finance their development projects. During a period of global crisis and intensified national competition, as in the 1980s, there were added pressures to maximize exports, reduce imports, and cut public spending. Even leftist governments must emphasize technological rationalization, industrial growth, profit maximization, and austerity—all consistent with capitalist priorities of securing a good climate for business investment but hardly congruent with the dynamics of social change and redistribution. Since Eurosocialist parties were bent on *attracting* more capital, they were generally solicitous of commercial banks, the multinationals, and the EEC. Thus, given the overriding importance they assigned to modernization at the outset, they were obviously prepared to adapt to the logic of capital—or, more accurately, to the logic of technocratic state capitalism—with all of its political implications.[65] The outcome was more than ironic: Socialist governance in southern Europe resulted in an even greater concentration of capital in both public and private sectors than was the case under conservative predecessors.[66]

As Eurosocialism relinquished any vision that went beyond this convergence of state and market, it inevitably abandoned any interest in the defense of labor, qualitative social change, and grassroots mobilization. Clearly, these commitments—vital to the prospects for democratic socialism—were destined to clash with the imperatives of economic restructuring. Indeed, Socialist governance coincided with the steady *decline* of labor and social movements, precisely the opposite of what jubilant supporters had expected when the parties came to power.[67] Following the example of social democracy, then, leftist governments once again appeared as rationalizing vehicles of capitalist production, political stability, and social integration. Despite the wave of labor protests against Eurosocialist initiatives, the reality was that the 1980s brought a strengthening of capitalist and pluralist-democratic institutions to the Mediterranean.

This stabilizing phenomenon was dialectically intertwined with the contours of party strategy. The Socialist victories, whatever they owed to popular movements and constituencies, took place almost exclusively within the domain of electoral politics. Parliamentary majorities were built through the ballot box after lengthy periods of electioneering. The overriding goal in each case was to conquer institutional power at the national level. Although this may have reflected important advances for the left—and initially helped to create a more participatory culture—the problem was that party structures were largely detached from local struggles, cut off from the flow of grassroots politics. As mass-based national organizations with societal priorities, the Socialists were engaged *in practice* with only one sphere of political activity: parliament, the party system, state bureaucracy. (Although Socialists did have a presence in local and municipal governments, this fact did not alter their basic detachment from grassroots movements nor the character of power that was wielded.) Sooner or later the parties made their peace with the pluralist world of interest group bargaining, patronage networks, and bureaucratic influence—that is, with the very corporatism and electoralism that typified social democracy.

The replay of this familiar predicament dramatizes the deep flaws of structural reformism as they have been played out within the socialist tradition.[68] What defines this strategy is a view of the electoral-parliamentary arena as the primary, if not sole, arena of social transformation. Although lip service may be paid to local movements and participatory structures outside or peripheral to the dominant public sphere, there is not much theory or practice *uniting* the dimensions of electoral politics and grassroots struggles. In this sense, it is possible to identify a broad legacy of futility that extends from Kautsky through Togliatti and Eurocommunism and, finally, Eurosocialism.[69]

The long record of historical evidence shows that parliamentary institutions tend to reproduce a division between party and movements, the state and the grassroots, elites and masses, no matter what group or ideology is hegemonic. Since participation is usually limited to voting, interest group bargaining, and trade union codetermination (where present), the idea of an autonomous social bloc of forces capable of radical action is essentially ruled out. The "electorate" is generally comprised of a fragmented, passive, often alienated mix of disparate groups and individuals unable to exert unified political leverage within or outside the power structure. Where socialist electoralism is converted into stable governance, as in Sweden (1940s-1970s), Germany (1970s), and Spain (1980s), the subversive potential of mass struggles is typically held in check or neutralized. Here parliamentarism carries forward and sometimes strengthens the political division of labor, thus narrowing and depoliticizing the public sphere.[70] Elite domination behind a socialist facade coexists with a very weak sense of party identification around ideology, programs, and issues—a trend indicated by research data.[71] Of course, this reflects the catchall pattern, with its emphasis on the role of mass media, personalities, and sideshows over efforts to confront urgent social problems. Commenting on the popularity of Gonzales in Spain, Donald Share observes, "Where catch-all electoral appeals are likely to capture votes from the inchoate political center, the importance of a charismatic and popular leader becomes enhanced."[72]

A related problem is that even massive shifts in parliamentary alignments—as occurred in France, Spain, and Greece—do not normally constitute any substantial attack on the centers of power and privilege that lie outside parliament and the party system. This point does not refer merely to the familiar argument that legislative bodies in the industrialized countries have declined in power relative to the executive branch. It is more a question of the enormous influence of economic, political, and social power beyond the full reach of parliaments: the multinationals, international banks, the military, the bureaucratic state itself. To reconstitute parliament according to the vision of structural reformism—to create a shifting equilibrium of electoral forces favoring the left—does not amount to a genuine transformation of class and power relations, nor is it likely to be a prelude to such a transition.[73]

The record of Eurosocialist parties shows that the single-minded pursuit of normal politics within complex legislative and bureaucratic systems has a definite institutionalizing and moderating impact over time, just as we saw in the case of social democracy and Eurocommunism. The decision to participate fully and not just tactically encourages a logic of structural adaptation and class collaboration endemic to catchall parties, which reproduce a common *modus operandi*: interest group conciliation, bureaucratic style, social conservatism, fear of instability and disruption. This recalls the Michelsian dilemma of how to sustain large-scale, mass-based electoral activity and organization without at the same time losing ideological dynamism—except that in modern pluralist systems the deradicalizing impulse may be even stronger (if still not quite an "iron law") than Michels's critique of early German social democracy suggests. The corporatist entanglement of parliament, the party system, interest groups, mass media, and the state apparatus is such that integrative pressures are more effective now than during earlier phases of capitalism. In any event, we have no historical instances of mass-based communist or socialist parties following an exclusively parliamentary strategy that were able to resist this institutionalizing pull.[74]

One consequence of electoral politics for Eurosocialism, therefore, was to legitimate the structures and norms of capitalist democracy. If the parliamentary arena is open enough to give expression to popular struggles, its stability ensures that radical incursions will go only so far—to the point where the integrity of the state system is threatened. An electoralism that rules out extra-parliamentary activity necessarily enforces the code of bourgeois hegemony. Here, as elsewhere, the intimate link between economics and politics is abundantly evident: Restructuring and parliamentarism are mutually reinforcing.

Yet electoral politics *does* allow for a certain conquest of governmental power along the lines of what happened in southern Europe. A modified power structure did emerge in the 1980s, permitting a wide range of democratic reforms while helping to destroy the previous legacy of right-wing authoritarianism.[75] At the same time, the question of fundamental social change was left up in the air. Going back to the 1930s, socialist governments have introduced technocratic planning mechanisms, public ownership and control of industries and banks, progressive taxation schemes, and welfare reforms in more than a dozen countries, but none of these governments has ever challenged the rules of capital accumulation or pluralist democracy.[76] The boundaries of structural reform seem rigidly fixed. Where mass constituencies are depoliticized and parliaments wield relatively little power, the most probable outcome—although hardly a radical one—is for a regrouping of privileged interests around the state and corporations, possibly under the banner of "socialism."

Still, it would be misleading to conclude that Eurosocialists were able to fully assimilate popular movements into a new corporatist bloc. Local insurgency persisted throughout the 1980s on many levels: labor protests against austerity, peace mobilizations, urban struggles, feminism, and so forth. Of course, *one* outcome of Eurosocialist retrenchment was the demobilization of movements within the orbit of party activity; movement demands and goals were either incorporated by electoral politics or closed off altogether by the turn toward productivism and corporatism. But such quiescence was not likely to endure for long in a context where ruling Socialist parties had lost their vision and where neo-liberal domestic policies were offered as the only alternative. The point is that Eurosocialism, within a few short years, actually stood as an obstacle to democratization and qualitative social change.

All of this raises once again the question of whether the mythical third road model is really possible, given the unyielding pressures of global capitalism and the barriers to change set by pluralist democracy. The obsolescence of Leninism and the Soviet experience for the industrialized societies, the marginalization of radical alternatives, and the seeming impotence of structural reformism calls for a fundamental rethinking of past Marxist strategies. What appears to be missing from each schema is a dialectical view integrating two distinct realms of politics: national and local, party and movements, institutions and community, parliament and grassroots assemblies. A radical-democratic approach of this sort is more compatible, at least in theory, with a genuinely transformative process grounded in forms of insurgency directed against the old centers of power.[77] Although consonant with the spirit of democratic socialism, this embryonic alternative—in all its multiple expressions—is probably best characterized as "post-Marxist." It is to this realm of possibility that we shall now turn.

Postscript

The resurgence of left-wing politics in Italy in the early 1990s, fueled largely by popular revolt against a corrupt and bureaucratic state, seemed to offer hope that the impasse of third-road socialism might finally be broken. From all appearances, more than a decade of steady European leftist decline was now halted: the PDS, surrounded by a plethora of small oppositional parties, moved to resurrect its electoral status. The December 1993 regional and local elections brought a refurbished Progressive Alliance to municipal power in many cities, including Rome, Naples, Trieste, Venice, and Genoa. The leftist share of the vote reached well over 50 percent in several large cities. Comprised of eight groups, ranging from the PDS to the *Verdi* (Greens), old-line Marxists in *Rifondazione Comunista*, and the anti-Mafia *La Rete* (The Network), the alliance was posed to capture national power— a task that would be made easier with the disintegration of the long-dominant Christian Democrats and growing hatred of the old *partitocrazia* with its scandal-ridden patronage systems. For the first time since 1947 the Italian left appeared ready to assume political hegemony. As PDS leader Achille

Occhetto observed in early 1994: "After years of struggle, we finally have in this country a fully mature left that is prepared to govern." Could the earlier, more grandiose promises of both Eurocommunism and Eurosocialism now be retrieved from the wreckage strewn about by 1980s-style conservatism?

The March 1994 general elections did in fact spell the collapse of the DC and the "center", but the left—with much of its momentum still intact—could not prevail in the face of an enormous right-wing avalanche that might well have completely reshaped the landscape of Italian politics. The rightists were able to mobilize vast support for three large organizations: the regionalist *Lega Nord* (Northern League), the neo-fascist *Alleanza Nazionale* (National Alliance), and the broad-based *Forza Italia!* (Go Italy!) led by the super-wealthy industrialist Silvio Berlusconi. Running a slick "anti-politics" campaign hostile to the discredited state system but still dedicated to "free-market" capitalism and a renewal of traditional values, this ideologically seductive yet fragile coalition won 366 seats in the 630-seat Chamber of Deputies (compared to 213 seats for the left). Such a stunning turn of events, made possible in part by the new American-style winner-take-all electoral arrangement, enabled Berlusconi to become Prime Minister within a month of the elections. While the old parties were thoroughly discredited in the wake of a massive 21-month corruption scandal implicating more than 3000 politicians, government officials, and business leaders, the right offered the glimpse of a rejuvenated social order and a new way of doing business; the left, for its part, suffered because it was still viewed by a majority of the electorate as hopelessly compromised with the past—not only ideologically but in its turgid style of political discourse and action. The PDS call for a "government of reconstruction" during the election campaign actually recalled earlier structural reformist slogans that were all too closely associated with an outmoded communist left. The triumph of image and spectacle in Italian politics, moreover, could only have favored the right with its preponderant control of financial resources and the mass media.

The sad irony for the left was that its most impressive electoral turnout since the mid-1970s could not be translated into national power. At the same time, it is important to ask what the historical significance of a left victory might have been in this context. Despite the deep political malaise in Italy, the left failed to present anything resembling an oppositional agenda. Thus the PDS, still fervently trying to distance itself from communism and the Soviet model, embraced the most neo-liberal of agendas: a mixed economy with a heavy dose of privatization, a pro-American foreign policy, full and uncritical acceptance of the European Community, worship of economic modernization with its fetishism of technology and material values. A pervasive technocratic ethos had overtaken the leadership of the PDS and most other groups in the left alliance. Obsession with institutional stability and economic growth—a legacy of structural reformism—might be compatible with electoral success, along with some reforms here and there, but the ideology contains little that would subvert or frighten the dominant interests. So the post-communist left, in Italy as in other European countries, seemed to have abandoned even that modest anti-system politics embraced by third-road models of the 1970s and 1980s.

6

SOCIALIST DECLINE AND THE RADICAL CHALLENGE

By the 1990s, little more than a century after its birth, the political legacy of modern socialism has essentially run its course: social democracy, communism, and successive efforts to achieve a "third path" all failed to move industrial society toward the Marxian vision of an egalitarian, democratic order. The socialist project has always been directed toward deep historical change: the abolition of classes and capitalist division of labor, workers' self-management, decommodification of production and social services, and socialization of public life. In its most utopian moments, this ideal embraced a thorough democratization of both state and civil society, institutional and cultural life. Twentieth-century reality, however, has produced some rude awakenings—Communist regimes crumbling under the weight of their own bureaucratic morass; Socialist parties and governments retreating toward neo-liberal celebration of the "free market," reprivatization, and austerity policies; and Third World forays into socialism obliterated by the relentless economic and political pressures of the world capitalist system. The final eclipse of Bolshevism that came with the downfall of the Soviet model symbolizes the end of an era, where "socialism" wound up being equated with an economics of growth and a politics of statism.

For a many years it has been obvious that the only transformative agenda that stands a reasonable chance of success, particularly in the industrialized countries, is designed around a radical-democratic extension of collective and cooperative forms in all spheres of life. If this is so, then it is necessary to fully dispel a whole set of promises inherited from the socialist tradition: its discursive universality, its identification with single classes and parties, its premise of a simple representation of (economic) interests, its blindness to multiple forms of domination, its unbridled productivism in a world of ecological limits. Indeed, the very aim of a unified socialist worldview, or politics, may be hopeless in a postmodern age where the reproduction of dispersed social interests, agencies, identities, and meanings holds sway on a global level. The historical vision of "socialism" as a teleological end may well have lost its once powerful theoretical and political attraction, never to be revived again by efforts to correct or reconstitute organizational forms, leadership, strategy or tactics.

The long historic struggle for a radically transformed society—for a truly liveable planet—is now compelled to move in the direction of new practices, meanings, identities and even labels beyond those associated with failed legacies of the past. Of course, the obsolescence of previous formulas does not mean that such history can simply be forgotten. On the contrary, important lessons can always be drawn from earlier failures, and, any new "syntheses" will have to build upon the best of what went before. Any unifying or "globalizing" element of the future will probably have to emerge within the *subjective* realm, around the motifs of ideology, culture, collective identities, and politics, rather than around imputed sociological categories of class, status, or material interests. Where plural identities, outlooks, and interests exist, as in the postmodern context, the only real basis of unity is likely to be a firm oppositional stance around general but nonetheless radical goals (full democratization, social wage, ecological sustainability), as Alain Touraine has suggested.[1] From this standpoint, the key issue for a post-Marxist politics may be the most difficult and critical of all: how to effectively subvert the modes of legitimation that have kept the structures of domination in place for so long. The deep and lingering malaise of contemporary politics, with its pervasive sense of powerlessness, cynicism, alienation, and loss of citizenship,[2] therefore becomes a focal point of radical-democratic renewal, since it is upon the revival of collective subjectivity that hopes for global change will depend.

Socialist decline is rooted in this catastrophic loss of agency: the old models could never effectively challenge powerful forms of ideological hegemony bolstered by corporatist integration, pluralist democracy, and technocracy, nor did they offer a democratizing alternative. As Joseph Femia observes, this recurrent problem is closely bound up with a Marxist tradition that, ironically enough, devalues the realm of politics. Thus,

"While Marxists tirelessly decry the hypocrisy and deficiencies of 'bourgeois' democracy, they have expended much less ink and energy on the development of a feasible alternative…. Such reticence owes much to the inescapable logic of economic determinism. If the mode of political life essentially reflects the material conditions of existence, then the classic political problems of power and authority are of secondary importance. Why devote attention to surface phenomena which only rarely affect the underlying reality?"[3]

Yet the decline of socialist politics is also, and more profoundly, a function of the crisis of modernity that is the inescapable fate of all industrialized societies. The growing contradictions of a gigantic capitalist technostructure bent on ever-expanded production and consumption, on growth-for-growth's-sake, on bureaucratic rationalization, on the domination of nature—all encased in a "normal" politics of electoral competition—cannot be separated from an understanding of the predicament of traditional leftism. If Enlightenment rationality bequeathed such contradictions in a fragile world of limits, it simultaneously brought into question the subversive role of political parties, trade unions, class agencies, and "scientific" discourses tied to the familiar modernizing schemas. All previously "successful" models of socialist transformation ultimately reproduced, in one fashion or another, a rationalizing and institutionalizing logic that underpinned ideological degeneration.

Dramatic changes in the postwar global economy have only exacerbated this logic. The remarkable growth of transnational corporations, and with it new levels of capital mobility, along with the international communications revolution, feeds into and accelerates strongly conflicting tendencies within modernity, transforming the very parameters of anti-system movements. One result is the weakening of single nation-states, parties, and classes as efficacious actors for change on the world scene. The transfigured global order is beset with its own crises stemming from national economic rivalries, massive uneven development between North and South, perpetuation of militarism, and ecological devastation. By the 1990s material, political, and cultural processes have become so globally intertwined that conventional Marxist assumptions about class struggles leading to anti-capitalist shifts in social and power relations of specific national regimes are now obsolete. If the post-Cold War historical conjuncture, owing to its explosive contradictions, refuses the easy triumph of a new world order on the basis of liberal capitalist hegemony, so too does it militate against prospects for a worldwide Marxist or socialist revival.[4]

At the same time, socialist decline should not be confused with the death of radical politics *tout court* or the exhaustion of leftist possibilities in a world of sharpening human misery and social polarization, of increasing authoritarian power that more often blocks democratic participation than not. Rather, the ebbing of socialist prospects might well clear new space for innovative theoretical and political departures, expanding upon a process that has been underway for at least three decades. The eclipse of traditional party-centered, hierarchical, and productivist models of change may represent the end of one epoch and the beginning of another in which elements of a radical-democratic alternative might finally galvanize political opposition. Such an alternative will probably transcend the boundaries of any single "model"; indeed, it will necessarily encompass multiple "alternatives," in contrast to the universalist aspirations of the organized socialist tradition. Yet such new departures will not spring up *de novo*, from an ideological vacuum: they have deep roots, as we have seen, in the European radical legacy going back to the syndicalists and council communists, and extending through Western Marxism, critical theory, and the resurgence of new oppositional currents since the 1960s.

The Radical Left: Survival and Rebirth

Except for a few isolated insurrections, radical-left politics from the 1920s to the 1960s was obliterated first by either fascism or Stalinism and then, especially after World War II, by the Keynesian-engineered welfare state. During this period, radical *theory* at least was kept alive by the stubborn persistence of Western Marxism and critical theory that derived much of its impetus from the neo-Hegelian revival of the early 1920s. Despite enormous internal differences, this current stood as a lonely but sometimes powerful voice against the bureaucratization of socialist and liberal politics both East and West. Against the truncated positivist Marxism of Soviet elites known as "dialectical materialism," with its emphasis on scientific laws and economic determinism, Western Marxism upheld a more open, eclectic, *critical* theory which seemed to be more compatible with the massive historical changes underway in Europe.

This "Western" alternative in fact originated in the work of diverse theorists before World War I, including Antonio Labriola, Gustav Landauer, Georges Sorel, Anton Pannekoek, and even anarchists like Sergei Kropotkin and Emma Goldman. It was extended during and after the war by some of the great luminaries of twentieth-century Marxism—Rosa Luxemburg, Karl Korsch, Georg Lukács, Antonio Gramsci, Wilhelm Reich, representatives of the early Frankfurt School, Herbert Marcuse, Erich Fromm, existential Marxists like Sartre, and early post-Marxists like Cornelius Castoriadis and André Gorz. What these theorists shared was a deep view of social transformation incorporating a fuller understanding of mass consciousness and collective subjectivity than was possible within orthodox Marxism. What this meant, above all, was an engagement with motifs that scarcely figured in the rigid framework of historical materialism: ideology, culture, psychology, everyday life. Proceeding from a heightened sensitivity to generalized forms of domination (bureaucracy, the authoritarian state, the culture industry, the patriarchal family), Western Marxism addressed revolutionary change as a function of deep transformations within civil society rather than of "objective" contradictions and crisis tendencies within capitalism as such. The explosive antagonisms between two rival classes, between proletariat and bourgeoisie, could not be expected to produce cataclysmic upheavals leading to socialism by itself; modernity introduced far more complex mediations and processes of change. In contrast to orthodox Marxism, which saw class consciousness as building naturally out of material forces, the neo-Hegelian tendency assumed that subversive consciousness—not a monopoly of the working class—was a matter of ongoing social *construction* within every realm of human existence.

Western Marxism, therefore, did not readily accept the hollow thesis of proletarian revolution: in Gramscian terms, workers were commonly victims of bourgeois hegemony—a dominant system of values, beliefs, attitudes, and myths reproduced through a variety of ideological and cultural mediations. The postwar failure of revolution in the West was understood as an historical *process* rather than as the more mechanistic betrayal of leaders, incorrect strategic decisions, or uncontrollable "external" forces. In the absence of capitalist laws of motion leading to crisis and transition, history was seen as an open-ended, relatively indeterminate flow of social forces with variable possible outcomes. Still committed to some variant of (democratic) socialism, Western Marxists believed that transformative ideals could be realized only when subordinate groups begin to penetrate the veil of ideological domination—"reification" for Lukács, "hegemony" for Gramsci, social and sexual repression for Reich, "technological rationality" for Marcuse. This was emphatically a matter of recovering a sense of collective self-activity in a world where ideological manipulation and control were becoming more visible. As Marcuse put it, "[T]he question once again must be faced: how can the administered individuals—who have made their mutilation into their own liberties and satisfactions, and thus reproduce it on an enlarged scale—liberate themselves from themselves as well as from their masters? How is it even thinkable that the vicious circle be broken?"[5]

Of course, the class dimension was never entirely discarded, and for some—Lukács and Gramsci, for example—it remained a central preoccupation. The emphasis on the social construction of reality and popular struggle within civil society led, predictably enough, to an embrace of cultural transformations, local autonomy, and democratic forms of self-management as the guiding motifs of revolutionary politics. Drawing from such diverse traditions as Hegelian philosophy, Freudian psychoanalysis, Weberian sociology, and some aspects of "existential" theory, Western Marxism was able to carve out an ideological (though clearly not political) presence outside and against both social democracy and communism well into the 1960s. To be sure, a variety of other currents—Trotskyism, anarchism, surrealism—helped, at different times, to keep the radical-left tradition alive. But the historical importance of Western Marxism cannot be stressed enough, for it served as a vital connecting link to post-Marxist currents that came later: the European extra-parliamentary opposition, the new left, new social movements, the Greens.

One theorist who personified this intellectual struggle was Cornelius Castoriadis, a co-founder of the seminal group *Socialisme o Barbarie* in the late 1940s and architect of a legacy that passed through many influences, from Marxism and council communism through Trotskyism and the new left. With Claude Lefort and others, he laid the groundwork (often under the pseudonyms Paul Cardan and Pierre Chaulieu) for a devastating leftist critique of Marxism many years before such assessments became popular in France, and well before left intellectuals in the U.S. had even discovered Marxism. In the spirit of European precursors like Luxemburg, Pannekoek, and Gramsci, Castoriadis was always driven by one passionate and overriding concern: the goal of socialist revolution as the culmination of mass self-activity.[6]

His analysis of bureaucratic rationalization, inspired by a reading of Weber and Merleau-Ponty, led Castoriadis to the conclusion that the underlying tendencies at work in the industrialized countries, both East and West, contrasted dramatically with what Marx had projected. Indeed, Castoriadis came to see bureaucracy itself as an all-encompassing phenomenon that would eventually dominate every aspect of social life and thus would, unless somehow reversed, obliterate the possibility of a critical mass consciousness.

If Marx reduced bureaucracy to the sphere of class relations, Castoriadis insisted that it develops according to its own logic of domination, in which the division between "directors" and "executants" reproduces itself independent of the forces of production. With advancing levels of industrialization, bureaucracy comes to embody the natural tendency of modern economies toward concentration of capital and power. In the West, Castoriadis wrote, "Capitalism has exhausted its historical role. It can go no further. It has created an international, rationalized, and planned economic structure, thus making it possible for the economy to be directed consciously and for social life to be directed freely."[7]

Castoriadis's hostility toward bureaucracy forced him to reject Soviet communism as well as Western capitalism; to be meaningful, revolution would have to come from below, through the autonomous struggles of the working class. Following Trotsky, he believed that the novel appearance of Stalinist bureaucracy had reversed every social gain of the Bolshevik Revolution. But whereas Trotsky argued that the USSR was a deformed workers' state that, with a return to Leninist leadership, could resume its socialist course, Castoriadis held that this "deformation" was permanent insofar as the bureaucracy (or party state) constituted an entirely new exploitative class system of its own. Against Trotsky's view that the Bolsheviks had overthrown capitalism with the introduction of collective property relations and centralized planning, Castoriadis insisted that the entire Soviet model—beginning with Lenin's vanguard party—created a form of bureaucratic domination *sui generis*. Stalinism was ultimately destined to carry out those functions associated with the rise of capitalism in the West: a distinct class system prevailed in each case even if its *form* (bureaucratic vs. market) differed profoundly.

Castoriadis's critical outlook led him to discard Marxism itself as the privileged theory of social change. It was clear to him by the late 1940s that Marxism had failed to exert itself creatively into the political context of France or elsewhere. Far from being a matter of theoretical nuance or adaptation to new historical conditions, the deficiencies of Marxism went to the very core of the theory itself—its scientific pretensions, its crude determinism, its productivism, its false claim to totality. The idea of a definitive, all-embracing theory was nothing but the fantasy of bureaucratic elites. By the 1950s Marxism had become a *conservative* theory: it did not transcend but actually *reflected* the categories of capitalist political economy, ending up as an ideological barrier to fundamental change. This critique of Marxism was not entirely original; it was, as we have seen, a staple of earlier radical traditions. What Castoriadis did, however, was forge the kind of eclectic *gauchisme* that would later feed into the explosive anti-authoritarian impulses of the 1960s. Disdaining reliance upon sacred texts, he sought to piece together the constituent elements of a post-Marxist theory appropriate to the phase of bureaucratic expansion in both the East and West.

The revolution Castoriadis and the *Socialism or Barbarism* group had in mind would lead to a system of self-managed workers' councils that would democratically transform both the economy and the state, abolishing social hierarchy in all spheres of life. Workers' struggles at the base would unleash the enormous creative power of the masses to make history against the claims and dictates of elites. Thus, "The goal of the socialist revolution must be the abolition of all fixed and stable distinctions between directors and executants in relation to both production and social life in general."[8] The insurgent consciousness and energy of the masses must be perpetually opposed to all established structures, leading to a "permanent self-institution of society" that would unfold outside and against the governing apparatus.[9]

Castoriadis often referred to the 1956 Hungarian Revolution as a model of this type of democratic socialist insurgency; it embodied the substance and form of workers' control directed against the Communist apparatus while offering a concrete alternative to bureaucratic rule. The Hungarian events, though short-lived, embodied the "clearest and highest expression of the tendencies and goals of the workers in our epoch. Its significance is utterly universal."[10] In Hungary, as in Germany, Italy, and Spain during the 1920s and 1930s, the structural basis of revolt was the factory councils as militant expressions of popular self-management. Castoriadis wrote that "to achieve the widest, the most meaningful direct democracy will require that all the economic, political and other structures of society be based on local groups that are concrete collectives, organic social units."[11] Reconstituted on new terrain, politics is accordingly diffused throughout civil society to the extent that "this network of general assemblies and councils is all that is left of the state or of power in a socialist society. It is the *whole* state and the *only* embodiment of power. There are no other institutions that could manage, direct, or make binding decisions about peoples' lives."[12]

Workers' struggles to overcome their alienation inevitably bring them into conflict with the imperatives of bureaucratic domination. Initially, Castoriadis viewed revolution as a process evolving organically out of the conditions of everyday proletarian life, much as Gramsci viewed the factory councils in Italy; capitalism generates the seeds of its own transcendence.

The *Socialism or Barbarism* group had taken an optimistic stance from its inception until the late 1950s, when the theme of depoliticization began to enter its discourse. In France as elsewhere in the West, large sectors of the labor movement were becoming domesticated—a phenomenon reflected in the deradicalization of both Socialist and Communist parties. Here Castoriadis referred to the dismal spectre of "so-called socialist parties participating in bourgeois governments, actively repressing strikes or movements of colonial peoples and championing the defense of the capitalist fatherland while neglecting even to make reference to a socialist system of rule."[13] With the goal of revolutionary change still so closely tied to the fate of the industrial proletariat, optimism readily gave way to pessimism and a sense of defeat, which in the end contributed to the collapse of *Socialism or Barbarism.*[14]

From the 1940s to the 1960s Castoriadis was clearly a powerful voice of theoretical renewal on the left, at a time when mainstream Marxism had reached its limit. He helped to keep alive the radical spirit through the decades when it appeared to have been crushed. At the same time, while Castoriadis strove mightily to distance himself from orthodox Marxism, his work nonetheless carried forward strong residues of the classical theory: centrality of the industrial proletariat as the agent of change, a focus on class struggle at the point of production, the primacy of material forces in history, and so forth. As he put it in 1960, "The fundamental contradictions of capitalism are to be found in production and work."[15] While he paid lip service to the role of social forces outside the sphere of production (for example, youth, minorities, women), he never incorporated these forces into a general understanding of social change. Still attached to traditional forms of class struggle, Castoriadis failed to explore the complex elements of social structure (beyond bureaucracy) or popular consciousness that mediate political conflict in the industrialized setting. Thus, while critical theorists of the Frankfurt School had already begun to explore mediations of this sort (the family, culture industry, mass media, education), these phenomena received surprisingly little attention in Castoriadis's work.

A related problem is that Castoriadis, while anticipating the new left critique of bureaucracy and its celebration of direct democracy, fell short of analyzing bureaucratic rationalization in relation to class forces and other forms of domination (including the state). Sweeping references to "the bureaucracy" and workers' struggles against bureaucratic rule, whether in the Soviet bloc or the West, suggest a rather mechanistic model of conflict and change, overlooking not only the intricate relationship between state and civil society but also the very differentiated character of bureaucracy itself. Large-scale organization turns out to be far more complex than Castoriadis assumed.

This raises a more general difficulty symptomatic of the *gauchiste* tendency: Insofar as socialist revolution was understood as a process whereby the goodness and vitality of civil society is counterposed to the tyrannical incursions of state power, political strategy is reduced to a spontaneist validation of local struggles, and little more. Indeed, Castoriadis offers hardly anything that might pass for a coherent strategy, an affliction that would persist throughout most of post-Marxist theory and practice from the 1960s onward. In his anxiety to sidestep the authoritarian outcomes of both social democracy and Leninism, Castoriadis fell into the same trap that immobilized the radical left. Rather than engaging the state system with the aim of democratically transforming it, he largely ignored it on the assumption that the spread of local councils would eventually force the state to crumble from its own historical obsolescence. Even granting the importance of such organs of popular control, this "strategy" is hopelessly inadequate in confronting the pervasive nature of state power in modern society.

While Castoriadis's contributions to the radical tradition were perhaps the most politically incisive during this period, they actually paralleled the evolution of *gauchiste* thought in France associated with Jean-Paul Sartre, Henri LeFebvre, and the *Arguments* group. More significantly, his work—despite its various shortcomings—anticipated the later revival of European radicalism: the "extraparliamentary opposition"; new working-class currents reflected in the work of André Gorz, Alain Touraine, and Serge Mallet, the postmodernism of Jean Baudrillard, Michel Foucault, and others, and the new social movement theorizing of Touraine.

An Extraparliamentary Radicalism?

The historical trajectory that moves from Western Marxism and the *gauchiste* critique to the more mature expressions of post-Marxist radicalism in the 1970s and 1980s inevitably passes through the explosive May 1968 Events in France. Perhaps the most cataclysmic moment in the global emergence of new left politics, the May Events proved to be a catalyst of the European extra-parliamentary opposition that reached its peak in France and Italy in the decade that followed.

More than anything, May 1968 represented a comprehensive social upheaval against the old forms of domination—capitalist, bureaucratic, cultural—and the values holding those forms together. The revolt began innocently enough, as a student protest carried out by the March 22nd Committee at Nanterre University on the outskirts of Paris. Bitter confrontations with university and local officials ensued, giving rise to a militant wave of struggles that spread throughout Paris. Within days a full-scale uprising was underway, involving student strikes, demonstrations mobilizing tens of thousands, university occupations, and massive street fighting that continued for most of May. Strike activity extended from the schools and streets to factories and offices, culminating in a general strike that engulfed not only Paris but the rest of France. Diverse constituencies were mobilized, well beyond the limits of normal politics, around distinctly *general* issues: the claim to rule, quality of work, character of education, cultural values. When the dust had settled in mid-June, France had come the closest of any advanced industrial country to a revolutionary overthrow of the power structure.

The May upheaval was clearly a *gauchiste* event that exploded beyond the perimeters of conventional politics. As Daniel Singer observed, it was of a cultural revolution precisely in the sense that it "fitted a revolt against a way of life, a social organization, a civilization."[16] It was, moreover, a democratic rebellion in the fullest and deepest sense: "The violent French outburst against the crippling society, however incoherent, was a reminder that millions of people are not resigned to having no share in the shaping of their own lives."[17] Although the events were marked by their outrageous spontaneity, the radical-left presence in the intellectual figures of Sartre, Gorz, and Castoriadis could easily be detected. From Sartre came the collective "existential" struggle to overcome alienation in a corrupt bureaucratic society. From Gorz and the new working class-theorists came the theme of total resistance linking immediate material demands with universal social and cultural goals, proletarian opposition with the strivings of progressive groups within the middle strata. From Castoriadis, as we have seen, came the famous critique of everyday life that was a hallmark of the May Events, along with an emphasis on popular self-management and institutions of dual power.

The French explosion, which seemed to follow its own compelling (yet ultimately self-destructive) logic, was a decidedly non-Marxist phenomenon that was far more urban spectacle than class struggle. In a country where the left was long dominated by the Communists and Socialists, stale proletarian formulas were rudely tossed aside in favor of fresh initiatives and experiences; the realm of party organizations, leaders, platforms, and strategies had little meaning for the assembled masses. This was the first widespread revolt to shake the foundations of a *modern* order and articulate the meaning of new forms of conflict and opposition in advanced capitalism. The events opened up a new phase of radicalism in the West, affirming the universal significance of a new left. In George Katsiaficas's words, "At the same time that the French movement was the *product* of global forces, it also acted as a *producer* of the worldwide turmoil of 1968. The May Events were internationally significant since the vast majority of the working class in France, unlike their peers in other industrialized countries, joined with the students and nearly made a revolution." Moreover, the insurgency "brought new forms of social organization into existence. A vision of the future where nations, hierarchies of domination, boredom, toil, and human fragmentation no longer would exist came to light during the general strike."[18]

Within several weeks the May insurrection ran up against the limits of its own spontaneity; refusal to enter the realm of normal politics had its price—in this case failure. Arthur Hirsch writes that "May was a revolution of consciousness without a revolution of structure, a cultural revolution without a political revolution."[19] Certainly, failure had much to do with the relentless and often hysterical opposition of the French Communists to what was happening—as well as to De Gaulle's skillful manipulation of the events, which enabled the power structure to reconstitute itself. But political success was never possible under any conditions given the movement's ideological and organizational diffuseness and, above all, its lack of coherent *strategy*. At least in Paris, the center of rebellion was the local and highly dispersed action committees. According to Daniel Cohn-Bendit, "They showed how simple it is to bypass the trade union and political bosses, how workers can spontaneously unite in action, without a 'vanguard' or a party."[20] True enough, but they were never able to create an alternative program and strategy that could supersede the obsolete models. In sum, the May Events incorporated both the strengths and weaknesses of French *gauchisme* to the fullest extent. If the insurgents were not able to conquer power and change society, they did offer a vision of a new era—and an inspiration for a rapidly growing extra-parliamentary opposition in other parts of the world.

Nowhere was this opposition stronger than in Italy, where the political upsurge of diverse groups—students, intellectuals, factory and technical workers—was in full swing by the late 1960s. The May upheaval in France served as a catalyst, in particular furnishing the spark that set off Italy's "hot autumn" of 1969, when mobilization of students and workers around a general strike nearly led to a duplication of the French events. Splintered and diffuse, the Italian *nuova sinistra* actually originated in the early 1960s when leftist opposition, defined mainly as "pro-Chinese," developed outside and against the deradicalized Communist and Socialist parties. By 1969 scores of new political groups to the left of the PCI appeared, with the typical accompaniment of newspapers, journals, and pamphlets representing a wide range of opinions; the number of active supporters of these groupings was estimated at two to three million. Spanning the ideological spectrum from Maoism to anarchism, the nascent extra-parliamentary left held a few basic ideas in common: revolution must be a deep process of social and cultural transformation; its center of gravity should be outside the sphere of conventional politics, with an orientation toward new structures of popular control; and the transition to an egalitarian, democratic order would be less a matter of economic crisis than of conscious, imaginative, and bold political activity. These ideas naturally brought the new groups into a head-on confrontation with the traditional left, giving rise to a period of intense ideological conflict around definitions of change, socialism, and revolution.[21]

The Italian student movement, at times the backbone of the new left, grew out of a critique of the elitist university system; it began with the Trento protests in 1965 and reached a peak during occupations at the Universities of Turin and Rome in 1968–69. Students, youth, and intellectuals played a catalytic role in the "hot autumn" explosions, much as student radicalism was a detonator for May 1968 in France. Central to the student movement in Italy, as elsewhere, was its attack on authoritarianism in all areas of life: the university and high schools, government, the Church, the family, and, of course, established leftist organizations like the PCI and PSI. This element of youth politics often took on anarchistic overtones, rendering unified collective action difficult if not impossible.

The largest student organization was the Milan-based *Lotta Continua*, which sustained an extra-parliamentary presence through the 1970s. Like other sectors of the radical left, it was loosely organized around small units, coming together only for mass actions and occasional conferences. For several years its overriding goal was to forge an "organic alliance" between students and workers, in which each group would concentrate on building its own struggles while uniting for common action—a *modus operandi* that ran counter to the old idea of university radicals going out to "organize" workers at the factory gates of Fiat or Pirelli. New left workers' organizations such as *Potere Operaio* (Workers' Power) and *Avanguardia Operaio* (Workers' Vanguard), while more tightly organized and disciplined than student groups, also looked to bypass the large parties and unions in favor of local forms such as the *comitati di base* (committees of the base) that had proliferated in factories throughout the north.[22] The *comitati* provided an arena in which workers could advance *control* issues and mount direct action tactics (sit-ins, organized slow-downs, wildcat strikes, street actions). But such committees, which recalled the factory council movement of an earlier era, either disappeared or became co-opted by the mid-1970s.

With few exceptions, groups within the Italian *nuova sinistra* gravitated toward the Chinese as opposed to the Soviet (and, of course, social-democratic) outlook: an emphasis on "cultural revolution," local democratic forms, and insurrectionary politics, rather than the "peaceful road to socialism." In the period 1968–1970 there was also widespread enthusiasm, among the most militant groups, for some strategy of armed revolutionary struggle inspired by the Maoist experience—a tendency prefiguring the later appearance of terrorist organizations like *Brigate Rosse* (the Red Brigades) and their support network *Autonomia*. Among other things, Maoism offered a thoroughgoing critique of the Soviet model and an inspiration for a more dynamic, creative Marxian socialism.[23] From the vantage point of that period, the Chinese road appealed to the extra-parliamentary left because it represented a systematic attack on the bastions of authoritarianism and elitism, concerns that were rarely taken up by European communists and social democrats. In its obsession with anti-bureaucratic struggles, Maoism often encouraged the spontaneism of the new left, where a strong attachment to the theories of Rosa Luxemburg, Rudi Dutschke, and Daniel Cohn-Bendit had already developed.

The cult of spontaneity, along with the disaggregation and semi-isolation of radical groups, hampered the maturation of the Italian *nuova sinistra* into a strategically effective movement. One side of Maoism was a sectarianism that hindered the search for an efficacious theory and politics appropriate to peculiarly European conditions. Indeed, the "Chinese" alternative often consisted of leftists mechanically repeating Maoist ideas as no more than exercises in simple repetition or scholastic purity, detached from any social context. One effort to synthesize new left tendencies into a unified extra-parliamentary formation was undertaken in 1969 by a group of Marxist intellectuals, many of them emigrés from the PCI, who founded *Il Manifesto* with the aim of creating a new "historical bloc" of social forces in Italy.

The guiding vision of *Il Manifesto*, beginning with the first publication of its journal in June 1969, was a small faction of PCI militants expelled from the party for oppositional activities in November 1969. They included Lucio

Magri, Rossana Rossanda, Aldo Natoli, Luigi Pintor, and Massimo Caprara, who at different points were joined by other prominent Marxists within and outside the PCI. They shared a radical critique of the PCI's structural reformism and its attachment to the Soviet Union, from which they set out to develop a new strategy relevant to the conditions of advanced capitalism—one that could furnish points of convergence for the new left. Within a few years a dynamic new radicalism was moving toward consensus by means of work being carried out in dozens of "Manifesto centers" throughout Italy; the key challenge was to lay the foundations of a truly mass-based socialist revolution in the West. It was Magri, deriving inspiration from Gramsci, who soon emerged as the leading theorist of the group. In a series of articles published in *Il Manifesto*, he called for a rejuvenated Marxism transcending the reformist economism of the traditional left, the anarchistic spontaneism of the new left, and the Jacobin-style elitism of the vanguard party.[24] As Magri and his comrades viewed it, the PCI's failure to sustain revolutionary politics stemmed from its inability to counter the enormous power of bourgeois hegemony in Italy, which in turn was a function of its narrow economism and parliamentarism. In the case of the student movement and the fragmented *groupuscules*, their spontaneism actually restricted the development of viable forms of collective power. As for Leninism, Magri saw great dangers in its reliance upon a vanguard of professional cadres because this heavy organizational presence undercuts popular energies and encourages the rise of new hierarchical structures.

The primary *Il Manifesto* assumption was that socialist revolution must be a profoundly democratic phenomenon, a process initiated and carried out by the masses themselves as they seek to break with established forms of domination. Change would pass through local organs of self-management (peoples' and workers' councils, action committees, cooperatives) that would constitute a system of "dual power" outside the existing state. But such embryonic forms were hardly enough: as the French events demonstrated, coordination and strategy must enter into the equation in order to build a framework of common action. For this a new type of party would be needed.

The *Il Manifesto* group wanted to replace the venerated Leninist concept of a vanguard party with that of a *mass* party—a sort of political bloc—grounded in a two-way linkage between constituent units and the larger structure, between popular organs and a central organization needed to provide a repository of theory and strategy. Following Gramsci, this meant a reshaping of the party's relationship to its mass base and external structures such as trade unions and coops; the connection would be more dialectical than the vanguard model. Furthermore, it meant far less preoccupation with the conquest of state power, in favor of transforming civil society along lines the of Gramsci's "war of position." In place of a cadre-based leadership there would be a more loosely defined "collective intellectual" comprised of representatives of *all* tendencies and staffed proportionately by leaders selected from their own constituencies on the basis of experience, knowledge, and familiarity with a specific discourse (around labor, education, women's issues, et cetera). The *Il Manifesto* vision was intended to furnish political coherence to what was a diffuse, atomistic, and often sectarian extra-parliamentary left, without at the same time obliterating local energies that were vital to its strength. The critical task was to forge an identity strong enough to provide a unifying strategy without destroying the popular, democratic character of its separate parts. This task, as it turned out, would not be an easy one.

The *Il Manifesto* quest for a new revolutionary synthesis broke down the traditional separation between pre- and post- insurrectionary change, between material and cultural phases of struggle, between the "war of position" and the "war of movement" in the Gramscian terminology. Given conditions of modernity and a diversified working class, as in most of Italy, it was necessary to spell out a new "point of convergence" for anti-capitalist forces around distinctly radical objectives. The left urgently needed an entirely reconstructed image of socialism that took into account the sphere of social relations, culture, and politics, as well as economic life.

Through the mid-1970s *Il Manifesto* remained a dynamic force within the Italian *nuova sinistra*; as a group, its efforts to articulate a renovated Marxist strategy for conditions of advanced capitalism were probably the most extensive of the period. The impact of *Il Manifesto* was felt much beyond its numbers, but within a few short years its role turned out to be far more intellectual than political. After publication of its "Theses" the group achieved a certain international status as architects of a neo-Gramscian theory,[25] but the goal of winning over a critical mass of Italian students and workers was never attained. For one thing, the extra-parliamentary left was beset with fragmentation, sectarianism, and localism—the same legacy that impeded the French movement. Further, *Il Manifesto* intellectuals did not generally come forth with effective *political* leadership in a way that could unify disparate tendencies. Equally important, the systematic assault on traditional social and authority relations that was so central to the group's theoretical initiatives did not become a significant priority for the *nuova sinistra*—even among groups stressing the role of "cultural revolution"—

until the rise of the feminist and ecology movements in the late 1970s.

Despite its flaws, the Italian extra-parliamentary opposition mobilized millions of people and left an indelible imprint on European politics: Above all it made a significant contribution in the global effort to create a transformative theory and practice grounded in the industrialized setting. Its "failure" must be situated in this context. As the introduction to the *Il Manifesto* "Theses" stated: "Strategy and organization cannot be simply the expression of a movement as it unfolds in action in one country at one particular historical moment. All this is the product of mediations between the present and past, between experiences derived from action and pre-existing theory in the course of struggles by the vanguard, the larger society, and the international movement."[26] Both the French and Italian *gauchistes* were in some measure heirs to the earlier radical-left tradition, with all of its tendencies toward dispersion and localism. Yet, as the experience of *Il Manifesto* shows, many groups never fully struggled free of the Marxist (or even Leninist) paradigm; witness the tortured vanguardism of many small Maoist and Trotskyist sects, not only in Italy but in France and elsewhere. As for *Il Manifesto*, it was a driving force behind the creation of PDUP (Democratic Party of Proletarian Unity) in 1972, whose idea, consonant with the group's outlook, was to establish a new revolutionary party committed to "democracy at the base" and a full break with the capitalist, bureaucratic system. PDUP promised a novel blend of electoral politics and grassroots activity, coordinated party strategy and local democracy, parliamentarism and mass mobilizations.

The leading figures of PDUP, while opposed to PCI strategy, argued that a broad left alternative in Italy would have to be erected around the Communists. (Extra-parliamentary groups like *Lotta Continua*, *Potere Operaio*, and *Avanguardia Operaio* maintained a firm rejectionist stance toward the PCI.) If the PCI could be pressured from the left, it might be forced to drop its *compromesso storico* tactics and move back into opposition. Given the depth of Communist deradicalization, however, this hope turned out to be an illusion. Running on a joint list with new leftists in 1976 and 1979, the PDUP was never able to win more than 1.5 percent of the vote. In 1983 it competed on a joint list with the PCI, by which time the struggling party had abandoned any pretenses of independence; during the 1980s most PDUP and *Il Manifesto* leaders had returned to the Communist fold, their presence never having gone much beyond their valuable intellectual work.

A more radical party, *Democrazia Proletaria* (DP), appeared in 1975 with the goal of carving out a dynamic sphere of extra-parliamentary opposition outside the PCI orbit. This effort, too, met with little success. Grounded in a more heterogeneous and militant assemblage of new leftists drawn from labor and the student movement, DP projected a revolutionary identity around which groups ranging from traditional Leninists to countercultural anarchists would be represented—an impossible vision, as it turned out. Running in its first three national elections (1976, 1979, and 1983), DP failed to win more than a half-million votes or return more than seven deputies to parliament. Although DP continued as a tiny radical party, by the early 1980s most *nuova sinistra* organizations had disappeared and the once hopeful extra-parliamentary opposition became little more than a historical memory; meanwhile the established left was able to reconsolidate its political position.

The eclipse of the Italian extra-parliamentary left was a function of several factors. Perhaps most important was the debilitating impact of left-wing terrorism in the late 1970s. Driven by a sense of political futility, thousands of radical activists were attracted to the ethos of armed struggle and a "strategy of tension" championed by underground groups such as the Red Brigades, Front Line, and the Armed Proletarian Nuclei. Supported by movement organizations like *Autonomia*, their strategy was to provoke class polarization and the collapse of system legitimacy that might open the floodgates of revolutionary insurgency.[27] Actions included bombings, kneecappings, and even murder of selected targets (including Prime Minister Aldo Moro in 1978). But the spread of violent tactics only served to bolster the ruling forces (including both the Christian Democrats and Communists) while demoralizing—and discrediting—the main new left tendencies. Even in the absence of a terrorist presence, however, the fate of extra-parliamentary radicalism surely would have turned out no different. Aside from its extreme fragmentation and spontaneism, the new left could never resolve its ambivalence concerning the vanguardist and hierarchical features of Marxism and Leninism: It was simultaneously Jacobin and democratic, workerist and countercultural, traditional and visionary. Meanwhile, not only the PCI and PSI but also the Greens and Radicals were able to siphon off this insurgent energy, or what remained of it, in the 1980s.

New Left as Counterculture: American Exceptionalism?

The familiar theme of "exceptionalism" in American history calls attention to the peculiar weakness of both Marxist theory and socialist politics in the U.S. throughout the twentieth century. Neither the Socialist Party (which reached its zenith before World War I) nor the Communist Party (which peaked in the 1930s) were able to establish a durable presence in either social movements or the political system; labor unions and popular struggles have historically made their peace with liberal capitalism.[28] The radical and Marxist intellectual culture has always been a marginalized force. During the postwar years Keynesian welfare state capitalism—combined with the permanent war economy—achieved seemingly unassailable hegemony. Since the time of Werner Sombart's original analysis of U.S. political idiosyncracies,[29] a good many reasons have been cited for this state of affairs: the extraordinary strength of American liberal ideology (owing mainly to the absence of feudalism), the open expanse of the frontier, widespread affluence, a divided working class owing to racism and immigration, and the uniquely deradicalizing consequences of the single-member winner-take-all electoral system. More recently, ideological closure resulting from Cold War consensus and corporatist integration has been identified as a key factor in the narrowing of real differences between Republicans and Democrats and the absence of any significant left formation in U.S. politics. American political culture has been fiercely utilitarian, competitive, individualistic, and, in its oppositional moments, also localist and populist.[30] Insofar as "socialism" was never widely considered a thinkable goal in American discourse, the progressive ideal was generally to create a more humane and liveable capitalism.

Popular struggles in the U.S., therefore, typically resisted the lexicon of fundamental change, class conflict, and insurrection; they have opted instead for either localist solutions or the normal routines of electoral campaigns, legislative reforms, and interest group politics. The search for radical alternatives on a national scale—or even a European-style social democracy—has been repeatedly frustrated.[31] If common patterns of social and political life today in the industrialized countries have begun to obscure the key features of U.S. exceptionalism, vast differences remain, and these differences help to explain the uniquely explosive, countercultural, and even populist character of the American new left. While "socialism" has been received quite differently in the U.S. than elsewhere, so too has the radical challenge.

Until the late 1980s the historical judgment passed on the American new left was a rather harsh one. Many critics, both left and right, viewed it as at best utopian, irrational, and reckless, at worst crude, violent, and willfully destructive. Most agreed that it amounted to something of a temporary childish phase of rebellion—the impetuous acting out of immature youths who, saturated with drugs, sex, rock music, and mysticism, were destined to self-destruct in a frenzy of rage, hedonism, and fanaticism.[32] New leftists were often described as self-righteous, dogmatic, and narcissistic. Verdicts of this sort were regular fare not only among mainstream writers like Lewis Feuer, Seymour Martin Lipset, Daniel Bell, Christopher Lasch, and Allan Bloom, but also among academic Marxists and traditional leftists who saw the sixties as an infantile distraction from the "real" world of class struggle, economic crisis, and struggle for state power.

Recent historical interpretations suggest that, on the contrary, new left politics was shaped by one overarching theme from beginning to end, from the civil rights movement to early SDS (Students for a Democratic Society) to the Columbia University uprising to the Yippie phase: the commitment to participatory democracy. What connected everything was a passionately anti-authoritarian ethos—a fascination with direct action, community, and self-activity that carried into virtually every arena of struggle. The sixties were marked by a utopian revival of democratic, popular, and even anarchist traditions that appealed especially to youth, students, and intellectuals. A widespread feeling was that utopian, communitarian ideals could be realized on a foundation of abundance that was already the heritage of American industrialism. The SDS, as James Miller shows, contained two broad impulses: a grassroots populism and civil rights empowerment.[33] Their *Port Huron Statement* embraced a Rousseauian fascination with direct democracy and social solidarity that, it was thought, could be achieved without confronting the power structure itself, exhibiting a naivete rarely visible in the European radical left. (In Europe democratic sensibilities generally embraced the more militant symbols of workers' control and autogestion.) Of course SDS was only a small part of the sixties panorama. There was also the counterculture, with its diffuse amalgam of cultural, political, and even spiritual influences that unfolded on an altogether different terrain: yippies, Diggers, communards, street people, and other marginalized elements of the youth scene immersed in alternative life-styles, theatrical politics, and revolt against leaders, heroes, and organizers. For many, cultural insurgency consisted of participation in "collective peak experiences."[34] The Berkeley Peoples' Park episode of May 1969 tapped these accumulated visions and sensibilities, and much more—including a turn toward "nature" and reclamation of public space consonant with the ideology of the later ecology movement. Indeed, countercultural motifs, reflected in such notions as the "Great Refusal" and consciousness transformation, seemed to permeate all movements of the time.

The sixties culture, in the U.S. as in Europe, was a fragmentary, pluralistic, and sometimes chaotic mosaic of rebellious impulses and currents that could never be incorporated into a single overarching "movement" of the sort identified with the Marxist left. In this sense, its embryonic postmodernism anticipated the later dispersion and localism of the new social movements. Yet the uniqueness of the American new left could not be denied. In Western Europe, as Ronald Fraser and David Caute stress, political history allowed for a rather different trajectory: an entrenched socialist tradition, where large social democratic and communist parties had long been fixtures of the system, meant that a more coherent revolutionary left could take shape, making possible (for a brief time) the coexistence of old and new lefts within the same movements.[35] But the European radicals, as we have seen, were hardly immune to the same centrifugal forces.

The *Port Huron Statement* was woven together on the basis of many influences that SDS activists believed would amount to a distinctly American radicalism. In it one could detect the influence of C. Wright Mills, Paul Goodman, Albert Camus, Erich Fromm, Allen Ginsberg, and Jack Kerouac.[36] SDS sought to transcend, however impressionistically, the limits of both liberalism and Marxism, indicating a restless, eclectic intellectual style and a willingness to experiment with new ideas. In contrast to their European conterparts, American new leftists had little respect for Marxism or Leninism—at least until the early 1970s. On the one hand, this meant a certain blindness to the past, to socialist history; on the other, it signified a healthy skepticism toward ritualized belief systems and correct ideological lines.

To a greater extent than in Europe, the new left in the U.S. derived its energy from the university campuses, which were, after all, a far more integral part of the social order. From the outset SDS and other groups assigned an important if not decisive role to students and intellectuals in the popular struggles of the time.[37] Ironically, it was the European new working-class theorists (Gorz, Touraine, and Mallet) who first systematically conceptualized the notion that the university was destined to be a dynamic center of radical initiatives in an increasingly complex capitalist society. Wedded to corporate and governmental priorities, yet the locus of a new generation of radical activists, the system of higher education was now more a site of ideological conflict and social transformation than an elite institution to be smashed. As the same time, new left emphasis on participatory democracy meant that intellectuals would not be welcomed in a Jacobin role; that model was too closely identified with the Marxist tradition and especially Leninist regimes.

International revolts in the 1960s, from France to Mexico, from Japan to the U.S., reflected a legitimation crisis that was probably as much cultural and political as economic. In the midst of chaos could be found a glimpse of a profoundly radical opposition, yet that opposition never generated an effective political assault on the bastions of power, in the U.S. or elsewhere. This was so for several reasons: failure to create durable forms of local organization; absence of a coherent ideology linking disparate groups and movements; fascination with dramatic, momentary actions at the expense of building institutions; fetishism of Third World models; and a base of support confined largely to campuses. In the end, the failure of the new left resulted from abandonment of three of its defining features—SDS as a national organization, the vision of revolutionary apocalypse, and the idea of a youth culture.[38]

In this context, it was hardly surprising that the American new left—again in contrast to its European counterparts—never really *attempted* to forge a social theory appropriate to its own experience. There was nothing in the U.S. resembling *Il Manifesto* or PDUP. (Of course, the nascent Marxist-Leninist currents like Progressive Labor and the Weathermen did offer a "theory," but one derived from external models.) Underlying the fiery rhetoric of total change was a spontaneism so strong that strategic thinking about social transformation (as opposed to mere tactical maneuvering) was virtually impossible. Nor did an imputed "global" solidarity furnish real answers: from issue to issue, from locale to locale, from country to country, each popular struggle went its own way.

While much of the American new left vanished or was left to atrophy, other parts—often shaped by a life-style-oriented countercultural ethic—persisted and even gained strength over time, although typically in new guise. The argument that sixties radicalism totally fell apart sometime between 1968 and 1970 was a myth. Amidst the turbulence of left sectarianism, organizational impasse, and a sometimes wildly self-indulgent counterculture, the "movement" was said by many (including sympathetic observers) to have disintegrated virtually overnight, giving way to co-optation, privatized forms of escape, religious cults, novel therapies, and (for some) return to traditional life-styles.[39] For example, Todd Gitlin found that with the passing of nationwide campus upheavals in May 1970 an "exhausted movement had lost its moral edge."[40] Government repression against the student, anti-war, and black liberation movements hurt, but the new left had in fact collaborated in its own demise; the dialectic of defeat was largely *internal*, an "implosion." Above all, SDS failed to supply the organization and leadership needed to keep centrifugal tendencies under control. Thus, "The riptide of the Revolution went out with the same force it had surged in with, the ferocious undertow proportionate to the onetime hopes."[41] Breakdown gave way to an incoherent "grab-bag of movements," a penchant for conventional life-styles, and the ubiquitous "transcendence industry."[42]

This "implosion" of the American new left, just when the European extra-parliamentary opposition was taking off, did reflect a building tension between the participatory impulse of the early SDS and the newly discovered vanguardism of the Marxist-Leninist groups. For one thing, the contempt that these groups had for "petty bourgeois" values, individualism, and formal democracy—not to mention the university setting itself—amounted to a rejection of the entire new left experience in favor of external constituencies (the proletariat, Third World peasants). The bankruptcy of sixties radicalism meant that it would be necessary to make a new start, inspired perhaps by Cuba or China or Vietnam. While in Europe radicals were struggling to confront or reshape the socialist tradition in different ways, in the U.S. vanguardism represented a facile solution to the chronic sixties quandary stemming from strategic confusion. The Marxist-Leninist response was to substitute organized cadres, party building, and "scientific" theory for the frustrating amorphousness of local struggles that seemed to lack political focus. The influence of Western Marxists and other theorists searching for a contemporary radical politics, grounded in conditions of advanced capitalism, was scarcely felt in the U.S.—until later, when the new left had ebbed.[43]

The desperate vanguardist search for political certainty in a chaotic world, however, turned out to be illusory. What Gitlin refers to as "pseudo-Leninism" was in reality a caricature of radicalism—indeed, a flight from politics—insofar as it rested upon a foundation of class guilt, name calling, and prefabricated phrases from other contexts substituting for genuine theory and practice. More than that, the Marxist-Leninist style of "desperado politics" was simply another expression of elitist arrogance toward the general population typical of the Jacobin style. At the same time, virtually *every* sixties current in the U.S. (yippies, SDS, Marxist-Leninist groups, the Weather Underground) shared the same afflictions. In various ways they had in common a romantic fascination with heroic vanguards; an organizational dilettantism that encouraged a scattered approach to politics; a detachment from local constituencies (except for students); the use of ritual phraseology in place of programmatic and strategic discourse. Moreover, it was relatively easy for activists to gravitate toward simplistic formulas readily available in orthodox Marxism, Leninism, and Maoism in the American setting where Marxism was so weak and the gulf separating "old" from "new" left was so vast.

In every case, when it came to pressing issues of long-term strategy there were surprisingly few statements or manifestos offering viable answers. (The *Port Huron Statement*, written in 1961, could not possibly have done this.) What were the main features of a rapidly changing social structure in advanced capitalism? What was the character of state power? What were the main forms of ideological control? How could a truly *new* left construct a bloc of forces around distinctly radical objectives? Indeed, what *were* the radical objectives? In Europe, as we have seen, major initiatives were undertaken toward achieving a radical synthesis appropriate to the modern context. But in the U.S. the new left responded to urgent political questions with silence, whereas the vanguard groups were content to apply formulas from another period (nineteenth century capitalism) or another geopolitical setting (Cuba, China, Vietnam, et cetera).

The disintegration of the new left phase of widespread popular revolt went much deeper than the collapse of SDS. Indeed, SDS was but a small, distorted part of the entire sixties scene, a kind of "young boys' network" increasingly cut off from the societal flow of energy and pressing concerns of students, youth, people of color, and women. The internal conflict within SDS was symptomatic of divisions within the entire new left, but it was only a single act in a whole drama. For better or worse, there was a rich multiplicity of realities that shaped insurgent activity during the sixties and later. In Wini Breines's words: "[T]here were many centers of action in the movement, many actions, many interpretations, many visions, many experiences. There was no unity because each group, region, campus, commune, collective, and demonstration developed differently, but all shared in a spontaneous opposition to racism and inequality, the war in Vietnam, and the repressiveness of American social norms and culture, including centralization and hierarchy."[44]

More significantly, the spirit of protest and revolt did not disappear with the death of SDS in 1969—nor with the Chicago events (at the Democratic Convention in 1968) or any other apocalyptic moment. The broader *meaning* of the new left cannot be grasped by a mechanistic "total break" thesis, according to which the "rebellious" sixties were immediately followed by the "passive" seventies, and that a failure of organizational resolve was at the center of this presumed collapse. What needs to be retained is a sense of history as *process* rooted in the unfolding of social forces, where past is connected to future, the sixties with the period that followed, the new left with the emergence of new social movements.

Despite their boundless energy, sixties movements were unable to consolidate local power bases; the dispersive force of spontaneism was far too powerful. A potential radical bloc existed, but lacking the necessary political translation it inexorably dissipated. The problem, however, was not the lack of centralized organization and leadership, nor was sectarianism the critical obstacle. For a new left that glorified participatory democracy and local community, no vanguard structure or leadership could have salvaged the radical initiatives of the moment, since the very effort to do so would have negated the essence of such initiatives. The disintegration of the new left, as it was conceived in the sixties, was a function of deeper problems at the level of theory and strategy: there was no overall sense of direction, blocked in part by the persistence of romantic fantasies and revolutionary visions unrelated to the actual forces at work. And this in turn could be partly attributed to the lingering influence of American exceptionalism.[45]

Still, in a relatively brief decade the new left ignited a phase of rebellion that touched the lives of millions in the U.S. alone. What then were the novel and enduring features of sixties radicalism? Beyond immediate tangible achievements—helping to force the U.S. military out of Indochina, pressing for social reforms and affirmative action, democratizing many institutions—what was truly original and significant about the new left? Tom Hayden argues that the period was unique precisely in its call for a politics of identity and authenticity that could no longer be expressed within either the liberal or socialist traditions.[46] Gitlin suggests that the peculiar blend of politics and culture—especially in music but also in life-styles—gave the new left a distinct, nearly messianic sense of mission.[47] Miller and others stress the recurring theme of participatory democracy. The most expansive account is probably that of George Katsiaficas, who situates the sixties within the European radical traditions of 1848, 1905, and 1917, with 1968 symbolizing yet another phase of universal struggles against domination.[48] These and other accounts point toward an understanding of the American new left (and European radicalism, too) as the initial expression of explosive new social forces growing out of the knowledge industry, the new middle strata, and marginal groups likely to reshape the contours of social change in the West.

To affirm the novelty of the new left is also to stress the immense gulf that separated the old from new lefts, the thirties from the sixties generation.

Although Maurice Isserman may be correct in pointing out that traditional socialist currents often played a creative role in the formation of the new left—the Socialist Workers Party is one example—this connection was always tenuous and strained at best. Surely, before the later turn toward Marxism-Leninsm, the differences were rather sharp. The traditional left still extolled the primacy of parties, unions, programs, and manifestos; the search for ideological certainty cloaked in the garb of "scientific" theory; faith in social progress made possible by economic growth underpinned by science and technology; attachment to mainstream social and cultural norms. In contrast, the new left was anarchistic in its quasi-existential desire for free self-expression and creativity, its attack on elitism, personality cults, and bureaucracy, in its passion for alternative lifestyles, and its willingness to break with old patterns and embark upon new social experiments. From this standpoint, it was above all a *countercultural* left that had no actual parallel elsewhere—a phenomenon once again rooted in the workings of American exceptionalism. The short-lived euphoria of new left politics meant a basic shift away from previous definitions of radicalism, especially those grounded in the Marxist tradition, and helped pave the way toward the more durable new social movements.

Social Movements and the Postmodern Dilemma

Against much received wisdom, the sixties legacy had a powerful impact upon the consciousness of those who were most engaged, and upon the various popular movements that flourished during the 1970s and 1980s. For the U.S., the findings of Jack Whalen and Richard Flacks put to rest the myth that new leftists were simply part of a generation of affluent students whose "alienation" soon gave way to high-powered careers, large incomes, traditional life-styles, and conservative beliefs once the drama of the sixties had run its course.[49] Instead, what emerges from their detailed study is a continuity, however partial and uneven, of ideas and even commitments, despite a profound change in the political milieu. Most ex-activists still distrusted authority, still rejected conventional life-styles, and still questioned materialist values, whether or not they remained politically active. The contours of American progressive politics in the 1980s, therefore, was probably shaped less by the limits of personal conviction than by various *contextual* factors, which, during the Reagan-Bush years, encouraged more low-key forms of activity. This was also true, to a lesser extent, in Europe with the triumph of

Thatcher and Kohl and the turn toward neo-liberalism by governing southern European Socialist parties. It might even be argued that the continuity
described by Whalen and Flacks reflected a certain *maturing* process, insofar
as a sense of "realism"—despite its reformist implications—replaced the earlier new left eschatology, with its naive faith in total, imminent change, its
glorification of marginalized strata, and its romantic attachment to insurrection and (in some quarters) "armed struggle."

Yet the implications of this analysis can be carried a step further: ideological continuity of the sort identified here may suggest other, more concrete
and structural links between the sixties and what followed. Like many
observers of the period, Whalen and Flacks do not fully explore the intricate
connections between new left radicalism and the proliferation of new social
movements during the succeeding two decades. The rhythm of grassroots
feminist, gay, peace, ecology, and urban protest movements that mobilized
millions of people *after* 1970 clearly could be traced to the pulse of the sixties. In the most global sense, as Katsiaficas argues, the new left and the new
movements both had roots in the struggle against the same general conditions: bureaucratization of authority relations, industrial and urban decay,
the ecology crisis, the arms race, widespread social anomie, and so forth.
Surely, the degree to which collective forms of action evolved mainly outside
the sphere of production, beginning in the sixties, would seem to affirm the
validity of this argument.

The new movements embraced themes that were already present, in less
developed form, in new left radicalism: a popular, grassroots insurgency
centered largely outside the dominant public sphere; an emphasis on qualitative or postmaterialist goals; a cultural radicalism; demands around
collective consumption; non-class-based identities.[50] At the same time,
although such thematic commonality lent historical meaning to the period,
the very *modalities* of movement activity shifted dramatically. The sixties
phase, in the U.S. more than in Europe, was characterized by a diffuse,
rapidly shifting, more or less rootless politics with its messianic ideologies
and rather exhibitionistic style (witness the Yippies). The later appearance
of social movements, however, introduced more durable, stable patterns of
action grounded in sustained local efforts to build organizations. In the new
movements there was less attachment to imported ideologies, less reliance
upon the university campuses as sources of mobilization. During the 1970s
and 1980s popular movements grew in numbers and also became more differentiated: the feminist, ecology, and peace/anti-intervention movements
each gave expression to multiple groups, ideologies, and *modus operandi*.

There was and continues to be a certain "global" dimension, however, that seems irrepressible, for new social movements are located at the core of social contradictions (class, bureaucratic, patriarchal, racial, ecological) that permeate industrialized society. The new left offered perhaps the first, albeit explosive, glimpse of cumulative struggles around these sites of conflict, which were fully grasped by neither liberalism nor Marxism, neither conventional wisdom nor any variant of the socialist tradition.

New movements expanded at a time when the growth of centralized power and the bureaucratization of public life led to a narrowing of political discourse, to a gulf between the national state apparatus and a more dynamic local sphere. In this context, an independent radicalism implied more than anything the struggle for empowerment, though a struggle confined primarily to civil society.[51] Although centered mainly in the advanced industrial countries, it has assumed an increasingly worldwide presence with the spread of non-governmental organizations (NGOs) and movements East and West, North and South. Marta Fuentes and André Gunder Frank write that "the new social movements today are by far what mobilizes most people in pursuit of common concerns. Far more than classical class movements, the social movements motivate and mobilize hundreds of millions of people in all parts of the world—mostly outside established political and social institutions that people find inadequate to serve their needs."[52]

In North America and Europe, the feminist and ecology movements took on particular significance, insofar as they both represented, in quite different ways, efforts to overcome alienation, social inequality, and domination. They advocated (in ideal form) not only democratization but recovery of the self in a world where economics had become globalized and politics deformed beyond the bounds of meaningful citizenship. Not coincidentally, feminist and ecological sensibilities intersected with, and were reinforced by, the radical side of the holistic transformation in therapy, healing, and health care originating in the counterculture. (In keeping with U.S. exceptionalism, this phenomenon was almost uniquely American.) Both feminism and ecology challenge established power relations in virtually all realms of life; both carried forward the strong communitarian impulses of the sixties; and both cut across class lines, status issues, and parochial interests.[53] Further, there is a prefigurative dimension that, in its more local-democratic moments, resisted the instrumentalism and productivism of both liberal capitalism and the socialist tradition.

This feminism-ecology nexus, which gave rise to new theoretical currents in the 1980s, could be said to form the core of a new movement paradigm, embracing but also going beyond identity politics. Once again, it was a convergence that seemed to have a peculiar resonance in American political culture.[54] It advanced a radicalism that *none* of the Marxist tendencies could have envisioned at earlier points in the twentieth century. As Murray Bookchin argues, its powerful insights "rendered the new left's anti-authoritarian outlook more explicit and more clearly definable by singling out hierarchical domination, not simply anti-authoritarian oppression." From this standpoint, ecology and feminism "were expanding the ideal of freedom beyond any bounds that had been established in recent memory. Hierarchy *as such*—be it in the form of ways of thinking, basic human relationships, social relations, and society's interaction with nature—could now be disentangled from the traditional class analyses that concealed it under a carpet of economic interpretations of society." Thus, general interests such as freedom and solidarity were now "*universal* interests that were shared by humanity as a whole." Consonant with his theory of social ecology, Bookchin insists that with these new movements "the revolutionary project could now be clearly defined as the abolition of hierarchy, the reharmonization of humanity with nature through the reharmonization of human with human, the achievement of an ecological society structured on ecologically sound technologies and face-to-face democratic communities." And, "feminism made it possible to highlight the significance of hierarchy in a very *existential* form.[55]

All this, of course, was an ideal construct that fell considerably short of permeating important spheres of discourse and practice. But new social movements did survive into the 1980s and 1990s, often extending their local presence even when the right won sufficient power to set the national agenda, as in the U.S., Germany, England, and Japan. In the U.S., grassroots politics, often in the form of "new populism" and Saul Alinsky-style urban community organizing, owed much of its dynamism to the absence of leftist parties and relative closure of the two-party system.[56] New movements were at the center of mass protest and popular struggles around a multitude of issues: the arms race, nuclear reactors, U.S. intervention in Central America, apartheid in South Africa, violence against women, abortion, gay rights, affirmative action, animal rights, housing, and toxic wastes to name the most significant. New movements were often the backbone of local communities and subcultures—for example, in the gay sections of San Francisco; alternative institutions such as cooperatives, underground media, bookstores, coffeehouses, and clinics; and electoral alliances with progressive agendas, including the Rainbow Coalition.

By the 1980s new opportunities appeared for social movements to converge around common agendas that could, on occasion, give rise to durable radical projects and organizations greater than the sum of their parts. Sometimes new movements came together on a shared terrain—for example, the Greenham Common movement in England during the early 1980s, where peace (anti-Euromissile) and feminist themes combined in an explosive fashion.[57] Other movements were part of a larger coalition-building process linking "old" and "new" concerns, traditional economic and post-material demands in the framework of sustained local efforts. One such instance is the Los Angeles-based Labor/Community Strategy Center, set up to create a grassroots environmental coalition merging ecological and class issues, local and global objectives, within the turbulent milieu of the inner city. The Center's environmental demands are conceived in the broadest of terms: Instead of an isolated specific focus (protecting endangered species, recycling, toxic wastes) characteristic of mainstream groups, the strategy is to forge a movement calling into question the whole logic of capitalist domination. A WATCHDOG organization, established to mobilize the urban poor in diverse sections of L.A. around multiple demands, maintains the premise that popular control of industrial production is a necessary basis for genuine long-range solutions. The broad goals are economic and political democracy built from the grassroots and a strategy of economic development that fosters material growth without sacrificing the environment. By creating space for a coalition of dispersed local movements, WATCHDOG aspires to emerge as a strong "counterforce" against the wealth and power of corporations.[58]

A similar project of empowerment and community-building was forged by a multiethnic, largely working-class movement of tenant families dedicated to saving their homes and neighborhoods that were threatened by a proposed freeway in the Silverlake district of L.A. In 1975 hundreds of tenants occupied housing owned by the state of California in the Route 2 corridor that was to be sold off after freeway plans were abandoned. When the bitter fight was concluded in the early 1980s, the families became owners of the housing either as individuals or through collective ownership in five cooperatives. After winning this battle, those tenants who became cooperative owners had to struggle with the task of collectively owning and managing their housing.[59] Defined around a mixture of housing, community, feminist, and environmental concerns, local coalitions of this sort—replicated in many cities around the U.S.—have in effect extended and deepened the scope of new social movements.

A sometimes forgotten outgrowth of the new movements is the critical forms of theoretical and political discourse they encouraged and nourished, both within and outside the university arena. Many elements of this highly eclectic and fragmented intellectual subculture—feminism, Western Marxism, poststructuralism, ecology, critical political economy—converge in different ways with the themes of the contemporary movements, which have a presence not only in higher education but in the media, the art world, trade unions, high schools, and even municipal governments. In the universities, the discovery of neo-Marxism and various offshoots of critical social theory by a generation of students, teachers, and scholars was inspired by new left preoccupation with ideology and consciousness, culture, social relations, and the larger problem of domination inherited from the anarchist and radical-left traditions. Creative scholarly enterprises, while all too often dull and abstruse, have challenged the old conceptual boundaries set by mainstream academic discourse, the new left, and traditional Marxism.[60] (As for the stale formulas of Marxism-Leninism, they have lost all resonance in the postmodern milieu.) Popular movements since the 1960s (again mainly in the areas of feminism and ecology) have derived much of their energy and continuity from the vast outpouring of books, journals, TV and radio offerings, college programs and courses, conferences, and lectures in most of the industrialized countries.

Of course, this energy and continuity has been anything but uniform; the fortunes of local movements ebb and flow. Moreover, the great diversity of new movements—as well as the blurring of lines between "old" and "new" movements—makes generalizations about bases of support, organizational styles, methods, strategies, and developmental potential hazardous at best: some look to direct action, others are more insular, still others are content to pursue moderate reforms within the electoral and legislative arenas. During relatively quiet periods, as in the 1980s, movements (whatever their goals) will commonly lose their subversive force as they become more atomized or enter into the more comfortable zone of normal politics. At the same time, Katsiaficas is correct to emphasize the radical *potential* of such movements, insofar as they can be located within emergent global forces of social conflict. If sixties radicalism was more turbulent and had more flair for the dramatic, new social movements carried forward a more sustained organizational presence, as well as a deeper oppositional theory *and* practice. But later social movements were no less dispersed than the new left.

Popular struggles spanning three decades have challenged an established but fragile Marxist tradition, with its familiar emphasis on class forces, parties, vanguards, and universal discourses. A new radicalism, uneven and lacking the strategic cohesion identified with social democracy and Leninism, points toward a multiplicity of fields of contention and mechanisms of change that could no longer be reduced to old-fashioned conceptual schemas. The complex and highly differentiated milieu of advanced industrial society has given rise to new modes of protest and revolt around plural forms of oppression, identities, and group interests; class forces no longer constitute a privileged agency of historical change. The era of new social movements is therefore also an emergent phase of post-Marxist radical theory and politics.[61] This momentous shift reflects a novel emphasis on the "micro" sphere of everyday life—including personal and cultural politics—that was largely ignored by socialist parties, unions, and governments trapped in a world of *haute politique.* Since the 1960s attention has turned to the concerns of identity and self-activity around gender, race, ethnicity, sexual preference, and even "nature" as a manifestation of postmodern consciousness that often took the form of a "politics of difference" or a "politics of identity." Stress was placed on cultural and political identities formed in the course of collective struggles against multiple forms of domination. Such a postmodern motif intersects with historical trends at work in post-Fordist society, with its increasingly complex social structure and cultural mediations, and its highly dispersed field of discourses that favors distinctly "local" over "Jacobin" agendas.[62]

But the logic of a postmodern shift contains its own severe difficulties regarding the way fragmented identities and worldviews are ultimately translated into effective mechanisms of change. As Steve Best and Douglas Kellner observe, "differences" can easily become fetishized, producing rigid ideological barriers between groups and a tendency toward liberal interest group politics.[63] Common goals and interests can be undermined by the peculiar strength of differences (speaking in a "different voice") so that politics takes on the character of style over content, form over concrete aims. Aside from whatever chauvinism or ethnocentrism this might foster, it can easily reinforce depoliticizing or separatist tendencies already at work within the dominant public sphere. When pushed to its extreme, postmodern politics—indeed, the whole legacy of new social movements—affirms a "radicalism" that sidesteps issues of power, privilege, and class in its articulation of parochial identities and post-materialist values. In this fashion, multiple sites of conflict can work against the development of a genuine transformative *politics.*

More specifically: when gender, racial, and ecological issues are removed from the class dimension of modern society they are inevitably robbed of their insurgent potential. If class is no longer the unitary subject posited by the socialist tradition, neither has its disappeared from view. Without labor as a critical site of popular opposition, all the accumulated energies of new movement constituencies will fail to advance the struggle for egalitarian class and power relations.[64] For this reason, the idea of a total postmodern "break" with conditions of modernity creates at least as many problems for radical politics as its solves. The new paradigm opens up a broader view of human emancipation but also makes more difficult the search for viable agents of social change and political strategy.

After the decline of the European extra-parliamentary left the closest thing to such a political translation of new movement radicalism has been the Green synthesis, which first emerged in West Germany during the early 1980s. Built around a confluence of local movements and citizens' initiatives, the Greens set out to incorporate essentially post-Marxist, post-materialist themes into a coherent party structure and electoral framework. Green parties across Europe were an outgrowth of the new left, the urban and environmental crises, and the decline of social democracy: many achieved significant electoral inroads by the late 1980s (notably in West Germany, Holland, Sweden, France, and Italy).[65] Based in a young, urban, and educated electorate anxious for fresh (if not radical) alternatives to mounting problems related to nuclear power, the arms race, urban blight, and ecological decay, the Greens looked to a movement-based "anti-party party" that would contend for power, but on its own terms. They were no *Volkspartei*, but neither were they an isolated opposition; they were not dedicated to politics-as-usual, but neither were they overly anxious about winning and wielding power. This was a rather novel experiment requiring an unprecedented balancing act.

Once the Green decision to participate fully in conventional politics was made, however, the familiar pressures of electoral politics and institutionalization came to the fore in a manner recalling the social-democratic predicament. The pressures were those of adaptation to established organizational routines and norms. Here the gradual ascendancy within the German Greens of the *Realo* (pragmatic, coalition-oriented) tendency over the *Fundi* (local, movement-oriented) outlook during the 1980s spoke volumes about the party's moderate trajectory. Deradicalization set in with each new electoral triumph, with each institutional advance made, with each step toward a "red-Green" coalition with the SPD—perhaps best reflected by the short-lived, disastrous alliance in Hesse in 1987.[66] As normal political routines came to dominate party life, the *Fundis* held out for a radical identity tied to the local movements, but this was hard to sustain in the wake of electoral success. The efforts of eco-socialists in the *Moderne Zeiten* group in Hamburg likewise met with defeat. Evolving out of a traditional Leninism, this tendency (led by Thomas Eberman and Rainer Trampert) sought to merge the concerns of the new movements with labor and post-materialist demands with Marxist sensibilities, but left-Green initiatives of this sort never generated much popular support.[67] A parallel development took place elsewhere, including the U.S., where a smaller Green nucleus seeking to make inroads into the electoral arena prevailed over movement-oriented activists and a marginalized "left" tendency influenced by neo-Marxism and social ecology. In West Germany, at least, the Greens expressed serious ambivalence about how far to continue along the road of normal politics: divisions and intense factionalization blocked consensus around strategy, leading to both local and national stalemate. As two observers comment, "This postindustrial framework party provided a dash of color, unconventionality, and high principle, but its ambiguity—at times hostility—toward pragmatic incremental reform through the laborious process of coalition-building defined its limits and may mark its demise."[68]

In Italy, where more than 2,000 environmental groups were formed in the wake of the Seveso dioxin incident in 1976, radical currents were attracted to the *Lega per l'Ambiente* and the *Liste Verdi* (Green Lists), which advocated "ecological renewal" beginning in the early 1980s.[69] The Italian Greens were able to build upon a strong legacy of extra-parliamentary opposition, the counterculture, a deep Marxist ethos, and strong urban protest movements frustrated with the record of the PSI and PCI on environmental issues. By 1986 the *Lega* membership numbered roughly 30,000. Constructed on the basis of these groups and the *Arcobaleno Verde* (Green Rainbow), a Green electoral coalition was able to win 600,000 votes (or 2.1 percent) in the 1985 local elections. In 1987, while the German Greens were polling 8.3 percent, the Italians won 2.5 percent—mainly on the basis of an emotional anti-nuclear campaign—in a fierce struggle to take votes away from the traditional left. As in West Germany previously, the outpouring of Green sympathies in Italy during the late 1980s coincided with the ebbing of the socialist tradition (even if this decline was not always precisely registered at the polls).

In response to the ecological challenge, some traditional leftist parties (notably the PCI and SPD) began to champion "green" themes in their electoral campaigns and legislative work, hoping to coopt those issues and prevent further erosion at the polls—and this worked to some extent. But even nominally socialist parties were hard put to overcome their deeply inbred patterns of hierarchy, routine, and above all productivism; the clash between instrumental pressures and ecological aims could not be resolved.

As for the European Greens in general, they have not been visibly successful in resolving the postmodern dilemma of how to press for multiple discourses and sites of conflict while simultaneously forging a common political strategy. As many Greens parties struggled heroically to combine local movements and normal politics, by the early 1990s the larger parties (including the German) were moving closer to the social democratic orbit while the smaller ones were still trying to achieve a national electoral breakthrough. Both the German and Swedish Greens, increasingly moderate in their outlook, lost their parliamentary representation in 1990 and 1991 respectively, although each retains an extensive local and regional presence. Also moving rightward, the two French Green parties (*Les Verts* and *Generation Ecologie*) combined to garner eight percent of the vote in the 1993 general election. As of the early 1990s the Italian Greens had lost any semblance of radical identity, which made it easier for them to enter broad coalitions with the PDS and even more moderate parties. Indeed, from Greece to Portugal the Green movement throughout southern Europe has not yet been able to establish much momentum. The situation in the north, however, is altogether different: Green parties in Sweden, Finland, Belgium, Holland, and Austria, as well as Germany, have constructed solid local and municipal bases of power. The German Greens polled more than fourteen percent of the vote in the 1993 state elections in Hamburg, while consistently receiving as much as twelve percent overall support in national surveys. Still, the distinctive Green radicalism of the mid-1980s seems to have lost its aura. One problem everywhere is that Green leaders, in reaching out to mainstream voters, have felt compelled to make ideological concessions and adapt to hegemonic political discourse in a number of areas: ecology, feminism, anti-capitalism, local democracy. (The vast array of problems that necessarily accompany the shift from movement to party is explored more fully in the epilogue.)

As postwar capitalism moved to stabilize itself on a foundation of centralized state power, Keynesian social policies, a militarized economy, and institutionalization of class conflict, the new left and new social movements, along with their various offshoots, made an indelible (though not always radical) imprint on the political landscape. Like similar movements of an earlier era, these contemporary modes of popular struggle have run up against the immense power of economic and political institutions—power that has restricted movement autonomy and, in many cases, has absorbed, isolated, or marginalized their oppositional thrust. Socialist decline has created space for new modes of opposition, but a truly radical and democratic opposition has evolved only sporadically and unevenly. Widespread insurgency has nonetheless persisted since the 1960s, shaped more often than not by the concerns set in motion by the new left: recovery of community, direct action, personal politics, consciousness transformation. This continuity pervades the diffuse postmodern spirit of the time, and is likely to extend well into the future. In Bookchin's words, "No radical movement of any importance in the future could ignore the ethical, aesthetic, and anti-authoritarian legacy created by the new left and the communalist experiments that emerged in the counterculture."[70]

The End of Socialism?

From all outward appearances, the socialist tradition remains very much alive despite the astonishingly rapid disintegration of the Soviet bloc. China, with a population numbering more than one-fifth of humanity, remains firmly under Communist governance. Ruling Communist parties, though weakened, still have a legitimate claim to power in North Korea, Vietnam, Cuba, and elsewhere. Socialists have won four consecutive national elections in Spain. Elsewhere in Europe, a mixture of social democrats, former communists, and independent leftists influenced by Marxism retain a solid electoral presence, locally and nationally, in scattered countries from Italy to Denmark, from Greece to Germany. The Canadian New Democrats achieved an electoral breakthrough in 1992 when they took power in Ontario, the country's largest province. Marxist inspired social movements, trade unions, and parties can be found in the vast majority of Third World countries. Even in Russia and Eastern Europe, there is an explosive backlash against capitalist "shock therapy" both among elites and the general population hoping to preserve elements of communism against predatory incursions of the world system. (In the U.S., true to its history of "exceptionalism," socialist currents remain virtually nonexistent within the public sphere.) Significantly, too, Marxist theory retains its prominent intellectual status in universities around the world; indeed, in some countries (including the U.S.), the tradition seems more popular than ever.

But this is only a small fraction of the larger picture: surface appearances barely conceal a deep historical decline of the socialist tradition that cannot be measured in labels, ideological rhetoric, and electoral statistics. Despite the failure of the post-sixties radical challenge to establish a leftist hegemony of its own, socialist politics is now mired in a profound impasse from which it is not likely to survive as a legitimate alternative to bureaucratic capitalism. More than anything the problem is one of goals and vision—and the capacity to achieve them—not flawed leadership, historical contingency, or even bad strategies. Nor is it a matter of the familiar "crisis of identity," though clearly enough that is a problem. My argument, based upon the analysis of the preceding chapters, is that the socialist tradition has exhausted its *political* vitality. Of course, this does not mean that Marxist inspired movements and parties will vanish overnight or that the theory and history of an entire tradition can be ignored *tout court*; neither of these is true.

Looking beneath the labels and claims of political elites, one is struck by the remarkable chaos and disintegration of a socialist tradition that not long ago could lay claim to universality and ascendancy in most regions of the world. Where once there were powerful anti-system impulses, today there is little but a sense of malaise and demoralization among even the most dedicated socialists. The collapse of communism has had much to do with this but, as we have seen, that is merely a surface phenomenon resulting from long-term developments. While the erstwhile Soviet bloc moves from chaos to chaos and crisis to crisis, the "stability" of Chinese communism remains highly misleading, insofar as outward harmony cloaks a new (and effective) form of bureaucratic-state capitalism that has little in common with Marxian ideals. The likelihood is that the few remaining Communist regimes will either follow the Chinese path or risk being overthrown in the fashion of some East European regimes. Even the label has become an embarrassment: Communist parties around the world, with the Italians as usual in the lead, have been scrambling to adopt new appellations and new "identities." But this search, too, barely conceals the underlying erosion of an entire socialist discourse and practice.

This predicament is most obvious in early 1990s Europe. The old Communist parties have desperately sought out new terrain: In Italy the PCI has become the PDS and is more frequently inclined to enter broad coalitions; in Spain the United Left was formed but remained a largely ineffective alternative to the PSOE; in Sweden the Communist Left Party VPK became just the Left Party (VP); and in Finland the former Communists became the Left Coalition. Meanwhile, popular support for these organizations under whatever banner has continued to erode. Thus, in the 1993

French general elections, the PCF wound up with only 9.2 percent of the vote. In the 1993 Italian municipal elections the PDS won just 8.8 percent of the vote in Milan, one of its strongholds, while the Refounded Communists polled 11.4 percent (making the overall former PCI total 20.2 percent in a city where it regularly received more than thirty-five percent). In the 1993 Spanish general elections the United Left was reduced to less than five percent of the vote and eighteen parliamentary seats. Even more than their electoral decline, however, these parties and alliances seemed to have lost any semblance of ideological vitality as they continued their shift rightward in a frenzied effort to garner votes and once again prove their credibility.

As for social democracy, only in a few instances (for example, Spain) was it able to capitalize on the sad plight of the communists. In most cases, it simply went further along the road of ideological moderation, governmental pragmatism, and (somewhat paradoxically) electoral decline. Much of this decline has resulted from the social democrats' failure, or perceived failure, to govern effectively. In some countries (Sweden, Germany, Denmark, France, and Italy), the Socialists had been in power or shared power over long stretches of time, so it seemed natural that blame for the economic downturn and crisis of the Keynesian welfare state would be placed on them. This was partly a function of pressures emanating from the world capitalist system, but it could also be seen as the inevitable backlash against parties that from the outset strongly emphasized governmental efficiency and economic growth.[71] Yet another factor contributing to the Socialists' loss of support was widespread corruption that took its toll above all in France, Italy, and Greece. But perhaps the biggest shock was the major electoral defeat suffered by the Swedish social democrats in the 1991 general elections. The SAP, which had governed the country almost continuously since 1932, was thrown out of office, receiving only 37.6 percent of the vote when it had never polled less than forty-one percent. Interestingly enough, during the preceding two years the SAP undertook a series of rather conservative policy initiatives (for example, around austerity measures) that departed even from its moderate social democratic legacy. In France the Socialist debacle was even worse: in the 1993 general elections the PSF was reduced to 17.6 percent of the vote, losing more than two hundred parliamentary seats in the process.

At the end of his book *Socialism: Past and Future*, Michael Harrington writes, "The question is: Can Socialism learn from the defeats and betrayals that resulted from its flawed understanding of its own profound truths? If not, socialism will turn out to be humankind's most noble and useful political illusion...."[72] Whatever its "profound truths"—and they have been many—it may well be too late for socialism to learn from its long history of "betrayals" and "defeats." Indeed, the predicament runs much deeper than the actions of leaders or losses in political combat. Perhaps those "profound truths" have turned into "illusions" precisely to the degree that the socialist tradition has become either a casualty of power or simply an extension of the whole project of capitalist modernization, or both. This manner of rephrasing Harrington's question brings us back to the intractable dilemma posed by Peter Gay at the outset: forced to choose between emancipatory ideals and instrumental methods in the perpetual struggle for power, socialists typically favored the later. The twin legacies of statism and productivism, along with the deradicalizing effects of parliamentarism, have rendered original socialist ideals no longer recognizable—witness the present-day experiences of Russia, China, and Spain. The very goal of "democratic socialism" no longer seems to make sense in the modern context, where that goal remains very much a part of the logic of rationalized growth and domination.

If such a logic fits the pattern of social-democratic and communist development in the twentieth century, it was always resisted by the radical left, with its emphasis on merging democratic means and ends; but this tradition, from the council communists to the Greens, has so far made little headway. At the same time, the persistence of a radical critique and opposition has illuminated the fatal weaknesses of the socialist tradition and helped clarify reasons for its decline. Grounded in Enlightenment rationality, it is a tradition wedded to the idea of human progress through expanded production and bureaucratic control over the state, civil society, and nature. It is an ideological discourse that in many ways has become inseparable from the very capitalist developmental model it originally set out to overturn. In the transformed setting of today, it offers few conceptual or strategic insights into the critical issues and challenges ahead that oppositional movements and parties will have to face: more complex forms of class struggle, bureaucratic domination, patriarchy, racial and ethnic divisions, the ecological crisis.

It follows that the modern alternative would be a different kind of "third road" than the ones pursued by Eurocommunists and Eurosocialists in the 1970s and 1980s; their "alternative" was all too quickly absorbed into the longstanding social-democratic model. A future third road will have to follow something akin to a radical-left path running between two increasingly anachronistic poles of development—the capitalist world order and a disintegrating socialist tradition.

A protracted radical-democratic struggle to overcome the mounting chaos and destruction of the world system will require a fundamental break with old institutions and values, although probably by means of a shifting balance of forces rather than a Jacobin conquest of state power. Moving from a transformative vision, it will have to bring into being new modes of production, work, consumption, leisure—and politics. This means an entirely new approach to development consonant with human needs, self-management, and ecological balance, tied to a system of socialized ownership, planning, and investment. At the bottom of all this, and a cornerstone of any post-Marxist radical strategy, is the process of *collective empowerment,* without which all other transformative projects become inert. The very thematic of empowerment and recovery of citizenship, linked as it is to multiple arenas of change, stands at odds with the main organized currents of the socialist tradition, which, whatever their material accomplishments, have more often than not *reinforced* and even extended the bureaucratic, patriarchal, and class forms of domination. Global movements for revolutionary change will therefore have to press for a broadening of local and individual realms of autonomy along with democratization of the public sphere in ways that can reverse the harmful effects of economic scarcity, institutional control, and cultural oppression. This epochal and ongoing battle, which began with the classical bourgeois revolutions, has become simultaneously more difficult and more urgent with the internationalization of economic, political, and cultural mechanisms of power. To conclude with the words of Immanuel Wallerstein: "To be anti-systemic is to argue that neither liberty nor equality is possible under the existing system and that both are possible only in a transformed world."[73]

7

EPILOGUE
The Global Crisis—Ecology and the Future of Socialism

IF MOVEMENTS FOR SOCIAL CHANGE IN THE ADVANCED INDUSTRIAL SETTING remain both numerous and vital, they are nonetheless socially and ideologically dispersed to an unprecedented degree, lacking a strategic coherence that was the hallmark of the social tradition. This fragmentation of leftist political culture appears to be endemic to the post-Fordist or postmodern context. While some movements have entered into mainstream discourse and institutional practice, others—usually those with more transformative ambitions—are local and insular in character, moving off in various directions while hoping to avoid the seductions of normal politics. This latter trajectory fits the radical side of the new social movements in Europe and North America but also around the world, which we explored in chapter six. More than ever, social change in the 1990s is shaped by multiple, overlapping and sometimes contradictory struggles around diverse themes and goals. Grounded in separate social realities, such movements typically have no pretense toward hegemony or universality. The collapse of communism and the recent accelerated decline of the socialist tradition analyzed in this book have given added life to this trend.[1] This poses new dilemmas for oppositional politics: concerns of power, governance, coalition building, and, most significantly, the very capacity of movements to carry out transformative ends.

These problems are further illuminated by the gravity of the global ecological crisis, as reflected in the depletion of natural resources; deforestation; thinning of the ozone layer; disruptive worldwide climate changes; poisoning of the air, water, soil, and food; and growing population pressures—all of which have destabilized the biosphere in ways that may be irreversible. The global crisis, which is simultaneously economic and environmental, demands a radical, universal response if meaningful social existence on the planet is to be preserved. The severity of the crisis is such that, unless drastic measures are taken within the next generation or so, it could be too late. As one prominent ecologist has lamented, our capacity to respond to the crisis "may ultimately decide whether human society will creatively foster natural evolution or whether we will render the planet uninhabitable for all complex life forms, including our own."[2] Thus, history forces a compelling question: Can movements for social change in the age of ecological crisis rise to this unprecedented challenge, transcending their highly scattered, localist, and even anti-political bent?

In the post-Cold War atmosphere, the global crisis has already begun to dictate a new paradigm of conflict and agenda of change, a phenomenon addressed obliquely at the Earth Summit gathering of 150 nations in Rio de Janeiro during June 1992. Yet the crisis itself, primarily a legacy of rampant industrialism in North America, Europe, and Japan, has been at least four centuries in the making. Today it is fueled by a number of interrelated factors: growth mania, fossil fuel driven economies, harmful technologies, consumerism, spread of military weaponry, and the intensified Northern exploitation of the South. Given this vast array of problems, the crisis has given rise to a culture of profound disempowerment—a pervasive sense that change is far beyond the realm of human control—that helps to define contemporary politics. Before the Earth Summit, which concluded as an embarrassing failure, efforts to analyze and solve the crisis were the domain largely of isolated, local ecology groups and small Green parties that appeared in Europe during the 1980s. The dominant political traditions—liberal-capitalist, communist, social-democratic—were thoroughly imbued with a commitment to industrial growth, which assumed a world of infinite resources and forever stable biosphere. Meanwhile, the new left, along with the new social movements it spawned, was never able to overcome the paralysis of localism and dispersion that was its defining *modus operandi* since the 1960s. And so the familiar destructive patterns of production and consumption continue to an ever greater extent on a world scale.

Dimensions of the Global Crisis

The self-perpetuating spiral of material and ecological decline is rooted in the growing contradiction between an imbalanced system of production, veering towards chaos, and an increasingly fragile biosphere. An abundance of scientific evidence suggests that the natural habitat, from oceans to rain forests to the atmosphere, cannot for long sustain the capitalist, industrialist drive toward endless material expansion, generalized domination, and the conversion of human beings and nature into commodities.[3] The logic of accumulation on a world scale, presided over by huge transnational corporations and powerful governments, guarantees uneven development and environmental decay. Corporations do not, and cannot, view any aspect of nature as having intrinsic value; the social effects of production (and consumption) scarcely enter into an equation that favors growth and profits over human outcomes. The pervasive motif, now and then modified by reforms and regulations, is to maximize the total quantity of commodities produced.

Although this dynamic dates back to the earliest phases of the industrial revolution, the crisis itself assumed new dimensions in the postwar years, with the intensification of worldwide capitalist expansion, the growth of transnational power, fierce competition between leading industrial countries, and the spread of information technology. More recently, the collapse of communist power and the end of the Cold War has signalled a resurgence of "free market" ideologies, which serve to further legitimate environmental plunder, especially in the Third World. Within this "new world order," the U.S. hopes to carve out a hegemonic position where national and corporate interests can be pursued as freely as possible. A major U.S. objective, shared by Democrats and Republicans alike, is to undermine rival international bases of power—whether in the form of competing capital, labor unions, social movements, or popular insurgency—in order to make easier the exploitation of resources.

Since the first world environmental meetings in Stockholm in 1972, the global crisis has worsened while the gap between North and South, with the exception of some newly developing countries like Taiwan and South Korea, has widened dramatically. U.N. reports in 1991 show that the difference between rich and poor nations has roughly doubled since 1961, with the top twenty percent of the world's population controlling eighty-three percent of the total wealth while the bottom twenty percent is left with only 1.4 percent. The richest now earn sixty times more than the poorest, due to the

North's continuing growth and resource consumption binge that shows no signs of abating. Thus, more that forty years of foreign "aid" engineered by the U.S. controlled World Bank and International Monetary Fund have only *exacerbated* uneven development and poverty in the Third World while wreaking ecological havoc everywhere. Lending practices of the industrial powers have trapped developing countries in a cycle of rising debt and economic decline, driving countries like Brazil, Mexico, and the Philippines further away from material stability and environmental sanity.[4] The South is presently transferring over 100 billion dollars each year to the North as a result of interest on debts to Northern banks, terms of trade losses, and assorted dividend and royalty payments. To this could be added billions of dollars that are lost through blocked access to global markets such as textiles, electronics, and autos, a phenomenon that will only worsen with the free trade initiatives of GATT (General Agreement on Tariffs and Trade).[5] Failure of the industrialized nations to make radical production and consumption changes in a world of increasingly scarce and blighted resources means that the poor, both North and South, will be squeezed even further.

In this century the idea of scientific and technological advance has been viewed by capitalist, Third World, and communist nations alike as a harbinger of material abundance and social progress. The historical reality, however, has been rather mixed: Economic growth and elevated levels of consumption for about ten percent of the world's population have been accompanied by greater inequality, frustrated ambitions of the many, concentration of power, and environmental degradation. In an era of ecological crisis, technology has been embraced as a kind of panacea by "experts" and citizens of all ideological persuasions. Here, too, the situation is far more complex than any form of technological optimism might indicate: Technology has enormous potential, but so long as its utilization is controlled by the transnationals and military it becomes merely one more ingredient in the process of global decline. Technology reinforces destruction of the biosphere as it speeds up destruction of the rain forests; produces massive nuclear and other toxic waste; spews thousands of chemicals into the air, water, soil, and atmosphere; and renders the exploitation of resources easier with each passsing day. The answer to the environmental predicament, then, lies in the realm of *politics*—not in science and technology.

Technology has given rise to an archipelago of hyper-developed urban regions around the world—regions where unprecedented affluence coexists with widespread poverty and disenfranchisement. In their ceaseless pursuit of growth, power, and new markets, transnationals have created super-metropolitan networks that employ technology in the service of corporate objectives that go far beyond the traditional nation-state framework. From Tokyo to São Paolo, from Seoul to Milan, from Mexico City to Los Angeles, a market and high-tech developmental strategy has excluded the input and needs of at least ninety percent of the populace. The search for integrated markets, rooted in easy access to raw materials, cheap labor, and a stable high-tech infrastructure, is expected to give rise to nearly one billion affluent consumers by the year 2020; the rest will be consigned to underclass status. As Riccardo Petrella observes, "On the one side we would see a dynamic, tightly linked archipelago of technologies constituting less than one-eighth of the world's population; on the other would be a vast, disconnected and disintegrating wasteland that is home to seven out of eight inhabitants of the Earth."[6] This harsh scenario, already a reality in many parts of the world, means that patterns of grossly uneven and unsustainable development will dramatically worsen during the next three decades. According to present U.N. statistics, more than one billion people live in dire poverty while 400 million are close to starvation. There are 100 million homeless around the world alongside 202 billionaires and three million millionaires.[7] So long as key investment decisions are made by elite industrialists and bankers, these patterns will never be overturned.

Meanwhile, the global military buildup and the spread of armed conflict that has defined the post-Cold War order only reinforces the general downward cycle of decay and instability. The Gulf War and events in Yugoslavia, both bloody and costly, might well augur a new period of regional conflict made more explosive by the readiness of political rivals to engage in military combat. By 1990 the total world expenditure on armaments was roughly one trillion dollars, the bulk of it produced and dispersed by the U.S., Russia, England, and France.[8] Mounting economic and political competition among nations, and *within* nations, both North and South—along with the ready availability of arms—stimulates this upsurge in militarism at a time when the East-West confrontation seems a dim memory and distinctly *ideological* conflicts have receded. Not only does the military represent an ethos of violence and authoritarianism, it also consumes scarce resources, redirects technological innovation away from public goods, exacerbates social problems, and damages the environment.

In the U.S., where about ten trillion dollars have been spent on the military since the end of World War II, Pentagon wealth and power now feed into a huge centralized monopoly that devours resources, peddles arms around the world, erodes democratic institutions, and pushes an aggressive foreign policy. Military Keynesianism, which in 1990 employed more than a half-million people to supply Pentagon acquisitions alone, amounts to an irrational use of capital in a period when the very material (and ecological) infrastructure of the country is in shambles. This downward slide will continue so long as the corporations find military production profitable and the worldwide struggle for high-tech supremacy does not wane.[9]

The modern crisis is not only global but is the expression of multiple forces that lie beyond the sphere of nation-state control. Fundamentally, this predicament is rooted in a sprawling production apparatus that has few boundaries and expands in a milieu where political opposition is at best feebly articulated. The corporate-state-military hold over industrial development, agriculture, banking and trade means that a shoddy economic discourse—narrowly confined to the sphere of growth, profits, interest rates, trade deficits and so on—generally prevails over the discourse of human needs and ecological sanity.

The social consequences of decline are clearly visible in the growing chaos of urban life, especially within and around the megacities; impoverishment on a world scale; strains in food production and distribution; worsening health indicators—for example, the drastic rise in cancer rates; and economic polarization that feeds into ethnic, religious, and other local conflicts. Mexico City perhaps best exemplifies this tendency. This megacity of twenty-two million people, forty percent of whom live in abject poverty, is faced with terrible overcrowding, unbreathable air, food distribution problems, increased outbreak of diseases, and social fragmentation. The Mexico City urban complex now experiences a nearly unbearable stress on land, capital resources, social relations, and, of course, the whole ecological support system.

Attitudes toward the global crisis among industrial, political, and intellectual elites in the industrialized countries, and most other countries as well, have been shaped by skepticism if not cynical detachment. With few exceptions, such elites owe their privilege and status to a corporate hegemony and expansion that places market priorities over human needs; the struggle for control over resources weighs far more heavily than solving environmental problems, which are predictably minimized. Moreover, the crisis itself does not appear to pose an imminent threat to human existence despite some forecasts of inevitable ecocatastrophe.[10] Rather than a volcanic eruption or cataclysmic finale, the crisis will more likely involve the long-term deterioration of the world economy and ecosystems over a period of several decades. In the absence of a shift to sustainable forms of development, beginning with the leading powers, the world is likely to see intensification of human misery (starvation, poverty, unemployment, crowding, worsening health, pollution), giving rise to higher levels of social conflict and political instability.

This contrasts with the familiar crisis scenario, according to which an imminent apocalypse will bring an end to life on the planet. It also contrasts with the familiar emphasis on isolated disasters like Bophal, the Exxon Valdez, Three Mile Island, and Chernobyl. The gradual decline of ecosystems means that the human condition will be more susceptible to global changes that take on the character of appearing to be outside the realm of popular intervention. Viewed in this way, the crisis is rooted in a long history of elite attempts to dominate the social and natural habitat that have produced a complex system of hierarchy, control, and economic privilege. Such attempts, however, have also given rise to explosive social contradictions.

New Sources of Conflict

In the great megacities of the world—and in smaller urban centers, too—social contradictions of the mounting global crisis are becoming more and more apparent: between the interests of the transnationals and the prevailing quality of life; between the system of production and the imperatives of nature; between the political capacity of local governments to act and the popular demands being placed upon them. The centrifugal tendencies are building. In urban areas like Manila, Seoul, Los Angeles, and Mexico City, there is a precipitous increase in unemployment, homelessness, civic violence, crime, and environmental decay, while at the same time social programs and services—needed now more than ever—are vanishing as the municipalities lose their power to intervene. The sprawling urban slums have reduced access to both material goods and political power, a situation that sooner or later fosters tension, protest, and insurrection of the sort witnessed in Los Angeles during April–May 1992. The megacities are becoming urban time bombs insofar as they reflect most brutally the vagaries of the global crisis. And it is here that the opposition to corporate domination is most likely to ferment and crystallize.[11]

The global crisis and the social polarization it generates constitute the main paradigm of contemporary popular movements. We can expect broad, militant, and often violent local struggles around material demands, empowerment, and ecological decay in a context where neither large corporations nor large governments can adequately respond to the pressures. New sites of popular intervention, both within and outside the institutional framework, will proliferate with the decline of old loyalties to states, parties, interest groups, and ideologies. There will be massive pressures for resource equity, democratic participation, and revitalization of urban space within the cities and on their periphery. As the crisis builds it lays the foundation for a potential convergence of interests among disparate social movements and NGOs: urban poor, labor, women, students, community and indigenous groups, environmental movements. Affected by the crisis at every turn, local residents have no choice but to respond to the disintegration of urban life. Material and ecological conditions are tightly intertwined, both North and South. In the North, however, the pattern of change most often fits the postmaterialist trajectory of new social movements, whereas in the South the struggles of the marginalized urban poor and labor occupy the center of the political stage. In both cases, however, conditions of environmental decay constitute the thread connecting multiple local struggles.

The phenomenon of local contestation takes many forms. In Berlin and Milan, there have been massive street mobilizations behind a variety of political banners. In Seoul, Bangkok, and Los Angeles, there have been insurrections taking the form of violent encounters. In Lima, on the other hand, people have created large grassroots networks in the Villa El Salvador district, where as of 1991 thousands of residents built twenty-six neighborhood schools, 150 day care centers, and 300 community kitchens while planting 500,000 trees and training hundreds of door-to-door health workers. These networks, duplicated in most urban areas around the world, are linked to broader struggles for local empowerment even where they may lack explicit political definition.[12] But urban insurrections, like earlier forms of "primitive rebellion," rarely possess coherent organizational forms or strategy—witness Los Angeles.

The spread of world cities characterized by mounting tension and conflict suggests that opposition, whether through community institutions or popular insurrection, will be a durable element of the global order. The examples of Lima, Bangkok, Seoul, Los Angeles, and Berlin will probably be reproduced many times in the coming decades. At a time when geographical boundaries are losing their importance, revolt in one locale can be inspired by the struggle in another to recuperate local urban spaces colonized by the corporations. The empowerment of grassroots movements is likely to occur insofar as government structures and party systems become assimilated into a neo-corporatist bastion of privileged interests that narrows the public sphere. The legacy of popular movements growing out of sixties radicalism, especially in North America and Europe, is already in place, though weakened by the late 1980s. At least in their more subversive incarnation, such movements challenged the institutionalized rules and norms of conventional politics; they offered a transcendent vision of change.[13] Today there are still many popular formations, including environmental groups, that correspond to (pre-political) images of oppositional cultures and communities. A shared motif is the struggle to preserve neighborhoods, fight ecological decay, and expand public services.[14] Their efforts to mobilize local resources, knowledge, and skills are pitted against the enormous power of the state, military, and corporations.

The persistence of local movements and networks around the world is but one phase in the development of a *politics* that can reverse the global crisis. It begins by broadening the sphere of critical discourse and democratic participation. The struggle for democratic empowerment is indeed a critical element in the worldwide spread of popular movements, East, West, and South.[15] At the same time, this phenomenon raises some difficult questions for the future: How far can such local forms of empowerment advance before they reach political limits? How can fragmented movements in geographically and culturally diverse settings hope to achieve the universal presence needed to subvert transnational corporate hegemony?

The Ecological Imperative

The modern crisis and the challenges it poses has inspired new ways of understanding the contours of social change. An ecological framework suggests that we must increasingly take into account the global forces at work (in production, communications, and environmental risks), as well as the distinctly *negative* consequences of modernity (quality of urban life, food production, health) that reflects the limits of both industrial growth and technology. Indeed, the entire classical industrial model that has brought centuries of imbalanced, uneven, and finally unsustainable development is being called into question. From this standpoint, the old syndrome of growth-centered industrialism appears obsolete whatever its ideological label. Within the assumptions of the growth model there is no way out of the crisis.

Viewed historically, the endless production of commodities inevitably and systematically came into conflict with the global ecological imperative.

Sooner or later the costs of random growth were bound to become greater than the benefits derived, especially in a period of untrammeled transnational power. The harsh side of industrialism reflects the degree to which the myth of progress associated with sheer production of wealth (measured without regard for social utility) has lost its relevance. An ecological outlook implies a final break with this myth, which, of course, still governs the thinking of corporate, political, and military elites. The crisis itself will ultimately force such a break.[16] As Ulrich Beck writes, "[I]ndustrial society destablizes itself through its very establishment.... People are set free from the certainties and modes of living in the industrial epoch—just as they were 'freed' from the arms of the Church into society during the age of the Reformation."[17] As a result, we are "concerned no longer exclusively with making nature *useful*, or with releasing mankind from traditional constraints, but also and essentially with problems resulting from techno-economic development itself."[18]

Before the 1960s political opposition in the West typically moved within the parameters of modernity: Even the most "revolutionary" strategies (for example, Leninism and council communism) sought to carry forward a simplified version of the Enlightenment tradition along with the growth model. They were class-defined and revolved around the concerns of production. During the past three decades opposition has more often taken the form of local, highly dispersed popular movements that resist clear definitions of constituency, organization, political strategy, and ideology.[19] Where movements began to stress grassroots citizen action over normal politics, collective over privatized consumption, and post-materialist values over strict economic rationality—as with feminist and environmentalist movements—the glimpses of a new post-Enlightenment tradition could be detected. The rupture with modernity paved the way toward a rejuvenated public sphere.

Dramatic changes in the world—globalization of the economy, massive assaults on the biosphere, the communications revolution, the collapse of communist regimes—have dictated an agonizing reappraisal of long-held theories about socialism, democracy, class conflict, and the role of ideology in social change. An ecological alternative suggests a complex mixture of local energies and global visions; it pits grassroots movements against the predatory interests of the transnationals. In its emphasis on the contradiction between capitalist industrialism and environmental sustainability, it expresses a key element in the limits of Marxism. Productivist as its core, the Marxist tradition failed to confront basic features of the global predicament: limits of industrial growth, the extent to which science and technology can lend themselves to social domination, universalization of costs and risks. In Northern countries, the decline of traditional left culture rooted in the industrial working class reinforced this theoretical inadequacy. The reality since the 1920s is that the main currents of organized Marxism and socialism have regarded modernity as a source of progress, embracing a utopian rationalism tied to the premises of capitalist expansion. Environmental problems (assuming they were even recognized) could be solved through a combination of proper technological innovations and managed economic growth, while nature remained a vital resource to be exploited for socialist goals.

By the 1990s the naiveté of such technocratic discourse had long become obvious. In acknowledging the failure of modernity to bring social progress—by conceding the limits of industrialism as such—ecological thinking pointed toward a post-Marxist radicalism grounded in a non-productivist dialectic.[20] Theorists like Paul Goodman, Ivan Illich, Murray Bookchin, Paolo Freire, Rudolf Bahro, E.F. Schumacher, and Theodore Roszak called attention to themes long buried within Marxism: human-scale organization, the recovery of equilibrium between human society and nature, direct forms of popular control, sustainable modes of economic development.[21] The critique of political economy (where retained) was extended into the sphere of nature, into everyday life. And it could be applied equally to both communist and capitalist forms of industrialism.

The main currents of the Marxian socialist tradition never considered the limits that nature imposes on economic and social development—hardly surprising given Marx's own contempt for nature "worship" and rural life, not to mention his productivist outlook. The assumption has been that capitalism is the sole determinant of environmental decay, obscuring a wider range of non-economic forces that feed into a phenomenon as complex as the global crisis.[22] One could go further: Marxism itself was historically immersed in the capitalist growth paradigm, the Promethean idea of mastering nature, to the extent it could never grasp how productive forces destroy planetary life-support systems. In effect, Marxism could never fully detach itself—its theories, strategies, and methods of struggle—from the imploding logic of capital accumulation in the epoch of industrial expansion.

Ecological theory does more than simply add a new dimension to Marxism; it suggests a holistic viewpoint that departs radically from the class-driven, productivist model. Industrial society is defined as a complex system of multiple and overlapping forms of domination extending to class, race, gender, authority relations, and increasingly, to nature. The notion that material affluence leads inexorably to social progress, to realization of the public good is necessarily overturned.[23] This model further stresses the role of cultural politics in broadening the public sphere where images and discourses are no longer, if they ever were, shaped by immediate class forces and politics. Thus politics is generalized into every arena of both state and civil society, beyond the institutional realm of governments, parties, and interest groups. In contrast to Marxism, ecological theory breaks with the Enlightenment impulse to conquer and domesticate nature: development entails adaptation rather than control, dispersion rather than concentration of power and hierarchy, sustainability rather than endless plunder. Twentieth-century history shows that the ethic of conquest leads to authoritarian politics, social domination, and ecological crisis. The demise of communist systems no less than the predicament of capitalist societies reflects this ongoing legacy.

Global Problems and Local Strategy

The urgency of the global predicament forces us to directly confront the issue of political strategy, defined here as a conscious, planned effort to merge thought and action within the sphere of politics, as part of the contestation for power that is a fundamental aspect of social change. The crisis demands not only a global vision but a global framework of action—an imperative that has not vanished despite the collapse of Leninism, the travails of Marxism, and the ideological power of postmodern discourse among the intelligentsia. In fact, the assault on universalistic motifs—proposed by postmodernism, new social movements, and localism—raises as many troublesome questions as it appears to resolve, especially in the industrialized countries where such counter-motifs have been influential.[24] In both Europe and North America, the strength of the ecology phenomenon stems from the strong appeal of localism often saturated with an anti-urban, back-to-the-land culture.

Reflecting upon the American experience, there is the perplexing question of how oppositional groups can pursue radical change within a political system that excludes real alternatives from serious debate. It has been difficult if not impossible for local movements to resist absorption or deradicalization.[25] For this and other reasons, the overriding environmental stratagem for more than a decade has been anything but localist or subversive: it has been profoundly mainstream, with an emphasis on interest group lobbying, professional staffing, fundraising, and the search for respectability. Such is the *modus operandi* of hundreds of top-down organizations like the Sierra Club, World Wildlife Federation, the Wilderness Society, and the Audobon Society. Mainstream environmentalism stresses piecemeal reforms within a context of limited governmental regulation and "private initiative." The all-consuming ethos of interest group managers is for compromise at every turn—understandable given their reluctance to alienate affluent member-ships, directors, donors, congressional leaders, and even corporate execu-tives. These managers readily go along with the myth that too much regulation threatens growth, jobs, and national security. And there is natu-rally a great fear of direct action, grassroots mobilization, or any type of con-frontation with the power structure. The deep cultural and structural transformation needed to overcome the downward ecological spiral is ruled out from the beginning.[26]

Yet localism remains very much alive in the U.S. and other industrialized societies, simply *because* the public sphere is so closed. The argument for sustainable development is increasingly forced outside the realm of normal politics: the party system, assisted by the mass media, manipulates con-sciousness and the rules of the game enough to suppress genuine conflict from public discourse, with the result that politics often degenerates into a spectacle tied to superficial images and symbols. In this milieu, a strictly electoral or institution-based strategy cannot go very far, hence the allure of a purely local approach that allows for more clarity of discourse and action. Ecology, with its penchant for nature fetishism and romantic solutions, is easily drawn in this direction.[27] Organizations fitting the localist pattern include Greenpeace, Earth First, the Greens (in some areas), and a multi-tude of community anti-toxic and anti-nuclear campaigns.[28]

The narrow range of public discourse in the U.S. was graphically illustrat-ed during the 1992 presidential election campaign. First, the enormity of the global crisis was essentially ignored by the three main candidates, even though one of the running mates (Al Gore) wrote a book, *Earth in the Balance*, that explored the crisis in great detail.[29] Although the familiar list of electoral issues (budget deficit, family values, free trade, personal charac-ter, et cetera) dominated the debates, Bill Clinton did offer modest proposals for pollution controls, consumer protection, and a shift toward cleaner fuel—but little else. Neither President Bush nor Ross Perot seemed particu-larly aware of the problem. More to the point, all candidates shared the national obsession with growth and more growth as the means to solving virtually *any* social problem, and all looked to revitalization of the corporate sector as the *sine qua non* of effective public policy.

Turning to a more specific example: The Los Angeles rebellion of April–May 1992 brought urban and racial problems (once again) to the forefront of national attention, yet the candidates had little to say about the mounting urban crisis beyond rhetorical gestures toward "jobs" and "growth." Aside from references to unproductive business schemes like enterprise zones, no comprehensive urban programs were unveiled. No analysis of the situation was offered, and no vision of a rebuilt infrastructure was presented. Just after the campaign President Bush, for his part, vetoed an already paltry twenty-eight billion dollar urban aid bill that had little more than symbolic value. Throughout 1992 the grinding issues of poverty, unemployment, homelessness, racism, and urban decay became, in effect, a submerged political discourse, a flight from probably the harshest manifestations of the global crisis. Politicians ignored the urban cauldron in their haste to win over the majority of Anglo, suburban, affluent voters— those most likely to go to the polls.[30]

President Clinton's electoral success stemmed from his ability to present himself as a new breed of Democrat—more concerned with stimulating business investment as a source of expansion and jobs than with the old "tax and spend" Keynesian liberalism. The function of government, according to Clinton, is to stimulate growth in the leading (for example, high-tech) industries and otherwise create a thriving economy with more investment, jobs, and revenues. While Clinton's neo-liberalism departs from the supply-side, trickle-down dogma of Reagan and Bush, it shares much in common with the "old" Democratic priorities of John F. Kennedy and Jimmy Carter, except that the end of the Cold War provides Clinton greater options. More significantly, Clinton's policies appeal to the affluent, including those seeking more disposable income and consumer goods.

Political and economic elites generally want growth for the U.S., at the expense of the rest of the world (or at least the Third World) and the global ecosystem. To sustain inherited patterns of privatized consumption, an auto-centered economy, militarism, and plunder of resources, the world system is doomed to imbalance, decay, and turbulence. With five percent of the world's population, the U.S. consumes about forty percent of all resources. (When Japan and the EEC countries are taken into account, those figures jump to fifteen percent and seventy percent respectively.) Each U.S. resident generates about thirty times the pollution of the average Third World resident. The U.S. produces one-half of all toxic waste and one-fourth of all carbon dioxide emissions. These figures are not decreasing, although Third World efforts to emulate Northern growth patterns can only exacerbate the crisis. (Of course, the South is a long way from catching up to the North: As of 1987, the average per capita income in the South was a meager 670 dollars, only six percent of the roughly 12,000 dollars per capita income in the North.[31]) Thus, as the majority of people in the North gorge while the majority of people in the South wind up severely deprived of basic goods and services, "development" today means an inevitable heightening of the crisis.

Since the public sphere in the U.S. marginalizes or trivializes discourse concerning the global crisis, ecology groups seeking to raise fundamental issues about the growth model are often drawn to grassroots politics. The two-party system, after all, is hardly an effective mechanism for social change. But there are other reasons why localism seems irresistible: eclipse of the communist model, the fragmented legacy of new social movements, a persistent anti-urban romanticism within the ecology movement. This is not an entirely negative phenomenon: Local strategy appears to be consonant with the deep Jeffersonian democratic tradition in American politics, with its emphasis on grassroots participation, protest, and community. It also spins off the new left radicalism of the sixties and seventies, with its attachment to populist and extra-institutional forms of activity. Above all, it seems to fit certain sensibilities of the ecology movement, which, in its radical expression, affirms a balance between society and nature, between human activity and the rhythms of the biosphere.[32] But this is only one side of the dialectic. If localism constitutes a necessary first stage in attacking the crisis, then the obvious question is: What next? Can localism represent a viable *political strategy*, or must it inevitably be confined to the realm of a dispersed, ineffective, pre-political rebellion?

The Limits of Localism

We have reached a point in worldwide industrial development where global ecological crisis, worsening by the day, forces serious appraisal of political methods, strategies, tactics, and even goals. If local movements reveal the shrinking capacity of normal politics, they nonetheless remain parochial, diffuse, and ideologically unfocused. Loose grassroots networks can win adherents and lay the foundations of community, but they lack the strategic direction and flexibility required for political effectiveness. The values of autonomy, identity, and spontaneity are not always compatible with norms endemic to the struggle for power, which have more in common with the bureaucratic model.[33] Confined to their social immediacy, local groups disengage themselves from a public sphere often regarded as hopelessly compromising; they want unmediated action and quick results. As Offe observes, "In their demands, new movements do not anticipate a lengthy process of transition, gradual reform, or slow improvement, but an immediate and sudden change."[34] From this standpoint, continuity (and success) depends upon the capacity of movements to congeal, merge, and build toward some form of political intervention.

Yet in the 1990s, after more than two decades of worldwide activity, environmental movements remain as localized and scattered as ever—at least those not already absorbed into mainstream politics. Localism moves along many paths: fixation on personal solutions (recycling, conservation), pursuit of single issues (tree planting, toxics, animal rights), a romantic attachment to nature (Earth First), "green" consumerism, new age spiritualism (goddess worship). These tendencies share a faith in the capacity of individuals or small groups to bring about change with minimal social conflict, along with a reluctance to identify corporations and other macro institutions as the *source* of the crisis. The predictable result is a flight from collective political action, as the ethos of harmony and individual "responsibility" prevails over that of struggle and confrontation.

The depoliticizing effects of localism are visible in the recent history of urban community organizing projects in the U.S.—many of them inspired by environmental ideals. What Sidney Plotkin calls "enclave" movements have grown rapidly in many cities, typically in response to the disintegration of urban life with its Hobbesian climate of fear and insecurity.[35] The enclave upholds a tenacious defense of neighborhood and community, of local space and identity, where these values are threatened by economic, political, and cultural incursions of all sorts. The inclination of city residents to rally around their vanishing sense of communal space is understandable enough. The problem is that, being largely defensive, such movements are organized to *avoid* the public sphere; they not only fear confrontation with the power structure, but change of any type. Insofar as it abandons any interest in transformative goals, this sort of possessive communalism turns out to be fiercely provincial if not conservative. In Plotkin's words, the enclave can become a "mini-fortress" that "tends toward a rigid and undifferentiated exclusionism." The result is a "consciousness reluctant to make social or moral distinctions between environmental dangers arising from modern physical and technical processes or urbanization and the more primitive fears of strangers."[36] There is clearly an empowerment process taking place in this context, but the question is: empowerment for what?

Local action, to be sure, cannot be dismissed as a complete failure. It does promise a rekindled sense of community that the chaos of urban life so often denies. It recaptures the spirit of Jeffersonian democracy. More than that, neighborhood struggles can often do much to *block* environmental destruction or threats of it—for example, around toxic landfills, nuclear reactors, incinerators, species extinction, and pesticide spraying. The problem is that local victories will mean little in cases where negative outcomes (for example, toxics) are simply transferred elsewhere. In any event, so long as local action fails to attack the web of corporate domination the systemic logic that feeds into the global crisis remains fully intact. All local groups eventually collide with, or become submerged by, social forces they cannot control. Meanwhile, the struggle for sustainable development is being lost.

The failure of local groups to expand outward, to engage the public sphere—to generate a transformative politics—testifies to the highly depoliticized nature of much ecological thought and action today.[37] The discourse of political strategy is inevitably enfeebled. Local "knowledge" is a vital ingredient of this equation, but without strategic form it becomes dissipated in the manner of enclave consciousness. Although dispersion seems appropriate to the postmodern mood of contemporary intellectuals and others, it works against the imperatives of political strategy and organizing, which is the terrain upon which the global crisis must ultimately be contested.

From Movement to Party?

In modern history the struggle to globalize local movements has become the domain of political parties, which have attempted to mobilize diverse interests for the purpose of winning and exercising state power. This was true of both the left and right, not to mention a good many political formations in between. The Marxian socialist tradition, whether in the form of electoral gradualism (social democracy) or vanguardism (Leninism), was always grounded in efforts to take control of the system of governance. From this standpoint, Marxism presented itself, as well as the capitalism it sought to transcend, as a global totality. The bourgeois social order, integrating all spheres of human life, had to be conceptualized by a grand theory and practice tied to the struggle of one great class (the proletariat) against another (the bourgeoisie). History was a protracted epic conflict between two rival systems of order and meaning. Particularly in the case of revolutionary socialism, politics took on the character of an all-powerful prime mover transcending and yet bringing together all fragments of social opposition. The Leninist model, as we have seen, embraced a strong millenarian and Jacobin drive giving decisive functions to the state.

The twentieth-century history of relations between movements and party has been a largely debilitating one for the movements; the parties have customarily taken control, especially where they succeeded in taking over state power. For social democracy, the hegemony of party over local struggles meant retrenchment of oppositional politics as the party became absorbed into corporate-state structures. For Leninism, on the other hand, the problems were twofold: contradictions inherent in bureaucratic centralism and the command economy, along with a monolithic belief system that delegitimated competing ideas. And efforts to carve out a third road alternative (Eurocommunism, Eurosocialism) failed to escape the deradicalizing logic of social democracy. In every case, original transformative goals, not to mention energies of popular movements, were lost in a maze of party-centered activity galvanized by a far-reaching theory. By the 1980s the failure of all these models was easy enough for anyone to see—first in the growing conservatism of European Socialist parties (for example, Germany, France, and Spain), second in the dramatic collapse of Soviet-type systems one after another. Given this legacy, the thematic of a globalizing theory retains little credibility today.

At the same time, increasing fragmentation of social movements in the face of a mounting global crisis poses the issue of political strategy and efficacy once again, which in turn raises the question of whether yet another forms of unifying intervention—beyond social democracy and Leninism—is available or possible. Obviously, the continuity and power of anti-system movements depends upon *some* degree of ideological and organizational coherence. Without such coherence opposition cannot unite around common goals, adapt to new conditions, and shape history; it can never become truly hegemonic. The modern context suggests that, for movements steeped in localism and parochial identity, dilemmas posed by engagement in normal politics cannot be evaded unless politics itself is somehow finally abandoned. The realm of normal politics includes elections, coalition building, party maneuvers, and, of course, compromise, which always introduces the risk of institutionalization.[38] There is the familiar danger of bureaucratic decline of the sort that has eroded socialist and communist identities since the 1940s.

For local movements, therefore, this merger process is fraught with ambiguity, insecurity, and imminent roadblocks. If grassroots struggles are diffuse and consumed with identity objectives, parties by definition are committed to winning power, to pursuing workable strategies and tactics. Movements jealously protect their own territories and identities against hierarchical and instrumental incursions of parties, however those parties may be ideologically defined. It follows that radical movements in particular will often resist the logic of electoral competition and interest group representation that is the hallmark of pluralist democratic politics. Such movements will prefer direct action over state governance, issue specificity over coalition building, and social protest over policy formation.

Yet the hope for radical, universal aims (ecological renewal, peace, gender equality) is negated by the absence of a comprehensive theory and practice. Dispersion without a unifying politics is bound to lead to futility. Even where local groups achieve a modicum of change or win limited victories, the result is usually neutralized in one way or another by corporate-state power: toxic wastes can be shifted from one area to another, the costs of pollution control passed on to consumers, the benefits of rent control undermined by condo conversions, the work of public clinics damaged by budget cuts, the efforts of cooperative producers stymied by the market, and so forth. Moreover, perfectly viable reforms are often nullified by bureaucratic obstruction. Within the inner city, too, disparate and sometimes conflicting neighborhood groups of blacks, Latinos, and Asian-Americans are often set against each other in the ongoing struggle for empowerment and reforms. There is a good deal of fragmentation *within* communities. In Los Angeles, for example, Latinos (comprising about forty percent of the population) have since the late 1960s created large community networks—neighborhood centers, clinics, co-ops—throughout much of the eastern part of the city, but Latinos as a whole remain powerless without a *political* formation linking the interests of disparate groups. Despite long years of protest and community building, the process of empowerment lags.

In the U.S. during the 1980s, one unifying force did seem to offer hope— the Rainbow Coalition, based in diverse local constituencies and linked to the presidential aspirations of Jesse Jackson. The Rainbow ideal was to crystallize the interests of dispossessed groups—labor, the poor, minorities, women, gays—within a single political vehicle that could contest power. By 1988, as the second of Jackson's candidacies was drawing to an end, the Coalition had built a solid presence in urban areas as well as the university and cultural sectors. This amounted to a breakthrough of sorts in American politics. The problem was that the bulk of political energy was funneled into the Democratic Party, which fit Jackson's long-term ambitions but ran counter to the professed grassroots politics of the Coalition. Radical goals were quickly compromised in the hopes of winning elite endorsements and funding. The Rainbow ultimately collapsed with the failure of Jackson's bid and, with it, the disappearance of the very few grassroots groups that were established in the process.[39] This effort to politicize local movements never burst outside of the boundaries of the established public sphere.

A more comprehensive synthesis of local movements and normal politics was attempted by the Greens in the early 1980s, first in West Germany, then in other parts of Europe, and finally in scattered countries around the world. Whereas the Rainbow Coalition downplayed ecological issues, the Greens brought them to the forefront of a radical vision connecting the rich variety of citizens' groups with an "alternative" electoral strategy. Greens championed the new politics of an anti-party party, flaunting institutional conventions (for instance, dress codes) while also taking the realm of power and governance seriously.[40] In West Germany, this formation challenged the SPD for support among liberal and progressive voters: Beginning with a series of impressive local and state campaigns, the Greens won representation to the national Bundestag in 1983 with twenty-seven seats and then expanded their regional and national strength during the 1980s. What most galvanized the Greens (particularly the radical faction) was the concept of an ecological mode of development, in which economy and nature would finally be in balance. While this concept lacked specificity, it was the first time any party confronted the environmental crisis head-on, as a matter of great urgency. For nearly a decade, as the German Greens won new victories, the growth of popular sentiment and the possibility of radical-democratic advances seemed to converge.

As the Greens won new increments of power, however, the temptations and pressures of normal politics began to erode party identity, chipping away at the organization's capacity to push for social transformation. As with the Rainbow Coalition, the grassroots component slowly disintegrated. The tension between *Fundi* (local, radical) and *Realo* (electoral, pragmatic) wings of the Greens was eventually resolved in favor of the latter, which argued for a moderation of programs, alignment with the SPD, and a strict institutional strategy. By 1990, with the onset of *Realo* hegemony and German reunification, the ideological decline of the Greens had reached a point where its identity separate from the SPD had largely vanished. In the

December 1990 federal elections the Greens dropped to 3.9 percent of the vote, below the five percent threshold for Bundestag representation, a failure that plunged party activists into further division and crisis. The *Realos* seized upon this defeat as a pretext for purging most of the *Fundis*, solidifying the Green metamorphosis into a regular social democratic party replete with mainstream ideology and a huge corps of professional politicians. A similar trajectory was duplicated elsewhere, though in less dramatic fashion.[41] Although centers of Green activity still flourished (witness the French Ecology Party), as an international phenomenon the radical side of ecological politics had faded by the early 1990s. As the Greens lost their original vision and zeal, the very idea of a party that could challenge growth-centered capitalist industrialism seemed more and more utopian, out of reach.

Crisis and Transformation

With the approach of the year 2000 the world order is becoming more imbalanced, fragile, and militarized than ever. Volcanic social eruptions in one city after another—Beijing, Seoul, Manila, Berlin, Los Angeles, Bangkok—reflect a new phase of polarization and conflict that accompanies global crisis. The postwar order dominated by two competing nuclear superpowers is now history. If the expansion of transnational corporate power with the globalization of economic markets signals further consolidation of capitalist hegemony, then the intensified rivalry among G-7 countries, the end of the Cold War, and intensification of North-South differences poses new threats to that hegemony. Further explosions could exacerbate the situation. The world system is shaped by modes of production and consumption that daily bring new pressures to an already enfeebled ecosystem; such pressures, as we have seen, emanate mostly from the industrialized powers.[42]

This global urgency compels all nations, North and South, to reassess developmental models that have been in place for decades and even centuries. The need for sustainable alternatives is now a matter of survival. As Martin Khor writes, "When viewed objectively, it is obvious that the levels of production and consumption in the North as a whole cannot be sustained; they will be brought down, either in a planned and orderly fashion or else eventually by ecological dictates when resources run out or the threshold of safety risks is crossed, in which case there will be social chaos."[43]

The question of how to break with old developmental patterns—how to plan for change at the global level—is a distinctly political matter. There are no technological or spiritual shortcuts. But oppositional movements, as we have seen, are highly localized and fragmented; their capacity to generate planning mechanisms at even regional or national levels is quite limited. While the total membership of NGOs is in the tens of millions, that number does not constitute a real political force. At the same time, because of the expansion of transnationals and sharpening of dependency relations inherent in the world system, most nations have lost autonomy and control over the course of events. International organizations like the World Bank, IMF, and GEF (Global Environmental Facility) are at the heart of the crisis and cannot be vehicles of sustainable economics and ecological balance. This leaves two possibilities: regional, national, and eventually international mergers of social movements and NGOs, or strong intervention by the U.N.—or some combination of the two. Lacking a system of global conflict-resolution, peacekeeping, and planning that can counter the power of transnationals (and the most influential nation-states), the crisis will veer more and more out of control. However imposing the global task might be, it will require a new type of international discourse, at once ecological and democratic, forged through popular struggles around the world. In Samir Amin's words, "A humane and progressive response to the problems of the contemporary world implies the construction of a popular internationalism that can engender a genuinely universalist value system...."[44]

Can the U.N. be the mechanism of such a profoundly radical transformation? Can an international system of governance along the lines of a progressive world government ever be established? If this is the main hope for avoiding chaos and catastrophe—and it can only work alongside simultaneous regional and national transformations—there seem to be few grounds for optimism. After all, the global corporations and their agents are gaining in power, while the U.N. is more than ever a tool of the G-7 countries (with the U.S. in the lead). Between 1946 and 1990 West European and North American nationals held seventy-one percent of the executive posts in charge of U.N. funds and specialized agencies, with American nationals holding roughly a quarter of the posts. Meanwhile, the proliferation of intense regional conflicts pitting nationalities and ethnic groups against each other militates against viable forms of universal cooperation.

The resurgence of nationalism in the 1980s, exacerbated by the spread of religious militancy and the breakup of the Soviet bloc, has profoundly negative consequences for the development of an ecological politics: it works against both the growth of local movements and the ethic of global cooperation. As the driving force behind anti-colonial struggles in the twentieth century, nationalism often had a powerfully transformative impact, as in Russia, China, Algeria, Vietnam, and Cuba. Today, however, it more often arouses a false sense of empowerment, in which the strength of nations is associated with the ideology of economic growth, authoritarian politics, fierce competition, militarism, and feelings of ethnic or racial supremacy. In this context, patriotism all too often emerges as a distorted search for the self or collective solidarity in a chaotic and hostile world.[45] These powerful sentiments obstruct a broader discourse that could address the global crisis, negating an international citizenship that could support the needed dramatic shift in priorities. The only countervailing tendency is that *all* nations, *all* groups, and *all* movements have a strong interest in reversing the ecological crisis.

As for the U.N., its high moral purpose—global cooperation, peacekeeping, amelioration of social problems—has scarcely been realized during the postwar years, even though a consensus within the General Assembly (now 179 nations) favors such proposals as a permanent U.N. military force and an international court with binding powers. Many U.N. partisans view these reforms as the first step toward a possible world government. Reflecting a post-Cold War shift of emphasis, the U.N. has mounted no less than thirteen peacekeeping operations in four years, all supported by the major powers. Still the world body is probably more undemocratic than ever: As the Gulf War mobilization showed, U.S. control of the Security Council served to undermine the role of the General Assembly, which was disenfranchised at the time key decisions were made. The U.S. can manipulate countries like Russia and China by recourse to economic pressures, while dependent countries (Egypt, Mexico, Brazil) must follow the dictates of the G-7 countries and the IMF or suffer dire economic and political consequences.

From the standpoint of ecological renewal, the U.N. was the focal point of new hopes at the 1992 Earth Summit in Rio de Janeiro. Never had so many countries gathered with such visionary ambitions: the Earth Summit was supposed to inaugurate a new era of eco-diplomacy, replete with new global institutions, discourses, symbols, practices, and social contracts. The global crisis was finally recognized as a severe threat to planetary survival.[46] More than 150 leaders assembled in Rio, all but a few of them dedicated to change, but in the end the Summit did little more than legitimate business-as-usual for the world economy, condoning long-established production and consumption patterns that coincide with the insatiable demands of growth economies. The U.S. was able to either manage consensus or block agreements at every turn—for example, on issues of bio-diversity, climate change, and toxic wastes. After all the documents and treaties had been signed, after 800 pages of the *Agenda-21* program for environmental action had been ratified, the Summit produced nothing to challenge the ecological status quo. In effect, the U.N. joined those rapacious corporate interests responsible for the crisis in the first place; deliberations were trapped in obsolete frameworks of discourse tied to the logic of the world market. A narrow, arrogant corporate ethic prevailed, despite the flowery rhetoric of change and sustainable development. Little attention was devoted to alternative energy sources, environmentally friendly technologies, strict regulating policies, more equitable resource distribution, or a break with polluting fuels.[47]

U.N. deliberations in Rio showed that we are far from an international community of interests that could override the power and self-interest of global industrial, banking, and political elites. The process also showed just how little democracy entered into the whole decision-making machinery behind the Summit. What emerged was a forum in which transnational corporate power was given *carte blanche* beneath the hyper-inflated verbiage of "green" transformation. Preparations for the Summit were conducted largely under the auspices of the Business Council for Sustainable Development, influenced by such companies as Chevron, Alcoa, Dow Chemical, Johnson and Son, Con Agra, and DuPont. Labor, citizens groups, and social movements had no input.

Given the oligarchical nature of the U.N., many environmental activists looked to the NGOs as the only hope for real change. In a separate, but still related, venue more than 30,000 citizens from around the world—most of them involved in one or more of the 750 NGOs—gathered in Rio to set up a grassroots alternative known as the Global Forum. The organizers believed that forces within "civil society," once empowered on a large scale, could for the first time set in motion an international movement comprised not only of environmental activists but also workers, people of color, indigenous groups, women, the poor, and others. The NGOs came to Brazil amid great fanfare, built networks, sponsored a two-week long Carnival, protested U.S. policies, and made grandiose plans for the future. The Forum attracted tens of thousands of participants and visitors from every social sector, offering space for cultural activity and political dialogue; an undeniably powerful spirit of cooperation defined the events. In the end, however, there remained a matter of politics: would the Global Forum be remembered as an initial step toward "saving the planet," or as just another environmental Woodstock?

Beyond the euphoria of the moment, the alternative scene in Rio turned out to have all the flaws of a spectacular, but decidedly non-political, event. The mood of celebration appeared to block serious political discourse from the Forum agenda. Political voices (especially radical ones) were marginalized, drowned out by the cacophony of utopian visions of love, harmony, and cosmic unity with nature, along with a wide assortment of chants, prayers, rituals, and exhortations to adopt better life-styles or learn more about green technology. The very idea of an NGO, moreover, was loosely construed to apply to nearly any grouping outside the governmental orbit: more than seventy percent were narrowly technical or non-political, while the corporate presence, which provoked debate and protest, was ubiquitous.

Before departing Rio many NGO activists vowed to continue the ecological struggle through "networking" and other activities. But the depoliticized groups that came away from the Global Forum did not seem to have the capacity for global action around a common set of goals. One transformative current that might have lent such integration to the Rio events and to the post-Rio possibilities was the European Greens. But their presence was hardly noteworthy: individual Greens from several countries attended, but they offered no unifying agenda of the sort initiated in Germany. Equally significant, groups broadly identified with the socialist tradition played practically no role. Various NGOs did become part of the formal U.N. apparatus, but, with the U.N. a tool of the rich and powerful nations, their space for radical intervention remains minimal. As the Summit revealed, the idea of equal access to the corridors of U.N. decision-making is a myth. For the U.N. to be an arena of far-reaching change, it would have to be reshaped in the direction of a democratic global parliament in which the poor Southern countries and NGOs around the world could fully represent those interests. There would have to be links between local groups and global structures.[48] This in turn would require a severe diminution of G-7 and transnational corporate power, along with a basic transformation of national and global structures.

In the end, the challenge of building a global network of NGO-type movements strong enough to overcome the destructive forces at work promises to be more challenging than it has been in single countries, where, so far, the results have not been inspiring. And, although the process of globalization has reduced the power of nation-states, they too remain a crucial arena of strategic change. The NGOs are comprised of thousands of single issue groups with few organic connections to one another. The gulf between labor and ecology, between religious (or "spiritual") and secular movements, or between urban and rural outlooks is not easily bridged. Nor is the chasm separating Northern and Southern countries, with their disparate world-views, interests, and priorities—as the Rio events demonstrated. At the same time, conceptual underpinnings of NGO politics would have to be revised: instead of a vision that locates movements strictly outside and against the state, it is necessary to identify how relations *between* civil society and the state can be elaborated in a transformative direction. One way or another, local movements will continue to have their own logic, their own turf, and their own goals, which no international meeting by itself can hope to tran-scend. But such movements will stagnate or disappear altogether if, sooner or later, they do not merge into larger structures or achieve at least interme-diate successes of the sort that gave historical definition to the socialist tra-dition.[49]

The Great Divide

As the global crisis intensifies, ecological politics is bound to play a decisive role in the unfolding of anti-system movements, both North and South. It promises to be the defining motif of a post-Cold War era of conflict in which East-West rivalries, along with traditional ideological formulas, pass into historical oblivion. For the moment, however, the only substantial popular force opposed to endless capitalist expansion consists of a scattering of local groups around the world dedicated to some vision of progressive change. Such groups typically lack global representation and ideological definition. Despite strong contributions of grassroots movements to empowerment, it is abundantly clear that global problems can never be solved though strictly local forms of action—although the local sphere may be the appropriate place to begin. Environmental issues are more global than ever, which means that crucial battles will be fought across national borders and across tradi-tional economic, political, and social boundaries. In this context the main currents of socialism appear politically obsolete.

In a context where the world market is more hegemonic than ever, partic-ular governments are increasingly unwilling to step forward or take initia-tives that will challenge corporate power, frighten capital markets, or undermine competitive advantage. Governments with diverse ideological labels, from Britain to China, from Italy to Brazil, remain captive to both the *logic* of transnational growth and the *ideology* of a self-correcting market. Like corporations, governments take a very short-sighted approach to development: they want growth, competitiveness, and quick returns on investments while steering away from a commitment to public values. Indeed, within the parameters of market ideology it is not easy to find the basis of a common good. And in a Hobbesian world system *all* countries are forced to scramble to protect their own (economically defined) interest by any means at their disposal, including military action.

The problem is that no global "invisible hand" exists, or can exist, to automatically correct the terrible consequences of rampant growth, so that in a period of mounting economic problems the environment will be either ignored or cosmetically touched up within a framework of corporate priorities. Since the Earth has finite resources and a fragile ecosystem, continuous development along the present path could soon take us beyond the point of no return. The annual rate at which the entire apparatus of production is destroying the global environment is so great that even ambitious reforms will make only a slight dent in the overall health of the planetary biosphere.

Conventional approaches to economic development—classical capitalist, social-democratic, communist, Third World—always stressed growth, to the near exclusion of "externalities," as the way out of the crisis (where crisis was even recognized). Growth was seen as a panacea, insofar as it could provide more jobs, prosperity, and a more dynamic social order in general.[50] But critical questions were rarely asked: what *kind* of jobs, what *kind* of production and consumption, what *kind* of goods—missiles or health clinics, submarines or schools? Such questions can no longer be ignored at a time when huge portions of GNP (both North and South) involve military production, wasteful commodities, and destructive technology that depletes scarce resources. Still another question must be addressed: How can science and technology be employed to help fight, rather than reproduce, conditions leading to ecological decay? Unless issues like this are directly confronted, gestures toward "sustainable development" will remain inconsequential, and the world market will continue to follow its own deadly logic.

The limits of political vision are detectable in the U.S. as a liberal "environmental" presidency replaces a Republican regime that viewed ecological reforms as a subversive threat not too far removed from the old Communist conspiracy. An example is Gore's book *Earth in the Balance*, with its proposal for a "Global Marshall Plan" in which the U.S., in tandem with the transnationals, assumes a leadership role in attacking the crisis. Gore is able to identify the most debilitating consequences of industrial growth, yet cannot locate a solution apart from the interests ("market forces") responsible for these consequences. Conceding the failure of the market to take into account ecological harm, Gore nonetheless can write, "As the world's leading exemplar of free-market economics, the United States has a special obligation to discover effective ways of using the power of market forces to help save the global environment."[51] Sadly, Gore's vision—reflected in a long list of imperatives for change at the end of the book—is neutralized by the free rein he gives to corporate power.

Looking ahead, any shift toward ecologically balanced development on a global scale, where limits to growth and an emphasis on social goods assumes primacy, will be difficult, costly, and painful for some. Clearly the most far-reaching adjustments will have to be undertaken by the G-7 powers, for it is *their* control of the world market and *their* command of resources and technology that now stands in the way of change. A fundamental shift means nothing less than a new relationship between society and nature, between development and the environment that goes beyond existing growth models, both capitalist and "socialist." It further calls into question the familiar crisis management scenario that simply moderates some of the worst excesses of corporate and military plunder while implicitly endorsing the failed paradigm itself.

In the mid-1990s there is no escaping the conclusion that political opposition barely exists as an organized global phenomenon. What makes the global crisis potentially catastrophic is the decline of left politics in the industrialized countries. The socialist tradition has for many decades embraced a statist, growth-centered ideology that allows little space for ecological rationality. In the 1980s, as we have seen, Socialist parties in France, Spain, Italy, and Greece, once in government carried out decidedly neo-liberal policies of technocratic efficiency and austerity. As for environmentalism, it is often immobilized by various depoliticizing tendencies: deep ecology, new age mysticism, romantic naturalism, a penchant for high-tech solutions, the ethic of personal responsibility. Such tendencies not only obscure the *material* dimension of the crisis but sometimes instill a sense of political fatalism, reflected, for example, in the idea of an impending, horrible ecological catastrophe.[52] Unfortunately, these ideologies seem to tighten their grip on popular consciousness the deeper the predicament becomes.

In the ecological tradition, moreover, there is a striking absence of alternative models of sustainable development congruent with a fully democratized social order.[53] Both classical anarchism and Marxism suffered debilitating *political* flaws of this sort, nullifying in part their transformative potential. New left radicalism, too, failed to articulate a transitional framework replete with a definition of economic and political forms appropriate to advanced industrialized society. Similarly, social movements that grew out of the sixties rarely looked ahead to a profoundly transformed society or, when they did, usually dwelled upon broad utopian ideals.

In Europe, the most ambitious effort to break this strategic impasse was mounted by the Greens. If the (radical) Greens put ecology at the center of their transformative project, they were still ecumenical enough to embrace the themes, if not the essence, of grassroots democracy, feminism, urban protest, peace activism, and so forth. Mirroring the postmodern milieu, their eclectic and dispersed radicalism was both strength and weakness: strength derived from their holistic breadth of analysis and vision, weakness born of a centrifugal pluralism that undercut strategic effectiveness. The familiar Green tension between grassroots struggles and normal politics created a dilemma that party leadership (as in the German case) could not easily resolve—a paradox sharpened by Green fixation on consensus building, process, and personal politics. And it was a dilemma, much like the one identified by Peter Gay at the beginning of this book, rooted in the dictates of winning and holding political power. This helps to explain why the Green momentum of the 1980s was rather quickly sapped, why a global alternative that could supersede the earlier Socialist and Communist Internationals seems a distant fantasy, at least from the vantage point of the 1990s.

The monumental shift from an obsession with growth to sustainability, from material exploitation to a system of balance and equity, from militarism to peaceful cooperation requires an equally profound and radical shift in the direction of ecological thinking. Such an agenda is shaped by the desire for a revitalized international system beyond a world order dominated by the industrial powers. Social movements and NGOs around the world have already *posed* this issues, but as of the mid-1990s they remain fragmented and weak, often reflecting the provincialism, enclave consciousness, and fear that increasingly shapes modern urban life in "new walled cities," where people seek illusory protection from a hostile, menacing, and polluted environment.[54] Universal discourses do not seem to offer a way out. With the socialist tradition in decline, oppositional movements lack the necessary political representation and global leverage that might some day be achieved through newly democratized international organizations that require anchorage in local, regional, and national forms of popular struggle. The question is whether they can acquire such representation and leverage in time.

Notes

Chapter 1
Introduction: Socialism, Democracy, and the Dilemmas of Power

1. Peter Gay, *The Dilemma of Democratic Socialism* (New York: Collier Books, 1962).
2. Ibid., p. 304.
3. This view differs from the common tendency to make a sharp break between Lenin and Stalin. See for example, Alex Callinicos, *The Revenge of History* (Cambridge: Polity Press, 1991).
4. Dusko Doder and Louise Branson, *Gorbachev: Heretic in the Kremlin* (New York: Penguin Books, 1990).
5. For more on this point, see Carl Boggs, *Intellectuals and the Crisis of Modernity* (Albany, N.Y.: State University of New York Press, 1993).
6. The early failure of Eurosocialism is charted by James Petras in "The Rise and Decline of Southern European Socialist Parties," *New Left Review* (July–August 1984).
7. Robert Michels, *Political Parties* (New York: Collier, 1962).
8. Adam Przeworski, *Capitalism and Social Democracy* (New York: Cambridge University Press, 1985).
9. For an excellent overview of American exceptionalism, see Seymour Martin Lipset, "Why No Socialism in the United States?," vol. 1 of *Sources of Contemporary Radicalism*, ed. Seweryn Bialer and Sophia Sluzar (Boulder: Westview Press, 1977), pp. 31–149.
10. Eric Foner, "Why Is There No Socialism in the United States?," in *The Future of Socialism*, ed. William K. Tabb (New York: Monthly Review Press, 1990).
11. Daniel Bell, *The End of Ideology* (New York: The Free Press, 1960).
12. Francis Fukuyama, *The End of History and the Last Man* (New York: The Free Press, 1992).
13. Ibid., p. 45.
14. Ibid., p. 289.
15. Ken Jowitt, "The Leninist Extinction," in *The Crisis of Leninism and the Decline of the Left*, ed. Daniel Chirot (Seattle: University of Washington Press, 1991), p. 84.
16. Chris Harman, "The State and Capitalism Today," *International Socialism* (summer 1991): pp. 33–34.
17. For a discussion on the global ecological crisis and its consequences for the future of socialism, see the epilogue.
18. Immanuel Wallerstein, "The Collapse of Liberalism," *Socialist Register 1992* (London: The Merlin Press, 1992), p. 107.
19. André Gorz, "The New Agenda," *New Left Review* (November–December

1990): p. 42.

20. See Ronald Aronson, "After Communism," *Rethinking Marxism* (summer 1992): p. 43.

21. See, for example, William Tabb's introduction to *The Future of Socialism*, p. 8.

22. Russell Dalton, *Citizen Politics in Western Democracies* (Chatham, N.J.: Chatham House Publishers, Inc., 1988), pp. 238–44.

23. See Claus Offe, "Reflections on the Institutional Self-Transformation of Movement Politics: A Tentative Stage Model," in *Challenging the Political Order*, ed. Russell Dalton and Manfred Kuechler (New York: Oxford University Press, 1990).

24. Samuel Bowles and Herbert Gintis, *Capitalism and Democracy* (New York: Basic Books, 1986), ch. 1.

25. See Joseph A. Schumpeter, *Capitalism, Socialism, and Democracy*, 3rd edition (New York: Harper and Row, 1950), and Robert Dahl, *Who Governs?* (New Haven: Yale University Press, 1961). For Dahl's considerably modified views, see his *Democracy and its Critics* (New Haven: Yale University Press, 1989).

26. C.B. Macpherson, *The Life and Times of Liberal Democracy* (New York: Oxford University Press, 1977), ch. 4.

27. Norberto Bobbio, *Which Socialism?* (Cambridge: Polity Press, 1988).

28. Perry Anderson, "The Affinities of Norberto Bobbio," *New Left Review* (July–August 1988): p. 29

29. For more on the concept of a radical-democratic model, see Ernesto Laclau and Chantal Mouffe, *Hegemony and Socialist Strategy* (London: Verso, 1985), pp. 149–93.

30. Sheldon Wolin, "What Revolutionary Action Means Today," in *Dimensions of Radical Democracy*, ed. Chantal Mouffe (London: Verso, 1992), pp. 242–51.

31. Ibid., p. 251.

32. John Keane, *Democracy and Civil Society* (London: Verso, 1988), p.15.

33. For a fuller discussion of the complexities of modern political strategy, see Laclau and Mouffe, *Hegemony and Socialist Strategy*, pp. 176–93. See also Murray Bookchin, *Remaking Society* (Montreal: Black Rose Books, 1989), pp. 159–204.

34. For a modern conceptualization of a shifting equilibrium of forces within the state system, see Nicos Poulantzas, *State, Power, Socialism* (London: New Left Books, 1978), pp. 123–60.

35. Laclau and Mouffe, *Hegemony and Socialist Strategy*, p. 180.

Chapter 2
The Marxist Origins: From Theory to Politics

1. Macpherson, *Life and Times of Liberal Democracy*, chs. 1–4.

2. Bowles and Gintis, *Capitalism and Democracy*, chs. 1–2.

3. Macpherson, *Life and Times of Liberal Democracy*, chs. 3 and 5.

4. Karl Marx and Friedrich Engels, "The Communist Manifesto," in *The Marx-Engels Reader*, ed. Robert C. Tucker (New York: W.W. Norton, 1972), pp.

331–62.

5. On Marx's theory of the state, see Hal Draper, *Karl Marx's Theory of Revolution* (New York: Monthly Review Press, 1978), and Martin Carnoy, *The State and Political Theory* (Princeton: Princeton University Press, 1984), ch. 2.

6. Marx, "The Civil War in France," in Tucker, *The Marx-Engels Reader,* p. 552.

7. Ibid., p. 555

8. Ibid., p. 557

9. Ibid., p. 557.

10. Stanley Moore, *Three Tactics: The Background in Marx* (New York: Monthly Review Press, 1963).

11. Engels clearly endorsed electoral politics in a pamphlet published just before his death in March 1895 in which he wrote, "With the successful utilization of universal suffrage...an entirely new method of proletarian struggle came into operation, and this method quickly developed further. It was found that the state institutions, in which the rule of the bourgeoisie is organized, offer the working class still further opportunities to fight these very state institutions." See "The Tactics of Social Democracy," in Tucker, *The Marx-Engels Reader*, p. 416.

12. See Moore, *Three Tactics*, pp. 37–61.

13. Ibid., pp. 11–33

14. Ibid., pp. 65–96.

15. I have developed this point further in "Revolutionary Process, Marxist Strategy, and the Dilemma of Political Power," *Theory and Society* 4, no. 3 (fall 1977): pp. 364–71.

16. This was the essence of Antonio Gramsci's later critique in "The Revolution Against *Capital*" contained in *Gramsci: Selections from Political Writings*, ed. Quintin Hoare (New York: International Publishers, 1977), pp. 34–37.

17. See Roger S. Gottlieb, *Marxism: Origins, Betrayal, Rebirth* (New York: Routledge and Kegan Paul, 1983), p. 51.

18. On the diverse Marxian attitudes toward parliamentary democracy, see Barry Hindness, *Parliamentary Democracy and Socialist Politics* (London: Routledge and Kegan Paul, 1983), ch. 1.

19. Leszek Kolakowski, *The Main Currents of Marxism*, vol. 2 (New York: Oxford University Press, 1981), p. 1.

20. Karl Kautsky, *The Class Struggle*, (New York: W.W. Norton, 1971).

21. On this point, see Massimo Salvadori, introduction to *Karl Kautsky and the Socialist Revolution: 1880–1938*, (London: New Left Books, 1979); Stephen Eric Bronner, *Socialism Unbound* (New York: Routledge, 1990), ch. 2; and Kolakowski, *Main Currents of Marxism*, ch. 2.

22. Salvadori, *Karl Kautsky and the Socialist Revolution*, p. 140. Although Kaustsky understood this process as one rooted in the dialectic of wage labor versus capital, he did argue for temporary alliances with progressive non-proletarian forces and parties in the struggle against Wilhelminian state domination. Also see pp. 150–52 of the above text as well as Gary P. Steenson, *Karl Kautsky, 1854–1938: Marxism in the Classical Years* (Pittsburgh: Universtiy of Pittsburgh

Press, 1978), pp. 112–14.

23. For a good overview of Kautsky's strategy, which reveals the absence of any cataclysmic crisis theory, see Salvadori, *Karl Kautsky and the Socialist Revolution*, pp. 59–73, and Bronner, *Socialism Unbound*, ch. 2.

24. Here, the objectivism of Kautsky's Marxism is more apparent: capitalist development bears the seeds of its own transcendence. On Kautsky's faith in science and "historical necessity," see Salvadori, *Karl Kautsky and the Socialist Revolution*, p. 33.

25. Karl Kautsky's *Dictatorship of the Proletariat* (Ann Arbor: University of Michigan Press, 1961), which wass written to show the necessary connections between socialism and democracy, clearly reveals this bias.

26. For a further elaboration of this point, see Hindess, *Parliamentary Democracy and Socialist Politics*, ch. 1.

27. See Salvadori, *Karl Kautsky and the Socialist Revolution*, p. 14.

28. Eduard Bernstein, *Evolutionary Socialism* (New York: Schocken Books, 1961). pp. 154, 163.

29. Lucio Colletti, in *From Rousseau to Lenin* (London: New Left Books, 1969), makes this point very convincingly.

30. For an extensive discussion of Bernstein's theory of the state, see Gay, *Dilemma of Democratic Socialism*, chs. 8 and 12. For a more comprehensive treatment, see Bronner, *Socialism Unbound*, ch. 3.

31. Bernstein, *Evolutionary Socialism*, p. 197.

32. Ibid., p. 149.

33. John H. Kautsky, "Karl Kautsky and Eurocommunism," *Studies in Comparative Communism*, 14, no. 1 (spring 1981): pp. 13–14. This abandonment of the last vestiges of Marxist "orthodoxy" (the dialectic, crisis theory, the notion of rupture) on the part of Karl Kautsky and others, needs to be seen as part of the general rightward trend in European social democracy during the 1920s.

34. V.I. Lenin, "'Left-Wing Communism: An Infantile Disorder," in *The Lenin Anthology*, ed. Robert C. Tucker (New York: W.W. Norton, 1975), pp. 550–618.

35. Lenin, "State and Revolution," in Tucker, The Lenin Anthology p. 381.

36. On the development of the pre-revolutionary Tsarist state, see Marcel Liebman, *The Russian Revolution* (New York: Vintage Books, 1970), chs. 1–3; and John Maynard, *Russia in Flux* (New York: Collier Books, 1962), chs. 9 and 10.

37. On Lenin's theory of the state, see Carnoy, *The State and Political Theory*, ch. 2; and A.J. Polan, *Lenin and the End of Politics* (Berkeley: University of California Press, 1984).

38. On Lenin's fascination with capitalist techniques, see Fred and Lou Jean Fleron, "Administrative Theory as Repressive Political Theory: The Communist Experience," *Telos*, no. 12 (summer 1972), pp. 63–92.

39. See Robert V. Daniels, *The Conscience of the Revolution* (New York: Simon and Schuster, 1960), chs. 3–6.

40. Contrary to the notion that there were "many Lenins," the overall theory and practice of Lenin and the Bolsheviks suggests a definite continuity. To look for scriptual variations in the writings of Lenin, and then weigh these against the

actual practice of the party, amounts to an exercise in scholasticism.

41. The common assumption that Leninist strategy was most effective when the state was strong does not seem to be valid; on the contrary, it is where political institutions were weak—where a crisis of authority deepened over a period of time, as in Russia—that Leninist revolutions have been most successful.

42. Georg Lukács, *Lenin* (Cambridge: MIT PRess, 1971).

43. On the manner in which democratic values outlined in *State and Revolution* were actually inverted by Lenin in practice, see Polan, *Lenin and the End of Politics.*

44. For Gramsci's insightful reflections on state and civil society in Russia, see "State and Civil Society," in *Selections from the Prison Notebooks*, pp. 235–37.

45. On the concept of a specific Marxist intellectual culture, see Alvin W. Gouldner, *The Two Marxisms* (New York: Seabury Press, 1980), ch. 5.

46. Lenin, "What is to Be Done?," in Tucker, *The Lenin Anthology*, p. 50. (Italics in original.)

47. Eric Olin Wright argues that Lenin—whatever his democratic vision—failed to confront the problem of organizational accountability, so consumed was he with the *class* basis of the state. See *Class, Crisis, and the State*, (London: New Left Books, 1979), pp. 194–204.

48. Like Kautsky and Bernstein, Lenin saw the transition to socialism as a process anchored in large-scale organization. Even in *State and Revolution* he argued that popular control was no longer possible under conditions of production in advanced industrial society, that "complex technical units" such as factories, railways, and banks could not operate without "ordered cooperation" and subordination.

49. See Michels, *Political Parties*, and Schorske, *German Social Democracy.*

50. Georges Sorel, *Reflections on Violence* (New York: Collier Books, 1950).

51. Georges Sorel, "Critical Essays on Marxism," in *From Georges Sorel*, ed. John L. Stanley (New York: Oxford University Press, 1976), pp. 111–75.

52. Rosa Luxemburg, "Organizational Questions of Russian Social Democracy," in *Selected Political Writings of Rosa Luxemburg*, ed. Dick Howard (New York: Monthly Review Press, 1971), pp. 283–306.

53. Luxemburg, "Social Reform or Revolution," in Howard, pp. 113–23. On Luxemburg's approach to parliamentarism and the liberal state, see Gay, *Dilemma of Democratic Socialism*, pp. 261–72; J.P. Nettl, *Rosa Luxemburg* (London: Oxford University Press, 1969); and Kolakowski, *Main Currents of Marxism–2*, pp. 76–88.

54. The truth of this observation was revealed, sadly enough, by the fate of the SPD itself after World War I when the party became a staunch defender of the status quo. Luxemburg herself was a victim of SPD authoritarian rule in 1919. For a greater elaboration of this point, see Schorske, *German Social Democracy*, and Roth, *The Social Democrats.*

55. Luxemburg, "Organizational Questions of Russian Social Democracy," in Howard, *Selected Political Writings of Rosa Luxemburg*, pp. 283–306.

56. Anton Pannekoek, "German Social Democracy," in *Pannekoek and the Workers'*

Councils, ed. Serge Bricianer (St. Louis: Telos Press, 1978), p. 57.

57. Pannekoek argued, along the line of Michels that social democracy "takes the form of a gigantic and powerful organization, almost a state within a state, with its own officials, finances, press, spiritual universe, and specific ideology (Marxism). By its general character, it is adapted to the pre-imperial peaceful phase." See "The World War and the Workers' Movement," in Bricianer, *Pannekoek and the Workers' Councils*, p. 140.

58. Pannekoek, "German Social Democracy," pp. 61, 65–67.

59. Pannekoek, "The World War and the Workers' Movement," in Bricianer, *Pannekoek and the Workers' Councils*, p. 140.

60. Pannekoek, "Tactical Differences with the Workers' Movement," in Bricianer, *Pannekoek and the Workers' Councils*, pp. 96–97. Pannekoek argued that although it could never be the locus of "class war" itself, electoral politics could enlighten workers about their class situation and therefore should not be rejected outright. The simplistic picture of council communism as "abstentionist"— a stereotype long cherished by Leninists and social democrats alike—is totally fallacious.

61. Pannekoek, "World Revolution and Communist Tactics," in *Pannekoek and Gorter's Marxism*, ed. D.A. Smart (London: Pluto Press, 1978), p. 116.

62. Pannekoek, "Principles of Organization," in Bricanier, *Pannekoek and the Workers' Councils*, p. 276.

63. This is the central theme of several essays written at various points in Pannekoek's life, assembled in the volume *Lenin as Philosopher*, (London: Merlin Press, 1975).

64. See the exploration of Pannekoek's ideas in Richard Gombin, *The Origins of Modern Leftism* (London: Methuen, 1975), pp. 87–97.

65. On Gramsci's theory of the factory councils, see pt. 2 of *Selected Writings 1910–1920*. See also Gwyn Williams, *Proletarian Order*, (London: Pluto Press, 1975), chs. 4–6, and Carl Boggs, *The Two Revolutions: Gramsci and the Dilemmas of Western Marxism*, (Boston: South End Press, 1984), ch. 2.

66. On this "prefigurative" dimension in Gramsci's view of the councils, see "Union and Councils" and "The Factory Council," in *Selected Writings*.

67. With the repression of the Turin councils, the defeat of revolutionary hopes in the period 1918–1921, and the subsequent rise of fascism in Italy, the limits of a strictly prefigurative strategy were dramatically revealed. Gramsci came to realize that the councils alone were not enough; the absence of centralized leadership left *Ordine Nuovo* impotent against its well-organized adversaries. After 1920, Gramsci began to devote more and more attention to the role of the political party—an emphaisis that permeated the later *Prison Notebooks*.

68. For a comparative analysis of the failures of European council movements, see Carl Boggs, "Marxism, Prefigurative Communism, and the Problem of Workers' Control," *Radical America* 11, no. 6 (November 1977), and 12 (February 1978).

69. Gramsci wrestled with many of these problems throughout the *Prison Notebooks*. See especially "Problems of Marxism," in S*PN*, pp. 381–419.

70. This denial of politics by the council theorists extended beyond their critique of parliamentarism to a rejection of the party form as such. This was the substance of Lenin's attack on "Horner" (Pannekoek) and other radical leftists in *Left-Wing Communism.*

71. On this point, see Boggs, "Revolutionary Process, Political Strategy, and the Dilemma of Political Power," op. cit.

72. The triumph of Jacobinism in Russian was not simply a question of historical conditions; in the absence of Lenin's vanguardist theory and practice, this outcome would have been impossible. The dialectical interplay of subjective and objective factors must form the basis of analysis.

73. This was one of Colletti's main criticisms of Bernstein's formula. See Colletti, *From Rousseau to Lenin,* p. 106.

74. This view was originally formulated by the Polish theorist Jan Machajski. For a summation of his views, see Gombin, *The Radical Tradition,* pp. 65–70.

Chapter 3
After Lenin: The Defeat of Democratic Socialism

1. On the statist myth of socialism, see Svetozar Stojanovic, *Between Ideals and Reality* (New York: Oxford University Press, 1973), ch. 3.

2. On the role of anarchism and syndicalism in the development of the radical left, see Richard Gombin, *The Origins of Modern Leftism.* (Harmondsworth, England: Penguin Books, 1975), ch. 4; and Daniel Guerin, *Anarchism* (New York: Monthly Review Press, 1970).

3. The democratic spirit of the Italian factory councils is captured in Paolo Spriano, *Occupation of the Factories* (London: Pluto Press, 1975), and Williams, *Proletarian Order.*

4. Robert Daniels, *Conscience of the Revolution* (New York: Simon and Schuster, 1960), esp. ch. 3.

5. On this point, see Lenin, "Left-Wing Communism: An Infantile Disorder," in Tucker, *The Lenin Anthology,* pp. 550–618.

6. For an analysis of the SPD along Michelsian lines, see Gay, *The Dilemma of Democratic Socialism*; Guenther Roth, *The Social Democrats in Imperial Germany* (Totowa, N.J.: Bedminster Press, 1963); and Carl E. Schorske, *German Social Democracy* (New York: John Wiley and Sons, 1955).

7. For Gramsci's critique of the socialist party, see "Towards a Renewal of the Socialist Party" and other essays in *Selections from Political Writings 1910–1920.*

8. See Roy Medvedev, *Leninism and Western Socialism,* (London: Verso, 1981) pp. 277–84.

9. On the theme of capitalist efficiency in Lenin, see Polan, *Lenin and the End of Politics.*

10. On the trajectory of social democracy between the wars, see Harrington, *Socialism Past and Future,* ch. 2; Albert S. Lindeman, *A History of European Socialism* (New Haven: Yale University Press, 1983), chs. 2–4; and William E. Paterson and Alastair H. Thomas, *Social Democratic Parties in Western Europe*

(New York; St. Martin's, 1971).

11. See C.A.R. Crosland's *The Future of Socialism* (London: Jonathan Cape, 1961) for a strong Bernsteinian argument in favor of reform over revolution.

12. Adam Przeworksi, "Social Democracy as an Historical Phenomenon," *New Left Review* (July/August 1980): pp. 42, 44.

13. For an overall critique of postwar social democracy, see Christiane Lemke and Gary Marks, eds., *The Crisis of Socialism in Europe* (Durham: Duke University Press, 1992), pp. 1–20.

14. Lenin's famous critique of reformism appeared first in his "What Is to Be Done?" See Tucker, *The Lenin Anthology*, pp. 12–114.

15. Frank Parkin, *Class Inequality and Political Order* (New York: Holt, Rinehart, and Winston, 1971), ch. 4.

16. The concept of the security state was developed by Joaquim Hirsch in his *Der Sicherheitstaat* (Frankfurt: Europaische Verlangsansalt, 1980). See also his "Fordist Security State and New Social Movements," *Kapitalistate* 10–11 (1983).

17. Gerard Braunthal, *The Western German Social Democrats, 1969–1982* (Boulder: Westview Press, 1983), pp. 262–63. On the limited nature of these reforms see Manfred G. Schmidt, "The Politics of Domestic Reform in the Federal Republic of Germany," *Politics and Society* no. 2 (1978): pp. 174–75.

18. Rudolf Bahro, "The SPD and the Peace Movement," *New Left Review* 112 (January/February 1982).

19. Norman Birnbaum, "The Crisis of the Social Democrats," *The Nation* (June 12, 1982) The "crisis of identity" theme was spelled out first by Richard Lowenthal in "Identität und Zukunft," *Die Neue Gesellschaft* no. 12 (January 28, 1981).

20. Standing apart from the SPD's general line were the Jusos, or Young Socialists, whose militant socialist politics attracted many students and intellectuals. The problem, however, was that the Jusos exerted little leftward influence upon the SPD as a whole. See Braunthal, *West German Social Democrats*, ch. 5.

21. On the relationship between the SPD and the Greens, see Diane L. Parness, *The SPD and the Challenge of Mass Politics* (Boulder: Westview Press, 1991), ch. 4, and Thomas A. Koelble, *The Left Unraveled: Social Democracy and the New Left Challenge in Britain and West Germany* (Boulder: Westview Press, 1992), ch. 6.

22. Oskar Negt, "The SPD: A Party of Enlightened Crisis Management," *Thesis Eleven* (1984), pp. 55, 57.

23. On the SPD's loss of image as a party of change, see Parness, *SPD and the Challenge of Mass Politics*, ch. 1, and Koelble, *The Left Unraveled*, pp. 55–56.

24. For an overall analysis of the decline of social democracy in the 1980s, see Thomas A. Koelble, "Recasting Social Democracy in Europe," *Politics and Society* 20, no. 1 (March 1992): pp. 51–70.

25. On corporatism, see Leo Panitch, "The Development of Corporatism in Liberal Democracies," *Comparative Political Studies* (April 1977): pp. 61–90.

26. See Koelble, *The Left Unraveled*, pp. 119–20.

27. For an analysis of PSI efforts to situate the party in the space between the DC and the PCI, see Gianfranco Pasquino, "La Strategia del PSI: Tra Vecchie e nuove Forme di Rappresentanza Politica," *Critica Marxista* 21, no. 1 (1983).

28. *La Repubblica* (November 26, 1982).
29. In order to resolve the PSI's "image" predicament, Craxi sought closer relations with European socialist leaders like Olaf Palme, Willy Brandt, Mario Soares, and Felipe Gonzales—presumably as part of his effort to transform the party into a modernizing agency. See David Hine, "The Italian Socialist Party Under Craxi: Surviving But Not Reviving," in *Italy in Transition*, ed. Peter Lange and Sidney Tarrow (New Haven: Yale University Press, 1979), pp. 139–41.
30. Gosta Esping-Anderson, *Politics Against Markets: The Social Democratic Road to Power* (Princeton: Princeton University Press, 1985), p. 312.
31. Ibid., chs. 9 and 10.
32. Michael Harrington, *Socialism Past and Future* (New York: Penguin Books, 1989), pp. 101–102.
33. On the Swedish welfare state, see Esping-Andersen, *Politics Against Markets*, ch. 5; and Ruth Sidel, *Women and Children Last* (New York: Viking Books, 1986), ch. 7.
34. Olof Palme, "Democratizing the Economy," in *Eurosocialism and America*, ed. Nancy Lieber (Philadelphia: Temple University Press, 1982), pp. 219–34.
35. Rudolph Meidner, "A Swedish Union Proposal for Collective Capital Sharing," in Lieber, *Eurosocialism and America*, pp. 25–34.
36. Anna-Grata Leijon, "Workplace Democracy in Sweden: Results, Failures, and Hopes," in Lieber, *Eurosocialism and America*, pp. 161–76.
37. See Colin Sparks and Sue Cockerill, "Goodbye to the Swedish Miracle," *International Socialist* (summer 1991): pp. 91–103.
38. The growth of working-class power in Western Europe from 1945 through the 1970s could be understood as a function more of sustained economic development than of particular social democratic policies. See Wolfgang Merkel, "After the Golden Age?: Is Social Democracy Doomed to Decline?," in *The Crisis of Socialism in Europe*, ed. Christiane Lemke and Gary Marks.
39. On the steady postwar growth of social democratic parties, see John D. Stephens, *The Transition from Capitalism to Socialism* (London: Macmillan, 1979), ch. 1.
40. From this viewpoint, the fate of social democracy was not a matter of certain electoral decisions or a shift away from labor in the postwar years, as Przeworski suggests. See *Capitalism and Social Democracy*, pp. 28–29.
41. The tendency to associate "decline" with simply loss of electoral support has led some observers to mistakenly assume that since social democratic parties often retain their electorial appeal the tradition itself is still as strong as ever. See, for example, Merkel, "After the Golden Age?: Is Social Democracy Doomed to Decline?" which shows that most parties have lost little electoral strength in the postwar period. But electoral strength and ideological direction or vitality should not be confused.
42. See Hirsch, "The Fordist Security State."
43. Robert Skidelsky, "The Decline of Keynesian Politics," in *State and Economy in Contemporary Capitalism*, Colin Crouch (New York: St. Martin's Press, 1979), pp. 71–76. See also the introductory essay by Crouch, "The State, Capital, and

Liberal Democracy."

44. Przeworski and Wallerstein suggest that indeed the main functional contribu-
    tion of Keynesianism was not economic but political insofar as it furnished the
    ideological basis of "class compromise" within "capitalist democracy." See
    Adam Przeworski and Michael Wallerstein, "Democratic Capitalism at the
    Crossroads," *Democracy* (July 1982): p. 54.

45. Koelble, "Recasting Social Democracy in Europe," pp. 51–52. See also Lauri
    Karvonen and Jan Sundberg, eds., introduction to *Social Democracy in
    Transition* (Brookfield, VT.: Dartmouth University Press, 1991).

46. Bo Rothstein, "Social Classes and Political Institutions: The Roots of Swedish
    Corporatism," in Karvonen and Sundberg, *Social Democracy in Transition*, pp.
    103–04.

47. Claus Offe, *Contradictions of the Welfare State* (Cambridge: MIT Press, 1984),
    p. 246

48. Jan Sundberg, "Participation in Local Government: A Source of Social
    Democratic Deradicalization in Scandinavia?" in Karvonen and Sundberg,
    Social Democracy in Transition, p. 138.

49. See A.J. Polan, *Lenin and the End of Politics* (Berkeley: University of California
    Press, 1984.)

50. On this point, see Roy Medvedev, *Lenisim and Western Socialism*, chs. 2–5.

51. On the early destruction of popular forces in the revolutionary process, see
    Daniels, *The Conscience of the Revolution*, chs. 4–7, and Paul Avrich, *Kronstadt
    1921* (New York: W. W. Norton, 1970).

52. On the development of the Left Opposition before and after the October
    Revolution, see Daniels, *Conscience of the Revolution*, chs. 3–6, and Maurice
    Brinton, *The Bolsheviks and Workers' Control* (London: Macmillan, 1970).

53. Lenin, in the period before his death, began to recoil from the behemoth he
    helped to create and expressed his misgivings about the bureaucratic tide
    already sweeping the party, but his belated protest could be little more than a
    feeble gesture. See Moshe Lewin, *Lenin's Last Struggle* (New York: Vintage,
    1969).

54. On the decline of the Soviets after 1917, see Oskar Anweiler, *The Soviets
    1905–1921* (New York: W.W. Norton, 1975).

55. See, for example, Polan, *Lenin and the End of Politics*, ch. 6.

56. Lenin, "State and Revolution", in Tucker, *The Lenin Anthology*, pp. 382–83.

57. Polan, *Lenin and the End of Politics*, ch. 3.

58. Joseph Stalin, *Problems of Leninism* (New York, 1933), p. 402.

59. Stojanovic, *Between Ideals and Reality*, ch. 3.

60. On Bukharin's contribution to the industrialization debates, see Stephen F.
    Cohen, *Bukharin and the Bolshevik Revolution* (New York: Vintage Books,
    1975), chs. 5 and 6; and Alexander Erlich, *The Soviet Industrialization Debate*
    (Cambridge: Cambridge University Press, 1960).

61. For an exhaustive treatment of the Soviet power structure, see Michel Tatu,
    Power in the Kremlin (New York: Viking, 1970).

62. Stojanovic contrasts the "bureaucratic-authoritarian" to the "democratic social-

ist" personality, noting that Lenin's concept of the professional revolutionary fit perfectly the former with its emphasis on iron discipline, sacrifice, and self-negation. See *Between Ideals and Reality*, ch. 8.

63. On the ritualization of Marxism in the U.S.S.R., see Herbert Marcuse, *Soviet Marxism*, pt. 1 (New York: Vintage, 1961).

64. On the concept of "state socialism," see David Lane, *The Socialist Industrial State* (Boulder: Westview Press, 1976). To the extent that such a concept is a contradiction in terms—socialism always implies democracy—then the notion of "bureaucratic centralism" as a system sui generis is to be preferred.

65. See Jowitt, "The Leninist Extinction," in Chirot, *The Crisis of Leninism*, pp. 74–99. See also Jowitt's *New World Disorder* (Berkeley: University of California Press, 1992).

66. On the absence of democratic participation in the U.S.S.R., see Lane, *The Socialist Industrial State*; Roy Medvedev, *Let History Judge* (New York: Vintage Books, 1973); Tony Cliff, *State Capitalism in Russia* (London: Pluto, 1974); Leslie Holmes, ed., *The Withering Away of the State?* (London: Sage Publications, 1981).

67. On the distinction between "technical" and "critical" intellectuals within Soviet-type systems, see George Konrad and Ivan Szelenyi, *Intellectuals on the Road to Class Power* (New York: Harcourt, Brace, Jovanovich, 1979), pp. 184–252.

68. On this point, see Jurgen Habermas, *Legitimation Crisis* (Boston: Beacon Press, 1973), pp. 68–75. As both Habermas and Marcuse observe, technological rationality tends to narrow the public sphere, undercutting prospects for democatization.

69. On the decay of Soviet society, see the contributions to Chirot, *The Crisis of Leninism*, chs. 1–4.

70. See Mihaly Vajda's excellent discussion of this theme in *The State and Socialism* (London: Allison and Busby, 1981), pp. 135–36.

71. On Gorbachev's shift, see Doder and Branson, *Gorbachev*.

72. For an analysis of the Gorbachev phenomenon, see ibid.; Stephen E. Hanson, "Gorbachev: The Last True Believer?," in Chirot, *The Crisis of Leninism*; Jerry Hough, *Russia and the West* (New York: Simon and Schuster, 1990); and the contributions to Tabb, *The Future of Socialism*, pp. 127–202.

73. Thus, Jowitt's thesis of a "Leninist Extinction," (in Chirot, *The Crisis of Leninism*), fails to take fully into account the extent to which these regimes were no longer really Leninist.

74. George Konrad, *Anti-Politics* (New York: Harcourt, Brace, Jovanovich, 1984).

75. On the collapse of legitimation in Soviet-type systems, see Chirot, "What Happened in Eastern Europe after the Revolutions," in Chirot, *The Crisis of Leninism*, pp. 3–32, and John Feffer, *Shock Waves: After the Revolution*, (Boston: South End Press, 1992), ch. 3.

76. See Daniel Singer, "Prometheus Rebound?," in Tabb, *Future of Socialism*, pp. 17–36.

77. On the failure within Marxism to generate a democratic socialist theory, see

Joseph Femia, *Marxism and Democracy* (Oxford: Claredon Press, 1993), ch. 3; and Bobbio, *Which Socialism?*

78. For an analysis of this phenomenon in Soviet-type systems, see Rudolf Bahro, *The Alternative in Eastern Europe* (London: New Left Books, 1978), pp. 30–37.

79. Richard Gombin, *The Radical Tradition*, ch. 2.

80. This failure of democratization in the West had much to do with the socialist fetishization of liberal democracy. See Alex Callinicos, *The Revenge of History*.

Chapter Four
The Third Road I: From Vanguardism to Eurocommunism

1. On the early differentiation between social democrats and communists, see Medvedev, *Leninism and Western Socialism*, ch. 1.

2. The best example is Trotsky's well-known analysis of Soviet bureaucratic degeneration in the 1930s. See his "Bureaucratism and the Revolution," and "The Degeneration of the Bolshevik Party," in *The Basic Writings of Trotsky*, ed., Irving Howe (New York: Vintage Books, 1965).

3. See Cornelius Castoriadis, *Political and Social Writings*, vol. 2 (Minneapolis: University of Minnesota Press, 1988); and Andre Gorz, *Strategy for Labor* (Boston: Beacon Press, 1964).

4. Stanley Aronowitz, *The Crisis in Historical Materialism* (New York: Praeger, 1981), pp. 124–30.

5. Togliatti's first efforts to articulate a distinctly "national road" go back to the 1944–45 period. See Palmiro Togliatti, *On Gramsci and Other Writings* (London: Lawrence and Wishart, 1979), esp. chs. 2 and 3.

6. I develop this argument further in *The Impasse of European Communism* (Boulder: Westview Press, 1982), chs. 2–4. See also Ernest Mandel, *From Stalinism to Eurocommunism* (London: New Left Books, 1978); and Henri Weber, "Eurocommunism, Socialism, and Democracy," *New Left Review* 110 (July–August 1978).

7. On early Comintern development, see Helmut Gruber, *International Communism in the Era of Lenin*, pt. 1 (New York: Fawcett Publications, 1967).

8. This declaration appeared in *l'Unita*, March 4, 1977, and was reprinted in *Italian Communists*, no. 1 (January–March 1977): pp. 123–24.

9. For a good summation of this process, see Neil McInnes, *The Communist Parties of Western Europe* (London: Oxford University Press, 1975), ch. 4.

10. On Togliatti's "via nazionale," see his *La via italiana al socialismo* (Roma: Editori Riuniti, 1964).

11. See George Ross, "The PCF and the End of the Bolshevik Dream," in *The Politics of Eurocommunism*, ed. Carl Boggs and David Plotke (Boston: South End Press, 1980), pp. 26–33.

12. Lucio Magri, "Italian Communism in the Sixties," *New Left Review* no. 66 (March–April 1971): pp. 40–42.

13. In the 1975 local elections for regional, provincial, and municipal offices, the PCI received 32.4 percent of the vote—an impressive gain over the 27.5 percent

won in 1972. More strikingly, it polled 34.4 percent of the vote in the 1976 national election, an unprecedented increase of 7.2 percent of 1972. Since 1976, however, the PCI's electoral status has steadily decline. For an analysis of PCI electoral growth through the Eurocommunist phase, see Giacomo Sani, "Italy: The Changing Role of the PCI," in *Communism and Political Systems in Western Europe*, ed. David E. Albright (Boulder: Westview Press, 1979), pp. 44–51.

14. See, for example, *Dialogue on Spain* (London: Lawrence and Wishart, 1976), based on interviews by Regis Debray and Max Gallo; and *Eurocommunism and the State* (London: Lawrence and Wishart, 1977).

15. *Dialogue on Spain*, p. 15.

16. The first major Soviet outburst was directed against Carrillo's *Eurocommunism and the State*, in the Moscow periodical *New Times* (July 1977), which accused the PCE leader of betraying "proletarian internationalism" and "denigrating real socialism" in those countries that have succeeded in creating a new society. For an account of this, see Ernest Mandel, *From Stalinism to Eurocommunism*, ch. 6.

17. Ibid., ch. 3. For a discussion of events and perspectives leading up to this conference, see Robert Levgold, "The Soviet Union and Western European Communism," in *Eurocommunism and Detente*, ed. Rudolf L. Tokes (New York: New York University Press, 1978).

18. Togliatti's strategically most important essays of this period were assembled by Luciano Gruppi in *Il compremesso storico* (Roma: Editori Riuniti, 1977).

19. On the frontist origins of postwar PCI strategy, see Giuseppe Mammarella, *Il partito comunista italiana* (Firenze: Vallecchi, 1976); Magri, "Italian Communism in the Sixties;" and Alastair Davidson, "The Italian Communist Party and Elections," in *Changing Campaign Techniques: Elections and Values in Contemporary Democracies*, ed. Louis Maisel (London, Sage Publications, 1976).

20. This point is developed by Herbert Marcuse in his *Soviet Marxism*, pp. 39–41.

21. For further analysis of this phenomenon, see Boggs, *The Impasse of European Communism*, ch. 2 and epilogue.

22. Such theoretical statements are repeated throughout Togliatti's writings, especially in the period 1958–1964. A good sampling is contained in *La via italiano al socialismo*—for example, pp. 179–82 and 192–96.

23. Probably Togliatti's most ambitious effort to build a connection between Gramsci and his own theory of structural reforms was his "Nel quarantesimo anniversario del partito comunista italiana," in Il Manifesto, *Da Togliatti al nuova sinistra* (Roma: Alfani Editore, 1975).

24. On the PCI's instrumentalized usage of Gramsci, see Boggs, *The Impasse of European Communism*, epilogue.

25. The discussion that led to the PCI's incorporation of "Gramscian" themes crystallized at the Tenth Party Congress in 1962. See "Report on the Debate of the Central Committee of the Italian Communist Party on the Twenty-Second Congress of the CPSU," *New Left Review*, nos. 13–14 (April–June 1962).

26. This was the essence of Berlinguer's three important *Rinascita* articles that appeared in the fall of 1973. These are reprinted along with a collection of other

speeches and documents in Antonio Tato, *La "questione comunista,"* vol. 2 (Roma: Editori Riuniti, 1975).

27. Enrico Berlinguer, "Report to the 15th National Congress of the PCI," *The Italian Communists,* no. 1 (January–June 1979): p. 8.

28. This post-Thirteenth Congress theoretical gestation took place mainly in the pages of *Rinascita,* where party leaders contributed to a long series of articles, many of which were assembled by various authors and published as anthologies. The most comprehensive of these volumes was Gruppi's *Il compromesso storico.* Others included Gruppi's *Togliatti e la via italiana al socialismo* (Roma: Editori Riuniti, 1977); and Pietro Ingrao's *Masse e potere* (Roma: Editori Riuniti, 1977). A more general sketch of the PCI's democratic road is contained in Giorgio Napolitano, *Intervista sul PCI* (Bari: Laterza, 1976)—an interview by E.J. Hobsbawn that was published in English as *The Italian Road to Socialism* (Westport, Conn.: Lawrence Hill, 1977).

29. Carrillo, *Dialogue on Spain,* p. 198.

30. The vote to dispense with Leninism at the PCE's Ninth Congress was 968 to 248; however, intense debate over this and related issues continued afterward. In the long run, according to many observers, the move toward "de-Leninization" was primarily a response to new democratizing impulses from the PCE's base.

31. See Georges Marchais, "Liberty and Socialism" and "In Order to Take Democracy Forward to Socialism, Two Problems are Decisive," in *On The Dictatorship of the Proletariat,* ed. Etienne Balibar (London: Unwin Brothers, 1977), esp. pp. 161–64 and 184–86. Balibar's defense of traditional Leninism is spelled out in the same volume, in "On the Dictatorship of the Proletariat." An excellent assessment of this debate in terms of its impact on PCF development is contained in Louis Althusser, "What Must Change in the Party," *New Left Review* no. 109 (May–June 1978).

32. Even the PCF's official departure from Leninism at the 22nd Congress angered many delegates who felt the party had abandoned its role as a class-based revolutionary organization. See Balibar, "On the Dictatorship of the Proletariat."

33. This line of thinking is particularly visible in the Soviet attack on Carrillo's theoretical work. One example was the editorial, "Contrary to the Interests of Peace and Socialism in Euope," *New Times* (June 1977).

34. A good overview of the Soviet approach is furnished by Levgold, "Soviet Union and Western European Communism," in Tokes, *Eurocommunism and Detente.*

35. Togliatti, *La via italiana al socialism,* pp. 181–82.

36. Pietro Ingrao, "Democrazia borghese o stalinismo? No: democrazia di massa," *Rinascita* (Feb. 6, 1976). An excellent elaboration of this point can be found in Ingrao's introduction to *Masse e potere.* For the PCE, see Carrillo, *Eurocommunism and the State,* pp. 89–91.

37. Guy Besse, "Reply to Balibar" in Balibar, *Dictatorship of the Proletariat,* p. 177.

38. Gruppi, "Partecipazione al governo, alternanza, compromesso storio," in *Almanacco PCI '79* (Roma: Fratelli Spada, 1979), p. 64.

39. Ibid.

40. Carlo Cardia, "Una proposta nuova nel 'dialogo' con il mondo cattolico," in *Almanacco PCI '79*, p. 58.

41. Carrillo, *Eurocommunism and the State*, pp. 101–02. Carrillo defined the "new political formation" as a "confederation of political parties and other forces" that would expand on the basis of growing socialist consensus.

42. Ingrao, *Masse e potere*, p. 43.

43. Fernando Claudin's critique of Eurocommunism on this score was valid for the PCF but much less accurate in the more ambiguous and complex cases of the PCE and PCI. See *Eurocommunism and Socialism* (London: New Left Books, 1978).

44. For an analysis of PCI alliance politics in the postwar period, see Stephen Hellman, "The PCI's Alliance Strategy," in *Communism in France and Italy*, ed. Donald L.M. Blackmer and Sidney Tarrow (Princeton, N.J.: Princeton University Press, 1975), esp. pp. 383–89.

45. According to Ingrao, the "crisis of institutions" in Italy had three dimensions: (1) the backwardness and inefficiency of the state bureaucracy; (2) the weakness of parliament relative to the executive; and (3) the immobilism of the political parties. *Masse e potere*, pp. 259–60.

46. Max Jaggi, Roger Muller, and Sil Schmid, *Red Bologna* (London: Writers and Readers, 1977), pp. 34–42. In Bologna there were 18 neighborhood councils with nearly 300 councillors—a more developed local network than existed in any other Italian city.

47. Ibid., pp. 199–200. See the interview with Bologna mayor Renato Zangheri.

48. Enrico Berlinguer, "Report to the 14th National Congress of the PCI" (March 18–23, 1975), *Italian Communists* no. 2 (March–May 1975): pp. 102.

49. Carrillo, *Triunfo* (July 3, 1976), p. 7, and *Il Manifesto* (November 1, 1975), p. 2, both quoted in Eusebio M. Mujal-Leon, "The Domestic and International Evolution of the Spanish Communist Party," in Tokes, *Eurocommunism and Detente*, pp. 243, 245.

50. The PCF officially rejected the goals of European integration, but after its support of the Joint Program (with the socialists) in 1972 it agreed in practice "to participate in the further extension of the EEC and its institutions." See Heinz Timmerman, "Democractic Socialists, Eurocommunists, and the West" in *The European Left: Italy, France, and Spain*, William E. Griffith (Toronto: D.C. Heath, 1979) pp. 180–84.

51. One of the first public statements endorsing the EEC came, predictably, from Giorgio Amendola. See "Working Class Initiative to Build European Cooperation," *Italian Communists* no. 3 (June–August 1975): p. 62.

52. The emphasis on ideological hegemony—and the looming but often distorted shadow of Gramsci—was clearly evident throughout Napolitano's *Intervista sul PCI* and in Carrillo's *Eurocommunism and the State*, ch. 3. See also Ingrao's *Potere e masse*, pp. 240–253.

53. For a discussion of Lenin's affirmation of state over civil society and its obsolescene for the advanced industrial setting, see John Keane, *Democracy and Civil Society* (London: Verso, 1988), pp. 117–20.

54. Ingrao, *Masse e potere*, pp. 42–47, 250–53, and 259–61. For a more general the-oretical discussion of the state that is compatible with this perspective, see Poulantzas, *State, Power, Socialism*, pp. 12–35, 154–57.

55. Ingrao, *Masse e potere*, pp. 240–41.

56. Ibid., pp. 250–53. This takes up the familiar Togliattian theme—the gradual modification of structures—and carries it one step further by arguing that the party itself should never be the exclusive agency of hegemony. Of all PCI theorists, Ingrao probably had the most elaborate views on the transition.

57. Carrillo, *Eurocommunism and the State*, pp. 27–28.

58. On the relationship between liberalism and socialism in this context, see Bobbio, *Which Socialism?* While never a member of the PCI, Bobbio in fact exercised considerable influence on the Italian left in areas of political strategy.

59. Here it is misleading to argue that Eurocommunist strategy was nothing more than a recycling of Kautskian social democracy simply because it shares the same parliamentarist illusions. For an example of this comparison, see "The Age of Reform," *Monthly Review* 28, no. 2 (June 1976): pp. 1–17.

60. Carrillo, *Eurocommunism and the State*, p. 28. It is necessary to recognize the differences here between chronic, ongoing crises that are endemic to capitalism—basic contradictions—and catastrophic crises of the sort that might lead to systemic collapse. The Eurocommunists recognized that first—indeed they based their strategy on it—but they insisted that global capitalism is strong enough to contain the latter.

61. Weber, "Eurocommunism, Socialism, and Democracy," p. 113.

62. Foremost among such themes was the Hegelian tradition, which exerted a compelling influence on the development of Italian Marxism beginning with the work of Antonio Labriola. See Paul Piccone, "Labriola and the Roots of Eurocommunism," *Berkeley Journal of Sociology* 22 (1977–78): p. 3–38.

63. As Pontusson notes, the Eurocommunist "need for consensus serves as a pretext to avoid the problem of coercion, and this is in part related to the way in which they [Eurocommunists] perceive the transition to socialism. See Jonas Pontusson, "Gramsci and Eurocommunism: A Comparative Analysis of Conceptions of Class Rule and Socialist Transistion," *Berkeley Journal of Sociology* 25 (1980): p. 223.

64. See Franco Rodano, *Sulla politica dei comunisti* (Torino: Boringheri, 1975), pp. 106–108.

65. On the primacy of this (structural reformist) definition of the "political" in Togliatti's strategic thinking, see Claudio Pavone, "Togliatti, la 'neutalità' dello stato e delle istituzioni," in Il Manifesto, *Da Togliatti alla nuova sinistra*, pp. 138–39.

66. It is worth mentioning here that Gramsci's own theoretical outlook suffered from a certain ambiguity and in some areas even a one-sidedness, especially in his approach to the state, where the influence of Lenin ran deep. In particular, Gramsci remained convinced that—given a favorable balance of political forces—a direct frontal assault on the bourgeois state was a strategic necessity. Once swept away, the old political order would be replaced by a qualitatively

new proletarian-socialist state the outlines of which were never specified.

67. Nicola Badaloni, "Gramsci and the Problem of Revolution," in *Gramsci and Marxist Theory*, ed. Chantal Mouffe (London: Routledge and Kegan Paul, 1979), p. 103.

68. Concerning strategic issues of socialist politics in Europe, see John D. Stephens, conclusion to *The Transition form Capitalism to Socialism* (London: Macmillan, 1977).

69. On this point, see Claudin, *Eurocommunism and Socialism*, pp. 102–04, and Lucio Colletti, "The Three Faces of the Italian Communist Party," *Telos*, no. 42 (Winter 1979–80): pp. 117–120.

70. In 1945 the PCI became the dominant governing force in Bologna, continuing to rule that city throughout the postwar years. See Jaggi, et. al., *Red Bologna*, and Gianluigi Degli Esposti, *Bologna PCI* (Bologna: Il Mulino, 1966).

71. On PCI decline during the 1980s, see Armen Antonian, *Toward a Theory of Eurocommunism* (New York: Greenwood Press, 1987), ch. 8. See also Tobias Abse, "Judging the PCI," *New Left Review* no. 154 (September–October 1985).

72. See Magri, "The European Left Between Crisis and Refoundation," *New Left Review* no. 189 (September–October 1991).

73. See Chris Bambery, "The Decline of the West European Communist Parties," *International Socialism* (Winter 1990). For a different, more optimistic view, see Luciana Castellina, "Remaining an Italian Communist: Reflections on the 'Death of Socialism,'" in Tabb, *The Future of Socialism*, pp. 37–47.

74. On the PCI and the women's movement, see Judith Adler Hellman, "The Italian Communists, the Women's Question, and the Challenge of Feminism," *Studies in Political Economy* (Spring 1984).

75. See Boggs, *Social Movements and Political Power*, pp. 67–74 for an analysis of this phenomenon.

76. Hellman, "The Italian Communists, the Women's Question, and the Challenge of Feminism," pp. 69–70.

77. Annarita Buttafuoco, "Italy: the Feminist Challenge," in Boggs and Plotke, *The Politics of Eurocommunism*, pp. 214–16. See also Biancamaria Frabotta, ed., *La politica del femminismo* (Roma: Savelli, 1978).

78. To argue that the PCI had become institutionalized was not to deny the party's extensive grassroots presence, which compared favorably with other Italian parties, nor its relatively open and participatory style in contrast to the Leninist model of organization. For a more favorable assessment of the PCI's approach to democracy, see Jaggi, et. al., *Red Bologna*, and Carl Marzani, *The Promise of Eurocommunism* (Westport, Conn.: Lawrence Hill, 1980).

79. Boggs, *The Impasse of European Communism*, pp. 57–63.

80. See George Ross and Jane Jenson, "The Tragedy of the French Left," *New Left Review* no. 171 (September–October 1988): p. 37.

81. Louise Beaulieu and Jonathan Cloud, "Political Ecology and the Limits of the Communist Vision," in Boggs and Plotke, *The Politics of Eurocommunism*.

82. On the point, see Daniel Cohn-Bendit, *Obsolete Communism: the Left Wing Alternative* (New York: McGraw-Hill, 1968), and Daniel Singer, *Prelude to*

Revolution (New York: Hill and Wang, 1970).

83. For a discussion of the PCF decline, see Bruno Buongiovanni, "The French Communist Party in the 1970s," *Telos* (Spring, 1983); George Ross, "The Dilemmas of Communism in Mitterand's France," *New Political Science*, no. 12 (1984); Cornelius Castoriadis, "The French Communist Party: A Critical Anatomy," *Dissent* (Summer 1979); and Daniel Singer, "The French Communist Party: On the Way Out?," *The Nation* (September 1, 1984).

84. Temma Kaplan, "Democracy and the Mass Politics of the PCE," in Boggs and Plotke, *The Politics of Eurocommunism.*

85. These Leninist "residues" finally came to the surface in 1984 when dissident PCE members set up an orthodox pro-Soviet party led by Ignacio Gallegos. It claimed 25,000 members, compared with 80,000 for the PCE.

86. Andre Gunder Frank, "Crisis of Ideology and Ideology of Crisis," in *Dynamics of Global Crisis*, ed. Samir Amin, et. al. (New York: Monthly Review Press, 1984), p. 148.

87. Immanuel Wallerstein, *Historical Capitalism* (London: Verso, 1983), pp. 85–92.

88. See Boggs, *The Impasse of European Communism*, ch. 3.

89 . See "Il PCI e le multinazionali," in Giacomo Luciani, *Il PCI e il capitalism occidentale* (Milano: Luganesi, 1977). There is also a brief discussion of this problem in Heinz Timmerman, "Democratic Socialists, Eurocommunists, and the West," in Griffith, *European Left*, pp. 180–85.

90. Lucio Libertini, "The Problem of the PCI," in *Eurocommunism: The Italian Case*, ed. Austin Ranney and Giovanni Sartori (Washington D.C.: American Enterprise Institute, 1978), p. 159.

91. On PCI electoral gains going through the phase of Eurocommunism see Albright, introduction to *Communism and the Political Systems of Western Europe.*

92. Ingrao, in *Masse e potere* (pp. 385–86), argued that a dialectical relationship between "central" and "local" forms must be characteristic of the democratic road, but he hedged by deffering construction of the local organs to a future moment when socialist democracy can presumably be posed.

93. Claus Offe, "Political Authority and Class Structures," in *Critical Sociology*, ed. Paul Connerton (New York: Penguin Books, 1976), p. 404. Italics mine.

94. On the limits of the parliamentary road, see Hindess, *Parlimentary Democracy and Socialist Politics*, conclusion.

95. Poulantzas, *State, Power, Socialism*, p. 209.

96. On the theme of PCI institutionalization, see Sidney Tarrow, *Peasant Communism in Southern Italy* (New Haven: Yale University Press, 1967), ch. 12; and Robert H. Evans, *Coexistence: Communism and its Practice in Bologna*, pt. 2 (Notre Dame: University of Notre Dame Press, 1967).

97. Eurocommunist tactics did in fact anticipate a leftward shift among state workers in the event of a leftist government, allowing for a smooth and continous transition to a new order of priorities, but this scheme was rarely discussed in any detail. On the limitaions of the PCI's approach to the public sector, see Paolo Flores and Franco Moretti, "Paradoxes of the Italian Political Crisis," *New*

Left Review no. 96 (March–April 1976): pp. 52–54.

98. See Degli Esposti, *Bologna PCI*, and Evans, *Coexistence*.

99. See, for example, Poulantzas, *State, Power, Socialism*, pp. 232–39; Piven and Cloward, *Poor People's Movements*, introduction; and Alan Wolfe, *Limits of Legitimacy* (New York: The Free Press, 1978), ch. 9.

100. Maria Antonietta Macciocchi, *Letters from Inside the Italian Communist Party to Louis Althusser* (London: New Left Books, 1973), pp. 94, 135–46, 205, 209–91.

101. Lucio Magri and Filippo Maone, "l'organizzazzione comunista: strutture e metodi di direzione," *Il Manifesto* (September 1969), pp. 29–32.

102. I first presented this argument in my article "Italian Communism in the Seventies," *Socialist Review*, no. 34 (July–August 1977): pp. 105–18.

103. See, for example, Togliatti, *La via italiana al socialismo*, pp. 192–93, 213–14.

104. Enrico Berlinguer, *La grande avanzata comunista* (Roma: Editori Riuniti, 1975), pp. 96–97.

105. Antonien, *Toward a Theory of Eurocommunism*, ch. 9.

106. Abse, "Judging the PCI," p. 40.

107. Luxemburg, "Social Reform or Revolution," in *Selected Political Writings of Rosa Luxemburg*, ed. Dick Howard (New York: Monthly Review Press, 1971), pp. 52–134.

Chapter 5
The Third Road II: The Rise and Decline of Eurosocialism

1. The only exception to this pattern—albeit a brief one—was the French communists' participation in national government during 1981–84. Their role, however, was one of a very junior partner to the socialists.

2. On the erosion of class conflict, see Etienne Balibar, "From Class Struggle to Classless Struggle?," in *Race, Nation, Class*, Etienne Balibar and Immanuel Wallerstein (London: Verso, 1991), pp. 153–184.

3. For an outline of basic Eurosocialist postulates, see Lieber, *Eurosocialism and America*, and Harrington, *Socialism Past and Future*, ch. 9.

4. On the relationship between the left and the French socialists, see Arthur Hirsch, *The French New Left*, pp. 208–14. For a general discussion of the radicalizing impact of new social movements on Socialist parties in the European contest, see Massimo Teodori, "New Lefts in Europe," in *Strategies and Impact of Contemporary Radicalism*, ed. Bialer and Sluzar (Boulder: Westview Press, 1977).

5. Byron Criddle, "The French Parti Socialiste," in *Social Democratic Parties in Western Europe*, ed. William E. Paterson and Alastair H. Thomas (London: Croom Helm, 1977), pp. 38–39.

6. George A. Codding, Jr. and William Safran, *Ideology and Politics: The Socialist Party of France* (Boulder: Westview Press, 1979), pp. 220–27.

7. Mark Kesselman, "Socialism Without Workers: The Case of France," *Kapitalistate* 10–11 (1983): pp. 17–19.

8. Jonathan Story, "Social Revolution and Democracy in Iberia," in Paterson and Thomas, *Social Democratic Parties in Western Europe*.

9. Stanley G. Payne, "Spain's Political Future," *Current History* (December 1982): pp.19–20. This growing detachment from the Marxist tradition did, of course, create various tensions and divisions within the leadership. See Donald Share, "Spain: Socialists as Neoliberals," *Socialist Review* (January–March 1988)

10. See Payne, "Spain's Political Future," and Share, "Spain: Socialists as Neoliberals," on this point.

11. Howard R. Penniman, *Greece at the Polls* (Washington D.C.: American Enterprise Institute, 1981), pp. 44–46.

12. Ibid., pp. 67–70.

13. This broadening of the public sphere could, in part, be attributed to the historic role of new social movements, See Teodori, "New Lefts in Europe," and Alain Touraine, *Return of the Actor* (Minneapolis: University of Minnesota Press, 1988).

14. Felipe Gonzales, quoted in Donald Share, *Dilemmas of Social Democracy* (New York: Greenwood Press, 1989), p. 139.

15. On the early development of the French socialist international outlook, see Diana Johnstone, *The Politics of the Euromissiles* (London: Verson, 1984), pp. 81–101.

16. Eurosocialist ideological and policy departures were outlined less in coherent theoretical statements than in speeches, pamphelets, and short articles. For an overview of Eurosocialist development, see Tom Gallagher and Allan M. Williams, eds., *Southern European Socialism* (New York: Manchester University Press, 1989).

17. Henri Weber, "French Employees Under Socialism," *New Policital Science* 12 (1984): pp. 46–47.

18. For some excellent analyses of this Mediterranean cycle of dependency and stagnation, see Giovanni Arrighi, ed., *Semiperipheral Development: The Politics of Southern Europe in the Twentieth Century* (Beverly Hills, Calif.: Sage Publications, 1985).

19. See Diana Johnstone's account in *In These Times* (May 2–8, 1984): p. 9.

20. As Kesselman notes, it was precisely this (social-democratic) Keynesian dimension of French socialist economic restructuring that set its austerity program apart from the strict market approach. See Mark Kesselman, "Capitalist Austerity Versus Socialist 'Rigeur': Does it Make a Difference?," *New Political Science* 12 (1984).

21. Daniel Singer, "Letter from Europe," *The Nation* (February 24, 1984). Singer wrote that in the Talbot situation the left government tried to use the CGT as a transmission belt for the purpose of restoring labor peace, but with only mixed success.

22. The PCF decision to leave the government was not a matter of basic differences with the socialists—they agreed on a program of economic and technological modernization—but involved largely secondary or tactical disagreements over austerity and other issues.

23. Diana Johnstone, "Mitterrand's New Curriculum," *In These Times* (Sept. 26–Oct. 2, 1984): p. 7.

24. Mark Kesselman, "Lyrical Illusions or a Socialism of Governance: Whither French Socialism?," *Socialist Register 1985–86* (New York: Monthly Review Press, 1986).

25. Chris Howell, "The Dilemmas of Post-Fordism," *Politics and Society* (March 1992), pp. 91–93.

26. Daniel Singer, "Bad News for French Socialists," *The Nation* (November 30, 1984).

27. Lucy Komisar, "Democracy First, Then Revolution," *The Nation* (February 11, 1984).

28. Adrian Shubert, "The Socialists and NATO: Bringing Spain Back into Europe," *The Nation* (December 1, 1985).

29. See Share, *Dilemmas of Social Democracy*, p. 105.

30. Michalis Sproudalakis, "The Greek Socialists in Action," unpublished manuscript (1985).

31. Allan M. Williams, "Socialist Economic Policies," in Gallagher and Williams, *Southern European Socialism*, pp. 194–95.

32. Nicholas Xenos, "The Greek Change," *Democracy* (Spring 1983): pp. 83–84.

33. For a report on the 1985 parliamentary elections, see Spyros Draenos, "PASOK's Triumph is Double-Edged," *In These Times* (June 26–July 9, 1985).

34. See Sharon Zukin, "French Socialists vs. Deindustrialization: The State in the World Economy," *Telos* (Spring 1983): p. 147.

35. The theme of economic modernization is discussed with reference to the French socialists by Kesselman, "Socialism Without the Workers," in *Socialist Register 1985–86*, pp. 23–24.

36. Diana Johnstone, *In These Times* (May 2–8, 1984): p. 9.

37. Daniel Singer, "Imagination Has Not Yet Taken Power," *The Nation* (January 29, 1983). Singer notes that the PSF chose to resort to Keynesian methods at a time when the crisis of capitalism was undermining the old solutions. One problem was that the Socialists had been unwilling to set forth programs that were unacceptable to business elites.

38. On this theme see Petras, "Rise and Decline of Southern European Socialist Parties," esp. pp. 51–52. There was surely a kernal of truth to Petras' generalization concerning decline of labor support, but this overlooked two points: first, the Eurosocialists did command substantial labor support and, second, the much stronger working-class base of previous Social Democratic and Labor parties failed to generate any real anti-capitalist initiatives.

39. Ibid., p. 40. See also Einar Bernstzen, "Democratic Socialism in Spain, Portual, and Greece," in Karvonen and Sundberg, *Social Democracy in Transition*.

40. Williams, "Socialist Economic Policies," in Gallagher and Williams, *Southern European Socialism*, p. 188.

41. Berntzen, *Democratic Socialims in Spain*, pp. 238–39.

42. On the phenomenon of corporatism in the European context, see Leo Panitch, "The Development of Corporatism in Liberal Democracies," *Comparitive Political Studies* (April 1977), pp. 61–90.

43. Alain Lipietz, "Which Social Forces are for Change?," *Telos* (Spring 1983): p. 29.

44. This democratizing process was particulary crucial to Spain and Greece, neither of which had experienced any long period of liberal-democratic development. For an analysis of the Spanish case, see Christopher Abel and Nissa Torrents, eds., *Spain: Conditional Democracy* (London: Croom Helm, 1984). See also Berntzen, "Democratic Socialism in Spain, Portual, and Greece," and Richard Gillespie, "Spanish Socialism in the 1980's," in Gallagher and Williams, *Southern European Socialism.* On the role of the PSOE in democratic transformation see Jose Maria Maravall, *The Transition to Democracy in Spain* (New York: St. Martin's Press, 1982). The PASOK contribution to Greek democratization is examined by Kevin Featherstone, "The Greek Socialists in Power", *West European Politics* 6, no. 3 (1983).

45. Kesselman, "Socialism Without the Workers," p. 35.

46. Roland Cayrol, "The Crisis of the French Socialist Party," *New Political Science* 12 (1984), pp. 9–12.

47. See, for example, Santiago Carrillo's bitter *Memoria de la Transicion* (Barcelona: Grijallo, 1983), and Manuel Azcarate's *Crisis del Eurocommunismo* (Barcelona: Argos Vergara, 1982).

48. Nicos Mouzelis, "Capitalism and the Development of the Greek State," in *The State in Western Europe*, ed. Richard Scase (London: Croom Helm, 1980), pp. 260–63.

49. Adamantia Polis, "Socialist Transformation in Greece," *Telos* 61 (Fall 1984): p. 107.

50. See Richard Gillespie and Tom Gallagher, "Democracy and Authoritarianism in the Socialist Parties of Southern Europe," in Gallagher and Williams, *Southern European Socialism*, pp. 163–87.

51. Geoffrey Pridham, "Southern European Socialists and the State," in Gallagher and Williams, *Southern European Socialism*, pp. 159–61.

52. Kevin Featherstone, "Socialist Parties in Southern Europe and the Enlarged European Community," in Gallagher and Williams, *Southern European Socialism*, pp. 247–70.

53. Werner J. Feld, *The Foreign Policy of West European Parties* (New York: Praeger, 1987), pp. 68–82.

54. As Diana Johnstone pointed out, the Mitterand government, despite its pretensions toward independence and neutrality, was completely subservient to U.S. global interests. See "How the French Left Learned to Love the Bomb," *New Left Review* (July–August 1984): p. 36.

55. Daniel Singer, "Mitterand: Middle of the Journey," *The Nation* (March 10, 1984).

56. Johnstone, *The Politics of the Euromissiles,* p. 133.

57. See, for example, Johnstone's report in *In These Times* (May 23–29, 1984): p. 7.

58. Shubert, "The Socialists and NATO."

59. Patrick Camiller, "Spanish Socialism in the Atlantic Order," *New Left Review* (March–April, 1986): pp. 30–31.

60. Johnstone, "A Greek Mystery," *In These Times* (Dec. 19–Jan. 8, 1984): p. 7.

61. John C. Loulis, "Papandreou's Foreign Policy," *Foreign Affairs* (Winter 1984–85): pp. 380–81.

62. Polis, "Socialist Transformation of Greece," p. 111.

63. Christos Lyrintzis, "PASOK in Power: The Loss of the Third Road to Socialism," in Gallagher and Williams, *Southern European Socialism*, pp. 37–48.

64. A clear articulation of the social-democratic outlook at the time, which argued that the "Atlantic Alliance must remain the fulcrum of American foreign policy," was Helmut Schmidt's "Saving the Western Alliance," *New York Review of Books* (May 31, 1984): pp. 25–27.

65. The issue was not whether the Mediterranean parties could move immediately toward socialism; this was obviously a utopian dream. The issue was whether the parties would have been able to make a significant beginning—whether, that is, they were moving in a transformative direction or in some other direction.

66. For an elaboration of this theme, see Daniel Singer, *Is Socialism Doomed?*

67. For a parallel interpretation of the modernizing role of the Mediterranean socialist parties, but one that is much less critical of their direction, see Franco Ferrarotti, "The Modernizing Role of the Working-Class Parties in Southern Europe," in *Democratic Socialism: The Mass Left in Advanced Industrial Countries*, ed. Bogdan Denitch (Totowa, N.J.: Allanheld Osmun, 1981).

68. On this point see Donald Share's discussion of the PSOE in its relationship to the labor movement, in *Dilemmas of Social Democracy*, pp. 124–31.

69. For a more general critique of structural reformism, see Boggs, *The Impasse of European Communism*, ch. 5.

70. See Gay, *The Dilemma of Democratic Socialism*, ch. 8, and Adam Przeworski, *Capitalism and Social Democracy* (New York: Cambridge University Press, 1985), ch. 1.

71. On the theme of party identification in Spain, see Share, *Dilemmas of Social Democracy*, p. 117.

72. Ibid., p. 121.

73. Hindess, *Parliamentary Democracy and Socialist Politics*, pp. 144–45.

74. On the institutionalization of Eurocommunist-style parties, see Boggs, *The Impasse of European Communism*, pp. 84–90.

75. Tom Gallagher and Allan M. Williams, "Southern European Socialism in the 1990s," in Gallagher and Williams, *Southern European Socialism*, pp. 271–77.

76. Przeworski, *Capitalism and Social Democracy*, pp. 29–46.

77. On the thematic of a radical-democratic strategy, see Laclau and Mouffe, *Hegemony and Socialist Strategy*, pp. 176–94.

Chapter 6
Socialist Decline and the Radical Challenge

1. Alain Touraine, *Return of the Actor* (Minneapolis: University of Minnesota Press, 1988), pp. 124–25.

2. Sheldon Wolin, "What Revolutionary Action Means Today," in *Dimensions of Radical Democracy*, ed. Chantal Mouffe (London: Verso, 1992).

3. Joseph Femia, *Marxism and Democracy* (Oxford: Claredon Press, 1993), p. 68.

4. John Urry, "The End of Organized Capitalism," in *New Times: The Changing Face of Politics in the 1990s* ed. Stuart Hall and Marin Jacques (London: Verso, 1990), pp. 94–102.

5. Herbert Marcuse, *One-Dimensional Man* (Boston: Beacon Press, 1964), pp. 250–51.

6. The bulk of Castoriadis' writings can be found in David Ames Curtis, ed., *Cornelius Castoriadis: Political and Social Writings*, vols. 1 and 2. (Minneapolis: University of Minnesota Press, 1988).

7. Castoriadis, *Political and Social Writings*, vol. 1, pp. 99, 101.

8. Ibid., p. 102.

9. Ibid., p. 33.

10. Castoriadis, *Political and Social Writings*, vol. 2, p. 57.

11. Ibid., p. 98.

12. Ibid., p. 132. Italics original.

13. Castoriadis, *Political and Social Writings*, vol. 1, p. 290.

14. For an excellent overview of the *Socialisme o Barbarie* group, see Arthur Hirsch, *The French New Left* (Boston: South End Press, 1981), pp. 108–36.

15. Castoriadis, *Political and Social Writings*, vol. 2, p. 228.

16. Daniel Singer, *Prelude to Revolution* (New York: Hill and Wang, 1970), p. 261.

17. Ibid., p. 263.

18. George Katsiaficas, *Imagination of the New Left* (Boston: South End Press, 1987), pp. 90, 102.

19. Hirsch, *The French New Left*, p. 148.

20. Daniel Cohn-Bendit, *Obsolete Communism: The Left-Wing Alternative* (New York: McGraw-Hill, 1968), p. 87.

21. On the development of the Italian new left, see Davide Degli Incerti, ed., *La sinistra rivoluzionaria in Italia* (Roma: Newton Compton Editori, 1975).

22. On the base committees in Italy, see Giuseppe Bianchi, et. al., eds., *I Cub: Comitati unitari di base* (Roma: Coines Edizioni, 1971), and Guido Romagnoli, ed., *Consigli di fabbrica e democrazia sindacale* (Milano: Mazzotta, 1976).

23. On Maoism as a source of theoretical and political revitalization for leftist movements and parties, see Stuart Schram, introduction to *The Political Thought of Mao Tse-Tung* (New York: Praeger, 1969).

24. For a summation of Magri's views in English, see his "Problems of the Marxist Theory of the Revolutionary Party," *New Left Review* no. 60 (March–April 1971), and "Italy, Social Democracy, and Revolution in the West," *Socialist Review*, no. 36 (November–December 1977).

25. On the "Theses", see *Il Manifesto*, nos. 1–4 (1969).

26. *Il Manifesto*, no. 1, p. 3.

27. On the "strategy of tension," see Gianfranco Sanguinetti, *On Terrorism and the State* (London: Aldgate Press, 1982), pp. 55–101.

28. See Piven and Cloward, *Poor People's Movements*, ch. 1.

29. Werner Sombart, *Why is There No Socialism in the United States?* (White Plains: M.E. Sharpe, 1976).

30. See Lawrence Goodwyn, *The Populist Moment* (New York: Oxford University

Press, 1978).

31. Eric Foner, "Why is There No Socialism in the United States?," in Tabb, *The Future of Socialism*, p. 269.

32. A notable exception to this dismissive attitude toward the new left was Wini Breines' *The Great Refusal: Community and Organization in the New Left, 1962–68* (New York: Praeger , 1982).

33. See James Miller, *Democracy is in the Streets* (New York: Simon and Schuster, 1987)

34. On this point see Jay Stevens, *Storming Heaven* (New York: Harper and Row, 1987), p. 293.

35. See David Caute, *The Year of the Barricades: A Journey Through 1968* (New York: Harper and Row, 1988), and Ronald Fraser, ed., *A Student Generation in Revolt* (New York: Pantheon, 1988)

36. See Miller, *Democracy in the Streets*, esp. chs. 6–8, for a more developed account of SDS theory and practice. See also Breines, *The Great Refusal*; and Kirk Sale, *SDS* (New York: Basic Books, 1973)

37. See, for example, Miller, *Democracy in the Streets*, ch. 9.

38. Richard Flacks, "What Happened to the New Left?," *Socialist Review* (January–March 1989): pp. 96–97.

39. On the "total break" thesis, see Todd Gitlin, *The Sixties* (New York: Bantam Books, 1987); David Farber, *Chicago '68* (Chicago: University of Chicago Press, 1988); and Tom Hayden, *Reunion: A Memoir* (New York: Random House, 1988).

40. Gitlin, *The Sixties*, p. 415.

41. Ibid., p. 420.

42. Ibid., p. 425.

43. The work of Herbert Marcuse in the 1960s and early 1970s was clearly one exception to this general theorical predicament, but Marcuse's work had virtually no strategic impact on new-left development. A major early attempt to establish a relationship between Marcuse and the new left was Paul Breines, ed., *Critical Interruptions* (New York: Herder and Herder, 1972).

44. Wini Breines, "Whose New Left?," *Journal of American History* (September 1988): p. 543.

45. This dynamic was intimately linked to the workings of anti-intellectualism in American political culture. See Richard Hofstadter, *Anti-Intellectualism in American Life* (New York: Vintage Books, 1966).

46. Hayden, *Reunion*.

47. Gitlin, *The Sixties*.

48. George Katsiaficas, *The Imagination of the New Left: A Global Analysis of 1968* (Boston: South End Press, 1987).

49. Jack Whalen and Richard Flacks, *After the Barricades: The New Left Grows Up* (Philadelphia: Temple University Press, 1989).

50. On the linkages between the new left and new social movements, see Boggs, *Social Movements and Political Power*, ch. 2.

51. On the theme of a revived sense of municipalism, see Murray Bookchin,

Remaking Society (Montreal: Black Rose Books, 1989), ch. 4.

52. See Fuentes and Frank, "Civil Democracy: Social Movements in Recent World History," in Amin, et. al., *Transforming the Revolution*, pp. 175–76.

53. Bookchin, *Remaking Society*, p. 157.

54. For a more negative assessment of major efforts to merge feminism and ecology, see Janet Biehl, *Rethinking Eco-Feminist Politics* (Boston: South End Press, 1991).

55. Bookchin, *Remaking Society*, p. 156.

56. On the new populism, see Harry Boyte, Heather Booth, and Steve Max, *Citizen Action and the New American Populism* (Philadelphia: Temple University Press, 1986).

57. See Alice Cook and Gwyn Kirk, *Greenham Women Everywhere* (Boston: South End Press, 1983).

58. Eric Mann and the WATCHDOG Organizing Committee, *L.A.'s Lethal Air: New Strategies for Policy, Organizing, and Action* (Los Angeles: Labor/Community Strategy Center, 1991).

59. See Allan Heskin, *The Struggle of Community* (Boulder: Westview Press, 1991).

60. On the role of critical intellectuals, see Boggs, *Intellectuals and the Crisis of Modernity*, ch. 5.

61. On post-Marxist radicalism, see Laclau and Mouffe, *Hegemony and Socialist Strategy*, ch. 4; and Boggs, *Social Movements and Political Power*, ch. 6.

62. On the postmodern shift in the realm of politics, see Stephen K. White, *Political Theory and Postmodernism* (New York: Cambridge University Press, 1991).

63. Best and Kellner, *Postmodern Theory*, pp. 213–14, 288.

64. On the necessity for integrating a class dimension into the thematic of new social movements, see Ralph Miliband, *Divided Societies* (New York: Oxford University Press, 1991), p. 110.

65. For an exhaustive overview of European Green development, see Mike Feinstein, *Sixteen Weeks with European Greens* (Naples, Fl.: Whitehall, 1992).

66. On the Greens-SPD coalition efforts in Hesse, see Parness, *The SPD and the Challenge of Mass Politics*, ch. 5.

67. The left Green tendency was first outlined by Thomas Eberman and Rainer Trampert in *Zukunft der Grünen: Ein realistisches Konzept fur eine radikale Partei* (Hamburg: Konkret-Verlag, 1984). See also Werner Hülsberg, "The Greens at the Crossroads," *New Left Review* (July–August 1985).

68. E. Gene Frankland and Donald Schoonmaker, *Between Protest and Power: The Green Party in Germany* (Boulder: Westview Press, 1992), p. 232.

69. See Mario Diani, "The Italian Ecology Movement: From Radicalism to Moderation," in *Green Politics One 1990*, Wolfgang Rudig (Edinburgh: Edinburgh University Press, 1990), pp. 153–76.

70. Bookchin, *Remaking Society*, p. 151.

71. Jonas Pontusson, "At the End of the Third Road: Social Democracy in Crisis," *Poltics and Society* no. 20 (1992): pp. 307–308.

72. Michael Harrington, *Socialism Past and Future* (New York: Penguin Books, 1990), p. 278.

73. Immanuel Wallerstein, "Antisystemic Movements: History and Dilemmas," in Amin, et. al., *Transforming the Revolution*, p. 36.

Chapter 7
Epilogue: The Global Crisis—Ecology and the Future of Socialism

1. For an excellent discussion of the crisis in the wake of Communist collapse, see Aronson, "After Communism," pp. 23–44.
2. Murray Bookchin, "A Philosophical Naturalism," *Society and Nature* (September–December, 1992): p. 60.
3. The massive abundance of evidence concerning global ecological decline can be found in dozens of sources. Some of the best include: Lester Brown, et. al., *State of the World* (New York: W.W. Norton, 1992); Helen Caldicott, *If You Love This Planet* (New York: W.W. Norton, 1992); Lynne Edgerton, *The Rising Tide: Global Warming and World Sea Levels* (Washington, D.C.: Island Press, 1991); Paul and Anne Ehrlich, *The Population Explosion* (New York: Simon and Schuster, 1990); Jeremey Legget, ed., *Global Warming: The Greenpeace Report* (New York: Oxford University Press, 1990); Francesca Lyman, et. al., *The Greenhouse Trap* (Boston: Beacon Press, 1990); Bill McKibben, *The End of Nature* (New York: Random House, 1989); Michael Oppenheimer and Robert Boyle, *Dead Heat: The Race Against the Greenhouse Effect* (New York: Basic Books, 1990); and Stephen H. Schneider, *Global Warming: Are We Entering the Greenhouse Century?* (San Francisco: Sierra Club Books, 1989).
4. On the growing North-South divide in the context of the ecological crisis, see Martin Khor Kok Peng, *The Future of North-South Relations* (Penang, Malaysia: Third World Network, 1992), ch. 3.
5. See Khor, ch. 5, and Caldicott, *If You Love This Planet*, pp. 140–48.
6. Riccardo Petrella, "Techno-Apartheid for a Global Underclass," *Los Angeles Times* (August 6, 1992).
7. Lester Brown, et. al., *Vital Signs: Trends that are Shaping Our Future* (New York: W.W. Norton, 1992), p. 110.
8. The actual figure is $394 billion, down slightly from the previous five years. But so many countries keep military data secret that accurate information cannot be assured; the actual figure is probably somewhat higher. See Brown, et. al., *Vital Signs*, p. 84.
9. Mike Klare, "It's Business as Usual," *The Nation* (February 3, 1992).
10. See, for example, McKibben, *The End of Nature*.
11. On urban crisis and the parameters of oppositional movements, see Margit Mayer, "Politics in the Post-Fordist City," *Socialist Review* (January–March 1991): pp. 105–124.
12. For a more extensive discussion of grassroots struggles around the world, see Alan B. Durning, "Grassroots Groups are Our Best Hope for Global Prosperity and Ecology," *Utne Reader* (July–August 1989): pp. 40–49.
13. On the visionary component of the new left, see Katsiaficas, *The Imagination of the New Left*; Wini Breines, *The Great Refusal* (New York: Praeger, 1983); and

Boggs, *Social Movements and Political Power*, ch. 2.

14. For examples of local organizing, see Harry Boyte and Frank Riesman, eds., *The New Populism: The Politics of Empowerment* (Philadelphia: Temple University Press, 1986). For a fascinating case study, see Allan Heskin, *The Struggle for Community*.

15. Andre Gunder Frank and Marta Fuentes, "Civil Democracy: Social Movements in Recent World History," in Amin, et. al., *Transforming the Revolution*, p. 178.

16. There are, of course, diverse views of crisis in general, and ecological crisis in particular. For two quite different, but in some ways complementary, approaches crisis see Ulrich Beck, *Risk Society* (London: Sage Publications, 1992), chs. 1 and 2; and Murray Bookchin, *Remaking Society*, ch. 1.

17. Beck, *Risk Society*, p. 14.

18. Ibid., p. 19.

19. On this aspect of new-movement theory, see Alain Touraine, *The Voice and the Eye*.

20. The relationship between ecology and post-Marxism is explored in Isaac Balbus, *Marxism and Domination* (Princeton: Princeton University Press, 1982), ch. 10; Bookchin, *Toward an Ecological Society* (Montreal: Black Rose Books, 1980), esp. pp. 193–286; and Andre Gorz, *Ecology as Politics*, pts. 1 and 2 (Boston: South End Press, 1980).

21. See, for example, Kirkpatrick Sale, *Human Scale* (New York: Doubleday, 1982).

22. An excellent discussion of points of encounter between ecology and Marxism is contained in Rainer Grundman, "The Ecological Challenge to Marxism," *New Left Review* (May–June 1991): pp. 103–20. For a reflection on the limitations of classical Marxism in confronting the environmental crisis, see James O'Connor, "Capitalism, Nature, Socialism: An Introduction," in *Society and Nature* (September–December 1992): pp. 174–202.

23. The myth that industrial growth and material affluence are connected to social progress is debunked by Paul L. Wachtel in *The Poverty of Affluence* (Philadelphia: New Society Publishers, 1989).

24. There are few good treatments of politics as an element of postmodern discourse. One notable exception is Steven Best and Douglas Kellner, *Postmodern Theory*, esp. ch. y. See also Stephen K. White, *Political Theory and Postmodernism*.

25. For an analysis of how local movements decline as they yield to the bureaucratic imperatives of organized politics, see Frances Fox Piven and Richard Cloward, *Poor People's Movements* (New York, Vintage Books, 1979), introduction and ch. 1.

26. Mark Dowie, "American Environmentalism: A Movement Courting Irrelevance," *World Policy Journal* 9, no. 1 (winter 1991–92): pp. 83–94. See in particular Dowie's insightful discussion of "third-wave" environmentalism, i.e., the marriage of ecological politics and neo-liberalism in the U.S.

27. See, for example, Sale, *Human Scale*; E.F. Schumacher, *Small is Beautiful* (New York: Harper and Row, 1973); and Hazel Henderson, *The Politics of the Solar Age* (New York: Doubleday, 1983).

28. Barbara Epstein presents a fascinating case study (the anti-nuclear movement in northern California) where localism shaped both the vision and the methods of struggle. See *Political Protest and Cultural Revolution* (Berkeley: University of California Press, 1991).
29. Al Gore, *Earth in the Balance* (Boston: Houghton Mifflin Co., 1992). This book is relatively strong on analysis but remarkabley weak in posing solutions.
30. The inescapable irony here is that Clinton's victory would have been impossible without substantial black (85 percent) and blue collar (55 percent) support.
31. Walter H. Corson, ed., *The Global Ecology Handbook* (Boston: Beacon Press, 1990), p. 44.
32 Probably the best and most elaborate treatment of the notion of balance between society and nature is Bookchin's *The Ecology of Freedom* (Palo Alto: Chesire Books, 1982), esp. ch. 12.
33. The view that political organization inevitably brings bureaucratization, first argued by the nineteenth century anarchists, and then by Robert Michels in *Political Parties*, is perhaps most cogently stated by Piven and Cloward, *Poor People's Movements*.
34. Claus Offe, "Reflections on the Institutional Self-Transformation of Movement Politics: A Tentative Stage Model," in Dalton and Kuechler, op. cit., p. 238.
35. Sidney Plotkin, "Community and Alienation: Enclave Consciousness and Urban Movements," in *Breaking Chains*, ed. Michael Peter Smith (New Brunswick, N.J.: Transaction Publishers, 1991), pp. 5–25.
36. Ibid, p. 18.
37. Dowie, in "American Environmentalism: A Movement Courting Irrelevance," offers a critique that is appropriate here: the search for ecological short-cuts, whether through technology, new-age spiritualism, or insider lobbying, always has depoliticizing effects.
38. See, for example, Offe, *Reflections on Institutional Self-Transformation*, pp. 237–45.
39. For a critique of Rainbow Coalition politics (from the left), see Adolph Reed, Jr., *The Jesse Jackson Phenomenon* (New Haven: Yale University Press, 1986).
40. On the emergence of the European Greens, see Rudolf Bahro, *From Red to Green* (London: Verso, 1984); Boggs, *Social Movements and Political Power*, ch. 5; and Werner Hulsberg, *The German Greens: A Social and Political Profile* (London: Verso, 1988).
41. For an exhaustive overview of European Green politics through 1992, see Feinstein, *Sixteen Weeks with European Greens*.
42. Khor, *The Future of North-South Relations*, esp. chs. 4 and 5. On the emergence of the world system in the context of ecological crisis, see Samir Amin, *Empire of Chaos* (New York: Monthly Review Press, 1992), ch. 1.
43. Khor, *Future of North-South Relations*, p. 56.
44. Ibid., p. 29.
45. Lauren Langman, "The Nation-State and the Self," (unpublished manuscript).
46. On the hopes and expectations that grew around the Earth Summit, see the contributions to Steve Lerner, ed., *Earth Summit* (Bolinas, Calif.: Common

Knowledge Press, 1991).

47. For a point-by-point critique of the Earth Summit, see the Greenpeace pamphlet *Beyond UNCED* (1992).

48. See Robert C. Johnson, "Lessons for Collective Security," *World Policy Journal* (summer 1991): pp. 572–73.

49. As Herbert Kitschelt suggests, the success of movement-oriented politics will depend upon the capacity of "left-libertarian" (i.e., Green) *parties* to expand. See "New Social Movements and the Decline of Party Organization," in *Challenging the Political Order*, pp. 179–208.

50. The theme of "growth equals better ecology," which permeates Gore's book, was the leitmotif of President Bush's appearance in Rio.

51. Gore, *Earth in the Balance*, p. 247.

52. See, McKibben, *The End of Nature*.

53. The avoidance of the "macro" dimenstion coincides with the familiar postmodern approach to politics, which typically seeks refuge in the comfort of "civil society" and its highly-fragmented spheres of thought and actions. See Best and Kellner, *Postmodern Theory*, pp. 283–94.

54. Dennis R. Judd, "The Rise of the New Walled Cities," in *Representing the City*, ed. Helen Liggett and David C. Perry (forthcoming).

Index